Lecture Notes in Computer Science 7597

Commenced Publication in 1973
Founding and Former Series Editors:
Gerhard Goos, Juris Hartmanis, and Jan van Leeuwen

Carlos A. Coello Coello   Julie Greensmith
Natalio Krasnogor   Pietro Liò
Giuseppe Nicosia   Mario Pavone (Eds.)

Artificial Immune Systems

11th International Conference, ICARIS 2012
Taormina, Italy, August 28-31, 2012
Proceedings

 Springer

Volume Editors

Carlos A. Coello Coello
CINVESTAV-IPN
Departamento de Computación
Av. Instituto Politécnico Nacional No. 2508
Col. San Pedro Zacatenco, Mexico, D.F. 07300, Mexico
E-mail: ccoello@cs.cinvestav.mx

Julie Greensmith
Natalio Krasnogor
University of Nottingham
School of Computer Science
Jubilee Campus, Wollaton Road, Nottingham, NG8 1BB, UK
E-mail: jqg@cs.nott.ac.uk; natalio.krasnogor@nottingham.ac.uk

Pietro Liò
University of Cambridge
Computer Laboratory
William Gates Building, 15 JJ Thomson Avenue, Cambridge, CB3 0FD, UK
E-mail: pl219@cam.ac.uk

Giuseppe Nicosia
Mario Pavone
University of Catania
Department of Mathematics and Computer Science
Viale A. Doria 6, 95125 Catania, Italy
E-mail: {nicosia,mpavone}@dmi.unict.it

ISSN 0302-9743   e-ISSN 1611-3349
ISBN 978-3-642-33756-7   e-ISBN 978-3-642-33757-4
DOI 10.1007/978-3-642-33757-4
Springer Heidelberg Dordrecht London New York

Library of Congress Control Number: 2012947655

CR Subject Classification (1998): I.6, I.2, J.3, F.1, F.2, I.5

LNCS Sublibrary: SL 1 – Theoretical Computer Science and General Issues

Typesetting: Camera-ready by author, data conversion by Scientific Publishing Services, Chennai, India

Printed on acid-free paper

Springer is part of Springer Science+Business Media (www.springer.com)

Preface

ICARIS, the International Conference on Artificial Immune Systems, is evolving. In the eight years since ICARIS was last hosted in Sicily, we have seen some dramatic changes within this field. It is intriguing to look back at the proceedings of the 3rd ICARIS from eight years ago and to compare them with ICARIS today. In 2004, the proceedings were dominated by engineering applications of immune inspired algorithms. The two keynote speakers, Dr. Alan Perelson and Prof. Robin Callard provided the only immunology-related talks, with the remainder of the conference focused on what we now term first generation AIS. The field now also encompasses the dynamic and innovative field of computational immunology, and the specialisms of the delegates have changed accordingly. ICARIS has evolved by introducing aspects of computational immunology, first as a stream within the conference and now as a full track within the program. This conference is composed of two tracks, Computational Immunology and Immune-Inspired Systems. ICARIS now acts as a mechanism by which researchers from both sides of AIS can come together to exchange knowledge and to form future collaborations.

Continuing in the spirit of ICARIS 2011 at the University of Cambridge, we adopted a two-track system, with each track running over two days. The Computational Immunology track was hosted on the first and second day of the conference. The submissions to this track consisted of extended abstracts and posters. From these we accepted 32 abstracts. We are delighted to have hosted a fascinating plenary lecture, given by Piero Mastroeni from the University of Cambridge, UK, on "Mathematical and Systems Biology Approaches to Understanding Infection, Immunity and Vaccination at the Single Cell Level". In addition to the plenary lecture, Heiko Muller and Luca Zammataro from the Italian Institute of Technology, Milan, Italy, delivered two tutorials for this session on sequencing data: "NGS: From the Sequencing Machine to the Data Archive" and "A Database for the Analysis of Mutation Spectra in Human Cancer and Immune Systems". An interactive poster session also formed part of this track.

The Immune-Inspired Systems track ran on days three and four of this conference. We accepted 19 full papers for this track, which were all double blind peer reviewed. In order to ensure the inclusion of the highest quality AIS papers, each submission had at least four reviews. Together with the full papers, we accepted 14 abstracts for this track. We invited the submission of abstracts to be published online, for oral or poster presentation, which are akin to the positional papers formerly featured as part of ICARIS. The invited tutorial for this track was presented by Christian Blum from the Universitat Politécnica de Catalunya, Spain, on the topic of "Swarm Intelligence". This ties ICARIS to the PPSN (Parallel Problem Solving from Nature) conference, held in Taormina right after ICARIS (1–5 September 2012). We hope that this helped to raise the interest of the natural computation community in AIS. An interactive poster session was given to showcase work in progress and to open up discussion among researchers. It was our great pleasure to host Stephanie Forrest, University of New Mexico, USA, who delivered a plenary lecture on "The Biology of Software", which we hope was of interest to participants of both tracks. Prof. Forrest is the recipient of the ACM Allen Newell Award and her research was instrumental in the rise of AIS as a unique field of scientific study. Her more recent research is currently making an impact on the Computational Immunology track of ICARIS.

The aim of this, the 11th ICARIS conference, was not only to strengthen the research for both tracks, but to forge strong links between the two communities. To this end the conference program contained a number of structured interactive events, some of which are new to ICARIS. On the second day of the conference we hosted a panel session dedicated to the "Advancement of Computational Systems Immunology and Immunoinformatics". We would like to thank the participants of this panel, including Hugues Bersini, Chang-Zheng Chen, Marc Thilo Figge, Stephanie Forrest, Koich Kobayashi, Melanie Moses, Veronique Thomas-Vaslin, and Jon Timmis. We offered delegates the opportunity to ask informal questions of the panel via 'speed networking'. This was done in order to encourage contribution from the less experienced members of our community, giving them the opportunity to speak to some of the world leaders in this field.

Poster sessions are becoming a popular mainstay of ICARIS. This year we further raised the profile of these poster sessions through the use of a poster introduction session, where each presenter had one minute and one slide to introduce their poster. The final crossover activity of ICARIS 2012 was the workshop on Bio- and Immune-Inspired Algorithms and Models for Multi-level Complex Systems for which five invited papers were presented: Giuditta Franco "A Computational Analysis of Repeat Sharing Gene Networks"; Raffaele Giancarlo and Filippo Utro "Stability-Based Model Selection for High Throughput Genomic Data: An Algorithmic Paradigm"; Niall Murphy and Alfonso Rodríguez-Patón "Distributed Computing with Prokaryotic Immune Systems"; Alberto Castellini, Vincenzo Manca and Mauro Zucchelli "Towards an Evolutionary Procedure for Reverse-Engineering Biological Networks", and Emanuela Merelli and Mario Rasetti "The Immune System as a Metaphor for Topology Driven Patterns Formation in Complex Systems".

Providing a balance between computational immunology and immune-inspired systems is not trivial and as an organizing committee we worked hard to correctly strike this balance. In these difficult economic times when it is becoming harder to fund large interdisciplinary projects, it is vital that as a community, we are capable of transferring knowledge among researchers. We hope that the additional activities further assisted in promoting interdisciplinary collaboration in AIS. As a sign of the progress in the field, since the first ICARIS event, we have seen an increasing number of students choosing computational immunology and immunoinformatics as their main PhD topics. There is also an important number of tenured positions at prestigious universities that involve research on such topics. Finally, we would like to thank the plenary speakers, panel participants, tutorial speakers, workshop speakers, the two program committees, and the delegates for their participation and input, resulting in a high quality, interesting, and engaging conference.

August 2012

Carlos A. Coello Coello
Julie Greensmith
Natalio Krasnogor
Pietro Liò
Giuseppe Nicosia
Mario Pavone

ICARIS 2012 Organizing Committees

ICARIS 2012 was organized and hosted by the Optimization and BioComputing Group of the Department of Mathematics and Computer Science, University of Catania, Italy. The University of Catania is the 29th oldest University in the world. Its establishment dates back to 1434.

Conference Chairs

Carlos A. Coello Coello	CINVESTAV-IPN, Mexico
Julie Greensmith	University of Nottingham, UK
Natalio Krasnogor	University of Nottingham, UK
Pietro Liò	University of Cambridge, UK
Giuseppe Nicosia	University of Catania, Italy
Mario Pavone	University of Catania, Italy

Publicity Chairs

Germán Terrazas Angulo	University of Nottingham, UK
Nareli Cruz Cortes	CINVESTAV-IPN, Mexico
Renato Umeton	MIT, USA

Organizing Committee Members

Giovanni Carapezza	University of Catania, Italy
Piero Consoli	University of Catania, Italy
Jole Costanza	University of Catania, Italy
Giovanni Murabito	University of Catania, Italy

Steering Committee

Peter Bentley	University College London, UK
Hugues Bersini	IRIDA, Belgium
Leandro de Castro	Mackenzie University, Brazil
Stephanie Forrest	University of New Mexico, USA
Emma Hart	Napier University, UK
Christian Jacob	University of Calgary, Canada
Doheon Lee	KAIST, Korea
Mark Neal	University of Wales, Aberystwyth, UK
Giuseppe Nicosia	University of Catania, Italy
Jon Timmis (Chair)	University of York, UK

Program Committee for Computational Immunology, Immunoinformatics, Theoretical Immunology, and Systems Immunology Stream

Colin C. Anderson	University of Alberta, Canada
Becca Asquith	Imperial College London, UK
Soumya Banerjee	University of New Mexico, USA
Sergio Baranzini	University of California San Francisco, USA
Nicole Baumgarth	University of California, USA
Catherine Beauchemin	Ryerson University, Canada
Hans Bitter	Roche Palo Alto, USA
Joseph Blattman	Arizona State University, USA
Gennady Bocharov	Russian Academy of Sciences, Russia
Ulisses M. Braga-Neto	Texas A&M University, USA
Robin Callard	University College London, UK
Raffaele Calogero	University of Turin, Italy
Michael P. Cancro	University of Pennsylvania, USA
Salvador Eugenio Caoili	University of the Philippines Manila, Philippines
Jonathan Carlson	Microsoft Research California, USA
Gastone Castellani	University of Bologna, Italy
Franco Celada	New York University, USA
Cliburn Chan	Duke University, USA
Chang-Zheng Chen	Stanford University, USA
Tong Joo Chuan	Institute for Infocomm Research, Singapore
Dmitriy Chudakov	Russian Academy of Sciences, Russia
Hilary Clark	Genentech - Roche Group, USA
Francesco Colucci	University of Cambridge, UK
Alberto D'Onofrio	IFOM-IEO Campus, Italy
Neil Dalchau	Microsoft Research Cambridge, UK
Anne DeGroot	University of Rhode Island, USA
David S. DeLuca	Broad Institute of MIT and Harvard, USA
Alexander Diehl	Buffalo Clinical and Translational Research Center, USA
Irini Doytchinova	Medical University Sofia, Bulgaria
Ken Duffy	National University of Ireland, Ireland
Deborah Dunn-Walters	KCL School of Medicine, London, UK
Omer Dushek	University of Oxford, UK
Sol Efroni	Bar Ilan University, Israel
Marc Thilo Figge	Hans-Knöll-Institute, Germany
Paola Finotti	University of Padua, Italy
Darren Flower	Aston University, UK
Nir Friedman	Weizmann Institute of Science, Israel

Carmen Molina-Paris	University of Leeds, UK
Melanie Moses	University of New Mexico, USA
Gioacchino Natoli	IFOM-IEO Campus, Italy
German Nudelman	Mount Sinai School of Medicine, USA
Yanay Ofran	Bar Ilan University, Israel
Osamu Ohara	RIKEN Yokohama Institute, Kazusa DNA Research Institute, Japan
Janet M. Oliver	The University of New Mexico, USA
Michal Or-Guil	Humboldt University Berlin, Germany
Anastasia Carla Pagnoni	University of Milano - Bicocca, Italy
Mirko Paiardini	Emory University, USA
Leila Perie	Utrecht University, Netherlands
Dimitri Perrin	Osaka University, Japan
Nikolai Petrovsky	Flinders University, Australia
Andrew Phillips	Microsoft Research Cambridge, UK
Philippe Pierre	Centre d'Immunologie, University of Marseille, France
Guido Poli	San Raffaele Hospital, Italy
G. P. S. Raghava	Institute of Microbial Technology, India
Srinivasan Ramachandran	Institute of Genomics and Integrative Biology, India
Shoba Ranganathan	Macquarie University, Australia
Timothy Ravasi	KAUST, Kingdom of Saudi Arabia
Roland R. Regoes	ETH Zurich, Switzerland
Ruy Ribeiroz	Los Alamos National Laboratory, USA
Benedita Rocha	Université Paris-Descartes, France
Luis M. Rocha	Indiana University, USA
Christian Schönbach	Kyushu Institute of Technology, Japan
Anurag Sethi	Los Alamos National Laboratory, USA
Alessandro Sette	La Jolla Institute for Allergy and Immunology, USA
Johannes Sollner	Emergentec Biodevelopment GmbH, Austria
Derek Smith	University of Cambridge, UK
Daron Standley	Osaka University, Japan
Stefan Stevanovic	University of Tuebingen, Germany
Sean P. Stromberg	Emory University, USA
Stephen Taylor	University of Oxford, UK
Paul G. Thomas	St. Jude Children's Research Hospital, USA
Véronique Thomas-Vaslin	CNRS-UPMC, France
Anna Tramontano	University "La Sapienza" in Rome, Italy
Rajat Varma	NIH, USA
Elena Vigorito	Babraham Institute and University of Cambridge, UK
Aleksandra Walczak	Ecole Normale Supérieure, France

Bridget Wilson	University of New Mexico Health Sciences Center, USA
Gur Yaari	Yale University, USA
Hong Yang	FDA, USA
Andrew Yates	Albert Einstein College of Medicine, USA
Alexey Zaikin	University College London, UK
Luca Zammataro	IFOM-IEO Campus, Italy
Guanglan Zhang	Dana-Farber Cancer Institute, Harvard University, USA

Program Committee for Immunological Computation, Immune-Inspired Engineering, Immune-Inspired Heuristics Stream

Uwe Aickelin	Nottingham University, UK
Paul Andrews	University of York, UK
Bruno Apolloni	University of Milan, Italy
Helio Barbosa	LNCC Brazil
Simone Bassis	University of Milan, Italy
Roberto Battiti	University of Trento, Italy
Peter Bentley	University College London, UK
Heder Bernardino Soares	LNCC Brazil
Tadeusz Burczynski	Cracow University of Technology, Poland
Zixing Cai	Central South University - Changsha, China
Sergio Cavalieri	University of Bergamo, Italy
George M. Coghill	University of Aberdeen, UK
Piero Conca	University of York, UK
Ernesto Costa	University of Coimbra, Portugal
Paulo Jose Costa Branco	Universidade Tecnica de Lisboa, Portugal
Vincenzo Cutello	University of Catania, Italy
Dipankar Dasgupta	University of Memphis, USA
Leandro de Castro	Mackenzie University, Brazil
Matteo De Felice	University of Rome "Roma Tre", Italy
Mario Di Raimondo	University of Catania, Italy
Yongsheng Ding	Donghua University - Shanghai, China
Benjamin Doerr	Max-Planck-Institut für Informatik, Germany
Marco Dorigo	Université Libre de Bruxelles, Belgium
Michael Elberfeld	Universität zu Lübeck, Germany
Fernando Esponda	University of New Mexico, USA
Stephanie Forrest	University of New Mexico, USA
Masoud Ghaffari	GE Aviation, USA
Maoguo Gong	Xidian University, China
Tao Gong	Donghua University, China and Purdue University, USA
Feng Gu	University of Leeds, UK
Walter Gutjahr	University of Vienna, Austria

Emma Hart	Napier University, UK
Andy Hone	University of Kent, UK
Christian Jacob	University of Calgary, Canada
Thomas Jansen	University College Cork, Ireland
Licheng Jiao	Xidian University, China
Colin Johnson	University of Kent, UK
Bruno Kyewski	German Cancer Research Center, Heidelberg, Germany
Henry Lau	University of Hong Kong, China
Doheon Lee	KAIST, Korea
Jay Lee	University of Cincinnati, USA
Yiwen Liang	Wuhan University, China
Jiming Liu	Hong Kong Baptist University, Hong Kong, China
Wenjian Luo	University of Science and Technology, China
Chris McEwan	Napier University, UK
Giuseppe Narzisi	Cold Spring Harbor Laboratory, USA
Frank Neumann	Max-Planck-Institut für Informatik, Germany
Mark Neal	University of Wales, Aberystwyth, UK
Robert Oates	University of Nottingham, UK
Richard E. Overill	King's College London, UK
Wei Pang	Jilin University, China and University of Aberdeen, UK
Elisa Pappalardo	University of Catania, Italy and University of Florida, USA
Andrea Roli	University of Bologna, Italy
Peter Ross	Napier University, UK
Sven Schaust	Gottfried Wilhelm Leibniz Universität, Germany
Susan Stepney	University of York, UK
Giovanni Stracquadanio	John Hopkins University, USA
Ying Tan	Peking University, Beijing, China
Alexander Tarakanov	St. Petersburg Institute for Informatics and Automation, Russia
Johannes Textor	University of Lübeck, Germany
Jon Timmis	University of York, UK
Andy Tyrrell	University of York, UK
Renato Umeton	MIT, USA
Mario Villalobos Arias	Universidad de Costa Rica, Costa Rica
Stefan Voss	University of Hamburg, Germany
Markus Wagner	University of Adelaide, Australia
Weichao Wang	University of North Carolina at Charlotte, USA
Carsten Witt	Technical University of Denmark, Denmark
Ning Xiong	Mälardalen University, Sweden
Christine Zarges	Technical University of Dortmund, Germany

Keynote Speakers

Stephanie Forrest   University of New Mexico, USA
Piero Mastroeni   University of Cambridge, UK

Tutorial Speakers

Christian Blum   Universitat Politécnica de Catalunya, Spain
Heiko Muller   Italian Institute of Technology, Center of
                            Genomic Science, Italy
Luca Zammataro   Italian Institute of Technology, Center of
                            Genomic Science, Italy

Panel Session Speakers

Hugues Bersini   Université Libre de Bruxelles, Belgium
Chang-Zheng Chen   Stanford University, USA
Marc Thilo Figge   Hans-Knöll-Institute, Germany
Stephanie Forrest   University of New Mexico, USA
Koichi Kobayashi   Harvard University - Harvard Medical School,
                            USA
Oliver Kohlbacher   University of Tübingen, Germany
Pietro Liò   University of Cambridge, UK
Melanie Moses   University of New Mexico, USA
Giuseppe Nicosia   University of Catania, Italy
Alex Sette   La Jolla Institute for Allergy and Immunology,
                            USA
Veronique Thomas-Vaslin   Université Pierre et Marie Curie, France
Jon Timmis   University of York, UK

Workshop Organizing Committee

Giuditta Franco   University of Verona, Italy
Giuseppe Nicosia   University of Catania, Italy
Mario Pavone   University of Catania, Italy

Sponsoring Institutions

TaoSciences Research Center, Italy
Angelo Marcello Anile Association

Table of Contents

Workshop on Bio- and Immune-Inspired Algorithms and Models for Multi-level Complex Systems Invited Papers

Face Recognition by Searching Most Similar Sample with Immune Learning

Tao Gong[1,2,3]

[1] College of Information S. & T., Donghua University, Shanghai 201620, China
[2] Engineering Research Center of Digitized Textile & Fashion Technology,
Ministry of Education, Donghua University, Shanghai 201620, China
[3] Department of Computer Science, Purdue University, West Lafayette 47907, USA
taogong@dhu.edu.cn

Abstract. Face recognition algorithms often have to filter out the disturbances of some conditional factors such as facial pose, illumination, and expression (PIE). So an increasing number of researchers have been figuring out the best discriminant transformation in the feature space of faces to improve the recognition performance. They have also proposed novel feature-matching algorithms to minimize the PIE effects. For example, Chen et al. designed a nearest feature space (NFS) embedding algorithm that outperformed the other algorithms for face recognition. By searching the most similar sample with immune learning, in this paper, a novel algorithm is proposed to filter out the disturbances of PIE for face recognition. The adaptive adjustment for filtering out the disturbance of PIE is designed with immune memory to maximize the success possibility for recognizing the faces. The clonal selection frame is used to search the most similar samples to the target face, and the selected antibodies are memorized as the candidates for the best solution or the second optimal solution. The proposed approach is evaluated on several benchmark databases and is compared with the NFS embedding algorithm. The experimental results show that the proposed approach outperforms the NFS embedding algorithm.

Keywords: Face recognition, most similar sample searching, immune learning, clonal selection, immune memory.

1 Introduction

Face recognition algorithms often have to solve problems such as facial pose, illumination, and expression (PIE), which many researchers tried to find the best discriminant transformation in eigenspaces to solve [1]. He et al. proposed locality preserving projection (LPP) to preserve the local structure of training samples [2]. Cai et al. use an orthogonal locality preserving projection (OLPP) for more local information [3]. The nonlinear dimensionality reduction methods, such as the global geometric frame-work [4] and the locally linear embedding [5], are useful for the discriminant transformation. Moreover, prior problems of class labels and small sample size (S3) have been studied with various approaches such as LDA [6], F-LDA [7], D-LDA [8], K-DDA [9], FD-LDA [10], and PCA [11].

C.A. Coello Coello et al. (Eds.): ICARIS 2012, LNCS 7597, pp. 1–13, 2012.
© Springer-Verlag Berlin Heidelberg 2012

The traditional LDA approach has a strong limitation on that the data distribution in each class is assumed to be of a Gaussian distribution [1]. Many researchers have tried to extract the regularity of face features and eliminate unwanted noises from eigenspaces. For example, Chen et al. designed a nearest feature space (NFS) embedding algorithm that outperformed the other algorithms for face recognition [1]. Rajagopalan et al. built an eigen-background space for background learning [12].

In this paper, in order to improve the discriminant effectiveness in face recognition, a novel face recognition algorithm is proposed. It will filter out the disturbances of the conditional PIE factors by utilizing adaptive memory and searching for the most similar sample by immune learning in the feature space of faces. The experimental experience inspires us that the various feasible filters are useful to recognize the different face images more correctly. So an adaptive filter is designed with the memory able to train the feasible filter parameters so that it can recognize the training sample correctly. It is assumed that the face recognition algorithm with the well-trained filters can recognize the testing face samples in the same classes as those of the trained samples. The experiments are utilized to verify the proposed algorithm and compare it with other state-of-the-art algorithms under same experimental conditions.

2   Related Work

A number of approaches that are inspired from biological immune systems have already been applied to the pattern recognition filed. The biological immune system has natural and powerful capability for pattern recognition, and has been utilized for the innate immune recognition [13], [14], regulation of adaptive immunity [15], [16], and immune learning and memory for better recognition [17]. C. A. Janeway et al. described the innate immune system as a universal and ancient form of host defense against infection, and innate immune recognition relied on a limited number of germline-encoded receptors [13]. These receptors evolved to recognize conserved products of microbial metabolism produced by microbial pathogens.

Based on immunological theories and phenomena, some artificial immune systems are designed to simulate the biological immune systems and solve problems such as image recognition and security in the computer world.

G.C. Luh et al. proposed a face recognition method based on artificial immune networks and principal component analysis (PCA) [18]. The PCA abstracted principal eigenvectors of the image in order to get best feature description, hence to reduce the number of inputs of immune networks. Henceforth these image data with reduced dimensions were input into immune network classifiers to be trained. Subsequently the antibodies of the immune networks were optimized using genetic algorithms. The performance of the method was evaluated by employing the AT&T Laboratories Cambridge database.

W.P. Ma et al. put forward a clonal selection algorithm for face detection, based on the antibody clonal selection theory of immunology [19]. The detector was fast and reliable, which could detect faces with different sizes and various poses with both indoor and outdoor scenes. The goal of the research work was to detect all regions that might contain faces while remaining a low false positive output rate. The algorithm firstly abstracted the face tem-plate and then realized the precise location of the face using clonal selection algorithm and template matching.

A. Watkins et al. proposed the inception and subsequent revisions of an immune-inspired supervised learning algorithm [20].

S.H. Yu et al. proposed an improved conserved self pattern recognition algorithm to analyze cytological characteristics of breast fine-needle aspirates (FNAs) for clinical breast cancer diagnosis [21]. A novel detection strategy by coupling domain knowledge and randomized methods was proposed to resolve conflicts on anomaly detection between two types of detectors investigated in their earlier work on Conserved Self Pattern Recognition Algorithm (CSPRA).

3 Immune Learning Model for Searching Most Similar Sample

Consider N d-dimensional samples $x_1, x_2, \ldots, x_N$, which constitute N_C classes of faces. Let x_j^i denote a sample in the feature space R^d representing the jth sample in the ith class of size N_i. It is assumed that each class has the same size. The known samples $x_1, x_2, \ldots, x_N$ are used to train the immune learning model, and the immune learning model is built on the clonal selection principle [22] and the strategy for searching the most similar sample of the unknown objects $o_\alpha, \alpha = 1, 2, \ldots, N_o$ in R^d.

3.1 Immune Learning Model on Clonal Selection

The clonal selection principle, which was proposed by N.K. Jerne [23], is about adaptive immunity. In some way there is the recognition of self components from non-selfs, and from the facts of immunological tolerance the recognition mechanism is laid down toward the end of embryonic life.

Based on the feature space R^d and the clonal selection principle, the immune learning model is comprised of five parts: 1) the feature space R^d; 2) the operator for acquiring the feature information of an object; 3) the operator for searching the most similar sample; 4) the object that will be recognized; 5) the result set for learning the object.

3.2 Improved Clonal Selection Algorithm for Face Recognition

The antigens $Ag_\alpha, \alpha = 1, 2, \ldots, N_o$ and the antibodies $Ab_m, m = 1, 2, \ldots, N$ are the two repertories of digit matrixes for the improved clonal selection algorithm. N is calculated as below, because all N_i are the same as mentioned before.

$$N = \sum_{i=1}^{N_c} N_i = N_c \times N_i \qquad (1)$$

In traditional clonal selection algorithms for pattern recognition, the affinity measure was calculated by using the Hamming distance (D_m) between the antigen Ag_α and an antibody Ab_m, according to the following formula [22].

$$D_m = \sum_{k=1}^{d} \delta_{mk}, \quad \text{where } \delta_{mk} = \begin{cases} 1, & \text{if } Ab_{mk} \neq Ag_{\alpha k} \\ 0, & \text{otherwise} \end{cases} \tag{2}$$

Here, Ab_{mk} represents the kth feature of the antibody Ab_m, and $Ag_{\alpha k}$ represents the kth feature of the antibody Ag_α.

The drawback of this affinity measure is that it is too simple for the face recognition algorithm to discriminate similar faces with the disturbances of PIE, because the binary coding of the face images causes the loss of some image pixel data. So the affinity measure is improved and calculated as below.

$$M_m = \sum_{k=1}^{Ltp} (\delta_{mk} + \rho_{mk}),$$
where
$$\delta_{mk} = \begin{cases} u, & \text{if } Ab_{mk} \pm \varepsilon \in Ag_\alpha \\ 0, & \text{otherwise} \end{cases},$$

$$\rho_{mk} = \begin{cases} v, & \text{if } Ab_{mk} \pm \varepsilon = Ag_{\alpha\omega}, Ab_{m(k-1)} \pm \varepsilon = Ag_{\alpha(\omega-1)} \\ v, & \text{if } Ab_{mk} \pm \varepsilon = Ag_{\alpha\omega}, Ab_{m(k+1)} \pm \varepsilon = Ag_{\alpha(\omega+1)} \\ v, & \text{if } Ab_{mk} \pm \varepsilon = Ag_{\alpha\omega}, Ab_{m(k-Ntp)} \pm \varepsilon = Ag_{\alpha(\omega-Ntp)} \\ v, & \text{if } Ab_{mk} \pm \varepsilon = Ag_{\alpha\omega}, Ab_{m(k+Ntp)} \pm \varepsilon = Ag_{\alpha(\omega+Ntp)} \\ v, & \text{if } Ab_{mk} \pm \varepsilon = Ag_{\alpha\omega}, Ab_{m(k-Ntp-1)} \pm \varepsilon = Ag_{\alpha(\omega-Ntp-1)}, \\ v, & \text{if } Ab_{mk} \pm \varepsilon = Ag_{\alpha\omega}, Ab_{m(k-Ntp+1)} \pm \varepsilon = Ag_{\alpha(\omega-Ntp+1)} \\ v, & \text{if } Ab_{mk} \pm \varepsilon = Ag_{\alpha\omega}, Ab_{m(k+Ntp-1)} \pm \varepsilon = Ag_{\alpha(\omega+Ntp-1)} \\ v, & \text{if } Ab_{mk} \pm \varepsilon = Ag_{\alpha\omega}, Ab_{m(k+Ntp+1)} \pm \varepsilon = Ag_{\alpha(\omega+Ntp+1)} \\ 0, & \text{otherwise} \end{cases} \tag{3}$$

$Ltp = Mtp \times Ntp$,
$u + v = 1$,
$1 \leq \omega \leq Ltp$.

Here, Mtp and Ntp represents the pixel lengths of the face images, Ab_{mk} represents the k-th pixel value of the antibody Ab_m for matching the face image, $Ag_{\alpha\omega}$ represents the ω-th pixel value of the antigen Ag_α for the face image, $Ag_{\alpha(\omega-1)}$ represents the left-neighbor value of the ω-th pixel value of the antigen Ag_α for the face image, $Ag_{\alpha(\omega+1)}$ represents the right-neighbor value of the ω-th pixel value of the antigen Ag_α for the face image, $Ag_{\alpha(\omega-Ntp)}$ represents the upper-neighbor value of the ω-th pixel value of the antigen Ag_α for the face image, $Ag_{\alpha(\omega+Ntp)}$ represents the bottom-neighbor value of the ω-th pixel value of the antigen Ag_α for the face image, $Ag_{\alpha(\omega-Ntp-1)}$ represents the left-upper-neighbor value of the ω-th pixel value of the antigen Ag_α for the face image, $Ag_{\alpha(\omega-Ntp+1)}$ represents the right-upper-neighbor value of the ω-th pixel value of the antigen Ag_α for the face image, $Ag_{\alpha(\omega+Ntp-1)}$ represents the left-bottom-neighbor value of the ω-th pixel value of the antigen Ag_α for the face image, $Ag_{\alpha(\omega+Ntp+1)}$ represents the right-bottom-neighbor value of the ω-th pixel value of the antigen Ag_α for the face image, and $Ag_{\alpha\omega}$ represents the ω-th pixel value of the antigen Ag_α for the face image. The neighbors of the kth pixel value of the antibody Ab_m for matching the face image use the same positioning method as the ω-th pixel value of the antigen Ag_α for the face image.

Based on the characteristics of the faces with the disturbances of PIE and the improved affinity measure, the clonal selection algorithm is modified for better application in the face recognition.

Input: The coding matrixes of the training samples $x_1, x_2, \ldots, x_N$, and the unknown objects $\{o_\alpha\}$.

Output: The type and coding matrix of the most similar sample for the objects $\{o_\alpha\}$.

Step 1: $\alpha = 1$, $\beta = 1$.

Step 2:   Filter out the PIE disturbances in the coding matrixes of the training samples $x_1, x_2, \ldots, x_N$, with the lowest parameter value $w_{\alpha\beta}$ $(1 \le \beta \le L)$ and the PIE-filtering function $f(\cdot)$. The parameters $w_{\alpha\beta}$ and L are calculated as below.

$$w_{\alpha(\beta+1)} = w_{\alpha\beta} + \Delta\lambda, \tag{4}$$

$$L = \left\lfloor \left| \frac{255 - w_{\alpha 1}}{\Delta\lambda} \right| \right\rfloor + 1. \tag{5}$$

where $\Delta\lambda$ is the step value for increasing $w_{\alpha\beta}$.

Step 3:   Acquire the antigen Ag^α of the sample $Ab^\alpha_{(N_p+1)}$ for recognizing. Here, $Ab^\alpha_{(N_p+1)}$ denotes the last sample for training in the class which has the αth object.

$$N_p = N_i - 1, i = 1, 2, \ldots, N_c. \tag{6}$$

Here, N_i is the same.

Step 4:   Initialize the memory repertory $AB_{1\alpha}$ of antibodies with the PIE-filtered coding matrixes of the first N_p ones among the antibodies of the training samples $x_1, x_2, \ldots, x_N$.

$$AB_{1\alpha} = \{Ab_{m\alpha}, m = 1, 2, \ldots, N_p\}, \tag{7}$$

Step 5:   Initialize the first population $P_{1\alpha}$ of N_p antibodies from the memory repertory $AB_{1\alpha}$ of antibodies. $AB_{t\alpha}, t = 1, 2, \ldots, N_g$ represents the tth-generation memory repertory of antibodies, and here $t = 1$. The generation number N_g of antibody clonal selection is calculated as below.

$$N_g = N_c. \tag{8}$$

Step 6:   Calculate the affinity $fit_{r\alpha}, r = 1, 2, \ldots, N_p$ between the last sample $Ab^\alpha_{(N_p+1)}$ for the class and any antibody Ab_{mr} in the memory repertory $AB_{1\alpha}$, and construct an affinity vector below.

$$fit_\alpha = \{fit_{r\alpha}, r = 1, 2, \ldots, N_p\}. \tag{9}$$

Step 7: Select n $(n < N_p)$ most matchable antibodies with the antigen Ag^α according to the affinity $fit_{r\alpha}$, and construct the new set S of antibodies below.

$$S = \{Ab_{m_{S_l}}, l = 1, 2, \ldots, n\}. \tag{10}$$

Step 8: The generation increases by 1, i.e. $t = t + 1$. Acquire the next N_p antibodies from the next memory repertory $AB_{t\alpha}$ of antibodies, and calculate the affinity $fit_{r\alpha}$ between the antigen Ag^α and any antibody Ab_{mr} in the memory repertory $AB_{t\alpha}$. Afterwards, mutate the N_p antibodies using the better antibodies in the set S instead of the worse antibodies in the next memory repertory $AB_{t\alpha}$ of antibodies. Then, produce the next-generation population $P_{t\alpha}$ through the clone of the better antibodies and the elimination of the worse antibodies.

Step 9: If $t < N_g$, then go to Step 6 again; else go to Step 10.

Step 10: $\alpha = \alpha + 1$. If $\alpha < N_o$, then go to Step 2 again; else go to Step 11.

Step 11: Calculate the correct recognition rate r_β for the parameter values $w_{\alpha\beta}$ below. N_r represents the sum of objects that are recognized correctly.

$$r_\beta = \frac{N_r}{N_o}. \tag{11}$$

Step 12: If $\beta + \Delta\lambda \leq L$, then $\beta = \beta + \Delta\lambda$, $\alpha = 1$, and go to Step 2 again; else go to Step 13.

Step 13: Compare the correct recognition rates $\{r_\beta\}$, and find the maximum $r_M = MAX\{r_\beta\}$ and the corresponding parameter values $\{w_{\alpha M}\}$. Then memorize the parameter values $\{w_{\alpha M}\}$.

Step 14: $\alpha = 1$.

Step 15: Filter the PIE disturbances in the coding matrixes of the training samples $x_1, x_2, \ldots, x_N$, and the unknown objects $\{o_\alpha\}$, with the best parameter value $w_{\alpha M}$ and the PIE-filtering function $f(\cdot)$.

Step 16: Initialize the memory repertory $AB_{1\alpha}$ of antibodies with the PIE-filtered coding matrixes of the first N_p ones among the antibodies of the training samples $x_1, x_2, \ldots, x_N$ according to (7).

Step 17: Initialize the first population $P_{1\alpha}$ of N_p antibodies from the memory repertory $AB_{1\alpha}$ of antibodies.

Step 18: Calculate the affinity $fit_{r\alpha}, r = 1, 2, \ldots, N_p$ between the antigen Ag_α and any antibody Ab_{mr} in the memory repertory $AB_{1\alpha}$, and construct an affinity vector according to (9).

Step 19: Select n $(n < N_p)$ most matchable antibodies with the antigen Ag_α according to the affinity $fit_{r\alpha}$, and construct the new set S of antibodies according to (10).

Step 20: The generation increases by 1, i.e. $t = t+1$. Acquire the next N_p antibodies from the next memory repertory $AB_{t\alpha}$ of antibodies, and calculate the affinity $fit_{r\alpha}, r = 1,2,...,N_p$ between the antigen Ag_α and any antibody Ab_{mr} in the memory repertory $AB_{t\alpha}$. Afterwards, mutate the N_p antibodies using the better antibodies in the set S instead of the worse antibodies in the next memory repertory $AB_{t\alpha}$ of antibodies. Then, produce the next-generation population $P_{t\alpha}$ through the clone of the better antibodies and the elimination of the worse antibodies.

Step 21: If $t < N_g$, then go to Step 18 again; else go to Step 22.

Step 22: If the coding matrix of the object o_α does not equal to the coding matrix of any sample in the training samples $x_1, x_2, ..., x_N$, the recognition type and the coding matrix of the object o_α are memorized into the set of the samples, and $N = N+1$.

Step 23: $\alpha = \alpha+1$. If $\alpha < N_o$, then go to Step 15 again; else go to Step 24.

Step 24: Calculate the correct recognition rate r_M for the parameter values $\{w_{\alpha M} \mid \alpha = 1,2,...,N_o\}$, and output the recognition type and coding matrix of the most similar sample for the objects $\{o_\alpha\}$. End.

4   Immune Model for Face Recognition

For face recognition, we propose a tri-tier immune model, which is comprised of native immune tier, adaptive immune tier, and parallel immune tier, as shown in Fig. 1. The native immune tier is used to recognize the known faces mainly by matching the known faces in the feature space of faces. The feature space is an important sample set for increasing recognition efficiency, and the recognition types and coding matrixes of the known samples are memorized into the feature space. The adaptive immune tier learns the unknown faces with the improved clonal selection algorithm. The learning is based on searching the most similar sample in the feature space of faces. The parallel immune tier is utilized to increase computing speed and keep the load balance for face recognition with parallel computing.

Furthermore, when the objects for face recognition are unknown, the immune learning of the adaptive immune tier and the immune computing of the parallel immune tier are used to search the most similar sample in the feature space by the improved clonal selection algorithm. If the searching processes return positive results, the unknown faces are recognized successfully. Besides, the matrixes of the faces are inserted into the feature space to make them become new samples. The mutation and selection of the improved clonal selection algorithm lead the searching to the best solutions according to the improved affinity. Based on the sample updating, the recognition type and the coding matrix of the new recognized faces are memorized after learning and recognition, so the unknown faces can become known ones in this way.

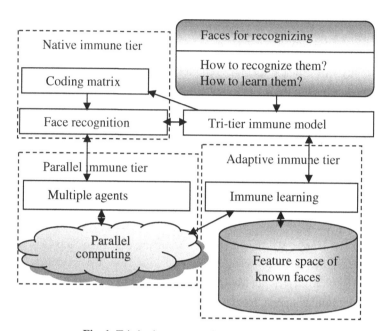

Fig. 1. Tri-tier immune model for face recognition

Finally, the learning and recognition of some unknown faces may be time-consuming and the real-time requirement needs faster responses. The parallel computing is one of good ways to increase the efficiency of face recognition and can keep the healthy load balance in most occasions.

5   Experimental Results

Experiments are conducted to test the effectiveness of the proposed algorithm. Several face benchmark databases, including ORL [24] and CMU [25], were utilized for evaluating the recognition performance. These data sets are briefly summarized as follows: First, the ORL face data set is comprised of 400 images and 40 individuals (10 images per person), with different PIE. Second, the CMU face data set consists of 68 people with PIE variations.

Before the comparison of recognition performance, a simple example is used to illustrate the class separability, the most similar sample searching, and the immune learning based on the improved clonal selection. With the Hamming-distance-based affinity measure and the binary coding of the images in the ORL face database, the testing results in Fig. 2 show that the recognition rate of the affinity measure with the Hamming distances is obviously lower than that of the improved affinity measure, because this affinity measure with the Hamming distance and the binary coding of images cause the loss of image information.

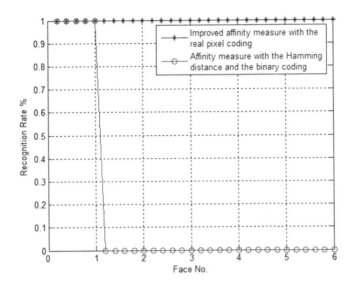

Fig. 2. Recognition rate comparison between the improved affinity measure with the real pixel coding and the affinity measure with the Hamming distance and the binary coding for the face example

In the experiments, some images are randomly selected from the face data sets as training set, with the diversity and typicality of the training samples kept, and the others are utilized for testing. The face images of size 92 by 112 were taken between April 1992 and April 1994 at the Olivetti Research Laboratory in Cambridge [24], and there are 10 different images of 40 distinct subjects, as shown in Fig. 3. For some of the subjects, the images were taken at different times, varying lighting slightly, facial expressions (open/closed eyes, smiling/non-smiling) and facial details (glasses/no-glasses). All the images are taken from a dark homogeneous background and the subjects are in up-right, frontal position (with tolerance for some side movement). The NFS-based recognition method, which was designed by Chen et al., cropped the original face images into the face-only ones to eliminate the influence of hair and background [1]. But this procedure is not necessary for the novel approach proposed in this paper, so the novel approach is simpler and more convenient.

All testing samples are matched with the training samples according to some matching rules. Each algorithm is executed 20 times to obtain the average rates. The recognition rates of several algorithms are compared with the proposed algorithm on various training samples for the benchmark databases are listed in Table 1, and 2. The standard derivations for these data sets are also compared in Table 3 to study the robustness of the proposed method. From these tables, the recognition rate of the proposed algorithm attains the maximum value and the standard derivation of the proposed algorithm is the minimum. Therefore, the performance of the novel face recognition approach based on the most similar sample searching and immune learning is the best among all tested.

Fig. 3. The original face images of size 92 by 112 for the examples of the ORL benchmark database

Table 1. The Highest Recognition Performance on the ORL Databases (Percent)

Dataset	ORL	
Method	4 Trains	5 Trains
PCA+LPPFace [1]	91.25(41)	97.00(51)
PCA+OLPPFace [1]	94.17(37)	97.00(22)
PCA+ONPDA [1]	91.92(61)	95.25(27)
PCA+MFA [1]	89.16(69)	95.00(69)
PCA+NFLE F1 [1]	94.17(41)	95.00(22)
PCA+NFLE F2 [1]	94.58(39)	97.00(24)
Novel face recognition approach	**100**	**100**

Table 2. The Highest Recognition Performance on the CMU Databases (Percent)

Dataset	CMU			
Method	6 Trains	9 Trains	12 Trains	15 Trains
PCA+LPPFace	67.72(56)	77.28(52)	85.95(61)	91.61(66)
PCA+OLPPFace	73.55(64)	76.15(66)	84.87(59)	90.77(70)
PCA+ONPDA	63.71(70)	71.90(70)	77.81(70)	88.28(67)
PCA+MFA	64.12(70)	73.94(70)	81.65(70)	88.32(70)
PCA+NFLE F1	75.45(62)	80.15(64)	88.53(70)	94.05(70)
PCA+NFLE F2	77.48(62)	80.15(64)	88.53(70)	94.05(70)
Novel approach	**100**	**100**	**100**	**100**

Table 3. The Average Recognition Rates and the Standard Derivations on Various Databases (Percent)

Dataset	ORL	CMU
Method	4 Trains	9 Trains
PCA+LPPFace	89.95 ± 1.3	72.78 ± 4.5
PCA+OLPPFace	92.37 ± 1.8	71.75 ± 4.4
PCA+ONPDA	89.92 ± 2.0	67.20 ± 4.7
PCA+MFA	87.16 ± 2.0	69.24 ± 4.7
PCA+NFLE F1	91.97 ± 2.2	75.55 ± 4.6
PCA+NFLE F2	92.38 ± 2.2	78.08 ± 4.5
Novel approach	$\mathbf{99.17 \pm 0.9}$	$\mathbf{97.65 \pm 2.4}$

Furthermore, the reasons for the failure of recognizing some faces are analyzed according to the disturbances of PIE and the limited number of training samples. For example, recognizing the faces in the ORL face database, the first four face images of No. 1-4 are used for training in the 4 trains, the face image No. 5 is used for additional training in the 5 trains, and the last two face images of No. 6 and No. 10 are not recognized correctly in the 4 trains. The possible reason for the failure of recognizing the face image of No. 6 is the obvious difference in their facial poses between this face image and the most similar face image No. 1 for training. The face image of No. 6 also has bigger difference in their expressions from the face image of No. 4 for training. The possible reason for the failure of recognizing the face image of No. 10 is the obvious difference in their illuminations between that face image and the most similar image No. 3 for training. However, when the additional sample of No. 5 is added for better training in the 5 trains, the face image of No. 6 can be recognized correctly and the face image of No. 10 is not recognized correctly yet.

6   Conclusion

In this study, the clonal selection frame has been modified for face recognition. The affinity measure of the clonal selection algorithm has been modified to represent the feature matching of the face recognition. The most similar samples are searched to recognize the classes of the target face images. This novel approach of face recognition needs no cropping of the face images, but the face recognition algorithm has been immunized against the disturbances of PIE. From the experimental results, not only the proposed approach has higher recognition rates for the ORL face database and the CMU face database, but also the training time of the proposed approach is less. In the future, the learning ability in the expandable feature space of face images will be addressed [26], [27]. Expandable feature dimensions for discriminating need to be found and analyzed to obtain more reliable results.

Acknowledgement. The work was supported in part by grants from the Shanghai Educational Development Foundation (2007CG42), Natural Science Foundation of Shanghai (08ZR1400400), and the Shanghai postgraduate education creative plan (SHGS-KC-2012OO3). I thank anonymous reviewers, IEEE Fellow Bharat Bhargava and IEEE Senior Members Zixing Cai and Yuhui Shi for their good advice on improving the research in this paper. I also thank my graduate student Long Li for his programming help.

References

1. Chen, Y.N., Han, C.C., Wang, C.T., et al.: Face Recognition Using Nearest Feature Space Embedding. IEEE Transactions on Pattern Analysis and Machine Intelligence 33(6), 1073–1086 (2011), doi:10.1109/TPAMI.2010.197
2. He, X., Yan, S., Ho, Y., et al.: Face Recognition Using Laplacianfaces. IEEE Transactions on Pattern Analysis and Machine Intelligence 27(3), 328–340 (2005), doi:10.1109/TPAMI.2005.55
3. Cai, D., He, X., Han, J., Zhang, H.: Orthogonal Laplacianfaces for Face Recognition. IEEE Trans. Image Processing 15(11), 3608–3614 (2006), doi:10.1109/TIP.2006.881945
4. Tenenbaum, J., Silva, V., Langford, J.: A Global Geometric Framework for Nonlinear Dimensionality Reduction. Science 290(22), 2319–2323 (2000)
5. Roweis, S.T., Saul, L.K.: Nonlinear Dimensionality Reduction by Locally Linear Embedding. Science 290(22), 2323–2326 (2000)
6. Belhumeur, P.N., Hespanha, J.P., Kriegman, D.J.: Eigenfaces vs. Fisherfaces: Recognition Using Class Specific Linear Projection. IEEE Trans. Pattern Analysis and Machine Intelligence 19(7), 711–720 (1997), doi:10.1109/34.598228
7. Lotlikar, R., Kothari, R.: Fractional-Step Dimensionality Reduction. IEEE Trans. Pattern Analysis and Machine Intelligence 22(6), 623–627 (2000), doi:10.1109/34.862200
8. Yang, J., Zhang, D., Frangi, A., et al.: Two-Dimensional PCA: A New Approach to Appearance-Based Face Representation and Recognition. IEEE Trans. Pattern Analysis and Machine Intelligence 26(1), 131–137 (2004), doi:10.1109/TPAMI.2004.10004
9. Etemad, K., Chellappa, R.: Discriminant Analysis for Recognition of Human Face Recognition. J. Optical Soc. Am. 14(8), 1724–1733 (1997)
10. Fortuna, J., Capson, D.: Improved Support Vector Classification Using PCA and ICA Feature Space Modification. Pattern Recognition 37(6), 1117–1129 (2004)
11. Swets, D., Weng, J.: Using Discriminant Eigenfeatures for Image Retrieval. IEEE Trans. Pattern Analysis and Machine Intelligence 18(8), 831–836 (1996), doi:10.1109/34.531802
12. Rajagopalan, A.N., Chellappa, R., Koterba, N.: Background Learning for Robust Face Recognition with PCA in the Presence of Clutter. IEEE Trans. Image Processing 14(6), 832–843 (2005), doi:10.1109/TIP.2005.847288
13. Janeway, C.A., Medzhitov, R.: Innate Immune Recognition. Annu. Rev. Immunol. 20, 197–216 (2002)
14. Kofoed, E.M., Vance, R.E.: Innate immune recognition of bacterial ligands by NAIPs determines inflammasome specificity. Nature 10394, 1–6 (2011)
15. Iwasaki, A., Medzhitov, R.: Regulation of Adaptive Immunity by the Innate Immune System. Science 327(5963), 291–295 (2010)
16. Huang, S.F., Wang, X., Yan, Q.Y., et al.: The Evolution and Regulation of the Mucosal Immune Complexity in the Basal Chordate Amphioxus. The Journal of Immunology 186(4), 2042–2055 (2011)

17. Yirmiya, R., Goshen, I.: Immune modulation of learning, memory, neural plasticity and neurogenesis. Brain, Behavior, and Immunity 25(2), 181–213 (2011)
18. Luh, G.C., Lin, C.Y.: PCA based immune networks for human face recognition. Applied Soft Computing 11(2), 1743–1752 (2011)
19. Ma, W.P., Shang, R.H., Jiao, L.C.: A Novel Clonal Selection Algorithm for Face Detection. In: Sattar, A., Kang, B.-H. (eds.) AI 2006. LNCS (LNAI), vol. 4304, pp. 799–807. Springer, Heidelberg (2006)
20. Watkins, A., Timmis, J., Boggess, L.: Artificial Immune Recognition System (AIRS): An Immune Inspired Supervised Machine Learning Algorithm. Genetic Programming and Evolvable Machines 5(3), 291–317 (2004)
21. Yu, S., Dasgupta, D.: Conserved Self Pattern Recognition Algorithm with Novel Detection Strategy Applied to Breast Cancer Diagnosis. Journal of Artificial Evolution and Applications, Special Issue on Artificial Evolution Methods in the Biological and Biomedical Sciences, 1–12 (January 2009)
22. de Castro, L.N., Von Zuben, F.J.: Learning and optimization using the clonal selection principle. IEEE Transactions on Evolutionary Computation 6(3), 239–251 (2002)
23. Burnet, F.M.: The Clonal Selection Theory of Acquired Immunity. Cambridge University Press, Cambridge (1959)
24. Samaria, F., Harter, A.: Parameterisation of a stochastic model for human face identification. In: Proceedings of 2nd IEEE Workshop on Applications of Computer Vision, pp. 138–142 (December 1994)
25. Sim, T., Baker, S., Bsat, M.: The CMU Pose, Illumination, and Expression Database. IEEE Trans. Pattern Analysis and Machine Intelligence 25(12), 1615–1618 (2003)
26. Gong, T., Cai, Z.X.: Artificial Immune System Based on Normal Model and Its Applications. Tsinghua University Press, Beijing (2011)
27. Fu, K.S., Cai, Z.X., Xu, G.Y.: Artificial intelligence principles and applications. Tsinghua University Press, Beijing (1988)

A Multi-Objective Artificial Immune System Based on Hypervolume

Thomas Pierrard[1] and Carlos A. Coello Coello[2,*]

[1] University of Nantes
Nantes, France
tom.pierrard@gmail.com
[2] CINVESTAV-IPN (Evolutionary Computation Group)
Departamento de Computación, Av. IPN No. 2508
Col. San Pedro Zacatenco, México, D.F. 07360, México
ccoello@cs.cinvestav.mx

Abstract. This paper presents a new artificial immune system algorithm for solving multi-objective optimization problems, based on the clonal selection principle and the hypervolume contribution. The main aim of this work is to investigate the performance of this class of algorithm with respect to approaches which are representative of the state-of-the-art in multi-objective optimization using metaheuristics. The results obtained by our proposed approach, called multi-objective artificial immune system based on hypervolume (MOAIS-HV) are compared with respect to those of the NSGA-II. Our preliminary results indicate that our proposed approach is very competitive, and can be a viable choice for solving multi-objective optimization problems.

Keywords: Multi Objective Optimization, Artificial Immune System, Hypervolume.

1 Introduction

For the last decades, metaheuristics have been widely used to solve multi-objective optimization problems (MOPs). The main advantage of metaheuristics in general, is that at each generation, the algorithm is able to provide solutions (exact or approximate) in a reasonably low amount of time, even if the problem has a highly nonlinear or very large search space. On the other hand, mathematical programming techniques may not work properly under certain conditions (e.g., in some highly nonlinear problems or when the objective function is not available in algebraic form). In spite of their theoretical limitations, metaheuristics tend to generate approximations of the global optimum that are generally sufficiently good to justify their use in a wide variety of practical applications.

* The authors acknowledge partial support of the UMI LAFMIA 3175 CNRS located at CINVESTAV-IPN. The second author also acknowledges support from CONACyT project no. 103570.

C.A. Coello Coello et al. (Eds.): ICARIS 2012, LNCS 7597, pp. 14–27, 2012.

From the many metaheuristics in current use, Artificial Immune Systems (AISs) are among the less commonly adopted for numerical optimization, in spite of their good performance in certain domains (see for example [1]). Here, we explore the performance of a multi-objective artificial immune system which incorporates a hypervolume-based selection mechanism (we call it MOAIS-HV). The aim is to show that this sort of approach can be a viable alternative for dealing with complex multi-objective optimization problems, even when facing a high number of objectives.

The remainder of this paper is organized as follows. Section 2 provides the basic concepts required to understand the rest of the paper. In Section 3, we provide a generic outline of multi-objective artificial immune systems (MOAISs). The previous related work is briefly reviewed in Section 4. Our proposed approach is described in detail in Section 5. A comparison of results between our proposed approach and NSGA-II is presented in Section 6. Finally, our conclusions and some possible paths for future research are provided in Section 7.

2   Basic Concepts

We are interested in solving problems of the type[1]:

$$\text{minimize } \boldsymbol{f}(\boldsymbol{x}) := [f_1(\boldsymbol{x}), f_2(\boldsymbol{x}), \ldots, f_k(\boldsymbol{x})] \tag{1}$$

subject to:

$$g_i(\boldsymbol{x}) \leq 0 \quad i = 1, 2, \ldots, m \tag{2}$$

$$h_i(\boldsymbol{x}) = 0 \quad i = 1, 2, \ldots, p \tag{3}$$

where $\boldsymbol{x} = [x_1, x_2, \ldots, x_n]^T$ is the vector of decision variables, $f_i : \mathbb{R}^n \to \mathbb{R}$, $i = 1, ..., k$ are the objective functions and $g_i, h_j : \mathbb{R}^n \to \mathbb{R}$, $i = 1, ..., m$, $j = 1, ..., p$ are the constraint functions of the problem.

To describe the concept of optimality in which we are interested, we will introduce next a few definitions.

Definition 1. Given two vectors $\boldsymbol{x}, \boldsymbol{y} \in \mathbb{R}^k$, we say that $\boldsymbol{x} \leq \boldsymbol{y}$ if $x_i \leq y_i$ for $i = 1, ..., k$, and that $\boldsymbol{x}$ **dominates** $\boldsymbol{y}$ (denoted by $\boldsymbol{x} \prec \boldsymbol{y}$) if $\boldsymbol{x} \leq \boldsymbol{y}$ and $\boldsymbol{x} \neq \boldsymbol{y}$.

Definition 2. We say that a vector of decision variables $\boldsymbol{x} \in \mathcal{X} \subset \mathbb{R}^n$ is **nondominated** with respect to $\mathcal{X}$, if there does not exist another $\boldsymbol{x}' \in \mathcal{X}$ such that $\boldsymbol{f}(\boldsymbol{x}') \prec \boldsymbol{f}(\boldsymbol{x})$.

Definition 3. We say that a vector of decision variables $\boldsymbol{x}^* \in \mathcal{F} \subset \mathbb{R}^n$ ($\mathcal{F}$ is the feasible region) is **Pareto-optimal** if it is nondominated with respect to $\mathcal{F}$.

---

[1] Without loss of generality, we will assume only minimization problems.

Definition 4. The **Pareto Optimal Set** $\mathcal{P}^*$ is defined by:

$$\mathcal{P}^* = \{x \in \mathcal{F} | x \text{ is Pareto-optimal}\}$$

Definition 5. The **Pareto Front** $\mathcal{PF}^*$ is defined by:

$$\mathcal{PF}^* = \{f(x) \in \mathbb{R}^k | x \in \mathcal{P}^*\}$$

We thus wish to determine the Pareto optimal set from the set $\mathcal{F}$ of all the decision variable vectors that satisfy (2) and (3). Note however that in practice, not all the Pareto optimal set is normally desirable (e.g., it may not be desirable to have different solutions that map to the same values in objective function space) or achievable.

When working with multi-objective optimization problems, there are two main aims: to generate solutions as close as possible to the true Pareto front and to have a set of nondominated solutions well distributed along the Pareto front.

3 Multi Objective Artificial Immune Systems

The immune system's role is to defend the body against infections. It has several defenses against outside attacks: the barrier of the skin, mucous membranes, and the passive system defense of cells, but the functioning of antibodies is its main element. Usually, when a foreign element is detected by the immune system, an immediate elimination reaction sets in. This reaction involves phagocytic cells and lymphocytes that circulate continuously throughout the body. This reaction is fast and called non-specific, meaning that the immune system attacks the antigen without knowing its nature.

Depending on the severity of the infection, this rapid and non-specific immune response may not be sufficient to eliminate the intruder. A second reaction, slower and more specific is then set up: it puts into play the recognition of the foreign element by immune cells. Following the recognition, immune cells specifically adapted for the destruction of the foreign agent (lymphocytes) will multiply rapidly. Some of these clones may be corrupt, and a risk of generating autoimmune cells occurs. The immune system is able to suppress self-generated cells (suppression of similar individuals). Subsequently, the organism keeps track of this encounter with the foreign element (thanks to the B cells). There is some form of memory in the immune system. This optimizes the specific immune response, which will be faster at a forthcoming encounter with the same foreign element.

In the design of a multi-objective artificial immune system (MOAIS), two sets of solutions are normally considered: *antibodies* (Ab) and *antigens* (Ag). The differences between them is defined by the designer of the algorithm, but normally one set represents "good" solutions (e.g., nondominated solutions to a multi-objective optimization problem) and the other represents "bad" solutions (e.g., the solutions that are dominated by others). The interactions between the solutions (e.g., Ag-Ab, Ag-Ag, and so on) are defined by an *affinity function.* It is normally the case that the measures of quality in which we are interested on (e.g., Pareto dominance and the spread of the solutions, in the case of multi-objective optimization) are embedded into the affinity function. Depending on the affinity value, a selection and a cloning process occurs, and then the clones are mutated. Finally, a certain strategy is used to generate the new population and to store the best solutions found so far (normally, an external archive that stores only nondominated solutions is adopted for this sake). Campelo et al. [2], provide a canonical algorithm of a MOAIS (see Algorithm 1).

Algorithm 1: Outline of a canonical MOAIS

---

1 Define the search space $\mathbb{S}$, objectives functions f_i, constraints g_j, h_k ;
2 $A(t = 0) \longleftarrow$ Initialize offline population;
3 $B(t = 0) \longleftarrow$ Initialize online population with random individuals;
4 **while** $\neg$ *stop criterion* **do**
5 $\quad$ Evaluate population $B(t)$ using f_i, g_j, h_k;
6 $\quad$ $B_1(t) \longleftarrow$ Define affinities($B(t), [A(t)]$);
7 $\quad$ $B_2(t) \longleftarrow$ Selection for cloning($B_1(t), [A(t)]$);
8 $\quad$ $B_3(t) \longleftarrow$ Proliferation and mutation($B_2(t)$);
9 $\quad$ $B_4(t) \longleftarrow$ Diversification & Suppression;
10 $\quad$ $B(t + 1) \longleftarrow B_3(t) \cup B_4(t)$;
11 $\quad$ $A(t + 1) \longleftarrow$ Update($A(t), B(t + 1)$);
12 $\quad$ $t \longleftarrow t + 1$;
13 **end**

It is worth noting that the canonical MOAIS of Campelo et al. [2] adopts the clonal selection priciple. The reason is that, most MOAISs currently available in the literature follow this principle.

Algorithm 1 first defines the problem, like all population-based algorithms (line 1). An archive is defined (line 2) in order to store the nondominated solutions found so far. The main (or internal) population is initialized (line 3) containing the solutions from the current generation. The main loop starts and performs the following steps until a stop criterion is met. The algorithm evaluates the online (or main) population (line 5) using the objective functions and constraints of the problem. Depending on the choices made, the solutions of the set B are analyzed and given an affinity value (line 6), the archive A can be used, for example, to define the new affinities between the current solutions and the best solutions found so far. Cloning selection is then triggered following either stochastic or deterministic rules (line 7), and based on affinities values or not. The cloning process is usually done based on the affinity values (proportional cloning), while the mutation of each individual can have several variants (line 8). The two previous steps constitute the so-called *clonal selection principle*. The diversification procedure (line 9) is not mandatory, and its goal is to maintain diversity in the population usually by creating new random individuals. Suppression is not mandatory either and can be applied to delete some individuals (responsible for autoimmune disorder), particularly to individuals that are not relevant for further optimization. The new population is generated taking into account the best clones (line 10), applying some predefined rules. Eventually, the archive is updated (line 11). At the end of the run, the archive will contain the set of nondominated solutions that constitutes our approximation of the true Pareto front of the problem.

4   Previous Related Work

An overview of MOAISs is provided in [3]. It shows that MISA (Multiobjective Immune System Algorithm), which was originally introduced in 2002 [4] is considered as the first Pareto-based MOAIS reported in the specialized literature[2] [6]. The algorithm is designed to fit the immune system metaphor and it follows the canonical algorithm previously presented. MISA uses Pareto ranking to classify solutions and to determine which of them will be cloned. The number of clones depends on antibody-antibody affinities. The clones are uniformly mutated according to their antigen-antibody affinities whereas other solutions use non-uniform mutation. An adaptive grid is used to ensure diversity in the (fixed size) external archive. Selection to access the archive is determined by some pre-defined rules based on Pareto ranking. The results obtained by MISA showed that the use of AISs for solving multi-objective optimization problems was a viable alternative. Over the years, several other MOAISs were introduced. The approaches that will be discussed here were selected based on the fulfillment of the five following criteria:

1. The approach follows the structure and behavior of a canonical AIS.
2. The approach does not adopt a recombination operator.
3. The approach allows the use of real-numbers encoding (as the approach proposed in this paper).
4. Its authors provide detailed results of the algorithm's performance.
5. The approach is relatively recent (2005 to date).

4.1   Vector Artificial Immune System (VAIS)

This approach was proposed in [7], and it uses a Pareto-based selection, cloning, mutation, suppression and an archiving process. For the nondominated individuals, fitness is determined by the strength defined in SPEA2 [8]. For dominated solutions, fitness corresponds to the number of individuals which dominate them. A suppression procedure is used for the archive as well as a diversification procedure by allowing a fixed number of random individuals to enter the archive.

---

[2] The first direct use of an artificial immune system to solve multi-objective optimization problems reported in the literature is due to Yoo and Hajela [5]. However, this approach uses a linear aggregating function to combine objective function and constraint information into a scalar value that is used as the fitness function of a genetic algorithm. Thus, this approach is really a hybrid algorithm and does not rely on Pareto optimality.

Results are compared with respect to the NSGA-II [9]. The authors show that VAIS can outperform NSGA-II in several unconstrained and constrained problems. However, it is worth noting that VAIS was not tested in the Deb-Thiele-Laumanns-Zitzler (DTLZ) test suite [10], which is a standard benchmark for multi-objective evolutionary algorithms (MOEAs).

4.2 Immune Dominance Clonal Multiobjective Algorithm/Nondominated Neighbor Immune Algorithm (IDCMA/NNIA)

The Immune Dominance Clonal Multiobjective Algorithm (IDCMA) was introduced in [11]. However, the difficulties of this algorithm for solving the DTLZ test suite [10], motivated the development of an improved version, which was called Nondominated Neighbor Immune Algorithm (NNIA), which was introduced in [12]. The selection mechanism which is responsible of choosing the set of candidates to be cloned, aims for the nondominated solutions. However, if the nondominated solutions are beyond a certain threshold, then the crowding distance is used. The archiving process uses the same methods to select candidates to enter the archive (i.e., nondominated solutions are always preferred). In NNIA, recombination is adopted. However, the authors also present results without the use of recombination (which is the reason why we selected this approach for this section). Nevertheless, the authors indicate that recombination provides a significant improvement of results for NNIA in some of the DTLZ test problems.

4.3 Immune Forgetting Multiobjective Optimization Algorithm (IFMOA)

This approach was introduced in [13]. In this case, the affinity assignment is based on the Pareto strength from SPEA2 [8]. This approach also adopts an antibody-antibody affinity which is inversely proportional to the sum of the two smallest Euclidean distances between an antibody and the rest of the population. The "immune forget unit" is a set of solutions that do not participate in the clonal proliferation. The results of this approach are compared with respect to MOGA [14] and SPEA2 on six unconstrained problems. The results presented by the authors show a good performance of IFMOA, but none of the test problems adopted is particularly difficult by today's standards in evolutionary multi-objective optimization.

4.4 Omni-aiNet

This approach was introduced in [15] and can be used for both single- and multi-objective optimization. First, all the individuals are cloned N_c times (N_c is a user-defined parameter). A random variation with rates inversely proportional to the affinity to the antigen is applied to each generated clone. Polynomial mutation is used to apply variations to the clones. Solutions are arranged in classes, so that the better the class, the smaller the variation. The algorithm adopts both suppression and diversification. Unfortunately, the authors provide results only with respect to those of another approach called *DT omni-optimizer*. Additionally, results are presented only in graphical form and for three problems. This does not allow to know how competitive is this approach with respect to state-of-the-art MOEAs.

Based on the previous discussion, it should be clear that most of the current MOAISs still adopt some form of Pareto ranking. Nowadays, however, several efforts have been focused on the development of indicator-based MOEAs. The main motivation for this is to overcome the poor performance exhibited by Pareto-based selection when dealing with problems that have four or more objectives [16]. Although several indicator-based MOEAs have been proposed in the last few years, no indicator-based MOAIS has been proposed so far, to the authors' best knowledge. We believe that the approach introduced in this paper is the first of such indicator-based MOAISs.

It is worth noting that not just any performance indicator can be adopted for selecting solutions. The most commonly adopted is an indicator known as **Hypervolume**.[3] The main advantage of the hypervolume indicator is that it has been proved that its maximization is equivalent to finding the Pareto optimal set [18]. This has been empirically corroborated [19] and, in fact, the maximization of this indicator also leads to sets of solutions whose spread along the Pareto front is maximized (although the distribution of such solutions is not necessarily uniform). Because of its popularity, we decided to adopt hypervolume for the MOAIS reported in this paper.

5   Our Proposed Approach

In this section, our proposed approach, called MOAIS-HV (HV stands for hypervolume) is described in detail. The main goal of the work reported here was to investigate the feasibility of incorporating a hypervolume-based selection into a MOAIS. It is worth noting that our proposed approach follows the main features of an AIS (we do not adopt any recombination operator, unlike most of the hypervolume-based MOEAs in current use).

5.1   Description of the Algorithm

The main idea of MOAIS-HV is to maintain an online population of antigens and antibodies. The antigens are considered to be the good solutions, and the antibodies are the bad ones. These two sets form two new subpopulations. The antigens are cloned (the best antibodies are cloned, too, if the number of antigens is insufficient) and a mutation operator is applied. If only one rank exists,

---

[3] The hypervolume (also known as the S metric or the Lebesgue Measure) of a set of solutions measures the size of the portion of objective space that is dominated by those solutions collectively [17].

candidates to be cloned are selected from individuals that contribute the most to maximize the hypervolume; otherwise, successive ranks are selected and hypervolume selection is only applied to the last one. The clones and the best antigens found are merged and the size of the main population is maintained by discarding individuals that contribute the least in maximizing the hypervolume. In the algorithm, the following notations will be used: Q, P: the main population and the pool, Ab, Ag: the sets of antibodies and antigens (subsets of Q), n: size of the main population, $m, ngen$: number of objectives and number of generations.

1. Initializing populations: Initialize population Q (Main population) by generating random individuals.
   $\rightarrow$ fixed size n.
   Initialize Antibodies population Ab to empty.
   $\rightarrow$ fixed size n.
   Initialize Antigens (or Archive) population Ag to empty.
   $\rightarrow$ fixed size n. Store the best individuals found so far.
   Initialize a pool P to empty (to store the clones).
   $\rightarrow$ fixed size $2 * n$.

2. Evaluate all individuals of the population Q.
   $\rightarrow$ Feasibility and objective values
   $\rightarrow$ Fast non-dominated ranking
3. "Split" the population Q into two sets:
   Constrained problems:
   Antigens:
   $\rightarrow$ Feasible and non-dominated
   Antibodies:
   $\rightarrow$ Infeasible and non-dominated
   $\rightarrow$ Feasible and dominated
   $\rightarrow$ Infeasible and dominated
   Unconstrained problems:
   Antigens:
   $\rightarrow$ Non-dominated
   Antibodies:
   $\rightarrow$ Dominated

4. Define Affinity for antibodies and antigens.
   Defining affinity on antibodies:
   For each antibody, select randomly one antigen in Ag. The affinity value of an antibody Ab is defined by its euclidean distance to the selected antigen Ag.
   Defining affinity on antigens:
   For each antigen, the affinity is based on its hypervolume contribution:
   The algorithm that computes the hypervolume contribution is shown in Algorithm 2.
   For both antibodies and antigens, the greater the affinity, the better.

5. **Clonal selection principle**
   Most of the population-based algorithms don't discard dominated individuals when selecting solutions to be cloned or mutated. The main aim in doing this is to keep some diversity in the population. After some experiments, the

---

Algorithm 2: Algorithm for computing hypervolume contributions

---

1 Input: Population Ag ;
2 Initialize Affinities(Ag) to 0.0 ;
3 **for** i *from 1 to m* **do**
4 | Sort Ag by obj i;
5 | **for** j *from 1 to Ag.size()* **do**
6 | | $Ag.ind[j].affinity += (Ag.ind[j].obj[i] - Ag.ind[j+1].obj[i])$;
7 | **end**
8 **end**
9 **for** j *from 1 to Ag.size()* **do**
10 | $Ag.ind[j].affinity += max_j(Aff(Ab_j))$;
11 **end**

---

choice for our algorithm was to select dominated solutions only if necessary (if non-dominated solutions are less than the number of clones). Some previous results have shown that cloning the antibodies gives worse results (convergence metric) than considering the best individuals found so far, the antigens. In order to fit to the immune system metaphor, one can consider here that if the main population already contains a certain number of antigens, it means that the immune system has already recognized some pathogen agents and it will use them to perform the cloning process (the antibody which reached the pathogen agent and is now considered as an antigen). The number of clones is usually defined as about 20% of the population. Nevertheless, a more thorough statistical analysis is still required and for now, we adopt a user-defined parameter to control the number of candidates. In the main population, the antigens and antibodies are classified according to their affinity. The first best NC solutions are chosen and for each of them, a different number of clones is calculated depending on their affinity. Moreover, these candidates are split into two sets $j = 1, 2$: the extreme solutions and the others. For each set, we define their total number of clones. The extreme solutions will be cloned more at the beginning and less at the end.

For each NC solution, the number of clones of each candidate (NCC) is given by:

$$NCC(A_{i,j}) = P_j * \frac{Aff(A_{i,j})}{\sum_{i=0}^{n_j} Aff(A_{i,j})} \quad \forall i,j$$

where: $A_{i,j}$ is the ith antigen or the ith antibody of the set j, P_j is the total number of clones for the set j, n_j is the number of candidates in the set j.

6. **Mutation**

Regarding mutation, two important choices have to be made:

- Mutation probability: It controls the probability to mutate one variable of a vector.
- Mutation step-size: It controls the degree of perturbation given to the variable selected to be mutated.

Concerning the mutation probability, the aim of this study is to simplify the algorithm in order to emphasize the combination MOAIS/Hypervolume and investigate this new idea. Furthermore, since we compare results with respect to NSGA-II, we decided to adopt its same mutation probability. Thus, the mutation probability mp remained fixed in the experiments reported next.

$$mp = \frac{1}{nreal}$$

7. Hybrid Mutation

Each time a variable has to be mutated, we compute the following value:

$$p\_mut\_type = \frac{1.0}{(1.0 + exp(-2.0 * (x + p)))}$$

where: $x = -6.0 + (t/ngen) * 12.0$, increasing with the number of generations. $p = -4.0 + ls * 8.0$, where ls is a parameter which determines the tradeoff between GL and GG.

While the algorithm is running, the probability to choose GL will increase and the mutation will perform more local searches. Local Gaussian mutation is performed following the formula:

$$x_i^* = x_i + (max_i - min_i) * 0.1 * \mathcal{N}(0, st_1)$$

Global Gaussian mutation is performed following the formula:

$$x_i^* = x_i + (max_i - min_i) * 0.1 * \mathcal{N}(0, st_2)$$

where: max_i, min_i are the bounds of each decision variable, x_i is the variable to be mutated, $\mathcal{N}(0, x)$ is the Normal distribution with mean 0 and standard deviation x, $st_1 \in [0.1, 0.5]$, parameter which controls the local Gaussian mutation step, $st_2 \in [0.5, 1.5]$, parameter which controls the global Gaussian mutation step.

8. Evaluate the pool: Objectives, feasibility.
9. Add the Antigens into the pool P
10. Non-dominated sorting in the pool P
11. Update the main population Q

The archiving process is quite simple but some choices have to be made when the archive is full and the candidates that aim to enter are non-dominated individuals. The main aim of the archive is to increase the value of the whole hypervolume at each generation. In order to achieve this, new individuals are added to the archive only if they dominate a previous individual. An archiving method is presented in [20] but the complexity is, once again, exponential with the number of objectives. Here, the hypervolume maximization of the archive will be ensured by only accepting individuals that dominate previous individuals. One drawback of this method is that we assume that the previous generation has a good spread to ensure that all the solutions of the Pareto front are reachable (relatively, because of the bounded size of the archive) - this is not so in most cases. The following method is adopted in order to find a good spread of solutions before accepting only individuals that will maximize the hypervolume:

12. Fill the main population with successive ranks from the pool P.
13. Split the population (Antigens & Antibodies)
14. Go to step 4 if the stop criterion is not met.
15. Return the antigen population as the approximation of the Pareto front obtained by the algorithm.

A MOAIS algorithm can be considered as a MOEA whose features are changed for selection, proliferation, mutation and archiving. In order to keep the comparison with NSGA-II as fair as possible, the implementation of the new algorithm is based on the data structures used in [9]. Other data structures used are simply arrays and the code is easily understandable and maintainable for further work (we adopted the code provided by Kalyanmoy Deb in http://www.iitk.ac.in/kangal/codes.shtml.

A competitive complexity is always hard to achieve when dealing with hypervolume, because of the high computational cost associated to it. Nevertheless, the complexity of the algorithm presented here is $\mathcal{O}(mn^3)$ and $\mathcal{O}(mn^2 logn)$ on average. This low complexity makes the algorithm suitable for real-world problems.

6   Comparison of Results

The aim of this document is to compare the results obtained by our proposed MOAIS-HV with respect to those of NSGA-II [9]. In order to allow a fair comparison, the same number of function evaluations was adopted for both algorithms. The same population size and the same number of generations were adopted for both algorithms.

We adopted both the Zitzler-Deb-Thiele (ZDT) test suite [21] (which contains bi-objective problems) and the DTLZ test suite [10] (which contains scalable problems that were implemented with 3 objectives, except for DTLZ4-4, which has 4 objectives). Due to space limitations, we only provide a summary of our results in Table 1. The performance measures adopted were hypervolume [17], inverted generational distance (IGD) [6] (which measures convergence) and spread [9] (which measures uniform distribution along the Pareto front).

As expected, MOAIS-HV performs better with respect to the hypervolume in all the test problems adopted, except for ZDT4, which is multi-frontal (i.e., it has several false Pareto fronts), which seems to produce some problems to our selection mechanism, although we still manage to produce a reasonably good final result. It is remarkable, however, that MOAIS-HV can produce good results in ZDT3, which has a disconnected Pareto front that normally produces problems to MOAISs (e.g., in [12] the authors have to rely on the use of recombination to properly solve this problem).

Something interesting is that the other convergence measure adopted (inverted generational distance) seems to contradict the hypervolume (which also measures convergence). The differences, however, are negligible in most cases, since both algorithms produce values close to zero in all cases. It is also interesting to note that the results obtained by our approach with respect to spread are quite competitive, although the hypervolume does not really emphasize uniform distribution of nondominated solutions.

Our results indicate that MOAIS-HV can produce very competitive results in both bi-objective and three-objective problems. This is remarkable if we consider that no recombination operator was adopted. It is also worth noting that we did

Table 1. Comparison of the average results obtained by NSGA-II and our proposed MOAIS-HV for the ZDT and DTLZ test problems. The reference point adopted to compute the hypervolume is provided in the last column.

Test problem	Spread		IGD		Hypervolume		
	NSGA-II	MOAIS-HV	NSGA-II	MOAIS-HV	NSGA-II	AIS-HV	Ref. point
ZDT1	2.54e-01	**1.91e-01**	1.98e-04	**1.67e-04**	8.88e-01	**8.92e-01**	(1.1, 1.1)
ZDT2	2.51e-01	**1.77e-01**	1.96e-04	**1.63e-04**	5.67e-01	**5.71e-01**	(1.1, 1.1)
ZDT3	**4.42e-01**	5.27e-01	**2.61e-04**	3.66e-04	1.115	**1.119**	(0.935,1.1)
ZDT4	**3.02e-01**	4.64e-01	**6.79e-04**	1.28e-03	**8.54e-01**	7.34e-01	(1.1, 1.1)
ZDT6	2.45e-01	**1.68e-01**	4.90e-04	**1.10e-04**	3.47e-01	**3.66e-01**	(0.935,1.1)
DTLZ1	**3.51e-01**	4.16e-01	**1.21e-03**	1.99e-03	**1.425**	1.422	(1.1, 1.1, 1.1)
DTLZ2	2.56e-01	**2.05e-01**	**1.23e-03**	1.25e-03	1.14	**1.16**	(1.1, 1.1, 1.1)
DTLZ2-4	**0.56**	0.69	**1.2e-02**	1.8e-02	4.60e-01	**4.65e-01**	(1,1,1,1)
DTLZ3	**3.52e-01**	8.58e-01	**1.28e-03**	8.14e-03	3.1002	**3.1003**	(5.0, 5.0, 5.0)
DTLZ4	2.74e-01	**1.92e-01**	**1.19e-03**	3.28e-03	**9.23e-01**	9.17e-01	(1.1, 1.1, 1.1)
DTLZ7	5.60e-01	**5.15e-01**	**1.25e-03**	1.33e-03	2.04	**2.05**	(1.1, 1.1, 7.0)

not include comparisons with respect to other MOAISs because most of them did not adopt the DTLZ test problems in their experiments.

Additionally, we included one example with four objectives (DTLZ2-4). Although the differences are marginal, it can be seen that our MOAIS-HV still provides better results than NSGA-II with respect to hypervolume. In fact, if we increase more the number of objectives, it is expected that the difference will become more significant very quickly, because of the fast degradation of Pareto-based selection.

7   Conclusions and Future Work

We have presented here what we believe to be the first indicator-based MOAIS. The aim of this work was to investigate the suitability of using hypervolume for designing a MOAIS that can be competitive with respect to state-of-the-art MOEAs.

Our preliminary results indicate that our proposed approach provides a competitive performance with respect to a state-of-the-art MOEA (NSGA-II) in a variety of difficult test problems that had not been used (in full) before for assessing performance of a MOAIS. It is also worth remarking that the hypervolume contribution discard process was simplified with the purpose of lowering the complexity of the algorithm. This was done, however, at the expense of decreasing the quality of the results. However, as part of our future work, we are interested in exploring the use of a faster algorithm for computing the hypervolume that was recently introduced in [22]. With this new algorithm we expect to produce a more competitive MOAIS, that has a lower computational complexity.

As part of our future work, we are also interested in adding new methods taken from the immune system metaphor for improving our results. For example, implementing an immune system memory seems to be relevant in order to avoid cloning candidates in bad regions of the objective space. Another interesting idea is to use a diversity function to add some random elements "between" two good solutions. These solutions would be nondominated solutions that were suppressed previously by the hypervolume discard process. Such a mechanism should improve the uniform distribution of solutions along the Pareto front obtained by our algorithm.

References

1. Zheng, J., Chen, Y., Zhang, W.: A Survey of artificial immune applications. Artificial Intelligence Review 34, 19–34 (2010)
2. Campelo, F., Guimarães, F.G., Igarashi, H.: Overview of Artificial Immune Systems for Multi-objective Optimization. In: Obayashi, S., Deb, K., Poloni, C., Hiroyasu, T., Murata, T. (eds.) EMO 2007. LNCS, vol. 4403, pp. 937–951. Springer, Heidelberg (2007)
3. Freschi, F., Coello Coello, C.A., Repetto, M.: Multiobjective Optimization and Artificial Immune Systems: A Review. In: Mo, H. (ed.) Handbook of Research on Artificial Immune Systems and Natural Computing: Applying Complex Adaptive Technologies. Medical Information Science Reference, pp. 1–21. Hershey, New York (2009) ISBN 978-1-60566-310-4
4. Coello Coello, C.A., Cruz Cortés, N.: An Approach to Solve Multiobjective Optimization Problems Based on an Artificial Immune System. In: Timmis, J., Bentley, P.J. (eds.) First International Conference on Artificial Immune Systems (ICARIS 2002), pp. 212–221. University of Kent at Canterbury, UK (2002) ISBN 1-902671-32-5
5. Yoo, J., Hajela, P.: Immune network simulations in multicriterion design. Structural Optimization 18, 85–94 (1999)
6. Coello Coello, C.A., Cruz Cortés, N.: Solving Multiobjective Optimization Problems using an Artificial Immune System. Genetic Programming and Evolvable Machines 6, 163–190 (2005)
7. Freschi, F., Repetto, M.: Multiobjective Optimization by a Modified Artificial Immune System Algorithm. In: Jacob, C., Pilat, M.L., Bentley, P.J., Timmis, J. (eds.) ICARIS 2005. LNCS, vol. 3627, pp. 248–261. Springer, Heidelberg (2005)
8. Zitzler, E., Laumanns, M., Thiele, L.: SPEA2: Improving the Strength Pareto Evolutionary Algorithm. In: Giannakoglou, K., Tsahalis, D., Periaux, J., Papailou, P., Fogarty, T. (eds.) Evolutionary Methods for Design, Optimization and Control with Applications to Industrial Problems, EUROGEN 2001, Athens, Greece, pp. 95–100 (2002)
9. Deb, K., Pratap, A., Agarwal, S., Meyarivan, T.: A fast and elitist multiobjective genetic algorithm: NSGA-II. IEEE Transactions on Evolutionary Computation 6, 182–197 (2002)
10. Deb, K., Thiele, L., Laumanns, M., Zitzler, E.: Scalable Test Problems for Evolutionary Multiobjective Optimization. In: Abraham, A., Jain, L., Goldberg, R. (eds.) Evolutionary Multiobjective Optimization. Theoretical Advances and Applications, pp. 105–145. Springer, USA (2005)
11. Jiao, L., Gong, M., Shang, R., Du, H., Lu, B.: Clonal Selection with Immune Dominance and Anergy Based Multiobjective Optimization. In: Coello Coello, C.A., Hernández Aguirre, A., Zitzler, E. (eds.) EMO 2005. LNCS, vol. 3410, pp. 474–489. Springer, Heidelberg (2005)

12. Gong, M., Jiao, L., Du, H., Bo, L.: Multiobjective immune algorithm with nondominated neighbor-based selection. Evolutionary Computation 16, 225–255 (2008)
13. Lu, B., Jiao, L., Du, H., Gong, M.: IFMOA: Immune Forgetting Multiobjective Optimization Algorithm. In: Wang, L., Chen, K., S. Ong, Y. (eds.) ICNC 2005, Part III. LNCS, vol. 3612, pp. 399–408. Springer, Heidelberg (2005)
14. Fonseca, C.M., Fleming, P.J.: Genetic Algorithms for Multiobjective Optimization: Formulation, Discussion and Generalization. In: Forrest, S. (ed.) Proceedings of the Fifth International Conference on Genetic Algorithms, pp. 416–423. University of Illinois at Urbana-Champaign. Morgan Kauffman Publishers, San Mateo, California (1993)
15. Coelho, G.P., Von Zuben, F.J.: omni-aiNet: An Immune-Inspired Approach for Omni Optimization. In: Bersini, H., Carneiro, J. (eds.) ICARIS 2006. LNCS, vol. 4163, pp. 294–308. Springer, Heidelberg (2006)
16. Knowles, J., Corne, D.: Quantifying the Effects of Objective Space Dimension in Evolutionary Multiobjective Optimization. In: Obayashi, S., Deb, K., Poloni, C., Hiroyasu, T., Murata, T. (eds.) EMO 2007. LNCS, vol. 4403, pp. 757–771. Springer, Heidelberg (2007)
17. Zitzler, E.: Evolutionary Algorithms for Multiobjective Optimization: Methods and Applications. PhD thesis, Swiss Federal Institute of Technology (ETH), Zurich, Switzerland (1999)
18. Fleischer, M.: The Measure of Pareto Optima. Applications to Multi-objective Metaheuristics. In: Fonseca, C.M., Fleming, P.J., Zitzler, E., Deb, K., Thiele, L. (eds.) EMO 2003. LNCS, vol. 2632, pp. 519–533. Springer, Heidelberg (2003)
19. Beume, N., Naujoks, B., Emmerich, M.: SMS-EMOA: Multiobjective selection based on dominated hypervolume. European Journal of Operational Research 181, 1653–1669 (2007)
20. López-Ibáñez, M., Knowles, J., Laumanns, M.: On Sequential Online Archiving of Objective Vectors. In: Takahashi, R.H.C., Deb, K., Wanner, E.F., Greco, S. (eds.) EMO 2011. LNCS, vol. 6576, pp. 46–60. Springer, Heidelberg (2011)
21. Zitzler, E., Deb, K., Thiele, L.: Comparison of Multiobjective Evolutionary Algorithms: Empirical Results. Evolutionary Computation 8, 173–195 (2000)
22. Bader, J., Zitzler, E.: HypE: An Algorithm for Fast Hypervolume-Based Many-Objective Optimization. Evolutionary Computation 19, 45–76 (2011)

A Comparative Study of Negative Selection Based Anomaly Detection in Sequence Data

Johannes Textor

Theoretical Biology & Bioinformatics
Universiteit Utrecht
Paudalaan 8
3584 CH Utrecht, The Netherlands
johannes.textor@gmx.de

Abstract. The negative selection algorithm is one of the oldest immune-inspired classification algorithms and was originally intended for anomaly detection tasks in computer security. After initial enthusiasm, performance problems with the algorithm lead many researchers to conclude that negative selection is not a competitive anomaly detection technique. However, in recent years, theoretical work has lead to substantially more efficient negative selection algorithms. Here, we report the results of the first evaluation of negative selection with r-chunk and r-contiguous detectors that employs these novel algorithms. On a collection of 14 datasets from real-world sources, we compare negative selection with r-chunk and r-contiguous detectors against techniques based on kernels, finite state automata, and n-gram frequencies, and find that negative selection performs competitively, yielding a slightly better average performance than all other techniques investigated. Because this study represents, to our knowledge, the most comprehensive one of string-based negative selection to date, the widely held view that negative selection is not a competitive anomaly detection technique may be inaccurate.

1 Introduction

One of the first immunological paradigms to be used as an inspiration for algorithm design was the paradigm of *negative selection*. In brief, the so-called *T-cells*, immune cells bearing diverse receptors highly specialized to recognizing specific molecular patterns, are born in the bone marrow and initially carry receptors generated by random recombination of DNA fragments. These T-cells are then exposed to normal proteins from the host organism (self) in an organ called the thymus. T-cells which react to such self proteins are eliminated, and only those that survive this process finally egress from the thymus and become part of the immune system.

Forrest et al. [1] abstracted this immunological principle into a simple anomaly detection algorithm: Based on pre-defined notions of a universe $\mathcal{U}$ and a set of patterns (detectors) $\mathcal{P}$, which each match a small subset of the universe, the algorithm first generates a set P of patterns that all fail to match the elements

C.A. Coello Coello et al. (Eds.): ICARIS 2012, LNCS 7597, pp. 28–41, 2012.
© Springer-Verlag Berlin Heidelberg 2012

of an input dataset $S \subseteq \mathcal{U}$ by rejection sampling. Then, each elements of another input dataset X is classified as anomalous if it is matched by any of the patterns in P and as normal, otherwise.

Initially researchers were enthusiastic about negative selection [2], however, performance problems soon became obvious [3]: For many datasets, the number of patterns necessary to achieve a good sensitivity rate is prohibitively large [4], while for others, it can take exponential time for rejection sampling to find even a single detector [5]. For these reasons, limited work has been done on evaluating especially string-based negative selection on real-world datasets, and such studies (e.g. [6], [7]) often lack a comparison to more standard anomaly detection techniques. In the case of string based negative selection, the only exception, to our knowledge, is the work of Stibor, who analyzed the performance of negative selection algorithms on four artificially generated binary datasets [8] and, in later work, compared the performance to Kernel density estimation [9].

In more recent work, Elberfeld and Textor [10,11] showed that the complexity issues pointed out by Stibor [12] can be solved, and negative selection with both r-chunk and r-contiguous patterns can be implemented in polynomial time. The main trick behind their work is the use of data compression techniques to avoid generating exponentially large detector sets explicitly. Theoretically, this approach should allow processing of sizable string-based datasets in reasonable time, even for large alphabets. Here, we report, to our knowledge, the first empirical results using these new algorithms. Our study employs 14 sequence datasets consisting of hundreds to thousands of sequences with alphabet sizes of up to 78. The performance of the negative selection algorithms is compared to that of 5 state-of-the-art anomaly detection techniques shown to perform competitively on 10 of these datasets in earlier work by Chandola et al [13].

The structure of this paper is as follows. In the upcoming section, we define the kind of classification problem we are solving and introduce our evaluation methodology. In Section 3, we give a brief overview of the classification algorithms we are employing. However, because the techniques we employ in this paper have all been described in great detail elsewhere, we give only a very high-level overview and refer the interested reader to the literature. Section 4 then describes the datasets we are using. Our experimental results are presented in Section 5. The paper concludes with a discussion of these results (Section 6).

2 Preliminaries

2.1 Problem Definition

Formally, the classification problem at hand can be defined as follows. Given an alphabet Σ, the input consists of two sets $S, X \subseteq \Sigma^*$. The set S is itself a subset of an unknown set (real self, ground truth) $\mathcal{S} \subseteq \Sigma^*$, and another set $X \subseteq \Sigma^*$. The algorithm's task is to decide, based on the information in S, for each $x \in X$ whether $x \in \mathcal{S}$ holds. The algorithms considered in this paper will do so by assigning to each $x \in X$ a value $\alpha(x) \in \mathbb{R}$ (anomaly score), quantifying the algorithm's confidence that x is an anomaly (i.e., $x \notin \mathcal{S}$). This type of a classification problem is usually referred to as "one-class classification" [14] and can also be viewed as a kind of semi-supervised learning [15,16]. In the following, S will also be referred to as "training data" and X as "test data".

Some of the algorithms we use, including negative selection, actually take strings of a fixed length ℓ as input. In that case, we transform the input dataset S into another set S^ℓ containing all substrings of length ℓ of all strings in S. To assign an anomaly score to a sequence $x \in X$, we first compute the anomaly score for each substring of length ℓ of x, giving a vector $(\alpha_1, \alpha_2, \ldots, \alpha_{|x|-\ell+1})$ of scores. Then, the final anomaly score α is defined as the logsum of the individual scores, i.e.

$$\alpha = \sum_i \log \alpha_i \ . \tag{1}$$

If some of the α_i are 0, we replace them with 10^{-6}. Of course, many other ways are conceivable to combine the sliding window anomaly scores into a single score [13]. We use the logsum here because it has been shown to perform well for the techniques studied by Chandola et al [13].

2.2 Evaluation Methodology

The results of our analysis were evaluated quantitatively as follows. First, like in Chandola et al. [13], we ranked all test sequences by their anomaly score and counted the percentage of true anomalies among the top n sequences, where n is the number of true anomalies in the test dataset X. Hence, a value of 1.0 would mean that the anomalous sequences are perfectly separated from the normal sequences, while a value of 0.0 would mean that the top n sequences are all false positives.

As a second evaluation metric, we used a receiver operating characteristic (ROC) analysis. A ROC curve visualizes the trade-off between sensitivity and specificity: For a given threshold θ for the anomaly score, one determines the false positive rate

$$\text{FP}_\theta = \frac{\# \text{ normal instances scoring higher than } \theta}{\# \text{ normal instances}} \tag{2}$$

and the true positive rate

$$\text{TP}_\theta = \frac{\# \text{ anomalous instances scoring higher than } \theta}{\# \text{ anomalous instances}} \ . \tag{3}$$

The ROC curve is then given by the points $(\text{FP}_\theta, \text{TP}_\theta)$ for all possible values of θ. The larger the area under the ROC curve (AUC), the better the performance of the classification algorithm. The ROC curve of a "classifier" that tosses a coin to determine the label of each $x \in X$ is a diagonal line from the origin to the point $(1, 1)$ with an AUC of 0.5. The ROC curve of a meaningful classifier should thus lie well above the diagonal and have an AUC higher than 0.5. A near-perfect classifier, which assigns almost all labels correctly for almost all parameters, has an AUC close to 1.

To compare the two metrics, we note that for our dataset, the percentage of true anomalies near the top is a "tougher" measure because our datasets contain only few anomalies. This means that a classifier which positions all anomalies near the top, with a few false positives in between, will get a very good AUC (near 1) but may still perform poorly in the true positive rate metric.

3 Algorithms

We start by briefly re-stating the definitions of negative selection algorithms with r-chunk and r-contiguous patterns (detectors). After that, we briefly explain the algorithms used by Chandola et al. [13], and refer the reader to that source for a more complete explanation. Note that Chandola et al. originally analyzed 7 different algorithms. However, two of those were shown to perform much worse than the other five on almost all datasets. Therefore, we excluded those algorithms from our analysis to obtain a more competitive reference base for our benchmark.

3.1 Negative Selection

Given are a universe $\mathcal{U}$, a pattern set $\mathcal{P}$ and a matching function that, for every $\pi \in \mathcal{P}$ and every $x \in \mathcal{U}$, determines whether π matches x or not. For any $S \subseteq \mathcal{U}$, let $\mathcal{P}[S]$ denote the set of patterns that do not match any $s \in S$, called the set of S-consistent patterns [17].

Definition 1 (r-chunk pattern). *An r-chunk pattern (d, i) is a tuple of a string $d \in \Sigma^r$ and an integer $i \in \mathbb{N}$. It matches a string $s \in \Sigma^\ell$ if $i \in \{1, \ldots, \ell - r + 1\}$ and the substring of s of length r starting at the i-th position is equal to d.*

When using negative selection with r-chunk patterns, we proceed as follows. For the input S, first generate $\mathcal{P}[S]$. Then, for each $x \in X$, the anomaly score is defined as the number of elements of $\mathcal{P}[S]$ that also match x. Hence, anomaly scores range from 0 to $\ell - r + 1$. For computing the logsum, we add 1 to each anomaly score.

Definition 2 (r-contiguous patterns). *An r-contiguous pattern is a string $d \in \Sigma^\ell$. It matches another string $s \in \Sigma^\ell$ if d and s are identical in at least r contiguous positions, i.e., if there is an $i \in \{1, \ldots, l - r + 1\}$ such that the substrings of length r of s and d starting at the i-th position are equal.*

For negative selection with r-contiguous patterns, we also first generate the set $\mathcal{P}[S]$ of S-consistent patterns. Then, for each $x \in X$, the anomaly score is defined as the largest number $r' \in \{0, \ldots, \ell\}$ such that there exists a pattern $\pi \in \mathcal{P}[S]$ that is identical to x in r' contiguous positions. Hence, anomaly scores range from 0 (we define that two strings are always identical in 0 contiguous positions) to ℓ. Again, we add 1 to all anomaly scores for computing the logsum.

Note that this type of anomaly score is somewhat different to what would typically be used in negative selection with r-contiguous detectors. Classically, one would simply determine whether or not there exists an S-consistent r-contiguous pattern that matches x. Our method generalizes this procedure in the following sense: If an r-contiguous pattern exists, then the anomaly score r' will be greater than or equal to r, otherwise it will be smaller than r.

We note that while the above explanations serve as a simplified description of our algorithms, we did in fact not generate the entire sets of S-consistent patterns, as these would have been prohibitively large, especially for the larger alphabets. Instead, we used the algorithms presented in earlier work by Elberfeld and Textor [11] and Liśkiewicz and Textor [17], which generate compressed representations of these sets. Further, note that Liśkiewicz and Textor [17] also presented an efficient algorithm to count the S-consistent r-contiguous patterns that match x, a number which they termed the *detector sampling distance*. We implemented this algorithm and found it to perform in almost all cases exactly like the corresponding r-chunk-based algorithm explained above. For this reason, we decided to use instead the simpler anomaly score for r- contiguous patterns discussed above. Our reference implementation (see end of this paper), however, contains both anomaly score versions as a basis for future work.

3.2   Algorithms Based on ℓ-grams

Like negative selection, the three algorithms of this group are applied by computing the logsum of anomaly scores for a sliding window of fixed size ℓ (see previous section). The easiest technique is the t-STIDE technique (stide) [18]. Here, the anomaly score is defined as

$$\alpha(s) = \frac{f(s)}{f(*)} \tag{4}$$

where $f(s)$ is the number of times that the string s occurs in the training data S, and $f(*)$ is the total number of strings of length ℓ in S. Note that for this score, higher numbers mean less anomalous sequences, which is also true for the following two techniques.

The other two algorithms in this group are based on finite state automata (FSA), which compute the conditional probability of the last symbol in the string given the $\ell - 1$ symbols preceding it. For instance, if the sequence AAAAA was followed most frequently by the letter B in the training data, then an occurrence of AAAAAB in the test data would get a high likelihood score and an occurrence of AAAAAC would get a low likelihood score. We refer to the literature for a detailed description on how this automaton is constructed [19]. The basic version of the algorithm (fsa) processes only windows from the test data that also occurred in the training data. Our third ℓ-gram based technique, FSA-z (fsaz), is a slight extension of FSA which assigns a likelihood score of 0 to unseen sequences instead of ignoring them.

3.3   Kernel Based Algorithms

In contrast to negative selection and ℓ-gram based techniques, kernel based algorithms treat the sequences as a whole instead of using a sliding window. Let

$u, v \in \Sigma^*$ be two strings, then the kernel function $\kappa(u, v) \in [0, 1]$ representing their similarity is defined as follows:

$$\kappa(u, v) = \frac{|\mathrm{LCS}(u, v)|}{\sqrt{|u|\,|v|}}, \tag{5}$$

where $\mathrm{LCS}(u, v)$ denotes the longest common substring (not necessarily starting at the same position) of u and v.

Based on this kernel function, we use the following two classifiers: (1) A simple kNN classifier (knn), where the anomaly score is the distance to the kth nearest neighbour in the training set; (2) a clustering algorithm (cls), which partitions the training data into k clusters using the CLARA k-medoid algorithm [20].

Of course, there exist a plethora of other possibilities to define string similarity functions for kernel classifiers, which we do not yet explore here. We limit ourselves to the longest common substring based kernel for the simple reason that it was previously shown to perform competitively on 10 of the 14 datasets that we will analyze [13].

4   Datasets

We evaluated all algorithms on 14 datasets in total, out of which we generated the first 4 ourselves, while the latter 10 datasets were taken from the work of Chandola et al [13]. The ratio of normal to anomalous sequences in all test dataset ranges between 1:10 and 1:20. Table 1 shows the basic properties of all datasets.

Table 1. Properties of the datasets used in our experimental evaluation. For each dataset, we list the alphabet size $|\Sigma|$, the mean length of sequences $\langle \ell \rangle$, as well as the sizes of the sets of training sequences (S), normal test sequences (X_{normal}), and anomalous test sequences $(X_{\mathrm{anomalous}})$.

class	dataset	$|\Sigma|$	$\langle \ell \rangle$	$|S|$	$|X_{\mathrm{normal}}|$	$|X_{\mathrm{anomalous}}|$
languages	hiligaynon	27	10	403	495	55
	latin	27	10	403	495	55
	plautdietsch	27	10	403	495	55
	tagalog	27	10	403	495	55
proteins	hcv	44	87	1423	1000	50
	nad	42	160	1685	1000	50
	tet	42	52	952	1000	50
	rub	42	182	559	500	25
	rvp	46	95	935	1000	50
syscalls	snd-cert	56	803	811	1000	50
	snd-unm	53	839	1030	1000	50
	bsm-week1	67	149	10	1000	50
	bsm-week2	73	141	113	200	10
	bsm-week3	78	143	67	1000	50

We point out that our evaluation method is a deterministic one, and that the training dataset S (which contain only normal sequences) and test dataset X (which contain mostly normal and some anomalous sequences in the ratio shown in Table 1) are pre-defined in each case. Therefore, the performance of an algorithm on a dataset S, X. is determined by a single run of the algorithm on that dataset. This is different from probabilistic evaluation methods like cross-validation, where training and test data are generated at random by splitting a basis dataset in two randomly chosen parts.

4.1   Languages

First we were interested how the algorithms would perform on a rather routine task, i.e., detection of short foreign-language snippets in an English-language background. In these datasets, all training and test sequences are of length 10. As training data, we extracted non-overlapping substrings of length 10 from the first two pages of Hermann Melville's classic novel "Moby Dick" [21], converting all letters to lower case, and collapsing all contiguous strings of non-letters to a single space. This yielded 403 strings for the input sample S. To generate normal test data, we applied the same procedure to the first chapter of the Book of John from the English Bible, giving 495 strings. As anomalous instances, we used the first 55 strings from the Book of John in the languages Hiligaynon (an austronesian language spoken in the Philippines), Latin, Plautdietsch (a northern German dialect), and Tagalog. Importantly, all these languages use the same alphabet – if this were not the case, then the anomaly detection problem would be rather trivial.

4.2   Protein Families

For the protein family datasets, Chandola et al. [13] obtained sequences from the five protein families HCV, NAD, TET, RVP, and RUB from the PFAM database [22]. Proteins from different families are expected to structurally differ from one another, which is reflected in their amino acid sequences.

The sequences obtained for each family were split into training data and the normal part of the test data. The test datasets were then augmented by anomalous instances by sampling 50 sequences from the respective other families.

4.3   Intrusion Detection

The intrusion detection datasets are of particular interest for our purpose, since the negative selection algorithm was originally conceived for intrusion detection, and it has been claimed that negative selection is inappropriate for this task [8]. However, as mentioned at the beginning of this paper, this claim was in large parts based on now disproved speculations about the algorithm's performance, while no direct empirical evidence was given except some experiments on artificially constructed datasets which had no relation to intrusion detection and which were not sequence data in nature. Presumably, the performance issues of classical negative selection algorithms impeded a more thorough investigation.

The intrusion detection datasets consist of sequences of UNIX system calls made by processes operating either normally or being hacked / under attack, an idea put forward by Forrest et al [23]. Each symbol of the alphabet encodes one type of system call. Two of the datasets (snd-unm and snd-cert) were generated by that group at the University of New Mexico[1], while three others (bsm-week1 through bsm-week3) were collected from a Solaris machine at the DARPA Lincoln Labs [24].

5   Experimental Results

5.1   Tuning Procedure

It is most meaningful to compare the results of machine learning algorithms when these have undergone a similar degree of tuning. The negative selection algorithms both have two parameters that can be used to control generalization, namely n and r, while the other algorithms have only one parameter each. To enable a fair comparison, we therefore chose to set the parameter n to a value determined by the structure of the dataset, namely the length of the shortest string. This is the maximum value for n and therefore also leaves a maximum number of choices for the parameter r; however, note that the classification results could in principle still be better for smaller n. In this manner, we set $n = 10$ for the language datasets (which only consist of strings of length 10) and $n = 6$ for the other datasets. The negative selection algorithm was then tuned by modifying the parameter r only.

Tuning was then performed separately for each dataset class (languages, proteins, and system calls) by, for each algorithm, determining that parameter which gave the best average detection rate among the top n sequences (our first metric). This led to the parameter settings shown in Table 2. Note that for all datasets used by Chandola et al [13], we determined the same "optimal" parameter settings for the datasets they analyzed, except for kNN where we consistently found a slightly better performance with $k = 1$ than with the parameter $k = 4$ that they used[2]. Therefore, we here report the results for $k = 1$.

5.2   Performance

The numerical results of our experiments are shown in Table 3 through Table 5.

Concerning the fraction of high-scoring true positives, the language datasets seem overall most difficult (perhaps due to their smallest size), followed by

---

[1] http://www.cs.unm.edu/~immsec/systemcalls.html

[2] More specifically, Chandola et al [13] state that they find similar performance for $k \leq 4$ but find performance to become worse for larger k.

Table 2. Parameter settings used to achieve the results shown in Table 3 through Table 5. For each technique, the parameters were tuned to yield the best average rate of true positives within the highest scoring input sequences.

	languages	proteins	syscalls
fsa	$\ell = 5$	$\ell = 6$	$\ell = 6$
fsaz	$\ell = 5$	$\ell = 6$	$\ell = 6$
stide	$\ell = 5$	$\ell = 6$	$\ell = 6$
knn	$k = 1$	$k = 1$	$k = 1$
cls	$k = 22$	$k = 32$	$k = 32$
rchunk	$r = 7$	$r = 5$	$r = 5$
rcont	$r = 7$	$r = 5$	$r = 6$

the anomaly detection datasets, while the protein family datasets seem easiest. Within the intrusion detection class, the DARPA datasets seem more difficult than the UNM datasets. All these observations are consistent with what was reported by Chandola et al [13]. The negative selection algorithms outperform all other techniques on the language datasets, come in second after kNN on the protein datasets, and score worst on the intrusion detection datasets where they come in 4th and 5th out of 7 techniques. A similar picture emerges when looking at the AUC metric, although the fraction of high-scoring true positives appears overall more informative for our benchmarking purposes.

The kernel based techniques exhibit the largest variation: They lag far behind on the language datasets, but are slightly ahead on the intrusion detection datasets, on which the negative selection algorithms show only average performance.

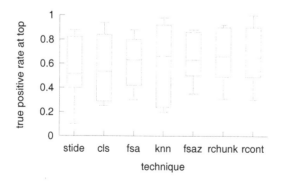

Fig. 1. Box plots depicting for each technique the minimum, maximum, interquartile range, and median across of the fraction of true anomalies among the top scoring test sequences for each of our 14 datasets (ordered by average performance)

Table 3. Results on language datasets. Above, bold numbers denote the best result in each row.

1. Fraction of true anomalies

	fsa	fsaz	stide	knn	cls	rchunk	rcont	avg
hiligaynon	0.51	0.51	0.53	0.29	0.23	**0.59**	**0.59**	0.48
latin	**0.55**	0.51	0.49	0.25	0.23	0.44	0.44	0.41
plautdietsch	0.35	0.40	0.40	0.28	0.20	**0.47**	**0.47**	0.37
tagalog	0.35	0.35	0.40	0.28	0.24	**0.49**	**0.49**	0.38
avg	0.44	0.44	0.45	0.28	0.22	0.50	0.44	0.50

2. Area under ROC curve

	fsa	fsaz	stide	knn	cls	rchunk	rcont	avg
hiligaynon	0.84	0.84	0.83	0.75	0.69	**0.92**	**0.92**	0.84
latin	0.85	0.85	0.85	0.72	0.67	**0.86**	**0.86**	0.81
plautdietsch	0.80	0.84	0.84	0.76	0.68	**0.90**	**0.90**	0.82
tagalog	0.79	0.80	0.81	0.73	0.70	**0.90**	**0.90**	0.81
avg	0.82	0.83	0.83	0.74	0.69	0.90	0.90	

Table 4. Results on protein family datasets. Bold numbers denote the best result in each row. The best AUC values were not highlighted because they are too similar across the columns.

1. Fraction of true anomalies

	fsa	fsaz	stide	cls	knn	rchunk	rcont	avg
rvp	0.88	0.86	0.86	0.84	**0.96**	0.90	0.90	0.89
rub	0.88	0.88	0.88	0.72	**0.92**	**0.92**	**0.92**	0.87
nad	0.66	0.62	0.60	0.48	0.72	0.68	0.68	0.63
hcv	0.88	0.88	0.88	0.62	**0.98**	0.90	0.90	0.86
tet	0.72	0.82	0.82	**0.86**	0.84	0.78	0.78	0.80
	0.80	0.81	0.81	0.70	0.88	0.84	0.84	

2. Area under ROC curve

	fsa	fsaz	stide	cls	knn	rchunk	rcont	avg
rvp	1.00	1.00	1.00	1.00	1.00	1.00	1.00	1.00
rub	1.00	1.00	1.00	0.99	1.00	1.00	1.00	1.00
nad	0.97	0.97	0.96	0.95	0.98	0.96	0.96	0.96
hcv	1.00	1.00	1.00	0.98	1.00	1.00	1.00	1.00
tet	0.99	0.99	0.99	1.00	1.00	0.99	0.99	0.99
	0.99	0.99	0.99	0.98	1.00	0.99	0.99	

Table 5. Results on intrusion detection datasets. Bold numbers denote the best results in each row.

1. Fraction of true anomalies

	fsa	fsaz	stide	cls	knn	rchunk	rcont	avg
bsm-week1	0.30	**0.50**	0.10	**0.50**	0.40	0.31	0.30	0.34
bsm-week2	0.42	0.48	0.26	0.42	0.54	**0.56**	0.50	0.45
bsm-week3	0.60	**0.64**	0.54	0.57	0.60	**0.64**	0.62	0.60
snd-cert	0.78	0.88	0.50	0.94	0.94	0.90	**1.00**	0.85
snd-unm	0.80	0.76	0.46	0.84	**0.92**	0.72	0.72	0.75
	0.58	0.65	0.37	0.65	0.68	0.63	0.63	

2. Area under ROC curve

	fsa	fsaz	stide	cls	knn	rchunk	rcont	avg
bsm-week1	0.87	**0.90**	0.55	0.74	0.68	0.64	0.53	0.70
bsm-week2	0.87	0.89	0.68	**0.90**	0.86	0.77	0.79	0.82
bsm-week3	**0.97**	**0.97**	0.80	0.92	0.90	0.82	0.78	0.88
snd-cert	0.95	0.96	0.94	**1.00**	**1.00**	0.96	**1.00**	0.97
snd-unm	0.99	0.99	0.96	**1.00**	**1.00**	0.86	0.98	0.97
	0.93	0.94	0.79	0.91	0.89	0.81	0.82	

5.3   Statistical Analysis

Figure 1 shows box plots of the minimum, median, maximum, and interquartile ranges of the true anomalies among the top scoring sequences across all datasets. Ordering the techniques by their average performance, we find negative selection with r-contiguous patterns to perform overall best. However, the difference to the runners-up r-chunk, FSA-z and kNN is quite small. We performed paired two-sided t tests to determine the statistical significance of these differences. The resulting p-values are shown in Table 6. Using a cutoff value of $p = 0.05$, we would conclude that negative selection with r-contiguous patterns performs significantly better than t-STIDE and clustering, while there is no significant difference to kNN, FSA, FSA-z, and to r-chunk pattern. Similarly, we would conclude that negative selection with r-chunk patterns performs significantly

Table 6. Resulting p-values of a two-sided t test of the null hypothesis that the corresponding pair of techniques give equal results on our 14 datasets. Those p-values that lie below a cutoff of 0.05 are highlighted in bold.

	fsa	fsaz	stide	knn	cls	rchunk
rcont	0.067	0.510	**0.012**	**0.026**	0.357	0.363
rchunk	**0.046**	0.502	**0.007**	**0.030**	0.363	

better than t-STIDE, clustering, and FSA, while there is no significant difference to FSA-z and kNN.

6   Discussion

To interpret our numerical results for the sliding window based techniques, it is instructive to adopt a characterization by Chandola et al. [13] according to which we can distinguish three types of substrings given a training set S, namely *unseen*, *seen-rare*, and *seen-frequent* substrings. First, note that negative selection algorithms are based only on unseen strings and do not distinguish at all between rare and frequently seen strings. In contrast, the t-STIDE, FSA, and FSA-z techniques do all assess the frequency of seen strings. Therefore, they use in principle more information than negative selection, except FSA which ignores unseen strings. That negative selection still performs competitively can be explained by noting that unseen sequences carry important information, a fact noted already by Chandola et al [13]. This is especially true for the language data, which has the smallest training sets. In this case, there is least information to be found in the frequency distribution of small substrings, explaining why negative selection performs best here. The short length of the input strings is also a problem for the kernel based techniques, which rely on pairwise comparison of the sequences, and therefore gain more information when longer sequences are compared. Thus, they perform very poorly on the language datasets but much better on the other datasets. This link between size of input data and the performance of the different classifiers would be interesting to explore in future work.

In summary, this paper presents what is, to our knowledge, the most comprehensive comparative evaluation of string-based negative selection algorithms on sequence data so far, and the first to use sizable non-binary alphabets. Overall, we found negative selection algorithms to perform competitively to state-of-the-art algorithms, and thus our results contradict earlier studies on artificially generated datasets where negative selection was found to perform very poorly compared to standard statistical techniques [9]. We believe this discrepancy to be mainly explained by the fact that the datasets used by Stibor [9] were generated by first sampling points from a connected shape in two-dimensional space, and then encoding those points as binary strings. In other words, the semantical nature of the data was "hidden" from the r-chunk and r-contiguous patterns, which were therefore not able to generalize properly. Because using r-chunk or r-contiguous patterns brings the assumption that close positions in the input data are more correlated than distant positions, we believe it to be more meaningful to evaluate these algorithms on data where this assumption actually holds, or where at least there is no good reason to assume that this assumption is violated. For the same reason, we agree with Stibor [8] that it is probably not a good idea to use r-chunk or r-contiguous patterns directly on IP packets.

Obviously, our analysis still represents just a starting point, and could be extended in several interesting ways. Our hope is that other members of the community will join us in our quest for a deeper understanding of the strengths and weaknesses of string-based negative selection, using the new tools that are now available. However, it must be said that the algorithms proposed in Elberfeld and Textor [10] and Liśkiewicz and Textor [17] are rather intricate, and implementing these algorithms was a significant part of the work that underlies this paper. The implementations are available as open source software and can be downloaded from the author's web page at www-binf.bio.uu.nl/textor/negativeselection.html.

References

1. Forrest, S., Perelson, A.S., Allen, L., Cherukuri, R.: Self-nonself discrimination in a computer. In: Proceedings of the IEEE Symposium on Research in Security and Privacy, pp. 202–212. IEEE Computer Society Press (1994)
2. Forrest, S., Hofmeyr, S.A., Somayaji, A.: Computer immunology. Communications of the ACM 40, 88–96 (1997)
3. Kim, J., Bentley, P.J.: An evaluation of negative selection in an artificial immune system for network intrusion detection. In: Proceedings of the Genetic and Evolutionary Computation Conference (GECCO), pp. 1330–1337. Morgan Kaufmann (2001)
4. D'haeseleer, P., Forrest, S., Helman, P.: An immunological approach to change detection: Algorithms, analysis, and implications. In: Proceedings of the IEEE Symposium on Security and Privacy, pp. 110–119. IEEE Computer Society (1996)
5. Timmis, J., Hone, A., Stibor, T., Clark, E.: Theoretical advances in artificial immune systems. Theoretical Computer Science 403, 11–32 (2008)
6. Hofmeyr, S.A., Forrest, S., Somayaji, A.: Intrusion detection using sequences of system calls. Journal of Computer Security 6, 151–180 (1998)
7. Balthrop, J., Esponda, F., Forrest, S., Glickman, M.R.: Coverage and generalization in an artificial immune system. In: Proceedings of the 2002 Genetic and Evolutionary Computation Conference (GECCO 2002), pp. 1045–1050 (2002)
8. Stibor, T.: On the Appropriateness of Negative Selection for Anomaly Detection and Network Intrusion Detection. PhD thesis, Technische Universität Darmstadt (2006)
9. Stibor, T.: An Empirical Study of Self/Non-self Discrimination in Binary Data with a Kernel Estimator. In: Bentley, P.J., Lee, D., Jung, S. (eds.) ICARIS 2008. LNCS, vol. 5132, pp. 352–363. Springer, Heidelberg (2008)
10. Elberfeld, M., Textor, J.: Efficient Algorithms for String-Based Negative Selection. In: Andrews, P.S., Timmis, J., Owens, N.D.L., Aickelin, U., Hart, E., Hone, A., Tyrrell, A.M. (eds.) ICARIS 2009. LNCS, vol. 5666, pp. 109–121. Springer, Heidelberg (2009)
11. Elberfeld, M., Textor, J.: Negative selection algorithms on strings with efficient training and linear-time classification. Theoretical Computer Science 412, 534–542 (2011)
12. Stibor, T., Timmis, J., Eckert, C.: The link between r-contiguous detectors and k-CNF satisfiability. In: Proceedings of the Congress on Evolutionary Computation (CEC), pp. 491–498. IEEE Press (2006)
13. Chandola, V., Mithal, V., Kumar, V.: A comparative evaluation of anomaly detection techniques for sequence data. In: Proceedings of the 2008 Eighth IEEE International Conference on Data Mining (ICDM 2008), pp. 743–748 (2008)

14. Moya, M.M., Hush, D.R.: Network constraints and multi-objective optimization for one-class classification. Neural Networks 9(3), 463–474 (1996)
15. Chandola, V., Banerjee, A., Kumar, V.: Anomaly detection: A survey. ACM Computing Surveys 41(3), 1–58 (2009)
16. Chapelle, O., Schölkopf, B., Zien, A. (eds.): Semi-Supervised Learning. Adaptive Computation and Machine Learning series. The MIT Press (2006)
17. Liśkiewicz, M., Textor, J.: Negative selection algorithms without generating detectors. In: Proceedings of Genetic and Evolutionary Computation Conference (GECCO 2010), pp. 1047–1054. ACM (2010)
18. Warrender, C., Forrest, S., Pearlmutter, B.: Detecting intrusions using system calls: Alternative data models. In: IEEE Symposium on Security and Privacy, pp. 133–145. IEEE Computer Society (1999)
19. Michael, C.C., Ghosh, A.: Two state-based approaches to program-based anomaly detection. In: Proceedings of the 16th Annual Computer Security Applications Conference, p. 21 (2000)
20. Jain, A.K., Dubes, R.C.: Algorithms for Clustering Data. Prentice Hall (1988)
21. Melville, H.: Moby-Dick, or, The Whale. Hendricks House, New York (1952)
22. Bateman, A., Birney, E., Durbin, R., Eddy, S.R., Howe, K.L., Sonnhammer, E.L.: The PFAM protein families database. Nucleic Acids Research 28, 263–266 (2000)
23. Forrest, S., Hofmeyr, S.A., Somayaji, A., Longstaff, T.A.: A sense of self for unix processes. In: Proceedings of the IEEE Symposium on Security and Privacy, pp. 120–128. IEEE Computer Society, Washington, DC (1996)
24. Lippmann, R.P., et al.: Evaluating intrusion detection systems – the 1998 DARPA offline intrusion detection evaluation. In: DARPA Information Survivability Conference and Exposition (DISCEX) 2000, vol. 2, pp. 12–26. IEEE Computer Society Press (2000)

Immune-Inspired Self Healing in Wireless Sensor Networks

TiongHoo Lim[1,3], HuiKeng Lau[1,4], Jon Timmis[1,2], and Iain Bate[1]

[1] Department of Computer Science, University of York
[2] Department of Electronics, University of York,
Heslington, YO10 5DD, UK
[3] Electrical and Electronics Engineering,
Institut Teknologi Brunei, Tungku Link, Gadong BE 1410, Negara Brunei Darussalam
[4] School of Engineering and IT, Universiti Malaysia Sabah,
88999 Kota Kinabalu, Sabah, Malaysia
{tl540,hl542,jon.timmis,iain.bate}@york.ac.uk

Abstract. Link failure and unreachable nodes due to interference from external devices are common problems in WSNs. These interferences can be a major inhibitor to node performance and network stability. In order to tolerate these failures, we propose an immune-inspired self healing system where an individual node can detect degradations in network performance, perform diagnostic tests, and provide automated immediate response to recover the network to a stable state. We evaluate and compare the performance of our approach with other routing protocols on a testbed environment using TelosB hardware motes.

Keywords: wireless sensor networks, error detection, error classification, error recovery, receptor density algorithm, routing protocol.

1 Introduction

Advances in microchip and communication technologies have enabled mass production of small and cheap devices called sensor nodes that are capable of sensing the environment and interact with each other. These nodes interact over the radio channel to form wireless sensor networks (WSNs) [1]. Each node can operate autonomously to monitor and collect data, and send the data packet over the wireless network via multi-hop routing protocols. To date, it has been used for indoor and outdoor applications such as remote patient health monitoring, fire search and rescue operation, and disaster management [1]. This type of application requires a specific level of quality of service (QoS) and availability of real-time data from the nodes to allow informed decisions and actions to be made.

An important issue is, real-world implementations of WSNs are usually difficult to control and susceptible to anomalies [19]. Anomalies, such as communication failure caused by battery depletion, component malfunction, human activity, obstruction, and interference, may occur in WSNs. This is in particular true when other devices operating at the same radio frequency as WSNs, e.g.

C.A. Coello Coello et al. (Eds.): ICARIS 2012, LNCS 7597, pp. 42–56, 2012.

IEEE 802.11 devices, are deployed very close to the sensor nodes [18]. The interferences created by these devices may exhibit unique and distinct characteristics that can be classified into different categories. In order for WSNs to operate over extended periods of time, individual nodes must be able to tolerate these interferences effectively. This can be achieved with a combination of detection, diagnostic and recovery mechanisms.

Over the years, many immune-inspired anomaly detection systems (ADSs) have been successfully applied to WSNs. This is partly motivated by the analogy between the characteristics of WSNs and the immune system. The Dendritic Cell Algorithm [8] and Negative Selection Algorithm [5] have been successfully applied to detect network and traffic anomalies. To be able to establish the anomalies that can lead to major failures is essential. Drodza et al. [4] applied the interaction between innate and adaptive immunity to classify the errors that can lead to degradation in packet delivery rate. However, these works mainly focus on detection, not on recovery. If real time remedial action is not performed, the network condition is likely to get worse. Recently, an automated response system based on Cognitive Immune System (CIS) has been proposed in [17] to network failure that assumed an accurate detection system is present to trigger the response system. However, detection without effective diagnosis of network disruptions is not sufficient to determine the underlying cause of the problem, and confirm the presence of the interference for an appropriate remedial action to be taken. These three actions have to be integrated into one component. In addition, for all these studies, the proposed solutions mainly focused on failure caused by malicious attacks. These attacks usually have unique features that can easily be detected. Little work has investigated anomalies due to interference in the operating environment, either using ADSs or with more conventional approaches. One of challenges in detecting anomalies due to interference is that the duration and occurrence for these type of anomalies are unpredictable and changes with time [14]. Thus, it is difficult to be detected and classified using existing AIS or conventional approaches [2].

In this paper, we propose an integrated immune-inspired Interference Detection and Recovery System (IDRS) based on CIS [3] to allow individual nodes to detect, diagnose and make decision as to how to response to network failure due to radio interference. The CIS postulates that the immune systems do not only protect the body, but it also performs body maintenance through the process of recognition, cognition and response, with respect to its environment [3]. Based on this principle, we combine the use of the Multi-modal Routing Protocol (MRP) [11] and the Receptor Density Algorithm (RDA) [15]. The MRP is a multi-modal routing protocol proposed to overcome transmission failure by providing automated responses based on existing routing protocols. The RDA is an artificial immune system algorithm based on a T-Cell signalling model with statistical kernel density function to detect anomalies [15]. The main contributions of this paper are 1) A novel distributed anomalies detection, diagnostic, and recovery system that can identify and respond to network anomalies caused by radio interference, 2) The application of the RDA as a diagnostic tool to identify the different types of interference in the radio channel and to aid recovery decision, and 3) A quantitative evaluation of the proposed IDRS.

The remaining of the paper is structured as follows. Section 2 formulates the problem before an insight into the design and implementation of the proposed IDRS design and algorithm is presented in Section 3. The accuracy, efficiency and reliability of IDRS are evaluated and discussed in Section 4. Section 5 ends the paper with the conclusion and future work.

2   Radio Interference in Wireless Sensor Network

Network failures in WSNs due to interference are common as WSNs uses the same radio frequency with other devices such as portable phones, microwave ovens, Bluetooth devices, and Wi-Fi networks. Lin et al. [13] has classified the radio interference in three distinct patterns namely: small fluctuation created by multi-path fading of wireless signals; large disturbance due to shadowing effect of the presence of obstacles; continuous large fluctuations caused by Wi-Fi devices. Each of these interference patterns can have different decremental effects on the Packet Sending Ratio (PSR). Recent work by Wang et al. [18] has shown that due to interference from a Wi-Fi network, packet loss in WSNs can reach up to 30%. To overcome this interference, the nodes may need to retransmit their packet, or even increase their transmission power in order to communicate with their neighbour. In other cases, when the interference source is strong, the node may need to establish a new route in order to send the packet. All these recovery steps may aggravate a congested network and reduce the availability and lifetime of the network if it is not executed according to the interference patterns.

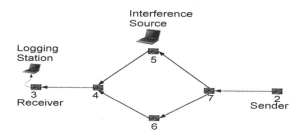

Fig. 1. Interference source is introduced near node 5 to disrupt the radio communication between node 2 and 3

To illustrate, six static and functionally homogeneous sensor nodes can be deployed in the topology shown in Fig.1. Each sensor node is capable of packet forwarding and produce network statistics. When a Wi-Fi device is placed close to node 5, the communication between node 5 and its neighbouring nodes (node 4 and 7) can be disrupted resulting in packet loss. As a result, the affected nodes will attempt to recover from the transmission failure by executing protocol-specific recovery functions such as retransmission, flooding and collision avoidance [16]. However, these responses are only effective if they are applied correctly, depending on the durations and intensity of the interference. Hence, it is not only a matter of detecting the presence of an anomaly, but also the cause of an anomaly, in order to make accurate and automated recovery decision.

3   IDRS: Interference Detection and Recovery Systems

The immune-inspired Interference Detection and Recovery System (IDRS) serves two purposes:

1. to accurately identify the interference that is affecting the communication between a node and its neighbour in a distributed manner,
2. to make autonomous decision on the recovery action to mitigate the effect of the interference, and improve the network reliability and efficiency.

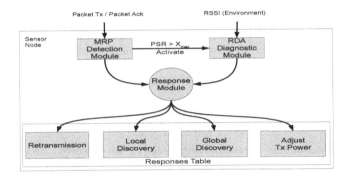

Fig. 2. The architecture of the CIS-based Interference Detection and Recovery System

The IDRS (Fig.2) consists of three modules, representing each stage in the CIS: MRP Detection Module (MDM), RDA Diagnostic Module (RDM), and Radio Interference Response Module (RIRM). Inputs to the IDRS are the PSR and the Receive Signal Strength Indicator (RSSI). These inputs can easily be obtained and calculated from the node. The MDM acts as the first line of defence to provide early detection and response to the interference when PSR is less than a predefined threshold value. If the condition does not improve, the MDM will activate the RDM to identify the type of interference based on the RSSI. Based on the results from both the MDM and the RDM, the RIRM will activate one or a combination of responses based the cognitive theory of *regeneracy* [3]. By using the close feedback loop provided by link layer, the effectiveness of the responses can be evaluated by the MRP. The cost of each response will be adjusted accordingly. Hence, IDRS is able to recognise and respond more effective from novel or existing interference based on the history of the response, and the strength and duration of the interference.

In the following subsections, a detailed description of the proposed IDRS Algorithm, in Appendix, is presented.

3.1   MDM: The MRP Detection Module

In WSNs, the packet reception ratio (PRR) is commonly used as a metric to detect network anomalies. The PRR is shared between neighbouring nodes [12]. This data is usually piggybacked on existing packet. However, in the presence of interference this data may be lost or corrupted. Hence, we advocate that the detection module should be implemented at the transmitting node. In the IDRS, we propose the use of the MRP [11] to detect the presence of interference based on the PSR and provide an initial response. The PSR is the total number of packets successfully send over the total number of attempts made in a given time window. The MRP detects deviation in the PSR and utilises the packet acknowledgement (P_{ack}) to provide network recovery responses [11] and to activate the RDM. Each route recovery response incurs a specific cost (RT_{cost} for *retransmission*, LD_{cost} for *local recovery*). Associated with each recovery response is a maximum cost threshold: RT_{max} for retransmission, and LD_{max} for recovery. The recovery response will only be selected if the cost of carrying out the response is lower than the maximum threshold. All these responses utilise the existing acknowledgement mechanisms on the link layer. As such, no additional communication overhead is incurred in the network. Work by Lim et al. [11] has demonstrated by employing MRP, significant network improvement has been achieved.

3.2   RDM: The RDA Diagnostic Module

To identify the cause of a transmission failure, the Received Signal Strength Indicator (RSSI) is used. Monitoring the RSSI in WSNs has been widely used to decide the required transmission power to transmit a packet [2,12]. However, as illustrated in Fig.3 (a_1) and Fig.3 (a_2), the RSSI values are sensitive to changes in environment. It has been demonstrated to be a challenging task to classify the RSSI values with traditional statistical techniques [2]. Small changes in the operating environment can trigger large variations in the RSSI, making it difficult to accurately determine the type of interference [9]. Here, we propose the use of the RDA [10,15] to filter the background noise and classify the interference. The RDA has been used to detect partial failure in swarm robotic system [10] and chemical substances [7] with high positive detection rate and low false detection rate. Its ability to recognise anomalies in a dynamic environment has motivated its application to WSNs.

The RDA was developed based on the immunological modelling on the activation of the T Cell Receptor (simply referred to as the *receptor* in this paper) when presented with antigen on the surface of an antigen presenting cell [15]. Depending on how often the receptor encounters the antigen, the receptor can become more sensitive or less sensitive (lower activation threshold) towards the antigen. To apply the RDA, the input data is divided into s discretised locations and a *receptor* $\mathbf{x}_s$ is placed at each of these locations. A receptor has a length $\ell = (\sqrt{2\pi})^{-1}$, a position $r_p \in [0, \ell]$, and a negative feedback $r_n \in (0, \ell)$. At each time step t, each receptor takes input $\mathbf{x}_i$ and performs a binary classification $c_t \in 0,1$ to determine whether that location is considered anomalous. The

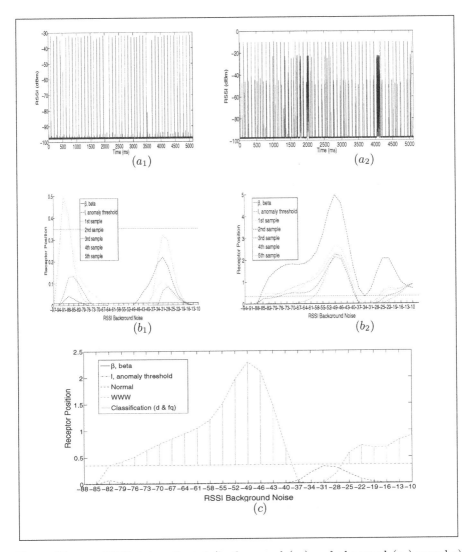

Fig. 3. The raw RSSI data collected (both normal (a_1) and abnormal (a_2) samples) from the radio interface are fed into RDA to product normal (b_1) and abnormal (b_2) signatures of activated receptors. Using the outputs generated by RDA, the interference can be classified into either Class I, II, or III based on the euclidean distance of the furthest activated receptor and the number of activated receptors above the threshold l, represented by the global maximum and vertical lines in (c) respectively

classification decision is determined by the dynamics of r_p and negative feedback $r_n \in (0, \ell)$.

The process for initialisation and classification of the RSSI values are described as follows:

Phase 1: Initialisation

1. Present the normal RSSI values $\mathbf{X}$ (Figure $3a_1$) to the RDA to generate its normal signature (Figure $3b_1$). For each receptor x , calculate the sum of stimulation $S(x)$ on each receptor x for each RSSI input x_i, $x_i \in \mathbf{X}$.

$$S(x) = \sum_{i=1}^{n} \frac{e^{\frac{-(x-x_i)^2}{2h^2}}}{h\sqrt{2\pi}} \tag{1}$$

where h is the kernel width and set to 5 in this paper, and n is the total number of normal RSSI values.

2. Calculate the negative feedback $r_n(x)$ for each receptor x. The base negative barrier β is set to a small value, 0.01 in this paper.

$$r_n(x) = \begin{cases} S(x) - \beta, & \text{if } S(x) \geq \beta \\ 0, & \text{otherwise} \end{cases} \tag{2}$$

Phase 2: Classification

1. Initialise the receptor position $r_t(x)$=0 for all receptors.
2. Based on the MAX($r_p(x)$) of normal signature, set the threshold value of the receptor length $\ell = (\sqrt{2\pi})^{-1}$.
3. Calculate the new receptor position $r_p(x)$ with current RSSI values $\mathbf{V}$.

$$K_s = \sum_{i=1}^{n} \frac{e^{\frac{-(x-v_i)^2}{2h^2}}}{h\sqrt{2\pi}}, \qquad r_p(x) = K_s - r_n(x) \tag{3}$$

where each RSSI value $v_i \in \mathbf{V}$.

4. Classify $\mathbf{V}$:
   A receptor is activated when

$$\mathbf{V} = \begin{cases} Normal, & \text{if } r_p(x) < l \\ Interference, & \text{otherwise.} \end{cases} \tag{4}$$

The classification of v to different classes of interference is based on two variables (Figure 3c):

- The difference between distance of the highest receptor position and ℓ ($\max(\ell - r_p(x))$), referred to as *Intensity*;
- The number of activated receptors, referred to as *Duration*.

3.3   RIRM: The Radio Interference Response Module

We assume that based on the RSSI and the PSR values, the interference can be classified into three classes according to the different duration (short or long) and intensity (weak or strong). Also, four different responses can be used to overcome the interference:

1. Retransmission (RT): Retransmission is the default action and activated when the MDM detects that the acknowledgement packet P_{ack} is not received and the cost of retransmission RT_{cost} has not exceed the threshold RT_{max}. This response is particularly effective when the interference noise signal is *weak* and *short* (CLASS I).

2. Local Discovery (LD): Local discovery is activated when the node failed to send the packet after several RT attempts (as indicated by PSR lower than 90%) or when the RDM identified a CLASS II interference. This response is best executed only when the next node is unavailable and the interference noise signal is *weak* and *long* (CLASS II).

3. Global Discovery (GD): This is usually the last option to take when the existing route is known to be unreliable. This action is usually taken when all the previous responses have failed, and there is no local node available to re-route the traffic, or the interference source is *strong* and *long* (CLASS III).

4. Transmission Power Control (TPC): This is an additional response to handle unavailable route cause by node failure or obstruction. It is a common approach to increase the transmission power in order to communicate with the next hop neighbouring node [2,12]. However, the use of higher transmission power can only be applied when necessary as it consumes more battery power and can interfere with other nodes. Hence, TPC is only applied when CLASS I interference is detected with the PSR is lower than 90% and the transmission power Tx_{power} is less than a predefine maximum power Tx_{max}.

To clarify, a decision tree, based on expert knowledge, is presented in Figure 4 to show the response strategy to be selected based on the current network environment.

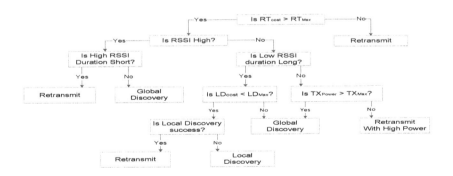

Fig. 4. Decision tree based on the RIRM and MDM to response to different interference

4   Experiments and Results

In order to evaluate the proposed IDRS, we conducted two experiments. The first experiment examines the effectiveness of the RDA classifier in the RDM whilst the second experiment evaluates the efficacy of the proposed IDRS when compared to other methods.

4.1   Evaluation of the RDM

In the RDM, we use over 850,000 RSSI readings to classify the interference into three classes: CLASS I, CLASS II, and CLASS III. The RSSI values are obtained from the TelosB radio module, exposed to different interference source. The spectrum of the RSSI values used is the range of -100dBm to -10dBm. This spectrum is uniformly divided into 30 slots and a receptor is used to represent each slot (the value x in Eq. 1).

In order to classify the interference into the three classes, an unsupervised K-mean clustering algorithm is applied to the set of training data (offline). The derived classes based on *Intensity* (**C1**) and *Duration* (**C2**) are in Table 1.

Table 1. Interference Class

Intensity, C1	Duration, C2	Class	Remarks
$0 < $ **C1** $ \leq 2.8$	$0 < $ **C2** $ \leq 5$	I	weak intensity, short duration
$2.8 < $ **C1** $ \leq 11.0$	$5 < $ **C2** $ \leq 16$	II	weak intensity, long duration
C1 $ > 11.0$	**C2** $ > 16$	III	strong intensity, long duration

We evaluate the performance of the RDM in TelosB mote based on *sensitivity* (Eq. 5) and *precision* (Eq. 6).

$$Sensitivity = \frac{TP}{TP + FN} \quad (5) \qquad Precision = \frac{TP}{TP + FP} \quad (6)$$

Sensitivity measures how well the RDM can correctly classify the interference source whilst *precision* measures the probability of a detected event is representing a true positive result rather than a false positive. *Precision* ensures the appropriate response is taken for the corresponding interference.

Experimental Setup: Two static nodes are deployed across a distance of 10 metres. One node is configured to transmit packets at the rate of 8 packets per second while sampling its radio channel at the rate of 1 KHz to collect the RSSI values and perform online detection.

Eight different network conditions are used to test the system namely: normal WSN communication, object blocking, jamming from another node, Wi-Fi traffics such as web browsing (WWW), slow video streaming, fast video streaming, slow file downloading, and fast file downloading. In each run, only one type of interference was injected into the network at periodic interval. This is done by placing a laptop next to the receiving node. Due to the limited log size in the motes, each experiment was run for 5 minutes to generate 2400 packets and is repeated 15 times.

Experimental Results: The results for the experiment are shown in Table 2. In the table, the RDM achieved a precision above 80% for most of interferences especially for interferences that have drastic impact on the PSR (PSR < 70%) such as blocking and fast download. These two types of interference require a different recovery approach. Hence, it is important to achieve a precision rate above 80% precision rate to allow a specific response approach to be taken when PSR < 75%. Although the false negative rate for Class II interference is high due to misclassification, its impact on the network PSR is less extreme with only up to 25% packet loss compared to blocking and fast download with packet loss above 30%. Beside, high accuracy in Class II interference is usually not required for accurate response as the sequential recovery step provided by the RIRM will eventually trigger the right response.

Table 2. The sensitivity and precision of the RDM in classifying different sources of interference. The RDM showed high sensitivity and precision for Class I and III interference.

Interference Source	Class Type	True Positive	False Positive	True Negative	False Negative	Sensitivity	Precision	PSR (Ave)
Normal	I	98	0	0	0	100.00%	100.00%	95%
Blocking	I	47	0	3	0	100.00%	**100.00%**	68%
Jamming	I	30	5	28	0	100.00%	**85.71%**	70%
WWW	II	12	10	7	8	60.00%	54.55%	80%
Slow Streaming	II	54	0	23	49	52.43%	**100%**	81%
Slow Download	II	14	5	2	4	77.78%	**73.68%**	76%
Fast Streaming	III	14	1	23	4	77.78%	**93.33%**	63%
Fast Download	III	39	8	13	6	86.67%	**82.98%**	45%

4.2   Evaluation of the IDRS

In this experiment, the performance of the IDRS will be compared to the Not So Tiny's AODV (NST) [6], the original MRP [11], and a modified MRP with TPC (M_{TPC}). M_{TPC} protocol is used to evaluate the benefit of boosting the transmission power with or without RDM. The performance of the routing protocols is evaluated based on the following metrics:

– **Packet Delivery Ratio (PDR)**: PDR represent the percentage of the number of packets received by the receiver, to the total number of packets transmitted by the sender. This metric measures the reliability of the routing protocol.

- **Transmission Overhead (TO)**: TO is defined as the average number of transmissions made by a node to deliver the packets to the receiver. This metric represents the efficiency of the routing. It can be calculated by dividing the sum of the transmissions made, including RT, LD and GD, to the total number of packets received.
- **Average Current Consumption (CC)**: CC can be determined by first calculating the total currents, $I_{total}(i)$ consumed in a node, i, by multiplying the number of packets transmitted to the current required to transmit one packet at that power level. A typical current consumption for transmitting a packet can be obtained from the Chipcon data sheet[1]. Finally, $I_{total}(i)$ can be used to determine the network average current consumption by multiplying $I_{total}(i)$ to the total of nodes in the networks.

Experimental Setup: Six static TelosB motes are placed 3 metres apart using the topology shown in Fig.1. The experiment is conducted at the centre of a room relatively free from uncontrolled radio sources to ensure its correctness and validity. The node transmission is set to minimum power using the same channel as the Wi-Fi in the room to treat it as a source of interference. The LLN is enabled to allow packet acknowledgement. During initialisation, node 2 is configured to collect temperature reading from the sensor and transmit the packet to node 3, at regular intervals of 256ms via the intermediate nodes. Once the network route has been established, and the normal signature has been collected by the RDM (after 30 seconds), different sources of interference are introduced into the network (close to node 5) at 30 seconds intervals. Each interference lasts for approximately 15 seconds. Each test is run for 10 minutes and is repeated 15 times.

Experimental Results: The results for this experiment are shown in Table 3. The results show that the IDRS outperformed the other three routing protocols in term of energy efficient (CC) when interference was introduced. Under the normal condition, all routing protocols consumed similar amount of energy to transmit one packet successfully. However, when interference was introduced, higher TO (up to an average of 14 transmissions per packet) has been observed in NST as NST requires to retransmit the packet before performing local discovery. The TO is significantly less for routing protocols with MRP especially for IDRS as highlighted in Table 3. As a result, less current is used to deliver a packet successfully.

When interferences with longer duration (CLASS II and CLASS III) are introduced, the IDRS consumed the least current as precise response can be executed by RIRM based on the diagnosis made by the RMD. For example, as shown in Table 4 with Class II interference, the IDRS performed less RT and TPC as the node was able to recognise the interference and performed LD immediately

---

[1] downloadable at http://www.ti.com/lit/gpn/cc2420

without executing RT and TPC. The RMD in the IDRS managed to effectively classify the interference as shown in class I, II, and III in Table 4. The total number of responses performed by IDRS is significantly less than the M_{TPC} and thus more energy efficient.

Table 3. The performance on the reliability (PDR), efficiency (TO) and energy usage (CC) for NST, MPR, M_{TPC} and IDRS under difference sources of interference

Radio Conditions	NST PDR (%)	NST TO	NST CC (mA)	MRP PDR (%)	MRP TO	MRP CC (mA)	M_{TPC} PDR (%)	M_{TPC} TO	M_{TPC} CC (mA)	IDRS PDR (%)	IDRS TO	IDRS CC (mA)
Normal	93.8	3.66	26.2	98.3	3.56	**25.9**	98.1	3.50	26.5	**98.4**	**3.49**	26.1
Class I	70.9	8.79	74.7	80.6	7.51	63.9	**84.9**	7.08	60.2	82.1	**6.55**	**55.7**
Class II	82.3	14.13	49.1	93.7	4.16	33.1	**96.9**	3.90	31.6	96.3	**3.78**	**31.0**
Class III	76.1	8.79	128.2	79.4	7.50	97.9	**87.1**	5.75	89.3	86.6	**5.36**	**83.6**

From Table 3, by increasing the transmission power as one of the response during Class I interference has improved the PDR by 5% on average compared to M_{TPC}. Although both M_{TPC} and IDRS exhibit similar PDR, IDRS has performed TPC less frequent than M_{TPC} during Class III error as Class I interference has been correctly classified by RDM as shown in Table 4 leading to better energy efficiency. Hence, the use of RDA to classify the radio signal noise pattern has not only allowed the system to response accurately with minimal energy consumption, but has also maintained a higher PDR.

Table 4. The execution of different responses with the interference classification in the IDRS, and without in the M_{TPC}. Results show that IDRS managed to execute the right response compared to M_{TPC}. Class III interference has been correctly classified resulting in higher number of Global discovery and lower number of high power transmission.

Radio Condition	Number of Response Executed RT IDRS	M_{TPC}	LD IDRS	M_{TPC}	TPC IDRS	M_{TPC}	GD IDRS	M_{TPC}	Interference Detected Class I	Class II	Class III
Normal	41	44	24	35	5	7	50	48	7	0	0
Class I	*113*	*174*	*52*	*92*	*33*	*12*	*342*	*404*	**59**	4	1
Class II	42	66	15	14	6	14	88	60	35	**15**	1
Class III	**164**	**193**	**108**	**145**	**15**	**44**	**121**	**219**	88	74	**82**

5   Conclusions

In this paper, we have presented an immune-inspired interference detection and recovery system (IDRS). This system consists of the MPR detection module, the RDA Diagnostic Module, and the Radio Interference Response Module. In the RDM, we have extended the usage of the RDA to diagnose certain types of interference. Our experimental results have demonstrated that RDA can effectively classify the interference based on the RSSI values. Together with the use of the MRP, an effective response to network anomalies due to interference can be achieved. The results show that the IDRS can improve the PDR by 11% and reduce the energy consumption by 25.5% with Class I interference, and 10.5% improvement in PDR and saving of 34.8% in energy with Class III interference. It can also be used to detect anomalies that affecting the mote's radio. As the signature of normal RSSI can be easily regenerated as required, the IDRS can be made to adapt to its changing environment. As future work, we will incorporate an adaptive tunable activation threshold based on its environment and performance.

References

1. Akyildiz, I.F., Su, W., Sankarasubramaniam, Y., Cayirci, E.: Wireless sensor networks: A survey. Computer Networks 38(4), 393–422 (2002)
2. Boers, N., Nikolaidis, I., Gburzynski, P.: Patterns in the RSSI traces from an indoor urban environment. In: The IEEE International Workshop on Computer Aided Modeling, Analysis and Design of Communication Links and Networks, pp. 61–65 (2010)
3. Cohen, I.R.: Tending Adam's Garden: Evolving the Cognitive Immune Self. Academic Press (2004)
4. Drozda, M., Bate, I., Timmis, J.: Bio-inspired error detection for complex systems. In: The 17th IEEE Pacific Rim International Symposium on Dependable Computing, pp. 154–163 (2011)
5. Drozda, M., Schaust, S., Szczerbicka, H.: AIS for misbehavior detection in wireless sensor networks: Performance and design principles. In: The IEEE Congress on Evolutionary Computation, pp. 3719–3726 (2007)
6. Gomez, C., Salvatella, P., Alonso, O., Paradells, J.: Adapting AODV for IEEE 802.15.4 mesh sensor networks: Theoretical discussion and performance evaluation in a real environment. In: The IEEE International Symposium on World of Wireless, Mobile and Multimedia Networks, pp. 159–170 (2006)
7. Hilder, J., Owens, N., Hickey, P., Cairns, S., Kilgour, D., Timmis, J., Tyrrell, A.: Parameter Optimisation in the Receptor Density Algorithm. In: Liò, P., Nicosia, G., Stibor, T. (eds.) ICARIS 2011. LNCS, vol. 6825, pp. 226–239. Springer, Heidelberg (2011)
8. Kim, J., Bentley, P., Wallenta, C., Ahmed, M., Hailes, S.: Danger Is Ubiquitous: Detecting Malicious Activities in Sensor Networks Using the Dendritic Cell Algorithm. In: Bersini, H., Carneiro, J. (eds.) ICARIS 2006. LNCS, vol. 4163, pp. 390–403. Springer, Heidelberg (2006)
9. Ko, J., Terzis, A.: Power control for mobile sensor networks: An experimental approach. In: The 7th Annual IEEE Communications Society Conference on Sensor Mesh and Ad Hoc Communications and Networks (2010)
10. Lau, H.K., Timmis, J., Bate, I.: Collective Self-detection Scheme for Adaptive Error Detection in a Foraging Swarm of Robots. In: Liò, P., Nicosia, G., Stibor, T. (eds.) ICARIS 2011. LNCS, vol. 6825, pp. 254–267. Springer, Heidelberg (2011)
11. Lim, T.H., Bate, I., Timmis, J.: Multi-modal routing to tolerate failures. In: The 7th International Conference on Intelligent Sensors, Sensor Networks and Information Processing, pp. 211–216 (2011)

12. Lin, S., Zhang, J., Zhou, G., Gu, L., Stankovic, J., He, T.: ATPC: adaptive transmission power control for wireless sensor networks. In: The 4th International Conference on Embedded Networked Sensor Systems, pp. 223–236 (2006)
13. Lin, S., Zhou, G., Whitehouse, K., Wu, Y., Stankovic, J., He, T.: Towards stable network performance in wireless sensor networks. In: The 30th IEEE Real-Time Systems Symposium, pp. 227–237 (2009)
14. Liu, H., Li, J., Xie, Z., Lin, S., Whitehouse, K., Stankovic, J.A., Siu, D.: Automatic and robust breadcrumb system deployment for indoor firefighter applications. In: The 8th International Conference on Mobile Systems, Applications, and Services, pp. 21–34 (2010)
15. Owens, N., Greensted, A., Timmis, J., Tyrell, A.: T Cell Receptor Signalling Inspired Kernel Density Estimation and Anomaly Detection. In: Andrews, P.S., Timmis, J., Owens, N.D.L., Aickelin, U., Hart, E., Hone, A., Tyrrell, A.M. (eds.) ICARIS 2009. LNCS, vol. 5666, pp. 122–135. Springer, Heidelberg (2009)
16. Perkins, C.E., Royer, E.M.: Ad-hoc on-demand distance vector routing. In: The IEEE Workshop on Mobile Computing Systems and Applications, pp. 90–100 (1999)
17. Schaust, S., Szczerbicka, H.: Applying Antigen-Receptor Degeneracy Behavior for Misbehavior Response Selection in Wireless Sensor Networks. In: Liò, P., Nicosia, G., Stibor, T. (eds.) ICARIS 2011. LNCS, vol. 6825, pp. 212–225. Springer, Heidelberg (2011)
18. Wang, Y., Wang, Q., Zeng, Z., Zheng, G., Zheng, R.: Wicop: Engineering wifi temporal white-spaces for safe operations of wireless body area networks in medical applications. In: The IEEE International Real-Time Systems Symposium, pp. 170–179 (2011)
19. Wu, Y., Kapitanova, K., Li, J., Stankovic, J., Son, S., Whitehouse, K.: Run time assurance of application-level requirements in wireless sensor networks. In: The 9th ACM/IEEE International Conference on Information Processing in Sensor Networks, pp. 197–208 (2010)

Appendix: The Algorithm

input : Packet Send P_s
output: Response Action

```
 1  while Packet Buffer is not Empty do
 2  │   Send Packet Ps and wait for acknowledgement Pack;
 3  │   if Pack is not received then                           ⎫  Activate MRM
 4  │   │    Calculate Packet Sending Ratio, PSR               ⎬  Detection
 5  │   else                                                   ⎭  Module.
 6  │   │    Decrease the cost for Retransmission, RTcost;
 7  │   end
 8  │   if PSR < 95% then                                      ⎫  Activate RDA
 9  │   │    Determine interference CLASS from RDM;            ⎬  Diagnostic
10  │   end                                                    ⎭  Module.
11  │   if not CLASS III and [PSR > 90% or RTcost < RTmax] and
12  │   Route is valid then                                    ⎫  Trigger
13  │   │    Retransmit;                                       ⎬  Retransmission
14  │   │    Increase the cost for Retransmission, RTcost;     ⎭  Response.
15  │   else if CLASS II and LDcost < LDmax then
16  │   │    Perform Route Discovery;                          ⎫  Trigger
17  │   │    Increase the cost for Local Discovery LDcost ;    ⎬  Local Discovery
18  │   │    if Route Discovery is Successful then             ⎭  Response.
19  │   │    │    Decrease the cost of Retransmission RTcost;
20  │   │    end
21  │   else if CLASS I and TxPower < TxMAX then               ⎫  Trigger Higher
22  │   │    Increase the Transmission power, Txpower;         ⎬  Transmission
23  │   │    Decrease the Retransmission Cost, RTcost;         ⎭  Power Response.
24  │   else                                                   ⎫  Trigger
25  │   │    Invalidate Route and Send Error for Global Discovery;  ⎬  Global Discovery
26  │   end                                                    ⎭  Response.
27  │   if Timeout then
28  │   │    Reinitialised
29  │   end
30  end
```

Algorithm 1: IDRS Algorithm with the combination of MRP and RDA

A Beginner's Guide to Systems Simulation in Immunology

Grazziela P. Figueredo, Peer-Olaf Siebers, Uwe Aickelin, and Stephanie Foan

Intelligent Modelling and Analysis Research Group, School of Computer Science,
The University of Nottingham, NG8 1BB, UK
{gzf,uxa,pos,sjf}@cs.nott.ac.uk

Abstract. Some common systems modelling and simulation approaches for immune problems are Monte Carlo simulations, system dynamics, discrete-event simulation and agent-based simulation. These methods, however, are still not widely adopted in immunology research. In addition, to our knowledge, there is few research on the processes for the development of simulation models for the immune system. Hence, for this work, we have two contributions to knowledge. The first one is to show the importance of systems simulation to help immunological research and to draw the attention of simulation developers to this research field. The second contribution is the introduction of a quick guide containing the main steps for modelling and simulation in immunology, together with challenges that occur during the model development. Further, this paper introduces an example of a simulation problem, where we test our guidelines.

1 Introduction

Some important advances in immunology were facilitated by the joint work of immunologists and mathematicians [1]. Many concepts existing in theoretical immunology are the result of mathematical models. Inumerous existing models in immunology are based on sets of ordinary differential equations (ODEs) [2,3]. This approach for immunology, however, in practice limits the modelling effort to simpler dynamics involving fewer immune elements such as cells or molecules and it only allows analysis at an aggregate level. Moreover, it is not trivial to model problems involving individual localisation, memory of past events (or states) and emerging properties mathematically [1]. Hence, systems simulation emerged as a complement of mathematics that allows to overcome some of these limitations. Moreover, systems simulation modelling methods are closer to the natural description of the system, without the need of an in depth understanding of mathematics [4].

Sauro *et al.* [5] debates the usefulness of simulation in contrast to reductionism in biology. In reductionism, the dynamics of complex systems can be understood from studying the properties of their parts [6]. In contrast to reductionism, in holism (in its methodological version) the properties of the parts contribute to our understanding of the whole, but the properties can only be fully understood

C.A. Coello Coello et al. (Eds.): ICARIS 2012, LNCS 7597, pp. 57–71, 2012.

through the dynamics of the whole [6]. Systems simulation is, therefore, based on holism. For biology, Sauro *et al.* [5] state that *"reductionism has proven to be a highly successful strategy and has enabled us to uncover the molecular details of biological systems in unprecedented detail"*. The success of reductionist methods raised some scepticism as to the need for alternative approaches, such as systems biology. The challenge for simulation is, therefore, to generate novel insights that cannot be uncovered just by looking at a phenomena using reductionism. Examples of successful simulation approaches that helped advance immunological research were introduced in [7]. The models reviewed simulate interactions of immune cells and chemical substances, humoral responses and drug testing. With these simulations it is possible to observe emergent behaviour in the systems, which is not feasible with reductionism.

As a first objective of this study, therefore, we want to show that there is a distinct place for simulation in the tool set that aids advances in immunology. Moreover we want to show that there is a wide range of problems in immunology to be tackled by computer scientists and simulation developers.

As there few examples on the methodology for constructing immune systems simulations [8,9,10], the second objective is to introduce general guidances for conducting simulation studies in immunology and outline the challenges that might be encountered during the development of a simulation model. These guidances adapted from the work developed by Robinson [11] for operational research, considering the characteristics observed in immune simulations. We complement the current methodologies for constructing immune systems simulations by presenting a framework containing a life-cycle with the main steps to be followed by any developer, independent of the simulation modelling method chosen.

The remainder of the paper is organized as follows. In Section 2 we review the main characteristics of the simulation methods used in immunology. In Section 3 we present the main steps and propose a life-cycle for conducting a simulation study for immune problems. In Section 4 we present a case study where we develop a system dynamics simulation model from the steps outlined. In Section 5, we present our conclusions and future work.

2   Simulation Methods

The choice of a modelling technique for a problem is driven by the resources available such as experimental data, an understanding of the mechanisms involved, the hypothesis to be tested and the level of abstraction needed to test the hypothesis. Once the conceptual model is defined, a simulation method needs to be chosen. There is a wide spectrum of simulation methods used in immunology. These methods are classified as static or dynamic, stochastic or deterministic, continuous or discrete. These methods model the system using either top-down or bottom-up perspectives. Static models help understand connections between system components, without explicitly representing time [12]. Dynamic models aid in understanding dynamic implications and consequences over time of a system structure [13]. Deterministic models do not contain any probabilistic components. Stochastic models, on the other hand, consider random components [14]. The characteristic of being continuous or discrete determine whether time and variables of the model change continuously or discretely. For example the age of an individual changes continuously in time, whereas the number of immune cells that die with age is a discrete value. Top-down approaches focus on the system at an aggregate level, while bottom-up approaches split the system in individual parts that will interact giving rise to the behaviour of the system as a whole [15].

Sauro *et al.* [5] mentions that the construction of models of biochemical and cellular behaviour has been traditionally carried out through a bottom-up approach, which combines laboratory data and knowledge of a reaction network to produce a dynamic model. This process, however, requires the reaction network to be known and the possibility to carry out the various laboratory experiments. Furthermore, the modelling relies on the fact that data from laboratory experimentation matches real-world phenomena, which is not always correct. Samples can be compromised during collection or during the experimentation process. In addition, although bottom-up approaches are very useful for immunology, there are circumstances where they can not be applied. Examples include when the reaction network process is not well understood, or laboratory experiments are known not to be able to reproduce the real-world reactions (for instance, given the environmental differences such as temperature). In addition, the authors argue that *"top-down modelling strategies are closer to the spirit of systems biology exactly because they make use of systems-level data, rather than having originated from a more reductionist approach of molecular purification"*. The conclusion reached in their study was that there is no best approach as it is preferable to view them as complementary. Their ideas match other studies in biology and other research areas, which investigate the merits of each approach and their combination for simulation [16]. To our knowledge, the most common system simulation approaches for immunology are Monte Carlo simulation, system dynamics, discrete-event simulation, cellular automata and agent-based simulation.

Monte Carlo simulations [17] are largely used in molecular theoretical immunology. These techniques generate random numbers and observe that fraction of the numbers that obey a certain property (of properties). These methods are suitable for obtaining numerical solutions for problems as an alternative to their analytical solution. The disadvantage of these methods are that they do not provide information of how the elements of the system change during the simulation (dynamics of the system). Instead, they focus on the determination of the system outcome given a certain input, not taking time into account.

System dynamics (SD) is a top-down modelling technique that uses stocks, flows and feedback loops as concepts to model the behaviour of complex systems in a stock and flow diagram. It is an aspect of systems theory that is initially applied in order to understand complex aggregate behaviours in industry [18]. Currently, SD is applied to any complex system characterized by interdependency, mutual interaction, information feedback and circular causality. System dynamics simulation (SDS) is a continuous simulation for an SD model. It consists of a set of ODEs that are solved for a certain time interval. These ODEs, however, are implicit in the system's structure and the relationships between the elements modelled can be established with experimental data. Some examples of SD applied to the immune system are found in [19,20].

Discrete-event simulation is also a top-down approach that models a system as a set of entities being processed and evolving over time according to the availability of resources and the triggering of events. The simulator maintains an ordered queue of events [21]. Each event occurs at an instant in time and marks a change of state in the system. It is process-oriented and the entities involved are passive [11], with no pro-activity. The entities are individually represented and can be tracked throughout the system simulation. The models are stochastic and outputs usually represent average values [22]. Examples of applications for the immune system are found in [23,24,25].

Cellular automata is a discrete model consisting of two main components. The first component is an infinite regular grid of cells, which constitutes the universe or space of the cellular automata. In computer simulations, however, due to space limitations, the cellular automata space is predetermined and finite. The second component is a finite automaton (or cell). Each cell from the grid contains a finite number of states and a predefined set of cells called *neighbourhood*. The communication of a cell with other cells within its neighbourhood is local, deterministic, uniform and synchronous [26]. Each cell is initialized with an initial state at time $t = 0$. As time advances, the cells are updated according to a fixed rule, which is, in general, a mathematical function. This rule defines the next state of each cell according to its current state and its neighbourhood states. Examples of several applications for the immune system are found in [7].

Agent-based simulation is a technique that employs autonomous agents that interact with each other [27]. The agents' behaviour is described by rules that determine how they learn, interact with each other and adapt. The overall system behaviour arises from the agents' individual dynamics and their interactions [21]. For immunology, it can amalgamate *in vitro* data on individual interactions between cells and molecules of the immune system to build an impression of the system as a whole. Cellular automata and agent-based simulation have some similarities such as individual rules and interactions between the individuals entities. Moreover, both are bottom-up approaches capable of representing emergent behaviour in the system. The entities in cellular automata, however, do not have memory and only interact with individuals from the predefined neighbourhood, as their location does not change. In agent-based simulation, on the other hand, the agents are individual entities with memory and are capable to interact with any other agent in the system. Several examples of agent-based models in immunology are found in the european virtual human immune system project (ImmunoGrid) [28].

By reviewing the simulation methods and some of their applications to immune problems, such as those from [7,23,24,25,29], it is possible to outline the benefits of simulation to immunology and, therefore, achieve our first objective of this work. Compared with real-world experimentation, simulation is time and cost-effective. Most laboratory experiments are expensive and have to be in agreement with ethical specifications. Furthermore, in a simulation environment, it is possible to systematically generate different scenarios, conduct and replicate experiments.

In the following section we fulfil our second research goal of this paper, which is to introduce a descriptive guide for the development of a simulation model in immunology and the challenges that might be encountered during this process. These guidances are kept general and can be applied to all simulation methods in immunology.

3   Steps in a Simulation Study

As there is not much done to established guidance to develop simulations for the immune system, we studied those developed by [11] for simulation in operational research problems and adapted them for simulations of the immune system. The adaptation was performed by studying several simulations under different approaches developed for the immune system, as mentioned in the previous section. In order to adapt the guidelines developed by [11], we observed the similarities and differences with operational research and outlined general steps for building immune simulations. These steps represent a life-cycle of a simulation and therefore the method we present is iterative. Furthermore, we discuss the pitfalls that might be encountered during the process, as shown below. In some of the steps, extra efforts specific to immunology were not added as we believe they are generic for any type of simulation.

1. Define the Objectives. Overall, the objectives are either to investigate a theory or propose a "what-if" scenario with no concern to ethics restrictions. The scenario proposed can either be based on experimental data or defined as an intuition of what might happen in reality. Furthermore, there are also cases where actual models do not match real-world experimentation and they need to be further investigated (in a simulation model). In addition, new hypotheses and research questions may be defined together with immunologists as simulation goals. The objectives come from real-world observation. We assume, however, that real-world observation and experimentation has been previously performed by immunologists.

2. Describe the System. In this step, it is necessary to use documents (immunology books and articles, transcripts of interviews with experts, etc.) describing how the immune elements to be simulated work and interact. The description of the system is based on knowledge acquired by theoretical work, real-world observation and laboratory experimentation. Due to the complexity of the elements and processes in the immune system, however, this knowledge is scarce. The immune system is far from being fully fathomable, and the descriptions found in literature are only partial representations and assumptions of what occurs in reality.

3. Investigate Existing Theories and Established Models. In order to build a new simulation model, it is common to look at the existing models and investigate their hypotheses, objectives, validation process and limitations. For some cases, these established models have somehow been validated against experimental data. With this practice it is possible to build a new model as an improvement of what has already been established in order to further investigate a certain immune process.

4. Use Experimental Data. Currently, most simulation models are built based on real-world observation and experimentation. There are some models, however, where there is no data available (for example, when Jerne's network theory was conceptualized [30]). These models are based purely on theoretical assumptions with the purpose of providing more insights about what happens in the real world. Furthermore, in the field of immunology, the non-existence of data can be due to the lack of understanding of a process, or a difficulty or even impossibility in collecting information with current technology. In other cases, a hypothesis is first formulated requiring experimental data to confirm it. There is, therefore, the need to collect this data. For instance, Foan *et al.* [20] implemented a system dynamics simulation of T cell subsets throughout a person's lifetime based on an established mathematical model developed by Balcheva [31]. The authors conclude that further validation of this model is necessary and so a novel data set should be collected as there are arguably more specific markers that could help to gain further insights from the model.

5. Build Conceptual Model. The conceptual model of a problem is an abstraction intended to contain the principal aspects observed in the real world, considering the necessary level of details [32]. In this step we formally define the model scope, the objectives previously outlined, the inputs and outputs and the simplifications. The process of creating a conceptual model evolves with decisions regarding the model scope and level of detail [11]. The acceptance of the conceptual model should be agreed with immunologists. According to Ulgen *et al.* [33], *"rigorous validation procedure for the conceptual model is as important as the verification and validation of the model because it saves time and redirects the simulation developers in the right direction before time is wasted in the study"*. Due to the limitations of a immune simulation, it is important to abstract the relevant real-world features and build a simple model. According to Kotiadis and Robinson [32], the importance of model abstraction *"relies on the fact that there is no need to model all that is known about the real problem. Simpler models are developed and run faster, they are flexible, require less data and results are easier to be interpreted"*. The nature of the immune problems thus implies that the model should be developed in order to address a few objectives, within a limited scope. The description of the system (and definition of the conceptual model) should therefore focus on the parts of the immune system (scope, elements, information available, assumptions, hypotheses) relevant to achieve the simulation goals. Daigle discusses the challenges of modelling immunology [34]. As it is a field in which information is still being gathered, simulations have to be updated frequently to suit new findings. Moreover, current computational resources and modelling techniques are in development. It is still thereby impossible to represent computationally an entire pool of cells of a typical immune response (around 10^{12} cells). In addition, immunological systems are mostly hierarchical, involving several layers and complex interactions between the elements of these layers.

6. Identify Elements, Parameters, Aggregates, etc. Already Established in Theory and Real-World Data. The study of the conceptual model provides a means to understand the problem and the best way to represent the elements of the system. This stage influences the choice of the most appropriate simulation approach. For example, if the in the conceptual model it is established the interactions of the simulation will occur at a cellular population level rather than an individual cell level, this might indicate that a top-down simulation approach would be more suitable to build the model.

7. Decide on the Most Appropriate Simulation Approach. This decision is made based on the characteristics of the problems, the research questions to be addressed, the scope, the level of aggregation and the experimental data available. Some of the most common approaches used in immunology are agent-based modelling and simulation, discrete-event modelling and simulation, cellular automata and system dynamics. Cellular automata is used for problems involving autonomous individual interactions within a neighbourhood placed in a lattice and emergent behaviour. Agent-based simulation is suitable for problems involving autonomous individual behaviour, elements spacial localization, memory and emergence. Discrete-event simulation tackles problems that are process-oriented, which have passive individual entities and chronological sequence of events. Furthermore, each event occurs at an instant in time and marks a change of state in the system. It can be used for any experiment where there is no need for continuous time. SD defines a system at a high level of aggregation and, therefore, it should be used when the research question involves patterns of behaviours and feed-back interactions between the aggregates. This approach is very useful to simulate dynamics of populations and interactions between different populations overtime. For example, interactions between tumours and populations of effector cells, populations of viruses and T cells, etc.

8. Represent Elements, Parameters, etc. Using the Appropriate Simulation Approach. Once the simulation approach is chosen, the elements defined in the conceptual model need to be translated into their correspondent implementation used by each approach, for instance, stocks, flows, parameters and information for SD or agents and rules for ABMS. This step is part of the construction of the simulation model, defined in the next step.

9. Build the Simulation Model. This stage includes the development of the computational implementation of the model in a simulation tool. The implementation is a software representation of the requisites defined in the conceptual model. The computational model is the final product to be used by the immunologists.

10. Verify the Model. The model verification is the process of ensuring that the model design has been transformed into a computer model with sufficient accuracy [11].

11. Validate the Model with Existing Theories and, if Available, Real-World Data. Validation ensures that the model is sufficiently accurate for the purpose at hand. For immunology it is acknowledged that models are not intended to be completely accurate for a number of reasons: (1) there is no real world data to compare against, (2) there is little data, (3) real-world data is inaccurate, (4) even if the data is accurate, the real world data is only a sample, which in itself creates inaccuracy. Verification and validation are continuous and iterative processes performed throughout the life cycle of a simulation study [11].

12. Experimental Design. The experimental design improves the experimentation process by the definition of sound experiments with trustworthy results. In this stage, the experimental factors that are most likely to lead to significant improvements are identified. This process is developed using data analysis, expert knowledge, preliminary experimentation and sensitivity analysis.

13. Experimentation. Experimentation is conducted following the experimental design guidelines. It can make use of multiple simulation replications; interactive experimentation (observing the simulation and making changes to the model to see the effects); batch experimentation (setting experimental factors and leaving the models to run for a pre-defined run length); comparing alternatives (where there is a limited number of scenarios to be compared) and search experimentation (when there is no predefined number of scenarios).

14. Result Analysis. Plots and statistics are collected during the simulation. The result analysis is the process that interprets results and the best way to present them.

15. Report Findings. After results are interpreted, there is the need to report the findings from the simulations. For immunology, it can be new insights, verification of a theory, etc.

16. Validate And add More Requisites with Immunologists. Building an immune simulation is an iterative process. Generally the model is built together with immunologists, and, in every step of the framework, the model elements should be verified with them.

The process of simulation is iterative, as shown in Figure 1. During the model development, additional data might become available, which changes the system description/objectives and impacts on every step of the process. Moreover, as validation occurs throughout the whole process, if any of the stages is not validated (data available, real world understanding and description, conceptual model, computer model, experimental design, etc), there is the need to go back and rethink the invalid state, which impacts on the subsequent steps.

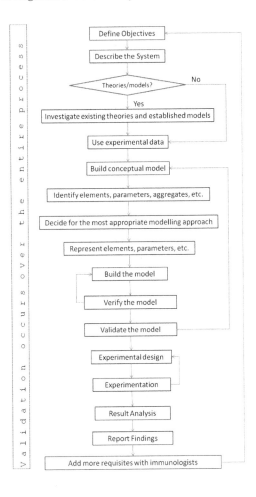

Fig. 1. Process of simulation study: the life cycle

4   Case Study

The objective of our case study is to exemplify how the steps defined previously can be employed to help in the development of a simulation for the immune system. The problem to be investigated is how the population of peripheral naive T cells evolve during the course of an individual's lifetime. The development of the simulation model is depicted below.

1. Define Objectives. The simulation goal is concerned with establishing an understanding of the peripheral naive T cell repertoire dynamics over time.

2. Describe the System. In the human body there is a type of white blood cell, namely the naive T cell, which plays an important role in the immune system by responding to new infections in the organism. Before an individual reaches the age of 20, the set of naive T cells is sustained primarily from thymic output. In middle age, however, there is a change in the source of naive T cells: as the thymus involutes, there is a considerable shrinkage in its T cell output, which means that new T cells are mostly produced by peripheral expansion. There is also a belief that some memory T cells have their phenotype reverted back to the naive proliferation cells type [35]. Furthermore, memory cells are originated from active T cells.

3. Investigate Existing Theories and Models. Immunologists found out that thymic contribution in an individual are quantified by the level of a biological marker called 'T cell receptors excision circle' (TREC). TREC is circular DNA originated during the formation of the T-cell receptor. The percentage of T cells possessing TRECs decays with shrinkage of thymic output, activation and reproduction of naive T cells [35]. This means that naive T cells originating from the thymus have a greater percentage of TREC than those originating through other proliferation and with time there is a depletion of naive T cells from thymus in the organism. There is an existing model proposed by Murray [35] that investigates the thymic output and decay of these cells mathematically with the use of an ODE system.

4. Experimental Data. TREC data collected by immunologists is presented by Murray *et al.* [35], which also develops an ODE system model for the dynamics of peripheral naive T cells. Furthermore, the authors provided us with data on active cells and total naive T cells in individuals with age ranging from 1 to 55 years. If we assume that this data has been validated by the immunologists and expresses what occurs in reality, we can use this information for the continuation of our investigations on naive cells from peripheral proliferation.

5. Conceptual Model. The population dynamics of the model is shown in Figure 2. We have four main populations of cells: naive from thymus (in the figure naive), naive from proliferation, active cells and memory cells. Naive and memory cells are sources of naive cells from proliferation. Active cells are sources of memory cells. The scope of the simulation, therefore, is limited to the dynamics of these four populations. The number of naive from thymus and active cells are given by real-world data collected by immunologists. The conceptual model and data used are the same as the those from the existing model proposed by Murray [35]. The objective is to determine what are the dynamics of the naive cells from peripheral proliferation with age under a systems simulation approach different from the ODEs simulation. Another goal is to determine the rates in which the naive cells from thymus and memory cells become naive cells from proliferation; and the rates in which active cells become memory cells.

6 and 7. Identify Elements, Parameters, etc. and Decide on the Most Appropriate Simulation Approach. As the investigations regard populations dynamics at a high level of aggregation, as defined in the conceptual model, we decided to build the simulation using the system dynamics approach, where the aggregates will be each different cell population and the feedback loops are those represented by the arrows in the conceptual model of figure 2.

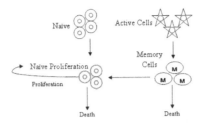

Fig. 2. Dynamics of Naive T cells

8. Represent Elements, Parameters, etc. Using the Appropriate Simulation Approach. As stated before, system dynamics models consist of stock, flows, information and feedback loops. The stocks of the simulation are the variables that accumulate over time; flows modify the stocks by adding or subtracting elements. For the simulation, therefore, the stocks will be the number of naive cells from proliferation and memory cells. The stock of naive cells from proliferation is modified by flows such as addition of new cells from thymus, peripheral proliferation and death, as shown in Figure 2 from the conceptual model. The memory cells stock is changed by the flows: active cells reversing into memory and memory cells death. Both naive and active cells are represented in the simulation as look up tables. Moreover, parameters representing rates in which flows modify the stocks need to be incorporated. These parameters are: $NaiveThymusProliferationRate$, $NaiveProliferationRate$, $NaiveProliferationDeathRate$, $MemoryToNPRate$, $MemoryDeathRate$ and $ReversionToMemoryRate$.

9. Build the Simulation model. The final SD model implemented is shown in Figure 3.

In the figure, the stocks are represented by the box ⬜, the flow variables are represented by the hourglass ⧗ , flow ⟹ , parameters ⟳ and information ⟶ . Information indicates that the stock value is used in the flow calculation. RealNaives and RealActives are look-up tables containing the experimental data.

9. Verify the Model. As the model studied is quite simple, we verified our implementation against the conceptual model. Further verification was performed during the experimental stage.

10. Validate the Model with Existing Theories and, if Available, Real-World Data. As we mentioned, the validation process is performed throughout all simulation development. We validate our results against the data set provided for the total number of naive T cells in the organism, as shown in the result analysis (step 12).

11. Experimental Design and Experimentation. For this case study we will run one experiment in which we adjust the parameters to fit the original data. The simulation was run for a period correspondent to sixty years.

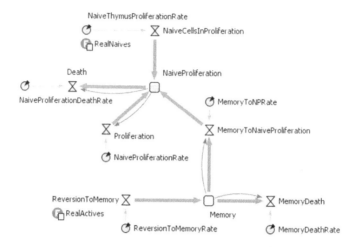

Fig. 3. SD built from naive T cells data

12. Result Analysis and Findings. We calibrated the simulation parameters against the data provided and the results obtained are shown in Figure 4(a). Figure 4(b) shows the results obtained in [35]. For both approaches, the total number of naive cells for the simulation are different for the first eighteen years and this difference as well as the parameters obtained need further investigation with immunologists. After twenty years, the numbers for the real data observed and the outcomes obtained are very close. Moreover, it is possible to observe how the population of naive cells from proliferation grows with time and is prevalent in the total naive cells cohort after fifty years.

13. Validate and Add More Requisites with Immunologists. Results (and parameters calibration) validation needs to be done with immunologists,

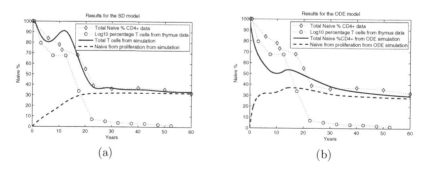

Fig. 4. Simulation results. For the SD simulation, the parameter values used are: NaiveThymusProliferationRate = 0.025, NaiveProliferationDeathRate = 0.017, MemoryToNPRate = 0.001, ReversionToMemoryRate = 0 and MemoryDeathRate= 0.05.

as well as new requisites do be added in the simulation model. There is the need to investigate whether the simulation models are informative and relatively accurate. Further research also needs to be done to explain the outcome differences for both models.

5   Conclusions

Although there are examples showing the success of simulation aiding advances in immunology, this set of methodologies is not popular among immunologists. The overall objective of our research, therefore, is to outline the potential contribution of simulation methods to help immunological studies and invite experts (simulation developers, computer scientists, etc) to build solutions in this field. For this paper, we had two research goals. The first goal was to show that there is a distinct place for simulation in the tool set used by immunologists and present the most common simulation approaches. As there are no general guidelines for the development of immune simulations, our second objective was to introduce our own guidances for conducting simulation studies in immunology and outline the pitfalls that might be encountered during the development of a simulation model. We achieved our first objective by arguing that popular methodologies used such as ODEs and reductionist methods have limitations that are overcome by simulation. Moreover, we argued that for many simulation methods, the problem representation is closer to the systems natural description. For our second goal, we studied several simulations using different approaches in the literature and outlined their common features. This helped us to develop a simulation lifecycle with several steps to be followed. These steps encompass common aspects to be considered during the development of immune simulations, independent of the simulation approach adopted. As future work we want to improve the lifecycle introduced and develop a decision framework that further helps with the choice of a simulation approach according to the problem presented. In addition, we aim at making our set of guidances more specific according to the simulation method used.

References

1. Louzoun, Y.: The evolution of mathematical immunology. Imm. Rev. 216, 9–20 (2007)
2. Gruber, J.: Models of Immune Systems: The Use of Differential Equations, http://www.lymenet.de/literatur/immundif.html (last accessed June 13, 2011)
3. Eftimie, R., Bramson, J.L., Earn, D.J.: Interactions between the immune system and cancer: A brief review of non-spatial mathematical models. Bull. Math. Biol. (2010)
4. Bonabeau, E.: Agent-based modeling: Methods and techniques for simulating human systems. In: Proc. of the National Academy of Sciences of the United States of America, vol. 99, pp. 7280–7287 (2002)

5. Sauro, H.M., Harel, D., Kwiatkowska, M., Shaffer, C.A., Uhrmacher, A.M., Hucka, M., Mendes, P., Strömback, L., Tyson, J.J.: Challenges for modeling and simulation methods in systems biology. In: Winter Simulation Conference, pp. 1720–1730 (2006)
6. Østreng, W.: Reductionism versus Holism – Contrasting Approaches? In: Consilience. Interdisciplinary Communications 2005/2006. Centre for Advanced Study, Oslo, pp. 11–14 (2007)
7. Fachada, N., Lopes, V., Rosa, A.: Agent-based modelling and simulation of the immune system: a review. In: EPIA 2007 - 13th Portuguese Conference on Artificial Intelligence (2007)
8. Kitano, H.: Computational systems biology. Nature 420, 206–210 (2002)
9. Kitano, H.: Systems biology: A brief overview. Science 295, 1662–1664 (2002)
10. Andrews, P.S., Polack, F.A.C., Sampson, A.T., Stepney, S., Timmis, J.: The CoSMoS process version 0.1: A process for the modelling and simulation of complex systems. Technical Report YCS-2010-453, Department of Computer Science, University of York (2010)
11. Robinson, S.: Simulation: The Practice of Model Development and Use. John Wiley and sons, Ltd. (2004)
12. Silva, P.S., Trigo, A., Varajão, J., Pinto, T.: Simulation – Concepts and Applications. In: Lytras, M.D., Ordonez de Pablos, P., Ziderman, A., Roulstone, A., Maurer, H., Imber, J.B. (eds.) WSKS 2010. CCIS, vol. 112, pp. 429–434. Springer, Heidelberg (2010)
13. Babulak, E., Wang, M.: 1. In: Discrete Event Simulation: State of the Art, pp. 1–8. InTech (2010)
14. Banks, J., Carson, J., Nelson, B., Nicol, D.: Discrete-event system simulation, 4th edn. Pearson (2005)
15. Macal, C.M.: To agent-based simulation from system dynamics. In: Proc. of the 2010 Winter Simulation Conference (2010)
16. Schieritz, N., Milling, P.M.: Modeling the forrest or modeling the trees: A comparison of system dynamics and agent based simulation. In: Proc. of the XXI Int. Conference of the System Dynamics Society (2003)
17. Metropolis, N., Ulam, S.: The Monte Carlo method. J. Amer. Stat. Assoc. 44, 335–341 (1949)
18. Forrester, J.W.: Industrial Dynamics. Pegasus Communications (1961)
19. Figueredo, G.P., Aickelin, U., Siebers, P.O.: Systems dynamics or agent-based modelling for immune simulation? In: Proc. of the Int. Conf. on AIS (2011)
20. Foan, S.J., Jackson, A.M., Spendlove, I., Aickelin, U.: Simulating the dynamics of T cell subsets throughout the lifetime. In: Proc. of the Int. Conf. on AIS (2011)
21. Siebers, P.O., Aickelin, U.: Introduction to Multi-Agent Simulation. In: Encyclopaedia of Decision Making and Decision Support Technologies, pp. 554–564 (2007)
22. Tako, A.A., Robinson, S.: Comparing model development in discrete event simulation and system dynamics. In: Rossetti, M.D., Hill, R., Dunkin, A., Ingalls, R.G. (eds.) Proc. of the 2009 Winter Simulation Conference, pp. 979–990 (2009)
23. Look, A.T., Schriber, T.J., Nawrocki, J.F., Murphy, W.H.: Computer simulation of the cellular immune response to malignant lymphoid cells: logic of approach, model design and laboratory verification. Immunology 43, 677–690 (1981)
24. Zand, M.S., Briggs, B., Bose, A., Vo, T.: Discrete event modeling of CD4+ memory T cell generation. The Journal of Immunology 173, 3763–3772 (2004)
25. Figge, M.T.: Stochastic discrete event simulation of germinal center reactions. Phys. Rev. E 71, 51907 (2005)

26. Wolfram, S.: Statistical mechanics of cellular automata. Rev. Mod. Phys. 5, 601–644 (1983)
27. Macal, C.M., North, M.J.: Tutorial on agent-based modeling and simulation. In: Proc. of the 2005 Winter Simulation Conference (2005)
28. ImmunoGrid. The European Virtual Immune System Project, www.immunogrid.eu (last accessed July 15, 2012)
29. Thorne, B.C., Bailey, A.M., Pierce, S.M.: Combining experiments with multi-cell agent-based modeling to study biological tissue patterning. Briefings in Bioinformatics 8, 245–257 (2007)
30. Jerne, N.K.: Towards a network theory of the immune system. Ann. Immunol (Inst. Pasteur) 125C, 73–89 (1974)
31. Baltcheva, I., Codarri, L., Pantaleo, G., Boudec, J.Y.L.: Lifelong Dynamics of Human $CD4^+CD25^+$ Regulatory T Cells: Insights from *in vivo* Data and Mathematical Modeling. Journal of Theoretical Biology 266, 307–322 (2010)
32. Kotiadis, K., Robinson, S.: Conceptual modelling: Knowledge acquisition and model abstraction. In: Madon, S.J., Hill, R.R., Mönch, L., Rose, O., Jefferson, T., Fowler, J.W. (eds.) Proc. of the 2008 Winter Simulation Conference, pp. 951–958 (2008)
33. Ulgen, O.M., Black, J.J., Johnsonbaugh, B., Klungle, R.: Simulation methodology - a practitioner's perspective. Int. Journal of Industrial Engineering, Applications and Practice 1 (1994)
34. Daigle, J.: Human immune system simulation: A survey of current approaches. Georgia State University (2006)
35. Murray, J.M., Kaufmann, G.R., Hodgkin, P.D., Lewin, S.R., Kelleher, A.D., Davenport, M.P., Zaunders, J.: Naive T cells are maintained by thymic output in early ages but by proliferation without phenotypic change after twenty. Immunology and Cell Biology 81, 487–495 (2003)

Clustering-Based Multi-objective Immune Optimization Evolutionary Algorithm

Wilburn W.P. Tsang and Henry Y.K. Lau

Department of Industrial and Manufacturing Systems Engineering,
The University of Hong Kong, Hong Kong
wilburn@graduate.hku.hk,
hyklau@hku.hk

Abstract. In everyday life, there are plentiful cases that we need to find good solutions such that risk, cost and many other factors are to be optimized. These problems are typical examples of multi-objective optimization problems. Evolutionary algorithms are often employed for solving it. Due to the characteristics of learning and adaptability, self-organization and memory capabilities, one of the biological inspired AI methods – artificial immune systems (AIS) is considered to be a class of evolutionary techniques that can be deployed for solving this problem. This paper aims to propose a new AIS-based framework focusing on distributed and self-organization characteristics. Population of solutions is decomposed into sub-populations forming clusters. Sub-populations in each cluster undergo independent evolution processes. These clusters are then combined and re-decomposed. The proposed mechanism aims to reduce the complexity in the evolution processes, enhance the exploitation ability and achieve quick convergence. It is evaluated and compared with representative algorithms.

Keywords: Artificial immune systems, Evolutionary Algorithm, Multi-objective optimization.

1 Introduction

In daily life, there are many different examples that aim to maximize or minimize several functions or parameters under a number of considerations and constraints. In area of logistics and supply-chain management, we may face with a lot of problems having the need to find the most advantageous solution such that the risk and the cost are minimized and the benefit is maximized.

In fact, almost all logistics and supply-chain related optimization problems concern more than a single objective. For example for a planner planning the delivery schedule of an online retailer, planner may wish to optimize the total transit time for the whole schedule, together with the total cost that may incurred in the delivery process. This requires the simultaneous consideration of several objectives which may be competing with each other.

In the development of algorithms or solution techniques for solving multi-objective optimization problems, researchers obtained their stimulation and inspiration mainly

C.A. Coello Coello et al. (Eds.): ICARIS 2012, LNCS 7597, pp. 72–85, 2012.

from different biological processes including the genetics and the immune system. Within the research field of multi-objective optimization algorithms, Evolutionary Algorithms have been considered to be very successful techniques in solving multiple-objective optimization problems. Artificial immune systems (AIS), the engineering analogue of the human immune system, is a technique that has drawn much interest in recent year in solving optimization problems. The appealing characteristics include learning, adaptation and memory abilities provided the main reasons for the recent attention. Good performance had been reported from the literature in solving single-objective optimization problem [1, 2]. For the multi-objective optimization problems, the interest and development can also be found in [3, 4].

The operation of the human immune system is inherently distributed with a network of agents who work and coordinate to achieve the stated goal. Each player carries partial information about the environment and then interacts with the local environment. Motivated by such phenomenon, in this study population of solutions is decomposed in the objective space into a number of sub-populations forming several clusters. Each cluster will undergo independent evolutionary process. At predetermined time, sub-populations are combined and re-decomposed into cluster again for the possible evolutionary process to continue. The processes will repeat until reaching the stopping criteria. The remainder of this paper is organized as follows: Section 2 defines the multi-objective optimization while Section 3 provides a summary on AIS and AIS-based multi-objective optimization algorithms. The methodology and the detail procedures of the proposed framework are discussed in Sections 4. Numerical studies are discussed in Section 5. Conclusion is finally given in Section 6.

2   Unconstrained Multi-objective Optimization

An unconstrained optimization problem is defined as the search for the best situation. With the given objective functions, multi-objective optimization problem requires the finding of vector of decision variables that optimizes these functions:

Maximum/ Minimum $\vec{f}(x) = [f_1(x), f_2(x), \dots, f_n(x)]$
Where $x = [x_1, x_2, \dots, x_n]$

Direct comparison by individual objective is not possible in multi-objective optimization. Solutions may be more favorable for some objectives but worst in others. It is difficult to determine whether a solution is better or worst. The Pareto dominance concept is employed by the academia to compare individual solution to see which one is better. Two solutions are compared on the basis of whether one solution dominates the other.

The evaluation is done through pair-wise comparison between two solutions (x and y). In case for maximization, the evaluation considers the following two conditions:

(1) x is no worse than y in all objectives
$$f_i(x) \geq f_i(y) \qquad \forall i = 1,2,..,n$$
(2) x is strictly better than y in some sense
$$f_j(x) > f_j(y) \qquad \exists j \in [1,n]$$

If both of the above conditions are met, solution x is said to be a dominant solution of y or solution y is dominated by solution x.

3   Immune Systems and Artificial Immune Systems

Human Immune Systems

Generally speaking, the most important function of the immune system is to protect us from incoming invaders. The immune system is a system with high complexity which is still under active research. It is considered to incorporate a number of molecules distributed around the body for developing various immune responses. These immune responses generated are targeted to recognize and attack organisms or invaders. T-cells together with B-cells are the two major players in the immune system. B cells secret specific antibodies against antigens which are being recognized. Helper T-cells act as the regulators in the immune system. It does not secrete antibodies but cytokines to influence the immune cell or organ to develop necessary immune response against the recognized antigen. Some T-cells actually can kill diseased cells once recognized [5]. Besides B-cell and T-Cell, there are still many specialized cells distributed around the body for generating various immune responses. Macrophages and neutrophils in the innate immune system are kind of phagocytic that ingest and engulf pathogens [6]. Dendritic cell is another phagocytic cell that is in contact with the external environment. Their main purpose is to function as antigen presenting cells whereby pathogen materials are presented on the surface to other cells of the immune system [7].

One of the appealing characteristics is its distributed nature. Immune cell are distributed around the body with no central control mechanism to dictate the. Each individual cell evolves independently to work out its function. The coordination of the response is the result of mutual communication and regulation which aroused from the interaction between different cells. Only partial information is available for the independents cells to analyze and work with, however this partial information is enough for the individual components in the whole immune system to work successfully and autonomously.

From Natural to Artificial Immune Systems

Owing to the appealing characteristics of human immune system including learning, adaptation, distribution, and information memory ability, the immune system provides a rich source of inspiration and stimulation to the development of novel problem solving methods. The use of artificial immune systems for new problem solving techniques and computation models is keeping on increasing. Immune-inspired techniques are now gaining much more popularity in a wide area of engineering application domain.

Although the biological immune system is under active research in the biological and medical areas, the actual working principles are still not well understood to a large extent. Most of current developments in AIS motivated from different observed immune principles. In particular, several immune principles, including clonal selection principles[8], immune network theory [9], negative selection mechanism [10], danger theory[11] and the like have attracted much attention from the research community. Practical implementations of AIS mainly focus on data analysis [1], anomaly detection [12], computer security [13], robotic and control [14] and optimization [15].

Immune-Inspired Algorithms for Multi-objective Optimization

In dealing with the multi-objective optimization, Evolutionary algorithms are always one of the most popular tools. There are a large number of proposed evolutionary algorithms targeting on the multi-objective optimization in the literature. Owing to the similarities between AIS and evolutionary algorithms and the potential benefit as listed in the beginning, the development of immune-inspired algorithms for multi-objective optimization has kept on increasing in recent years.

In decades ago, immune-inspired idea was mainly used as a collaborative feature in the evolutionary or genetic algorithms. Early attempts aimed to apply observed functions or principles to handle specific part of the algorithm. Clonal selection principle was employed in the Hybrid I-PAES [16] as the local search operator. The first attempt to adopt solely AIS shall be the work in [17, 18]. Application of Clonal selection principle, previously applied to general optimization problems, was extended to multi-objective case. The idea was almost exactly the same as in the single-objective case. Besides the clonal selection principle, several other immune principles were then employed. The Multiobjective Immune Algorithm (MOIA) proposed by [19] further mimicked several other immunological models including the gene conversion, nucleotide addition and the germ-line DNA library in the variation scheme. The adoption of these principle is rather complex. The development of some of these principles was withdrawn from the research interest.

Besides the clonal selection principle, immune network theory was another widely-used mechanism to be adopted in the immune-inspired algorithms. This theory was originally aimed to handle the diversity issue in multi-objective optimization. Vector Artificial Immune System (VAIS) as proposed in [20] was an extension of the aiNET to multi-objective situation. Network suppression operation from the immune network theory is introduced to suppress similar solutions in the survival or memory archiving stage with reference to the Euclidean distance in the objective space to prevent over-representation. Non-dominated Neighbor Immune Algorithm (NNIA) by [21] and Evolutionary Multi-Objective Immune Algorithm (EMOIA) by [4] had put forward another step in implementing the immune network theory for the network suppression process. The NNIA algorithm applied the immune network theory starting from the selection to the mutation stage. The selection operation selected isolated non-dominated solutions to enhance the evolution in the minority searching areas. The EMOIA algorithm tried on a more comprehensive adaptation of the immune network theory. The use is extended to the cloning process of the antibodies. The implementations of the immune network theory in most of the previous studies were only suppression in nature. In [22], a more comprehensive network interaction was implemented in the optimization algorithm. Stimulated activation from suppression operation was employed to enhance the exploitation power.

As AIS is still considerably new to multi-objective optimization, more effort could be put to develop and evaluate the potential gains. Past development focused mainly on the adoption of clonal selection principle and the immune network theory which in turncentered largely on the learning and adaptability nature of AIS. The distributed nature of the AIS is still a new area for immune-inspired algorithm in optimization.

4   Clustering-Based Evolutionary Algorithm

This study builds on the success in the past study in the adopting the network interaction in multi-objective optimization [22], stimulated network activation in addition to the network suppression was applied in the immune-inspired algorithm to enhance the exploitation process. Distributed nature is another appealing characteristic in AIS. There is no central decision point or overall information about the environment. Each individual component in the immune system obtains only partial information. And thus they coordinates and responses independently as accordance to their partial information. In case for the evolutionary process in multi-objective optimization, majority of solutions are dominated by neighboring solutions rather than by distant solutionsin fitness evaluation. And in the suppression process, again the solutions are mainly suppressed by nearby solutions. The core influence in the fitness evaluation process and suppression process are coming from the group of nearby solutions. Thus partial information regarding the groups of nearby solutions shall already provide sufficient information for individual solution in the evolutionary process.

Using the Pareto dominance concept for the fitness evaluation, fitness of individual solutions requires the comparison with the whole population separately. So if there is n solution in the current population, (n-1) comparisons would therefore be required for computation of the fitness for each candidate solution. This process often uses considerable computation resource, so it always draws significant research interest from the academia. The distributed nature of AIS provides the real hope in reducing the use of computation resource in fitness evaluation. Current population will be segregated into several clusters, the fitness of individual solutions within each cluster will base only on the solutions in the local environment within each cluster. That means in the computation of the fitness of each individual solution, the solution will need to compare with much fewer solutions. Assume c clusters are formed from the current population and the number of solution in each cluster is very similar, (n-1) comparisons could reduce to approximately (n/c - 1) comparisons for each evaluation. The use of computation resource could therefore be greatly reduced by such clustering technique. Although this example is over-generalized, the gain offered is obvious.

In evolutionary algorithms for multi-objective optimization, region-based concept was initialized by the PESA family. The initial effort was targeted only in the memory archiving process. Adaptive grid was adopted by PAES [23] in which objective space was divided into several hyperboxs. In the memory archiving process, the number of individual in each hyperboxs is used as one of the criteria for archiving. This region-based concept was further emphasized in subsequent development. In PEAS-II [24], the region-based concept was brought to the selection process. The application aimed to bias the selection for solutions in the less crowding regions. Region-based concept was applied in the sense that the selection unit changed from the solution itself to the hyperboxes in objective space. In this study, we go another step forward to introduce the region-based concept into the whole evolution process by means of the clustering evolution technique. The proposed clustering method provides not only the benefit from reduced usage of computation resource, but could also facilitate the region based evolution which helps to achieve quick convergence in the evolution process.

Two phase algorithm is proposed to implement the aforementioned clustering evolution technique. The two phases are called (1) the external phase and (2) the local phase. Both phases will include a number of distinct processes. The external phase focuses on the memory update operation. Current non-dominated solutions found in the local phase will be evaluated to update the fixed size memory population. Current population will then segregated in the external phase and passed to each cluster for the local phase to begin. Evolutionary processes will be carried out independently in each cluster in the local phase. Details of the algorithm are discussed below and shown in figure 1.

Initialization

If the resulting solution set is expected to have N solutions, a random population with size greater than N will be created in the initialization process. For simplicity, 2N solutions are to be generated. The population will be in real-value coding. Initial fitness and affinity will then assigned to each solution in the population. As in many other multi-objective optimization algorithms, Pareto ranking strategy, as proposed by [25], will be adopted for the fitness evaluation.The fitness assignment by Pareto rank divide the population into different levels by finding the non-dominated individuals in the population iteratively with the first set assigned with rank 1, the second set assigned with value rank 2 and so on. To reduce the unnecessary segregation, the segregation in the proposed algorithm will be restricted to three levels. Lower fitness value is preferred in the algorithm. Affinity of a solution, the measure of the diversity, is computed as the sum of the Euclidian distance in the objective space of the two nearest solutions from the non-dominated solutions set in the current population. Higher affinity value is preferred in the algorithm.

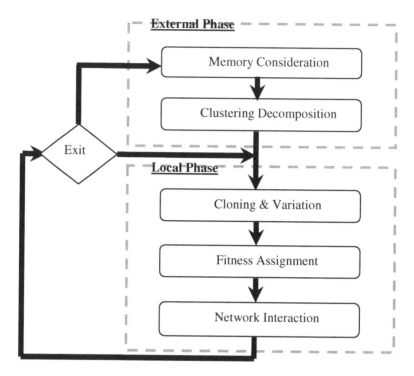

Fig. 1. Flow-Chart of the Clustering Algorithm

After the generation of the random population, solution with rank 1 is retained. All other solutions are discarded immediately. If the size of the retained population is larger than the expected size of resulting solution set (N), the selection scheme will be applied to bound the size of the population. The selection priority is set to be the higher affinity value of the solutions.

Clustering

After the initialization, the current solutions will undergo the clustering process. Segregation of the current population is based on the objective space. If the number of objectives is more than two, two of the objective functions are randomly selected for the segregation process to prevent the number of cluster created increase significantly with the increase in the number of objectives. For each of the selected objective function, the objective space will be divided into two sub-divisions, so a maximum of four divided spaces will be formed. The evolution population will be evaluated and assigned to the appropriate cluster as accordance to their objective values. The decomposed population is then sent to the local phase. Each cluster runs in its local phase in which the normal evolutionary processes including cloning, variation and network interaction take place.

Cloning, Variation and Fitness Assignment
The clone size for the group of current population in each cluster depends on its fitness and affinity. Non-dominated solutions in the cluster concerned are reproduced in n_{cs} clone. Other solution may select for the cloning process subject to the maximum clone size (n_{mcs}) available in each cluster. Both n_{cs} and n_{mcs} are user-defined parameters. For the other solutions, the priority is based on the affinity of the solutions. After the cloning process, the clone is subject to variation process.

No specific mutation and recombination schemes are explicitly defined in this algorithm. Different mutation and recombination strategies can be deployed. In the latter experiment, polynomial mutation and simulated binary crossover are used as the mutation and recombination schemes. The major reason behind the choice is that these strategies have been adopted in many other evolutionary algorithms. The fitness assignment scheme is the same as in the discussion of the initialization process. The fitness assignment scheme aforementioned is assigned as accordance to the whole population. In the local phase of the proposed algorithm, the fitness assignment scheme will focus only on the current population within the segregated cluster.

Network Interaction
In AIS, the inherent network suppression operator provides a means to manage the diversity for the current population. Solutions 'recognize' each other if they are close enough. Solution once recognized may be suppressed or activated by the recognized solutions. In the network interaction process, this study modified the strategy as proposed in [22] where the suppression operations are carried out in the objective space and variable space separately with potential activation strategy.

The triggering point for the suppression operation in the objective space is the recognition among the solutions. Solutions with distance fall within the sensory range (λ) of another solution will be recognized by the other solution (equation 2). The sensory range will be iteratively adapted automatically within the evolutionary process for each cluster (equation 1). The suppression operation in the objective space focused on solutions which are having a higher fitness or lower affinity value. And so solution will suppress other recognized solutions if they have a higher fitness value or a lower affinity value.

$$\lambda_i = \frac{\max(f_i(x)) - \min(f_i(x))}{No\ of\ non-dominated\ solutions} \tag{1}$$

Let x,y be two solutions. x is said to recognize y (in objective space)

$$\text{if and only if } \sqrt{\sum_{i=1}^{m}(f_i(x) - f_i(y))^2} \leq \sqrt{\sum_{i=1}^{m}(\lambda_i)^2}, 1 \leq i \leq m \tag{2}$$

where m is the number of objective

As in the variable space, the operation for the suppression process is almost exactly the same as in the objective space. The only difference is rested on the recognition criteria. Individual objective values are used by suppression in objective space. Here the decision variable value will be used instead of the objective values. Recognized and dominated solution will be suppressed and the suppression will trigger the activation of non-dominated solution. The activation is achieved through the generation of new solution on the high-potential solution space (equation 3).

$$SOL_n = SOL_p + (SOL_p - SOL_s) \times R \qquad (3)$$

where SOL_n is the new solution, SOL_p is the parent solution, SOL_s is the originally suppressed solution and R is the random number.

Evolutionary Process and Memory Consideration
Each cluster will undergo independent evolutionary process including cloning, varia-tion, fitness assignment and network interaction. At predetermined time, in general a number of M generations, sub-populations are combined and loop back to the external phase for the memory update consideration.

Memory population helps to provide the direction for subsequence evolution and to act as a storage space for the current best group of solutions. Thus memory population is considered to be a very crucial aspect in evolutionary process in multi-objective optimization. However in general, the group of current best solution may exceed the expected size of the resulting solution set. Archiving approaches were developed to bind the size of the memory population. Such approaches shall stress on both conver-gence and diversity in the memory population. In this algorithm, the archiving ap-proach adopted is same as many other immune-inspired algorithms for multi-objective optimization. Only the non-dominated solutions can be stored in the memo-ry population. If the size of the current best solutions exceeds the bound, network suppression will be carried out to suppress similar solution so as to reduce the capaci-ty back to the expected size.

After the updating process, the solution set is re-decomposed into cluster for the possible local phase to continue. The processes of the external phase and local phase repeat until reaching the termination criteria. After the end of the evolution process, the population will undergo final memory update process in which the resulting memory population represents the resulting solution set of the algorithm.

5   Numerical Experiments

Numerical experiment is conducted to evaluate the proposed algorithm with other algorithms proposed in the literature. In particular, the performance is compared with two immune algorithms, NNIA [21] and MISA [18] and three well-known multi-objective evolutionary algorithms, NSGA-II [26], SPEA2 [27] and PESA-II [24]; and, with a suite of six test functions.

Test Functions
The suite of test problems should capture a wide variety of characteristics of different problems. In this numerical experiment, six test problems reported in the standard multi-objective optimization literature [28, 29] are selected. The first five test prob-lems are taken from the ZDT test suite, namely, ZDT1, ZDT2, ZDT3, ZDT4 and

ZDT6. All test problems from the ZDT test suite are having only two objectives. To examine for other cases, one test problems is taken from DTLZ test suite, namely the DTLZ4. Details of these six test problems can be referred to [28, 29].

Key Performance Indicators

In approximating the Pareto-optimal set, we would like to attain two aims. The resulting solution set shall minimize the distance to the Pareto-optimal set and obtain a finite set of well-distributed trade-off front to approximate the true Pareto-optimal set. Such aims are again multi-objective. Two different key performance indicators are employed to measure the performance of the algorithms on these two different aims. Inverted generational distance (IGD), proposed in [30], measures the average distance between the solutions in the true Pareto-optimal set and the closest solution in the obtained non-dominated set. Beside convergence, this indicator measures also diversity and completeness of the obtained solution set. Hypervolume, proposed in [31], measures the dominated volume from the obtained solution setin the objective space. This indicator measures both the diversity and the convergence of the obtained solutions. The reference point was set to be much greater than the upper boundaries and the algorithm outlined in [32] is adopted for the calculation of the Hypervolume.

Experimental Setup

The proposed algorithm is benchmarked with two immune-inspired algorithms and three evolutionary-based algorithms. The choice of the algorithms is based on the representativeness in the research community. The proposed algorithm is implemented with Matlab with $n_{CS}=5$ and M=3. The Matlab version of the NNIA is modified from [33]. MISA is implemented with Matlab in accordance to the steps stated in [18] with necessary amendments. Other algorithms including NSGA-II, SPEA2 and PESA-II are implemented by [34]. The termination criterion of each run is set to a given number of evaluations which indirectly ensure a fair comparison. For the ZDT problem, 10,000 evaluations are allowed. While for the DTLZ test problems, 20,000 evaluations are allowed. Moreover, the size of the memory populations is kept the same in this experiment. The size is preset to be 50, i.e. N=50.

Experimental Result and Discussion

For comparison, 15 independent runs had been conducted. The results with immune-inspired algorithms are shown in Tables 1 and 3, while the results with the evolutionary algorithms are shown in Tables 2 and 4.

For the comparison with immune-inspired algorithms, the result was positive. The proposed algorithm was shown to outperform the other immune-inspired algorithms based on the experimental result. The proposed algorithm attained best performance in four out of the six test problems in both IGD and Hypervolume. Even for the

Table 1. Comparison with immune-inspired algorithms in IGD

	Our Algorithm	NNIA	MISA
	Mean, (Standard Deviation), [Failure rate]		
ZDT1	1.1×10^{-3} (1.8×10^{-2})	4.3×10^{-4} (3.4×10^{-5})	4.5×10^{-3} (1.3×10^{-3})
ZDT2	9.3×10^{-4} (4.6×10^{-4})	1.3×10^{-3} (2.2×10^{-3}) [40%]	9.9×10^{-3} (3.5×10^{-3})
ZDT3	1.5×10^{-3} (1.0×10^{-3})	1.7×10^{-3} (1.4×10^{-3})	3.2×10^{-3} (2.2×10^{-3})
ZDT4	8.3×10^{-3} (5.5×10^{-3})	1.3×10^{-2} (1.4×10^{-2}) [40%]	1.3×10^{-2} (5.2×10^{-3})
ZDT6	6.9×10^{-4} (4.6×10^{-4})	7.8×10^{-4} (1.6×10^{-4})	1.8×10^{-2} (2.8×10^{-3})
DTLZ4	3.4×10^{-3} (1.0×10^{-3})	1.7×10^{-2} (1.9×10^{-2}) [33.3%]	2.8×10^{-3} (7.0×10^{-4})

Table 2. Comparison with evolutionary algorithms in IGD

	Our Algorithm	NSGA-II	SPEA2	PESA-II
	Mean, (Standard Deviation), [Failure rate]			
ZDT1	1.1×10^{-3} (1.8×10^{-2})	4.4×10^{-4} (3.7×10^{-5})	4.8×10^{-4} (1.9×10^{-4})	2.9×10^{-3} (2.1×10^{-3})
ZDT2	9.3×10^{-4} (4.6×10^{-4})	1.1×10^{-3} (2.1×10^{-3})	3.4×10^{-3} (3.4×10^{-3})	1.7×10^{-3} (1.3×10^{-3})
ZDT3	1.5×10^{-3} (1.0×10^{-3})	8.6×10^{-4} (1.1×10^{-3})	4.7×10^{-4} (7.3×10^{-4})	2.4×10^{-3} (2.5×10^{-3})
ZDT4	8.3×10^{-3} (5.5×10^{-3})	4.2×10^{-3} (3.2×10^{-5})	1.0×10^{-2} (6.8×10^{-3})	8.5×10^{-3} (3.9×10^{-3})
ZDT6	6.9×10^{-4} (4.6×10^{-4})	1.6×10^{-3} (3.1×10^{-4})	3.5×10^{-3} (6.3×10^{-4})	8.2×10^{-4} (2.3×10^{-4})
DTLZ4	3.4×10^{-3} (1.0×10^{-3})	3.2×10^{-3} (3.5×10^{-4})	1.9×10^{-2} (1.7×10^{-2}) [20%]	1.3×10^{-2} (NA) [93%]

Table 3. Comparison with immune-inspired algorithms in Hypervolume

	Our Algorithm	NNIA	MISA
	Mean		
ZDT1	3.58	3.64	3.27
ZDT2	3.25	2.72	2.36
ZDT3	3.83	3.85	3.52
ZDT4	3.00	2.86	2.62
ZDT6	2.74	2.72	1.83
DTLZ4	7.08	6.06	7.03

Table 4. Comparison with evolutionary algorithms in Hypervolume

	Our Algorithm	NSGA-II	SPEA2	PESA-II
	Mean			
ZDT1	3.58	3.64	3.63	3.49
ZDT2	3.25	3.23	2.98	3.08
ZDT3	3.83	3.92	3.93	3.74
ZDT4	3.00	3.33	2.98	3.17
ZDT6	2.74	2.67	2.57	2.72
DTLZ4	7.08	7.16	6.24	5.48

remaining two test problems, the difference between the proposed algorithm and the best algorithm was very small. Both metrics evaluate not only the convergence, but also diversity and completeness of the solution set. For test problems ZDT3 and DTLZ4, IGD and Hypervolume shows different outcome. However as the numerical different on the result of both metric for these two test problems is so small, we may still consider that both metric provide similar result in the experiment. Thus the proposed algorithm was a better algorithm in comparison with the other immune-inspired algorithms. It is also observed that NNIA perform better than the MISA, though NNIA has difficulties in finding the approximate Pareto optimal solutions in three of the test problems. The failure rate represents the percentage of independent run where the resulting solution set obtained contain only one solution. To benchmark also with the popular tools for multi-objective optimization, the proposed algorithm was compared with three well-known evolutionary algorithms. Out of the suite of six test problems, the proposed algorithm shown to achieve good performance even compared with these popular tools in multi-objective optimization. The proposed algorithm attained the best performance in two test problems in both IGD and Hypervolume. Although the NSGA-II attained the best performance in half of the test problems, the proposed algorithm was able to achieve very similar result in all these test problems.

The standard deviation of both the IGD and Hypervolume measures for all algorithms was very small. That means all algorithms in concern achieve constant result in different initial random numbers. The proposed algorithm was able to find favorable result in every trial for all the test problems. However for NNIA, SPEA2 and PESA2 (three of the five algorithms under the comparison) have difficulties in finding the acceptable solution set in three of the test problems. This may present some limitation for these algorithms in solving solve of the multi-objective optimization problems.

6   Conclusion and Future Work

Biological processes often provide sources of inspiration and stimulations for the development new models, algorithms and computation paradigms for solving complex problems. AIS is one of such systems that has gained huge interest in recent decades. This study is motivated by the distributed nature of the immune network and an AIS-based optimization algorithm is developed with the adoption of the clustering evolution technique that aims at mimicking the distributed nature of the biological immune systems. Details of the algorithms were discussed in Section 4 with its performance benchmarked with a number of representative and well-known algorithms in Section 5. The proposed algorithm performs better than other similar AIS-based methods in solving multi-objective optimization problems. As in most other studies we started by considering problems with two to three objectives. In reality, multi-objective systems shall comprise problems with many-objectives, often more than three. While the study of many-objective optimization is at its early stage, we focus our future research on the development of bio-inspired algorithms for solving many-objective problems.

References

1. Watkins, A., Timmis, J.: Exploiting Parallelism Inherent in AIRS, an Artificial Immune Classifier. In: Nicosia, G., Cutello, V., Bentley, P.J., Timmis, J. (eds.) ICARIS 2004. LNCS, vol. 3239, pp. 427–438. Springer, Heidelberg (2004)
2. Timmis, J.: Artificial immune systems - today and tomorrow. Natural Computing 6, 1–18 (2007)
3. Brabazon, A., O'Neill, M.: Biologically Inspired Algorithms for Financial Modelling. Springer, Berlin (2006)

4. Tan, K.C., Goh, C.K., Mamun, A.A., Ei, E.Z.: An evolutionary artificial immune system for multi-objective optimization. European Journal of Operational Research 187, 371–392 (2008)
5. Timmis, J., Andrews, P., Owens, N., Clark, E.: An interdisciplinary perspective on artificial immune systems. Evolutionary Intelligence 1, 5–26 (2008)
6. Roitt, I., Brostoff, J., Male, D.: Immunolohy, 6th edn., Mosby (2001)
7. Satthaporn, S., Eremin, O.: Dendritic cells (I): biological functions. J. R. Coll. Surg. Edinb. 46, 9–19 (2001)
8. Burnet, F.M.: The Clonal Selection Theory of Acquired Immunity. Cambridge University Press (1959)
9. Jerne, N.K.: Towards a Network Theory of the Immune System. Annual Immunolgy 125(C), 373–389 (1974)
10. Dasgupta, D., Ji, Z., Gonzalez, F.: Artificial immune system (AIS) research in the last five years. In: IEEE Congress on Evolutionary Computation 2003 (CEC 2003), pp. 123–130. IEEE (2003)
11. Matzinger, P.: The danger model: a renewed sense of self. Science 296, 301–305 (2002)
12. Greensmith, J., Aickelin, U., Cayzer, S.: Introducing Dendritic Cells as a Novel Immune-Inspired Algorithm for Anomaly Detection. In: Jacob, C., Pilat, M.L., Bentley, P.J., Timmis, J.I. (eds.) ICARIS 2005. LNCS, vol. 3627, pp. 153–167. Springer, Heidelberg (2005)
13. Kim, J., Bentley, P.J.: The Human Immune system and Network Intrusion Detection. In: 7th European Congress on Intelligent Techniques and Soft Computing, EUFIT 1999 (1999)
14. Lau, H.Y.K., Wong, V.W.K.: A strategic behavior-based intelligent transport system with artificial immune system. In: Proc. of IEEE International Conference on Systems, Man and Cybernetics, pp. 3909–3914. Springer (2004)
15. Lau, H.Y.K., Tsang, W.W.P.: A Parallel Immune Optimization Algorithm for Numeric Function Optimization. Evolutionary Intelligence 1, 171–185 (2008)
16. Cutello, V., Narzisi, G., Nicosia, G.: A Class of Pareto Archived Evolution Strategy Algorithms Using Immune Inspired Operators for Ab-Initio Protein Structure Prediction. In: Rothlauf, F., Branke, J., Cagnoni, S., Corne, D.W., Drechsler, R., Jin, Y., Machado, P., Marchiori, E., Romero, J., Smith, G.D., Squillero, G. (eds.) EvoWorkshops 2005. LNCS, vol. 3449, pp. 54–63. Springer, Heidelberg (2005)
17. Coello Coello, C.A., Cortés, N.C.: An approach to solve multiobjective optimization problems based on an artificial immune system. In: Timmis, J., Bentley, P.J. (eds.) Proc. of the First International Conference on Artificial Immune Systems (ICARIS 2002), pp. 212–221 (2002)
18. Coello Coello, C.A., Cortés, N.C.: Solving multiobjective optimization problems using an artificial immune system. Genetic Programming and Evolvable Machines 6, 163–190 (2005)
19. Luh, G.-C., Chueh, C.-H., Liu, W.-W.: MOIA: multi-objective immune algorithm. Engineering Optimization 35, 143–164 (2003)
20. Freschi, F., Repetto, M.: Multiobjective Optimization by a Modified Artificial Immune System Algorithm. In: Jacob, C., Pilat, M.L., Bentley, P.J., Timmis, J.I. (eds.) ICARIS 2005. LNCS, vol. 3627, pp. 248–261. Springer, Heidelberg (2005)
21. Gong, M., Jiao, L., Du, H., Bo, L.: Multiobjective Immune Algorithm with Nondominated Neighbor-Based Selection. Evolutionary Computation 16, 225–255 (2008)

22. Tsang, W.W.P., Lau, H.Y.K.: Enhanced Network Interaction in Multi-Objective Immune Optimization Algorithm. In: 8th International Conference on Optimization: Techniques and Applications (ICOTA8), Shanghai, China (2010)

23. Knowles, J.: The Pareto Archived Evolution Strategy: A New Baseline Algorithm for Pareto Multiobjective Optimisation. In: Proc. of the 1999 Congress on Evolutionary Computation (CEC 1999), pp. 98–105. IEEE (1999)

24. Corne, D.W., Jerram, N.R., Knowles, J., Oates, M.J.: PESA-II: Region-based Selection in Evolutionary Multiobjective Optimization. In: Spector, L., Goodman, E.D., Wu, A., Langdon, W.B., Voigt, H.-M., Gen, M., Sen, S., Dorigo, M., Pezeshk, S., Garzon, M.H., Burke, E. (eds.) Proc. of the Genetic and Evolutionary Computation Conference (GECCO 2001), pp. 283–290. Morgan Kaufmann (2001)

25. Goldberg, D.E.: Genetic Algorithms in Search, Optimization and Machine Learning. Addison-Wesley Longman Publishing Company, Boston (1989)

26. Deb, K., Agrawal, S., Pratap, A., Meyarivan, T.: A Fast Elitist Non-Dominated Sorting Genetic Algorithm for Multi-Objective Optimization: NSGA-II. In: Deb, K., Rudolph, G., Lutton, E., Merelo, J.J., Schoenauer, M., Schwefel, H.-P., Yao, X. (eds.) PPSN 2000. LNCS, vol. 1917, pp. 849–858. Springer, Heidelberg (2000)

27. Zitzler, E., Laumanns, M., Thiele, L.: SPEA2: Improving the Strength Pareto Evolutionary Algorithm. Swiss Federal Institute of Technology (2001)

28. Deb, K., Thiele, L., Laumanns, M., Zitzler, E.: Scalable multi-objective optimization test problems. In: Proc. of the 2002 Congress on Evolutionary Computation (CEC 2002), pp. 825–830. IEEE (2002)

29. Zitzler, E., Deb, K., Thiele, L.: Comparison of multiobjective evolutionary algorithms: empirical results. Evolutionary Computation 8, 173–195 (2000)

30. Bosman, P.A.N., Thierens, D.: The balance between proximity and diversity in multiobjective evolutionary algorithms. IEEE Transactions on Evolutionary Computation 7, 174–188 (2003)

31. Zitzler, E., Thiele, L.: Multiobjective Evolutionary Algorithms: A Comparative Case Study and the Strength Pareto Approach. IEEE Transactions on Evolutionary Computation 3, 257–271 (1999)

32. Fleischer, M.: The Measure of Pareto Optima Applications to Multi-objective Metaheuristics. In: Fonseca, C.M., Fleming, P.J., Zitzler, E., Deb, K., Thiele, L. (eds.) EMO 2003. LNCS, vol. 2632, pp. 519–533. Springer, Heidelberg (2003)

33. Gong, M.: NNIA Toolbox Version 1.0 (2006), http://see.xidian.edu.cn/iiip/mggong/Projects/NNIA.html

34. Nebro, A.J., Durillo, J.J.: jMetal (Metaheuristic Algorithms in Java) Version 1.5. Sourceforge.net (2008)

Petri Nets Approach to Modeling
of Immune System and Autism

Anna Gogolinska[1,2] and Wieslaw Nowak[2]

[1] Faculty of Mathematics and Computer Science, Nicolaus Copernicus University
ul. Chopina 12/18, 87-100 Toruń, Poland
[2] Institute of Physics, Nicolaus Copernicus University
ul. Grudziądzka 5, 87-100 Toruń, Poland
{leii,wiesiek}@fizyka.umk.pl

Abstract. Algorithms based on graphs and networks offer great potential for modeling of physiological processes. In this paper bipartite graphs called Petri Nets (PN) are presented and their utility in modeling of the immune system is highlighted. We present our improved PN model of the immune system. The coupling between fever and autism is studied using this model. It is shown that fever may shift the level of IL-1, IL-6 cytokines in autistic subjects closer to standard physiological values. This is in accordance with a recent observation that fever improves behavior of autistic children, reported in medical literature.

Keywords: Immune system, Petri nets, Computer modeling, Fever, Autism.

1 Introduction

The immune system (IS) is a very complex object. It consists of hundreds of types of cells, interactions, control mechanisms finely tuned to protect an organism against pathological factors. We are still far from understanding this extremely important biological phenomenon. Computer models help a lot to comprehend better both homeostatic properties of IS and its activity during various diseases [1-3]. Such diverse topics as immune cell signaling [4] and a role of IS in cancer are studied [5]. Main methodological approaches based on ordinary differential equations, cellular automata and multi-agent models of IS have been recently reviewed [6]. The most up-to-date progress may be found in ICARIS conference proceedings [7].

One of the promising approaches to systems biology is a formalism of Petri nets (PN) proposed by Carl Adam Petri in 1962 [8]. Originally this theory was intended for modeling of chemical reactions using simple graphs, but due to its simplicity, robustness and straightforward interpretation PNs have been quickly transferred to studies of other complex processes [9-10]. For example, PNs were used in homeostasis analysis [11], regulatory processes [12] and modeling of metabolic pathways [13]. More recent references may be found in the excellent book by Koch *et al.* [14].

C.A. Coello Coello et al. (Eds.): ICARIS 2012, LNCS 7597, pp. 86–99, 2012.
© Springer-Verlag Berlin Heidelberg 2012

In 2004 Na *et al.* [15] for the first time introduced a simple model of the immune system (IS) using PNs formalism. They applied fuzzy-continuous PNs formalism to create three networks describing (a) lymphocyte Th1 and Th2 selection step, (b) *humoral* and (c) *cellular* immune response. That model was restricted only to major immune system's cells types and their interactions. Later it has been extended by the same authors through adding some cytokines. However, this extension has been limited to the proliferation of T lymphocytes phase of the immune response [16-17] only. In the recent paper [18] we have introduced much more elaborated model of IS using a similar PNs approach. Here we will further extend our model and apply it to study an anticipated coupling between fever and relieve of autism symptoms. This work illustrates the advantages and potential of using PNs in studies of IS.

This paper is organized as follows: after a brief introduction to the formalism of Petri nets and the architecture of IS, we describe the current PN model of IS and results of our simulations. The aim was to test the behavior of IS, modeled as PN, when both elevated temperature effects and pathological levels of cytokines, characteristic for autism, are simultaneously present. We conclude the paper with a perspective on the future application of the present PN model of IS.

2   Petri Nets Basics

Petri nets are bipartite graphs. There are numerous types of PNs [14]. Here we use Place-Transition Petri nets with weights. Basic definitions are following.

Def 1. A Petri net graph is a 3-tuple *(P,T,F)*, where:

- *P* is a finite set of places (indicated in figures by squares)
- *T* is a finite set of transitions, such that $P \cap T = \emptyset$ (indicated by circles)
- *F* is a set of directed arcs, $F \subseteq (P \cup T) \otimes (T \cup P)$, satisfying:
- $F \cap (P \times P) = F \cap (T \times T) = \emptyset$.

We do not have any action in that network – it is only a steady framework. To have an action we need tokens (indicated in figures by large dots). States of Petri net are described by distribution of tokens over the places called marking. Places may contain one or more tokens and then they are called marked.

Def 2. A marking of net N is mapping $M:P \rightarrow \{0, 1, 2, 3, \dots\}$.

Def 3. Petri net is a set (P, T, F, M_0) where M_0 is an initial marking.

Def 4. For each element $a \in T$ we can define a set of input places $\bullet a = \{p \in P; (p,a) \in P\}$ (a set of places from which an arc runs to transition *a*) and set of output places $a \bullet = \{p \in P; (a,p) \in P\}$ (a set of places to which arcs run from transition *a*).

Def 5. The weight is a function: $W:F \rightarrow \{1,2,3...\}$, it assigns a natural number (except 0) to arcs. The default weight of an arc is 1.

A transition t may fire in a marking M if the number of tokens in every input place p of transition t is equal or greater than the weight $W(p)$ assigned to an arc between the place p and the transition t in the marking M. The transition t consumes tokens from the input places p and puts them into the output places q – the number of tokens transferred is described by the weights of arcs involved.

Using these definitions one can analyze complex sets of chemical reactions, biological interactions, relations in engineering systems, etc., creating an appropriate graph and using an adequate system of places and transitions. In that way numerous processes and dynamics of complex systems may be studied. There is quite advanced theory of PNs, interested readers may find more details in articles [19-20].

3   PN Models of the Immune System

The immune system (IS) plays a critical role in defense against pathogens [21-22]. In recent years our understanding of IS components has increased tremendously [23], but unified, mathematical models of this complex set of places and interactions, critical for proper functioning of higher living organisms, are rather rare [7, 24-25]

Two major parts of the immune system can be distinguished [21]: (1) the *humoral* immunity and (2) the *cellular* immunity. Main elements of the *humoral* immunity are antibodies produced in the cells of the B lymphocyte (B cell). The *humoral* immunity is specialized against pathogens living in fluids. The *cellular* immunity involves the activation of macrophages, natural killer cells (NK), antigen-specific cytotoxic T-lymphocytes (Tc), and the release of various cytokines in a response to an antigen. This part of IS is specialized against pathogens living in cells. Alternative division of the immune response is also used [21-22]: (a) the *innate* IS which provides immediate, non-specific defense against infection, (b) the *adaptive* IS which consists of specialized cells and processes that recognize and respond to a pathogen in a specific way. This subsystem is more complex than the *innate* IS. Here we present a rough PN model of the *adaptive* IS including a small part of the *innate* IS. We show, that this PN computer code is a useful tool for modeling the coupling between autism and fever.

4   A Model of Immune System Based on Petri Nets

Papers [15-17] served as a basis for preparation of a more elaborate model of IS [18]. Our model offers the following improvements: it is more "up-to-date", for example, Na *et al.* didn't consider roles of the cytokines in the *cellular* and *humoral* immune response [15]. The present model contains new knowledge on the mechanism of lymphocyte activation. Moreover, in our PN model of IS two completely new networks (Fig. 1, Part A, E) describing the role of the dendritic cells (antigen recognition and presentation) and macrophages have been added.

Table 1. A list of cytokines having elevated levels in autistic IS

Cytokine	Source	Target	Stimulation of other cytokines	Comment	Place
IL-4	Th0, Th2	Th0→Th2, B, Macrophages		antiinflammatory	92
IL-5	Th0, Th2	B			93
IL-13	Th0, Th2	B, Monocytes			94
IL-2	Th0, Th1	Th0→Th1, Tc			55
INF-γ	Th0, Th1	Tc, NK, Macrophages	IL-1, IL-6, TNF	Antiviral; cause of fever	56
TNF-α	Macrophages, Monocytes	Macrophages, T and B with other cytokines	IL-2, INF-γ, IL-1, IL-6 (Macrophages)	cause of fever; proinflammatory; triggered by LPS and INF-γ	90
IL-1β	Macrophages, Monocytes	T, B	IL-2, INF-γ, IL-1, IL-6 (Macrophages)	cause of fever; proinflammatory; triggered by LPS and INF-γ	88
IL-6	Macrophages, Monocytes	B, T→Tc		cause of fever; triggered by IL-1 (mostly) and INF-γ, TNF, LPS	89
MCP-1	Macrophages, Monocytes	T, B		Proinflammatory	

Our model (see Fig. 1ab) consists of five sub-nets representing: (A) the dendritic cells activation, (B) Th lymphocytes activation, (C) the cellular response, (D) the humoral response and (E) a part of activity of the macrophages. Networks A-D can be unified into one, big network, representing the adaptive immune system and this net was presented in [18]. Since then we have extended our model. In the sub-net D, representing the humoral immunity, a fragment corresponding to the activation of B cells by Th2 cells has been extended. To study a relation between IS and autism we have added a new part (E). This subnetwork represents the role of macrophages in IS, but here their role is reduced to a part corresponding to carefully selected cytokines. Polypeptides, probably related to ASD (autism spectrum disorder) according to the recent literature [26], are listed in Table 1. Probably not only the cytokines specific to an *adaptive* immune system appear to be relevant for autism, but cytokines produced by macrophages have impact on this condition as well. That's why we have added this part to the extended IS model. The sub-net (E) showing cytokines' production by macrophages is shown in Fig. 2. Table 2 contains a description of places and transitions.

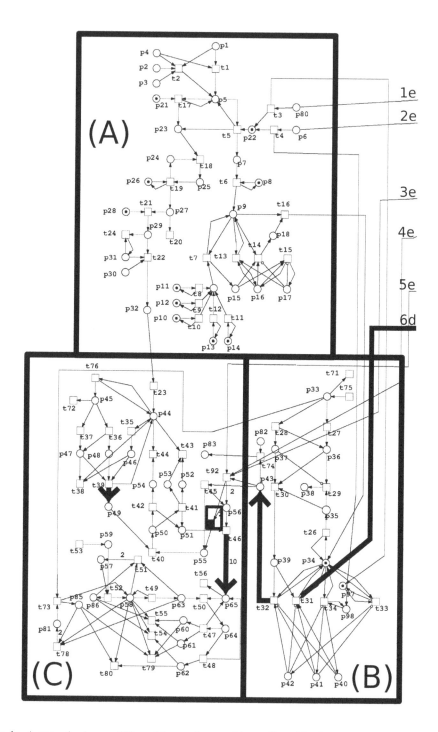

Fig. 1a. A general scheme of IS model, arcs for transitions affected by fever are shown in bold

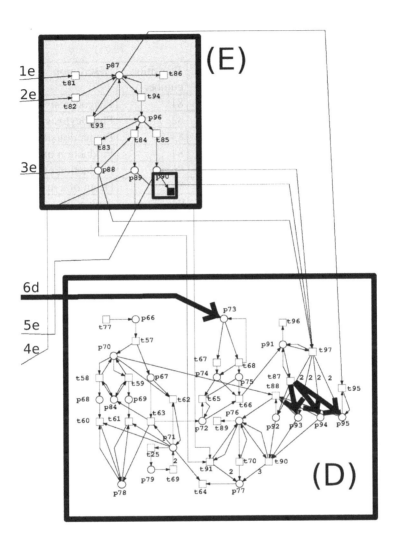

Fig. 1b. A general scheme of IS model, arcs for transitions affected by fever are shown in bold

Table 2. Description of places and transitions in the model of macrophage response (subnet E in Fig. 1b)

Place number	Descritpion	Transition number	Descritpion
87	Macrophage	81	Phagocytosis
88	IL-1	82	Phagocytosis
89	IL-6	83	Production of cytokine
90	TNF-α	84	Production of cytokine
96	Macrophage producing cytokines	85	Production of cytokine
		86	Death of a macrophage
		93	Activation
		94	Activation

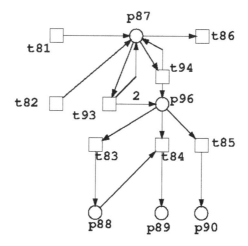

Fig. 2. Sub-net (E): the PN model of a production of cytokines by macrophages

Our Petri networks were created using public domain software SNOOPY [27]. This software was used to perform the initial analysis as well. Our IS nets (in SNOOPY format) is freely available on the website www.mat.umk.pl/~leii/. To improve the analysis further we wrote our own code in which an algebraic representation of Petri nets has been used. The software can simulate performance of a network more efficiently and gives information about markings in every step of the simulation.

5 Why the Elevated Body Temperature Relieves Symptoms of Autism? The PN Model

Autism Spectrum Disorder (ASD) is a range of severe medical conditions without known etiology and cure. These are a developmental disorders characterized by social and communication impairments, coupled with restricted range of interests and activities. Many studies suggested that genetic mutations in regions coding proteins that are responsible for brain development play a major role [28]. Some works put attention on infectious factors [29]. An integrated theory of autism is still in early phase of development [30].

In early 1980 it has been noticed that symptoms of ASD may be temporarily alleviated during periods of high fever (viral infections, body temperature elevated by 1.5-2 deg C). The children with elevated temperatures were reported to exhibit longer attention spans and increased social interactions than were typically observed in their behaviors. The symptom remission occurred at the onset of fever and persisted for 1 – 3 days following after return of the temperature to normal level [31].

There is no consensus explaining this observation, but there are high hopes that solving this puzzle may pave the way for new strategies in treatment of ASD [32-34]. It is known that the immune and central nervous systems are functionally connected [35]. The coupling is perhaps mediated by circulating cytokines.

Authors of recent papers speculate that fever may induce better activity of functionally impaired locus coeruleus-noradrenergic (LC-NA) system [36]. Neuronal communication may be also affected in a complex way by the level of cytokines in the brain [37]. The tight coupling between nervous system and IS is firmly confirmed [38].

One should note that the fever is a natural mechanism supporting the immune response. Some elements of IS, indicated in Fig. 1, are sensitive to rise of the temperature. What is important, the fever doesn't cause new interactions directly, but it stimulates different processes and increases their rates [39]. At the higher temperature the dendritic cells migrate faster to the region of the infection [40]. The fever increases an activity of the Tc lymphocytes [39, 41], their differentiation, proliferation [39, 42-44] and persistence [45-46]. It also facilitates the Th cell activation [45]. The fever does not have a direct impact on B cells, but through a stimulation of Th lymphocytes, it increases the B cells activation and production of the antibodies as well [39, 41, 47]. Thus, it is possible that changed proportions of various cytokines (including interferons) and/or chemokines, have beneficial effect on activity of ASD nervous system and synaptic connections.

Here we propose that PN model of IS provides a practical and useful formalism for testing this and similar hypotheses. In our previous paper [18] we have shown at the level of a PN model that fever increases the number of Th lymphocytes. In this work we assess to what extent fever may affect concentrations of cytokines (IL-1, IL-6, TNF-α) which are known to have abnormal levels in brains of persons with ASD [48]. In addition, using the present PN model of IS we have checked the effects of correlations between fever and "autism" on the level of IFN-γ (Fig. 1 part C, place 56).

We have added the effect of fever to our model via an enforced modification of arcs' weights. It is perhaps the simplest way to represent qualitative changes, which are caused by the elevated body temperature. The transitions corresponding to the presented effects of fever were identified in the model and the weights of arcs, connecting those transitions to appropriate places, were arbitrarily increased. Those "fever affected" arcs are represented in Fig. 1 by bold arrows. Not all effects of fever are present in the model directly, because in our study of ASD we wanted to simulate only a general state of IS to which the fever leads.

In order to mimic IS of autistic individuals the weights of transitions leading to the production of cytokines IL-1, IL-6, TNF-α in the part E (macrophages) are again arbitrarily set to be a factor of 2 higher than those in "non-autistic" individuals. Thus, the levels of these cytokines are higher, in qualitative accordance with experiments [49]. No experimental data are available to set this levels in a more quantitative way.

5.1   The Simulation Protocol

We start simulations of PN dynamics by an assignment of markings to places of the IS model. The dynamics, i.e. changes of a number of tokens in particular places, was monitored using a separate special purpose code developed in-house. Some 4000 steps imitating arbitrary span of time were calculated. Since the selection of competitive transitions was random, we have averaged results of 500 such simulations for each of four cases studied. We have modeled: (1) non-autistic, (2) non-autistic with fever, (3) autistic, (4) autistic and fever variants of IS Petri networks. Results of modeling are presented in Fig. 3. Statistical errors are presented in Fig. 3a and 3d.

5.2   Results of PN Modeling

In Fig. 3a an average amount of probably the most important cytokine IL-1 is presented for all cases studied. Both *cellular* and *humoral* immune responses were included in the PN model. One can see that amounts of IL-1 for the healthy children having fever and without it are similar. But for children with autism the effect of fever is quite significant: while for autistic children the IL-1 levels continuously rise, in cases having fever, this concentration achieves a constant level. What is more important, the fever causes the level of IL-1 in autistic subjects to be more similar to the level "observed" in healthy children (Fig. 3a). IL-1 exhibits pro-inflammatory activity and according to [50] a high level of IL-1 is not good for the nervous system. Thus, fever in autistic children leads to change in a good direction: lowering of IL-1 level .

However, in this network we had problems with homeostasis. One may extrapolate that IL-1 level corresponding to the autistic case will grow to infinity over time. That is why we modified the model of IS. We have added two transitions (black arrows in black frames, in parts (C) and (E), Fig. 1). These transitions represent collectively all remaining mechanisms of degradation/inactivation of cytokines INF-γ and TNF-α, respectively. The effect of this modification can be observed in Fig. 3b. A general behavior is similar to Fig. 3a but now a better homeostasis for "autism" is achieved. This example illustrates a problem of proper construction of PN for each case studied.

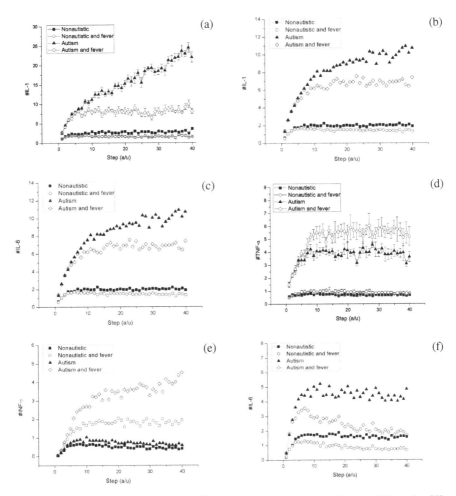

Fig. 3. Results of simulations: (a) levels of IL-1, bars represent statistical errors (b) levels of IL-1 with additional transitions, (c) levels of IL-6, (d) levels of TNF-α, (e) levels of INF-γ, (f) levels of IL-6 but only during the *humoral* response

IL-6 is also is pro-inflammatory cytokine and according to [50] it may adversely affect functioning of the brain. In Fig. 3c the same IS cases are analyzed and similar changes as those for IL-1 are observed. This cytokine was studied in greater detail – since much longer simulations were generated (data not shown). Despite of this elongated time the homeostasis wasn't perfect. Probably our simplified method of accounting for cytokines decay is too simple.

TNF-α is pro-inflammatory cytokine as well, and one could expect that a lower level of this compound during the fever might lead to better condition of an autistic brain. Our data show that the TNF-α levels in autistic IS are sensitive to fever indeed

(Fig. 3d), but contrary to this expectation, the TNF-α concentration <u>increases</u> during inflammation. In a normal brain TNF-α level increases during fever to much lower extent.

In the literature neuroprotective function of INF-γ is discussed [50]. We have monitored the levels of this compound during IS activity. Data presented in Fig. 3e indicate that in organisms without fever amounts of INF-γ are similar in both healthy and autistic children. Fever causes increase of INF-γ levels and this effect is much stronger for autistic individuals.

In certain medical conditions only *humoral* response of the IS is present. We have checked dynamics of IL-6 levels in such a case. Results (Fig. 3f) are very interesting: the fever causes enormous change in the autistic IS case. Due to the effects of fever the level of IL-6 in an autistic child is almost the same as in the healthy child. That is a promising result. May be not all cases of fever induced improvement in mental abilities of autistic children are related to the same type of fever. Perhaps in some cases only a part of IS responses to inflammation or the other pirogen, and thus the change in the behavior is seen. When whole IS is reacting to the external stimulus the effect of fever of autism is negligible. This observation requires more systematic experimental studies of normal/autistic children.

General findings in the model are: the fever usually changes the amount of cytokines and brings it closer to a level observed in healthy children (in almost all cases studied) or changes are qualitatively the same for the healthy and autistic children. Unfortunately, we have still problems with the homeostasis in the PN model. Adding two new transitions had improved the situation but problems are still present.

6   Conclusions and Prospects

PNs are useful tools for modeling of complex biological and medical phenomena. These models may be helpful in network based medicine [51] and in development of new drugs and new treatment strategies. In this paper we show that our relatively simple PN model of IS led to discovery of new couplings between fever, autism and cytokine levels in the brain. Thus the code provides a tool for new studies in the ASD area and IS properties. There is a wide area for future improvements of such PN based systems biology models and the work in this direction is currently done in our laboratory.

Acknowledgements. We thank for the support from Polish Funds for Science (grant No. N519 578138).

Literature

1. Forrest, S., Beauchemin, C.: Computer immunology. Immunological Reviews 216, 176–197 (2007)
2. Bernaschi, M., Castiglione, F.: Design and implementation of an immune system simulator. Computers in Biology and Medicine 31, 303–331 (2001)

3. Burroughs, N., Ferreira, M., Oliveira, B., Pinto, A.: Autoimmunity arising from bystander proliferation of T cells in an immune response model. Mathematical and Computer Modelling 53, 1389–1393 (2011)
4. Goldstein, B., Faeder, J.R., Hlavacek, W.S.: Mathematical and computational models of immune-receptor signalling. Nature Reviews Immunology 4, 445–456 (2004)
5. Eftimie, R., Bramson, J.L., Earn, D.J.D.: Interactions between the immune system and cancer: a brief review of non-spatial mathematical models. Bulletin of Mathematical Biology 73, 2–32 (2011)
6. Li, X., Wang, Z., Lu, T., Che, X.: Modelling immune system: principles, models, analysis and perspectives. Journal of Bionic Engineering 6, 77–85 (2009)
7. Liò, P., Nicosia, G., Stibor, T. (eds.): ICARIS 2011. LNCS, vol. 6825. Springer, Heidelberg (2011)
8. Petri, C.A.: Kommunikation mit automaten (1962)
9. Zurawski, R., Zhou, M.C.: Petri nets and industrial applications: A tutorial. IEEE Transactions on Industrial Electronics 41, 567–583 (1994)
10. Peterson, J.L.: Petri Net Theory and the Modeling of Systems. Prentice-Hall Inc., Englewood Cliffs (1981)
11. Sackmann, A., Formanowicz, D., Formanowicz, P., Koch, I., Blazewicz, J.: An analysis of the Petri net based model of the human body iron homeostasis process. Computational Biology and Chemistry 31, 1–10 (2007)
12. Grunwald, S., Speer, A., Ackermann, J., Koch, I.: Petri net modelling of gene regulation of the Duchenne muscular dystrophy. Biosystems 92, 189–205 (2008)
13. Genrich, H., Küffner, R., Voss, K.: Executable Petri net models for the analysis of metabolic pathways. International Journal on Software Tools for Technology Transfer (STTT) 3, 394–404 (2001)
14. Koch, I., Reisig, W., Schreiber, F.: Modeling in systems biology: The Petri Net Approach. Springer, London (2011)
15. Na, D., Park, I., Lee, K.H., Lee, D.: Integration of Immune Models Using Petri Nets. In: Nicosia, G., Cutello, V., Bentley, P.J., Timmis, J. (eds.) ICARIS 2004. LNCS, vol. 3239, pp. 205–216. Springer, Heidelberg (2004)
16. Park, I., Na, D., Lee, K.H., Lee, D.: Fuzzy Continuous Petri Net-Based Approach for Modeling Helper T Cell Differentiation. In: Jacob, C., Pilat, M., Bentley, P., Timmis, J. (eds.) ICARIS 2005. LNCS, vol. 3627, pp. 331–338. Springer, Heidelberg (2005)
17. Park, I., Na, D., Lee, D., Lee, K.: Fuzzy Continuous Petri Net-Based Approach for Modeling Immune Systems. In: Apolloni, B., Marinaro, M., Nicosia, G., Tagliaferri, R. (eds.) WIRN 2005 and NAIS 2005. LNCS, vol. 3931, pp. 278–285. Springer, Heidelberg (2006)
18. Gogolinska, A., Ochmanski, E., Nowak, W.: Petri Nets in Immunological System Modeling. In: Ochmanski, O., Penczek, W. (eds.) Matematyczne Metody Modelowania i Analizy Systemow Wspolbieznych, MASYW 2010, pp. 35–46 (2012)
19. David, R., Alla, H.: Discrete, continuous, and hybrid Petri Nets. Springer (2005)
20. Reisig, W.: Petri nets: an introduction. Springer-Verlag New York, Inc. (1985)
21. Male, D.: Immunology: an illustrated outline. Mosby Ltd. (2004)
22. Parkin, J., Cohen, B.: An overview of the immune system. The Lancet 357, 1777–1789 (2001)
23. Paul, W.E.: Fundamental immunology. Wolters Kluwer/Lippincott Williams & Wilkins (2008)
24. Germain, R., Meier-Schellersheim, M., Nita-Lazar, A., Fraser, I.: Systems Biology in Immunology: A Computational Modeling Perspective. Annual Review of Immunology 29, 527–585 (2011)

25. Yan, Q.: Immunoinformatics and systems biology methods for personalized medicine. Methods in Molecular Biology (Clifton, NJ) 662, 203–220 (2010)
26. Ashwood, P., Wills, S., Van de Water, J.: The immune response in autism: a new frontier for autism research. Journal of Leukocyte Biology 80, 1 (2006)
27. Rohr, C., Marwan, W., Heiner, M.: Snoopy - a unifying Petri net framework to investigate biomolecular networks. Bioinformatics 26, 974 (2010)
28. Freitag, C.M.: The genetics of autistic disorders and its clinical relevance: a review of the literature. Molecular Psychiatry 12, 2–22 (2006)
29. Patterson, P.H.: Maternal infection and immune involvement in autism. Trends in Molecular Medicine 17, 389–394 (2011)
30. Duch, W., Nowak, W., Meller, J., Osiński, G., Dobosz, K., Mikołajewski, D., Wójcik, G.: Consciousness and attention in autism spectrum disorders. In: Proceedings of Cracow Grid Workshop 2010, pp. 202–211 (2011)
31. Curran, L.K., Newschaffer, C.J., Lee, L.C., Crawford, S.O., Johnston, M.V., Zimmerman, A.W.: Behaviors associated with fever in children with autism spectrum disorders. Pediatrics 120, e1386 (2007)
32. Molloy, C., Morrow, A., Meinzen-Derr, J., Schleifer, K., Dienger, K., Manning-Courtney, P., Altaye, M., Wills-Karp, M.: Elevated cytokine levels in children with autism spectrum disorder. Journal of Neuroimmunology 172, 198–205 (2006)
33. Chez, M.G., Dowling, T., Patel, P.B., Khanna, P., Kominsky, M.: Elevation of tumor necrosis factor-alpha in cerebrospinal fluid of autistic children. Pediatric Neurology 36, 361–365 (2007)
34. Parker-Athill, E.C., Tan, J.: Maternal immune activation and autism spectrum disorder: interleukin-6 signaling as a key mechanistic pathway. Neurosignals 18, 113–128 (2010)
35. Pickett, J., London, E.: The neuropathology of autism: a review. Journal of Neuropathology & Experimental Neurology 64, 925 (2005)
36. Mehler, M.F., Purpura, D.P.: Autism, fever, epigenetics and the locus coeruleus. Brain Research Reviews 59, 388–392 (2009)
37. Szelényi, J.: Cytokines and the central nervous system. Brain Research Bulletin 54, 329–338 (2001)
38. Quan, N., Banks, W.A.: Brain-immune communication pathways. Brain, Behavior, and Immunity 21, 727–735 (2007)
39. Hasday, J.D., Fairchild, K.D., Shanholtz, C.: The role of fever in the infected host. Microbes. Infect. 2, 1891–1904 (2000)
40. Ostberg, J.R., Gellin, C., Patel, R., Repasky, E.A.: Regulatory potential of fever-range whole body hyperthermia on Langerhans cells and lymphocytes in an antigen-dependent cellular immune response. J. Immunol. 167, 2666–2670 (2001)
41. Jampel, H.D., Duff, G.W., Gershon, R.K., Atkins, E., Durum, S.K.: Fever and immunoregulation. III. Hyperthermia augments the primary in vitro humoral immune response. J. Exp. Med. 157, 1229–1238 (1983)
42. Mullbacher, A.: Hyperthermia and the generation and activity of murine influenza-immune cytotoxic T cells in vitro. J. Virol. 52, 928–931 (1984)
43. Duff, G.W., Durum, S.K.: Fever and immunoregulation: hyperthermia, interleukins 1 and 2, and T-cell proliferation. Yale. J. Biol. Med. 55, 437–442 (1982)
44. Kluger, M.J.: Is fever beneficial? Yale. J. Biol. Med. 59, 89–95 (1986)
45. Meinander, A., Soderstrom, T.S., Kaunisto, A., Poukkula, M., Sistonen, L., Eriksson, J.E.: Fever-like hyperthermia controls T Lymphocyte persistence by inducing degradation of cellular FLIPshort. J. Immunol. 178, 3944–3953 (2007)

46. Evans, S.S., Wang, W.C., Bain, M.D., Burd, R., Ostberg, J.R., Repasky, E.A.: Fever-range hyperthermia dynamically regulates lymphocyte delivery to high endothelial venules. Blood 97, 2727–2733 (2001)

47. Huang, Y.H., Haegerstrand, A., Frostegard, J.: Effects of in vitro hyperthermia on proliferative responses and lymphocyte activity. Clinical & Experimental Immunology 103, 61–66 (1996)

48. Ashwood, P., Corbett, B.A., Kantor, A., Schulman, H., Van de Water, J., Amaral, D.G.: In Search of Cellular Immunophenotypes in the Blood of Children with Autism. PLoS ONE 6, e19299 (2011)

49. Cohly, H.H.P., Panja, A.: Immunological findings in autism. International Review of Neurobiology 71, 317–341 (2005)

50. McAfoose, J., Baune, B.: Evidence for a cytokine model of cognitive function. Neuroscience & Biobehavioral Reviews 33, 355–366 (2009)

51. Zanzoni, A., Soler-López, M., Aloy, P.: A network medicine approach to human disease. FEBS Letters 583, 1759–1765 (2009)

Mathematical Implementation of Interaction between Malaria and Immune System

Cicero Hildenberg Lima de Oliveira, Thayna Baptista Moroso,
Fabio Hugo Souza Matos, Carolina Yukari Veludo Watanabe,
Ciro Jose Egoavil Montero, Carlos Alberto Tenorio de Carvalho Junior,
Hugo Fernando Maia Milan, and Fernando Berton Zanchi

Federal University of Rondonia, Electrical Engineering,
Porto Velho, Brazil
{berg,carolina,ciro.egoavil,tenorio}@unir.br,
{thayna_moroso,fabio_hugo08,fbzanchi}@hotmail.com,
hugofernando@gmail.com
http://www.eletrica.unir.br/

Abstract. Malaria is a serious disease with a high developing in the
world. It still major public health problem. In 2008, 109 countries were
declared as endemic to the disease, 243 million malaria cases were reported causing nearly a million of death, primarily of children under 5
year; nearly 3000 children die every day in Africa. In Brazil, Amazonia
is the area that presents the highest number of cases and consequently
having many cases of morbidity and mortality, especially when we deal
with the Malaria caused by the Plasmodium falciparum. The parasite
in the human organism attacks liver cells and erythrocytes. Plasmodium
falciparum is the deadliest protozoan because attacks a high number of
erythrocytes at any evolutionary phase, making the person susceptible
to others disease. The human immune system (HIS) operates in the invasion of this parasite (innate system) and during its development in
the organism (adaptive system), it is responsible for finding and neutral-
izing cells that are infected to prevent their proliferation, avoiding the
disease or the death of the patient. The complex biology of Plasmodium
falciparum and its interaction with the HIS are the motivation of this
work. Therefore, with mathematical models and computer simulations
which have been growing considerably in the medical science area, this
work presents a model to contribute quickly and trustfully for this interaction. The mathematical modeling used is structured by non-linear
ordinary differential equations of first-order that describes the action of
the HIS to eliminate the protozoa. We have performed several simulations to investigate the behavior of the protozoa front of the human
organism without the action of the HIS, and the results were compared
to the behavior with the action of the HIS.

Keywords: Malaria, Plasmodium falciparum, Erythrocytes, Human
Immune System (HIS), Mathematical Models.

C.A. Coello Coello et al. (Eds.): ICARIS 2012, LNCS 7597, pp. 100–110, 2012.
© Springer-Verlag Berlin Heidelberg 2012

1   Introduction

The increasing technological development that has been occurred in the current days has in general a connotation very important for science, especially when dealing with stochastic approximations or mathematical models that try to predict biological phenomenon.

Among the sciences of human knowledge, the medical science have used mathematical and computational tools as a strong support, trying in this manner, to resolve problems that in a not so distant past, was based on acquired empiricism as inherent truth.

Biomedical Engineering is then the multidisciplinary area which associates the exact science with health principles, aiming to develop innovative technologies applied to the prevention, diagnosis, diseases therapy, as well as monitoring physiological parameters.

In the area of human physiology, there are development of models in the nervous and immune systems [1], which with differential equations [11], analyze the participation of different nervous system cells in response to a stimulus from or not a disease, creating a range of analyzes from the various forms of interaction between the immune system and the antigen, which has served to encourage new theories in triggering the disease [10].

In this scenario, our work aims at modeling using differential equations, as the basis for biological aspects, of the infection process of the *Plasmodium falciparum*, obtaining a dynamic system related to the autoimmune response. Thus, this tool aims to present models that simplify the quantitative analysis of humoral and cellular immunity responses to infection with *Plasmodium falciparum*.

This work is organized as follows. Section II includes de biological of the parasite necessary for understanding this work. Section III describes the mathematical model implemented. Section IV has the simulation of a mathematical model. Section V presents the simulation results obtained with the model proposed and section VI the plans of future works.

2   Biological Background

Malaria is an infectious disease whose etiological agent is a parasite of the genus *Plasmodium* [5]. The natural transmission of malaria occurs through the bite of infected female mosquitoes of the Anopheles genus [6].

When the human is inoculated subcutaneously by the bite of the female mosquito of the Anopheles genus, there is an invasion of about 15-200 sporozoites [7] (extracellular infective forms of the *Plasmodium*) which are housed in the mosquito's salivary glands.

The sporozoites come in the bloodstream and disappear as fast as it came, penetrating in hepatocytes [3], where occurs the exo-erythrocytic cycle, which lasts six days for the species *P. falciparum* [5] [6]. These evolve into the merozoite form. At this moment, when they leave the liver, occurs the invasion of erythrocytes by the parasite. It should be noted that each hepatocyte ruptured releases about 40,000 merozoites due to *P. falciparum*. [7].

Plasmodium falciparum is the only one that attacks all stages (ages) of erythrocytes, thus there is a percentage of parasitized cells very high, and therefore, this parasite infections result in considerable levels of anemia since the beginning of infestation.

This is one of the reasons why malaria caused by *P. falciparum* to be one of the most serious, because it may have microvascular disease onset.

However, the major virulence factor of *P. falciparum* is the adhesion of parasitized erythrocytes by mature stages of the endothelium of small blood vessels, particularly of post-capillary venules.

This factor known as cytoadherence is considered as a fundamental factor in the pathological process, its due to it the central event of the pathophysiology of severe malaria, since the production of proinflammatory cytokines by host cells [16], such as tumor necrosis factor, is stimulated by soluble products, particularly glycosylphosphatidylinositol, released by the parasite at the end of blood schizogony [12]. The elevated levels of tumor necrosis factor induce the expression of some endothelial receptors such as intercellular adhesion molecules and E-selectin, providing the cytoadherence, and associated to fever, hypoglycemia, and anemia [5].

Due to cytoadherence the parasite develops inside the red cell for a period ranging from 48 to 72 hours, until cause its rupture, releasing new merozoites which will invade new red blood cells. The rupture and subsequent release of parasites in the bloodstream are reflected clinically by the onset of the malarial paroxysm (periodic fever peaks of malaria), which will be repeated with the end of the new cycle (in two days, with infection due to *P. falciparum*). [12] [13] [18].

That's when the parasite is exposed to the immune system due to its development phase.

The immune system is one of the more complex systems that exist in nature, which is a fundamental activity to protect the organism against infinity of attacks from various organisms to foreign substances to the environment. The immunity against malaria is a combination of genetic resistance, resulting from mutations found in the human genome, innate immunity and acquired immunity. [11]

When an organism is attacked by a foreign agent (pathogen), the first to start a sort of reconnaissance of area is the innate immune system, but it does not have a specific answer, but depending on the case he can defend the organism [9]. This immunity against malaria parasites can be classified into two types, one due to resistance to infection with the genetic bases [15] and another due to cell-mediated immune mechanisms [18].

The natural resistance may be related to genetic characteristics of the host [18] that can prevent the invasion of erythrocytes by merozoites. Thus, decreases the number of parasites within infected erythrocytes, or may cause damage in the release of these merozoites [12][13] that compose the schizont, reducing the ability of these parasites to invade other red blood cells after the disruption and release of the infected cell, interfering in the maintenance of the life cycle of the parasite [19] [20].

The cell-mediated resistance is developed against all foreign molecules to the host [21] and this resistance is the result of the phagocytosis of free parasites in the blood, the merozoites, process accomplished by neutrophils, monocytes and macrophages, which also phagocytosis infected erythrocytes acting on activation of NK cells (Natural Killer) [18] [16] [17]. Cytokines released by various cell types also participate in these mechanisms act against free parasites and / or infected erythrocytes [14].

In the other hand, the adaptive system becomes active when the first cannot neutralize or even protect [12]. His action is more effective and objective, thus resulting in a more effective response. He is the one that accredits the organism to recognize and respond to foreign bodies, even if they have never been found before in the environment.

Humoral immunity is a subdivision of acquired immunity where the immune response is achieved by molecules in the blood, known as antibodies. They are produced by B lymphocytes (cells formed in the bone marrow), much important in the control and action to pathogens that are in the bloodstream, which differs from cellular immunity, mediated by cells originating in the thymus, reason for been called T cells [9] [8].

3 Mathematical Model

Through the detailed description of the *Plasmodium falciparum* behavior in humans and the interaction of parasite with the immune system, we present a mathematical model to describe the dynamics of the immune response through the stimulation caused by the introduction of sporozoites in human bloodstream. Models such as [2] show the possibility and difficulties, because they are complex interactions of the visualization and interpretation of biological phenomenon.

The model adopted in this work is based on an individual being inoculated by plasmodium for the first time, in other words is an individual not immune (as travelers migrants from non-endemic areas) that will be considered the occurrence of paroxysms characteristic of malaria. Your immune system will recognize the invasion for the first time in his memory.

For the development process was necessary a separate study of the parasite dynamics and the immune system to obtain a setting amount of the complex interaction between the two.

When the parasite invades the human body, it looks for an appropriated place for its replication. Assuming that the host immune system is unable to respond the stimulus, it is possible to study the dynamics of the parasite and, after his understanding, incorporate the immune system action.

Thus, the dynamics of the parasite may be described through the following flow diagram in the Figure 1.

Therefore, based on [2], the dynamics of *Plasmodium falciparum* can be described by the first order ordinary differential equations below the Figure.

$$\frac{dM}{dt} = (\mu_G + \alpha_M)cT - \mu_M M \tag{1}$$

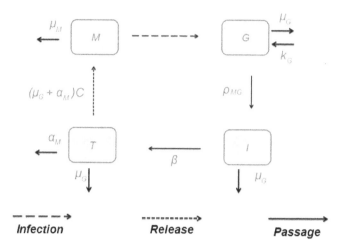

Fig. 1. Schematically the interaction of *Plasmodium falciparum* on infected human

$$\frac{dG}{dt} = k_G - \rho MG - \mu_G G \tag{2}$$

$$\frac{dI}{dt} = \rho MG - \beta I - \mu_G I \tag{3}$$

$$\frac{dT}{dt} = \beta I - (\mu_G + \alpha_M)T \tag{4}$$

Where M, G, I and T represent the concentrations per mm^3, at time t, of the merozoite, red blood cells (target cells of merozoites), erythrocytes infected by the parasite and red blood cells in the terminal, respectively.

The rates per capitals of natural mortality of merozoites, healthy erythrocytes, infected and in the terminal are, respectively, μ_M and μ_G and α is the mortality rate of red blood cells in the terminal phase because infection by merozoites. The replacement rate of erythrocytes is the k_G, a constant value to keep a constant population of cells for homeostasis.

The attack rate in the erythrocytes by merozoites is represented by ρ and the transfer rate of infected red blood cells for the terminal state is β. And finally, the replication rate of the merozoite is $(\mu_G + \alpha)C$, this rate is constant because replication varies from differences of the erythrocytes as specified in Section II.

The humoral and cellular response to infection by *Plasmodium falciparum*, as described in Section II, can be described by a dynamic system with immune system cells represented by S, its replacement rate is k_S, and its mortality rate per capita is μ_S, with μ_S^{-1} being the average life span of cells type S. The immune system can be described as a below differential equation:

$$\frac{dS}{dt} = k_S - \mu_S S \tag{5}$$

As the diagram (Figure 1) for the simulation, there is considered merozoites into the bloodstream and therefore the immune systems interaction with the parasite occurs when happens its first replication, so the cells of the S type will be activated only in the compartment T. We considered the immune system represented by humoral and cellular response and components of the innate immune system.

By the above considerations of system activation, and the models created for the parasite and immune system, the dynamics interaction of *Plasmodium falciparum* with the defense line of human can be described below by differential equations:

$$\frac{dM}{dt} = (\mu_G + \alpha_M)cT - \mu_M M - \epsilon_M SM \tag{6}$$

$$\frac{dG}{dt} = k_G - \rho MG - \mu_G G \tag{7}$$

$$\frac{dI}{dt} = \rho MG - \beta I - \mu_G I \tag{8}$$

$$\frac{dT}{dt} = \beta I - (\mu_G + \alpha_M)T - \sigma_G ST \tag{9}$$

$$\frac{dS}{dt} = k_S + \varphi T - \mu_S S \tag{10}$$

Where ϵ_M and σ_G are the deactivation rates of the merozoites and erythrocytes in a terminal state, respectively, caused by the action of the immune system. We

Table 1. Initial conditions and parameters

Parameter	Value	Unit	Reference
μ_G	0.01	$1/day$	estimated
μ_M	0.01	$1/day$	estimated
μ_S	0.01	$1/day$	estimated
α_M	0.1	$1/day$	estimated
ϵ_M	0.01	$1/cell \cdot day$	estimated
c	$8.0 < c < 32.0$	cell	estimated
σ_G	0.01	$1/cell \cdot day$	estimated
ρ	0.00005401	$1/cell \cdot day$	estimated
β	0.5	$1/day$	estimated
k_G	0.01	$cell/day$	estimated
k_S	0.01	$cell/day$	estimated
φ	0.01	$1/day$	estimated

also have a proliferation rate φ of immune cells, which is given by the number of dead cells or in a terminal.

The Table 1 presents the initial conditions and the values to the parameters used in the simulations.

4   Implementation

As can be noted, the proposed set of equations to model the physiological effect of the interaction between malaria and the human body is composed entirely of first order differential equations.

To effectuate the solution of this system, it is usual to use numerical methods. One of the simplest and most widespread in the literature is the Finite Difference Method (FDM) [22][23]. To its use, the time derivatives are considered as variations ($\Delta\phi/\Delta t$). Thus, it is essential to have the knowledge of the system at a given initial time [24].

From the initial instant [23][24], all the other points are approximate, considering that $\phi(t) = f(\omega) \cdot \Delta t + \phi(t - \Delta t)$. With these relations, was scheduled a graphical interface to assist in the results interpreting, where the starting points and the variables are inserted and containing, in its programming, all the equations in their formulation by the finite difference method [24].

5   Numeric Results

Two biological characteristics of the *Plasmodium falciparum* partially explain the major virulence of this species: the ability to produce large numbers of merozoites at the end of the hepatic schizogony and the ability of these merozoites of invade erythrocytes of all ages.

To show the dynamics of the model, consider the cases of the inactive immune system and subsequently the immune system acting on the parasite dynamics.

As the literature reports and was discussed earlier the cellular immunity as the humoral immunity are involved in immunity against malaria, the relative importance of each one in the process of protection against the disease is not well established. Thus, to study the interaction of the immune system with the parasite *Plasmodium falciparum*, it was considered a general system not subdivided.

In all cases we will consider a dimensional area based on the proportional quantity to the dynamic time considered.

Case 1: In the first case is simulated the blood schizogony considering that the hepatic schizogony has already happened. It will be considered the number of merozoites per schizont tissue of 40,000, for a quantity of red blood cells per mm in the bloodstream of 5,000,000, with a proportion of 40 to 5,000.

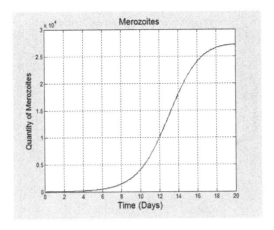

Fig. 2. Number of merozoites x time with the Immune System INACTIVE

The figure below may be explained by the cytoadherence, that is the major virulence factor of the *P. falciparum*, saving proportions of the anterior graph.

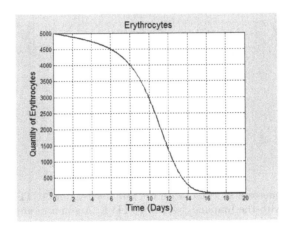

Fig. 3. Number of Erythrocytes x time with the Immune System INACTIVE

The following figure shows the comparison between the terminal and infected cells with some anticipation of the terminal cells that can be interpreted by observing the patient's peripheral blood, where usually finds only young tropho-zoites, which has a typical ring signet shape, and gametocytes.

Case 2: We will consider from now on the immune system acting in full. The figure below presents the growth of merozoites, by his side the dynamic behavior of the erythrocytes through merozoites growth and the last figure the action and trigger of the immune system through this interaction.

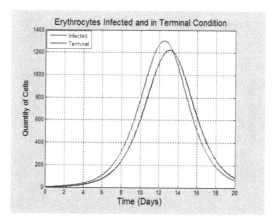

Fig. 4. Number of cells (Infected and Illness) x time with the Immune System INACTIVE

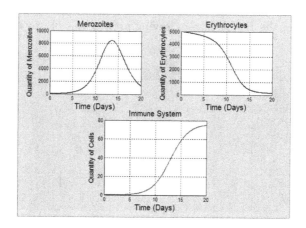

Fig. 5. Number of merozoites x time with the Immune System ACTIVE; Erythrocytes x amount of time with the Immune System ACTIVE; Amount of immune cells x time

The figure shows the period comprising the tenth and fifteenth day of massive intravascular hemolysis or fever hemoglobinuric (blackwater fever) which may result depending on the infestation hyperparasitism above 100,000 parasites per microliter of blood, without mention of course the classic symptoms of the paroxysm which are accompanied by chills, malaise, headache and muscle and joint pain. During this period starts a high fever, which produces dinamia and prostration; this phase is also observed a period of profuse weats that with the action of the immune system is possible to observe the progressive improvement of general condition that coincides in which febrile every 48 hours.

In clinical practice this is uncommon in individual continuously exposed to malaria, infection may be completely asymptomatic in semi-immune individuals with low parasitaemia [4].

6 Conclusion

This is an initial work with several considerations, one of them is considerate the immune system acting entirely without the specificities of the cellular and humoral immunity system. The main objective of this work is to show the possibility of modeling biological interactions by differential equations and try to approximate the biological reality culminating with the reactions of the organism when it is infected by the parasite.

New tests need to be performed for a better approximation to the biological systems and thus create the possibility of predicting the interaction of the immune system with a vaccine.

The great advantage of being able to have a numerical method and predict the phenomenons that may occur, even if they are not deterministic, because there are many variables operating in this dynamic, is to have more tools for comparisons and analysis to assist in important decisions about this parasite that causes so many evils to the brazilian population as well as other populations that suffer with this disease.

References

1. Yang, H.M.: Comparison between Shistosomiasis Transmission Modelling Considering Acquired Immunity and Age-structured Contact Pattern with Infested Water. Math. Biosc. 184, 1–26 (2003)
2. Barrozo, S., Yang, H.M.: Desenvolvimento de um modelo para resposta imunlógica primária célula-mediada. Tendências em Matemática Aplicada e Computacional. 7(1), 31–41 (2006)
3. Chitnis, C.E., Blackman, M.J.: Host cell invasion by malaria parasites. Parasitology Today 16, 411–415 (2000)
4. Da Silva-Nunes, M., Ferreira, M.U.: Clinical spectrum of uncomplicated malaria ub senu-immune Amazonians: beyond the "symptomatic" VS "asymptomatic" dichotomy. Mem. Inst. Oswaldo Cruz 102, 341–347 (2007)
5. World Health Organization. Severe falciparum malaria. Transactions of the Royal Society of Tropical Medicine and Hygiene 94(supl. 1), S1/1–S1/90 (2000)
6. Cooke, B.M., Wahlgren, M., Coppel, R.L.: Falciparum malaria: sticking-up, standing out and outstanding. Parasitology Today 16, 416–420 (2000)
7. Vieira, P.P., Ferreira, M.U., Alecrim, M.G., Alecrim, W.D., Da Silva, L.H., et al.: pfcrtpolymorphism and the spread of chloroquine resistance in Plasmodium falciparum populations across the Amazon Basin. Infect. Dis. 190, 417–424 (2004)
8. Bezzi, M., Celada, F., Ruffo, S., Seiden, P.E.: The transition between immune and disease states in a cellular automaton model of clonal immune response. Physica A: Statistical and Theoretical Physics 245(1-2), 145–163 (1997)
9. Sompayrac, L.M.: How the Immune System Works. Wiley, John & Sons (2008) (incorporated)

10. Janeway, C., Murphy, K.P., Travers, P., Walport, M., Janeway, C.: Immunobiology, 5th edn. Garland Science, New York (2001)
11. Edelstein-Keshet, L.: Mathematical Models in Biology, New York. Birkhauser Mathematics Series (1988)
12. Zorzeno, R.M.S., Pinho, S.T.R., Ferreira, C.P., da Silva, P.C.A.: On the study of the dynamic aspects of parasitemia in the blood cycle of malaria. Europen Physcial J. Special Topics 143, 125–134 (2007)
13. Molineaux, L., Diebner, H.H., Eichner, M., Collins, W.E., Jeffery, G.M., Dietz, K.: Parasitology 122, 379–391 (2001)
14. Adams, J.H., Blair, P.L., Kaneko, O., Peterson, D.S.: An expanding ebl family of *Plasmodium falciparum*. Trends Parasitol 17(6), 297–299 (2001)
15. Al-Yaman, F., Genton, B., Anders, R., Taraika, J., Ginny, M., Mellor, S., Alpers, M.P.: Assessment of the role of the humoral response to *Plasmodium falciparum* MSP2 compared to RESA and SPf66 in protecting Papua New Guinean children from clinical malaria. Parasite Immunol. 17(9), 493–501 (1995)
16. Anders, R.F., Smythe, J.A.: Polymorphic antigens in *Plasmodium falciparum*. Blood 74(6), 1865–1875 (1989)
17. Aribot, G., Rogier, C., Sarthou, J., Trape, J., Balde, A., Druilhe, P., Roussilhon, C.: Pattern of immunoglobulin isotype response to *Plasmodium falciparum* blood-stage antigens in individuals living in a holoendemic area of Senegal (Dielmo, west Africa). Am. J. Trop. Med. Hyg. 54(5), 449–457 (1996)
18. Artavanis-Tsakonas, K., Riley, E.M.: Innate immune response to malaria: rapid induction of IFN-gamma from human NK cells by live *Plsmodium falciparum*-infected erythrocytes. J. Immunol. 169(6), 2956–2963 (2002)
19. Ayi, K., Turrini, F., Piga, A., Arese, P.: Enhanced phagocytosis of ring-parasitized mutant erythrocytes: a common mechanism that explain protection against falciparum malaria in sickle trait and beta-thalassemia trait. Blood 104(10), 3364–3371 (2004)
20. Babiker, H., Ranford-Cartwright, L., Currie, D., Charlwood, J., Billingsley, P., Teuscher, T., Walliker, D.: Random mating in a natural population of the malaria parasite *Plasmodium falciparum*. Parasitology 109 (pt 4), 413–421 (1994)
21. Bachmann, A., Predehl, S., May, J., Harder, S., Burchard, G.D., Gilberger, T.W., Tannich, E., Bruchhaus, I.: Highly co-ordinated var gene expression and switching in clinical *Plasmodium falciparum* isolates from non-immune malaria patients. Cell Microbiol. 13(9), 1397–1409 (2011)
22. Butcher, J.C.: The Numerical Analysis of Ordinary Diferential Equations. John Wiley and Sons Inc., NY (1987)
23. Dormand, J.R.: Numerical Methods for Diferential Equations, A Computational Approach. CRC Press, NY (1996)
24. Hildebrand, F.B.: Finite-Difference Equations and Simulations, Section 2.2. Prentice-Hall, Englewood Cliffs (1968)

Computing Longest Common Subsequences with the B-Cell Algorithm

Thomas Jansen[1] and Christine Zarges[2]

[1] University College Cork, Department of Computer Science, Cork, Ireland
t.jansen@cs.ucc.ie
[2] University of Warwick, Department of Computer Science, Coventry CV4 7AL, UK
zarges@dcs.warwick.ac.uk

Abstract. Computing a longest common subsequence of a number of strings is a classical combinatorial optimisation problem with many applications in computer science and bioinformatics. It is a hard problem in the general case so that the use of heuristics is motivated. Evolutionary algorithms have been reported to be successful heuristics in practice but a theoretical analysis has proven that a large class of evolutionary algorithms using mutation and crossover fail to solve and even approximate the problem efficiently. This was done using hard instances. We reconsider the very same hard instances and prove that the B-cell algorithm outperforms these evolutionary algorithms by far. The advantage stems from the use of contiguous hypermutations. The result is another demonstration that relatively simple artificial immune systems can excel over more complex evolutionary algorithms in the domain of optimisation.

1 Introduction

When hard optimisation problems need to be solved in practice often general randomised search heuristics are applied. While they are routinely outperformed by the best problem-specific algorithms if such problem-specific solutions are available they come with the advantages of being relatively easy to apply and to adapt to new and complex problems. Equally important, they usually deliver good solutions in acceptable time. Many different such randomised search heuristics are known. Many of them are nature-inspired heuristics, among them simulated annealing [14], ant colony optimisation [11], evolutionary algorithms [10] and artificial immune systems [9].

Evolutionary algorithms are inspired by the process of natural evolution. They work on a population of candidate solutions that undergo random variations and selection. Variation operators include mutation where a single candidate solution is randomly perturbed and crossover, where two or more candidate solutions are randomly combined into a new one. All candidate solutions are evaluated and assigned a fitness value. Selection favours candidate solutions with larger fitness. Obviously, the metaphor of natural evolution lends itself naturally to the task of optimisation.

C.A. Coello Coello et al. (Eds.): ICARIS 2012, LNCS 7597, pp. 111–124, 2012.

Artificial immune systems are inspired by the natural immune system of vertebrates and modelled after various immunological theories [9,25]. The metaphor of the natural immune system makes their application most natural in anomaly detection and classification. However, there are many artificial immune systems for optimisation, e. g., CLONALG [4], opt-aiNet [3], the B-cell algorithm [21], MISA [7], and OPT-IA [8]. Apart from opt-aiNet, which is inspired by immune network theory, these algorithms are based on the clonal selection principle [2], a theory which describes the basic features of an adaptive immune response to invading pathogens. The algorithms model immune cells to represent candidate solutions. These proliferate and are subject to a hypermutation process implying mutations at very high rate in comparison to evolutionary algorithms. The design of the mutation operator can be inspired by various types of immune cells. Here we consider the B-cell algorithm [21]. This particular immune-inspired algorithm has been subject of theoretical analysis before [5] and has proved to be particularly capable of efficiently solving combinatorial optimisation problems. The B-cell algorithm has been proven to perform equal or even better than more complex evolutionary algorithms on the well-known vertex cover problem [16].

We consider the B-cell algorithm on a different combinatorial optimisation problem, namely the longest common subsequence problem. In this problem one is given a set of m sequences of potentially different length over a common finite alphabet Σ, i. e., $X_1, X_2, \ldots, X_m \subseteq \Sigma^*$. Depending on the application Σ may be as small as $\Sigma = \{0, 1\}$ (common for binary files) or $\Sigma = \{A, C, G, T\}$ (common in bioinformatics) or as large as the set of all characters in some encoding like ASCII or UTF-8 (common for text files). By $|Y|$ we denote the length of a sequence Y, i. e., $|Y| = l$ for $Y = y[1]y[2] \cdots y[l] \in \Sigma^l$. A sequence $Y = y[1]y[2] \ldots y[l] \in \Sigma^l$ is called a subsequence of a sequence $X = x[1]x[2] \cdots x[n] \in \Sigma^n$ if there are indices $0 < i_1 < i_2 < \cdots < i_l \leq n$ such that $y[j] = x[i_j]$ holds for all $j \in \{1, 2, \ldots, l\}$. For example, AAGG is a subsequences of ACAAGATG while AAAAGG is not. The sequence of indices proving that Y is a subsequence of X may not be unique. In our example, one can demonstrate that AAGG is a subsequence of ACAAGATG by means of $1, 3, 5, 8$ as well as by means of $1, 4, 5, 8$. A sequence Y is a common subsequence of $X_1, X_2, \ldots, X_m$ if it is a subsequence of X_i for all $i \in \{1, 2, \ldots, m\}$. It is a longest common subsequence if all common subsequences of $X_1, X_2, \ldots, X_m$ do not have greater length.

In the general case, the problem is NP-hard [22]. Using a dynamic programming approach one can compute a longest common subsequence in time $O\left(\prod_{i=1}^{m} |X_i| \right)$ [6]. This implies that the problem can be solved in polynomial time if the number of sequences m is a constant, in particular it can be solved in quadratic time for two sequences. The complexity of the general problem motivates the use of heuristic algorithms and developing fast heuristics for the longest common subsequence problem is still an active research topic [24,26,27]. One heuristic approach employing evolutionary algorithms reports that evolutionary algorithms yield excellent results in practice [13,20]. A subsequent theoretical analysis, however, revealed that the performance of a large class of evolutionary algorithms is extremely bad even for problem instances that are easy to solve using the problem-specific algorithm based on dynamic programming [18]. We revisit this analysis and analyse the B-cell algorithm for exactly the same instances.

We prove that the B-cell algorithm fails to be efficient if started with random candidate solutions but is very efficient if started with trivial empty candidate solutions. This coincides with the empirical observation that evolutionary algorithms perform better if started with trivial empty candidate solutions [20]. However, we prove that for evolutionary algorithms the performance on the considered instances is still very bad even with this initialisation. This proves that artificial immune systems, in particular the B-cell algorithm, can be a simple and very efficient alternative to evolutionary algorithms and that they are able to outperform these by far.

2 Notation, Algorithms, Problem and Encoding

We consider the longest common subsequence problem over an arbitrary finite alphabet Σ. Let $X_1, X_2, \ldots, X_m \subseteq \Sigma^*$ denote the problem instance we consider. We define $n := |X_1|$ and assume without loss of generality that X_1 is the shortest sequence in the problem instance, i. e., $|X_1| = \min\{|X_1|, |X_2|, \ldots, |X_m|\}$.

In order to make a combinatorial optimisation problem amenable for solution by means of randomised search heuristics a problem-encoding is needed. This problem encoding defines the search space S, i. e., the set of all candidate solutions, as well as an objective function f such that an optimal solution has maximal function value under f. We use the encoding defined by Jansen and Weyland [18], which in turn is motivated by the encoding used by Hinkemeyer and Julstrom [13,20].

The search space is $S = \{0, 1\}^n$, where $n = |X_1|$ is the length of a shortest sequence in the input. Note that n is an upper bound on the length of a longest common subsequence. Let $X_1 = x[1]x[2] \cdots x[n] \in \Sigma^n$ denote the letters in the sequence X_1. For a search point $s = s[1]s[2] \cdots s[n] \in \{0, 1\}^n$ let $I_1 = \{i_1, i_2, \ldots, i_l\} \subseteq \{1, 2, \ldots, n\}$ (with $i_1 < i_2 < \cdots < i_l$) denote the positions of 1-bits in s, i. e., $s[i] = 1$ for all $i \in I_1$ and $s[i] = 0$ for all $i \in \{1, 2, \ldots, n\} \setminus I_1$. The search point s encodes the sequence $x[i_1]x[i_2] \cdots x[i_l]$, a subsequence of X_1. We use $c(s)$ to refer to the sequence encoded by s, i. e., $c(s) = x[i_1]x[i_2] \cdots x[i_l]$. Clearly, the all zero bit string encodes the empty sequence, i. e., $c(0^n) = \varepsilon$, and the all one bit string encodes X_1, i. e., $c(1^n) = X_1$. If $c(s)$ is a subsequence of all $X_1, X_2, \ldots, X_m$ we say that s encodes a feasible solution, otherwise $c(s)$ is infeasible. Observe that the all zero bit string 0^n encodes the trivial feasible solution.

An objective function f needs to assign values $f(s)$ to search points s such that a longest common subsequence has maximal value. In order to guide the search one would like to have larger values for longer common subsequences. Moreover, one would like that infeasible solutions are assigned smaller values than feasible solutions. To this end Hinkemeyer and Julstrom [13,20] define a rather complicated function that we call f_{HJ} here. Jansen and Weyland [18] consider this function and define two more, called f_{MAX} and f_{LCS}, respectively. The function f_{MAX} captures the main ideas of f_{HJ} in simpler form while f_{LCS} is impractical and merely of theoretical interest. In the following definition let $c(s)_{(k)}$ denote the prefix of length k of the sequence $c(s)$.

The function f_{HJ} explicitly distinguishes feasible from infeasible solutions. Infeasible solutions are assigned negative values, feasible solutions positive values. The values increase with increasing length of the common subsequence. The function f_{MAX} determines the maximal length k of a prefix of $c(s)$ such that $c(s)_{(k)}$ is a common subsequence of $X_1, X_2, \ldots, X_m$. The remaining suffix of $c(s)$ does not contribute to feasible solution. This is penalised by subtracting its length from the function value. The function f_{LCS} provides a search heuristic with the maximal amount of information possible. It yields as function value the length of a longest common subsequence of $c(s), X_1, X_2, \ldots, X_m$ (again penalising infeasible solutions). Since the evaluation of f_{LCS} requires solving the longest common subsequence problem it cannot be used in practice and is merely of theoretical interest.

Definition 1. *Consider the instance* $X_1, X_2, \ldots, X_m \in \Sigma^*$ *with* $n = |X_1|$ $= \min\{|X_1|, |X_2|, \ldots, |X_m|\}$. *For* $s \in \{0,1\}^n$ *let* $k(s)$ *be the number of sequences from* $X_1, X_2, \ldots, X_m$ *such that* $c(s)$ *is a subsequence.*

Let $MAX(c(s), X_1, X_2, \ldots, X_m) = \min\{\max\{k \mid c(s)_{(k)} \text{ is subsequence of } X_i\}$ $\mid i \in \{1, \ldots, m\}\}$ *and let* $LCS(c(s), X_1, X_2, \ldots, X_m)$ *be the length of a longest common subsequence of* $c(s), X_1, X_2, \ldots, X_m$.

$$f_{HJ}(s) = \begin{cases} 3000(|c(s)| + 30k(s) + 50) & \text{if } |c(s)| = n \text{ and } k(s) = m \\ 3000(|c(s)| + 30k(s)) & \text{if } |c(s)| < n \text{ and } k(s) = m \\ -1000(|c(s)| + 30k(s) + 50)(m - k(s)) & \text{if } |c(s)| = n \text{ and } k(s) < m \\ -1000(|c(s)| + 30k(s))(m - k(s)) & \text{if } |c(s)| < n \text{ and } k(s) < m \end{cases}$$

$$f_{MAX}(s) = MAX(c(s), X_1, X_2, \ldots, X_m) - (|c(s)| - MAX(c(s), X_1, X_2, \ldots, X_m))$$

$$f_{LCS}(s) = LCS(c(s), X_1, X_2, \ldots, X_m) - (|c(s)| - LCS(c(s), X_1, X_2, \ldots, X_m))$$

We consider the B-cell algorithm as defined by Kelsey and Timmis [21]. It has a population of μ candidate solutions and employs contiguous somatic hypermutations as well as standard bit mutations as variation operators. In these hypermutations a contiguous region in a bit string is selected and each bit in this region is inverted with a fixed probability r. Clark, Hone and Timmis [5] point out that for the extreme case $r = 1$ the algorithm may be unable to locate a global optimum. Jansen and Zarges [19], however, proved in a theoretical study good performance with this extreme case $r = 1$ and point out that r should be at least very close to 1 to maintain the main advantages of this mutation operator. Moreover, good performance for vertex cover is also achieved with this parameter setting [16]. Therefore we also consider the algorithm only for $r = 1$ and omit this parameter in the following description. The values of $\mu, \lambda \in \mathbb{N}$ are parameters of the algorithm.

Algorithm 1 (The B-Cell Algorithm)

1. **Initialisation**
   Select $x_1, x_2, \ldots x_\mu \in \{0,1\}^n$.
2. **Repeat**
3.   **Clonal selection and expansion**
   For each $i \in \{1, 2, \ldots, \mu\}$
       For each $j \in \{1, 2, \ldots, \lambda\}$: Set $y_{i,j} := x_i$.
4.   **Standard bit mutation**
   For each $i \in \{1, 2, \ldots, \mu\}$
       Select $j \in \{1, 2, \ldots, \lambda\}$ uniformly at random.
       For each $k \in \{1, 2, \ldots, n\}$: With probability $1/n$, invert the bit $y_{i,j}[k]$.
5.   **Hypermutation**
   For each $i \in \{1, 2, \ldots, \mu\}$
       For each $j \in \{1, 2, \ldots, \lambda\}$
         Select $p \in \{0, 1, \ldots, n-1\}$ uniformly at random.
         Select $l \in \{0, 1, \ldots, n\}$ uniformly at random.
         For each $k \in \{0, 1, \ldots, l-1\}$
           Invert the bit $y_{i,j}[1 + ((p+k) \bmod n)]$.
6.   **Selection**
   For each $i \in \{1, 2, \ldots, \mu\}$
       If $f(x_i) \leq \max\{f(y_{i,1}), f(y_{i,2}), \ldots, f(y_{i,\lambda})\}$
       then set $x_i := y_{i,j}$ where $f(y_{i,j}) = \max\{f(y_{i,1}), f(y_{i,2}), \ldots, f(y_{i,\lambda})\}$.
7. **Until STOP.**

The initialisation is either done randomly, i.e., $x_1, x_2, \ldots x_\mu \in \{0,1\}^n$ are identically and independently distributed according to the uniform distribution, or deterministically using the trivial empty candidate solution, i.e., having $x_1 = x_2 = \cdots = x_\mu = 0^n$. We do not discuss the choice of an appropriate stopping criterion. Instead we adopt the usual perspective when analysing random search heuristics [1] and analyse the number of function evaluations made until an optimal search point is found for the first time. We refer to this number as optimisation time and are interested in its mean value, the expected optimisation time, as well as its distribution.

We compare the performance of the B-cell algorithm on the longest common subsequence problem with the performance of the same large class of evolutionary algorithms that was analysed by Jansen and Weyland [18], defined as Algorithm 2.

Algorithm 2 (Generic Evolutionary Algorithm)

1. **Initialisation**
   Select $x_1, x_2, \ldots x_\mu \in \{0,1\}^n$.
2. **Repeat**
3.   **Variation**
   For each $i \in \{1, 2, \ldots, \lambda\}$
       Select $z_1 \in \{x_1, \ldots, x_\mu\}$ uniformly at random.
       With probability p_c

> *Select $z_2 \in \{x_1, \ldots, x_\mu\}$ uniformly at random.*
> *For each $j \in \{1, 2, \ldots, n\}$*
>   *Select $y_i[j] \in \{z_1[j], z_2[j]\}$ uniformly at random.*
> *For each $j \in \{1, 2, \ldots, n\}$: With probability $1/n$, invert the bit $y_i[j]$.*
> *Else (with the remaining prob. of $1 - p_c$)*
>   *Set $y_i := z_1$.*
> *For each $j \in \{1, 2, \ldots, n\}$: With probability $1/n$, invert the bit $y_i[j]$.*

4.   **Selection**

> *Sort $x_1, \ldots, x_\mu, y_1, \ldots, y_\lambda$ descending according to fitness breaking ties by sorting $y_1, y_2, \ldots, y_\lambda$ in front of $x_1, x_2, \ldots, x_\mu$, breaking remaining ties uniformly at randomly.*
> *Replace $x_1, \ldots, x_\mu$ by the first μ elements from this sorted sequence.*

5.   *Until STOP.*

The generic evolutionary algorithm defined as Algorithm 2 covers a wide range of different evolutionary algorithms, from the simple and well-known (1+1) EA (with $\mu = \lambda = 1$ and $p_c = 0$, see e.g. [12]), over the (1+λ) EA (with $\mu = 1$, $\lambda > 1$ and $p_c = 0$, see e.g. [15]), the (μ+1) EA (with $\mu > 1$, $\lambda = 1$ and $p_c = 0$, see e.g. [28]) to steady state GAs (with $\mu > 1$, $\lambda > 1$ and $p_c > 0$, see e.g. [17]).

As for the B-cell algorithm (Algorithm 1) we consider random initialisation as well as initialisation with only trivial empty candidate solutions. We use the same perspective for the analysis, of course, counting the number of function evaluations until an optimal solution is found for the first time.

In the following two sections we present results on the performance of the B-cell algorithm and the class of evolutionary algorithms covered in Algorithm 2. In doing so we follow the analysis of Jansen and Weyland [18] for the evolutionary algorithms, i.e., we consider precisely the same instances here that they proved to be hard for evolutionary algorithms. These are four instances, two for f_{LCS} and two that work for the two other functions, f_{HJ} and f_{MAX}. The first two instances are used to show that the evolutionary algorithms fail to locate an optimal solution efficiently. We call these instances E_{MAX} and E_{LCS}. The other two instances are used to show that the evolutionary algorithms even fail to approximate an optimal solution up to a factor of $2 - \varepsilon$ (for any constant $\varepsilon > 0$). We call these two instances A_{MAX} and A_{LCS} and define all four instances in the following definition. All instances are defined over the binary alphabet $\Sigma = \{0, 1\}$. They all assume that the length of the shortest sequence n is a multiple of some integer k. It is easy to generalise the definitions to arbitrary values of n by considering the alpha $\Sigma = \{0, 1, 2\}$ and appending to X_1 the shortest possible sequence of 2 such that the total length is a multiple of k. Note that at most 2^{k-1} needs to be appended. This does not change anything in a significant way and is omitted in the following in order not to unnecessarily complicate the notation. All examples, however, assume that n is sufficiently large.

Definition 2. *For the definition of E_{MAX} let n be a multiple of 32. The instance consists of $X_1 = 0^{(8/32)n} 1^{(24/32)n}$ and $X_2 = 1^{(24/32)n} 0^{(5/32)n} 1^{(13/32)n}$.*

For the definition of E_{LCS} let n be a multiple of 40. The instance consists of $X_1 = 0^{(24/40)n}1^{(16/40)n}$ and $X_2 = 1^n0^{(13/40)n}$.

For the definition of A_{MAX} let $\varepsilon > 0$ constant, $l := \lceil(3/\varepsilon) - (1/2)\rceil$ and n be a multiple of $8l$. The instance consists of $X_1 = 0^{(1/l)n}1^{((l-1)/l)n}$ and $X_2 = 1^{((l-1)/l)n}0^{(5/(8l))n}1^{((4l-3)/(8l))n}$.

For the definition of A_{LCS} let $\varepsilon > 0$ constant, $l := \lceil(5/(2\varepsilon)) - (5/4)\rceil$ and n be a multiple of $16l + 8$. The instance consists of $X_1 = 0^{((l+1)/(2l+1))n}1^{(l/(2l+1))n}$ and $X_2 = 1^n0^{((14l+5)/(16l+8))n}$.

3   Performance with Random Initialisation

In this section we consider the B-cell algorithm (Algorithm 1) and the evolutionary algorithms (Algorithm 2) with random initialisation, i. e., all candidate solutions are initially selected independently and uniformly at random from $\{0,1\}^n$. For this case the evolutionary algorithms have been analysed by Jansen and Weyland [18]. Therefore, we can cite their result (Theorem 5 in [18]).

Theorem 1. *The probabilities that an evolutionary algorithm as defined in Definition 2 using random initialisation finds an optimal solution for the instance E_{MAX} with f_{HJ} or f_{MAX} or an optimal solution for the instance E_{LCS} with f_{LCS} within t function evaluations are $t \cdot e^{-\Omega(n)}$ for all settings of p_c, $\mu = n^{O(1)}$ and $\lambda = n^{O(1)}$.* □

We see that evolutionary algorithms fail to solve a rather simple problem instance. Note that the problem-specific algorithm solves this instance in time $\Theta(n^2)$. We prove that the B-cell algorithm is also very inefficient here.

Theorem 2. *The probabilities that the B-cell algorithm (Definition 1) using random initialisation finds an optimal solution for the instance E_{MAX} with f_{HJ} or f_{MAX} or an optimal solution for the instance E_{LCS} with f_{LCS} within t function evaluations are $t \cdot e^{-\Omega(n)}$ for all settings of $\mu = n^{O(1)}$ and $\lambda = n^{O(1)}$.*

Proof. Consider E_{MAX} and observe that the longest common subsequence is $1^{(24/32)n}$ which is encoded by $0^{(8/32)n}1^{(24/32)n}$. Any bit string s that contains a 1-bit among the first $(8/32)n$ positions encodes a common subsequence of length at most $(18/32)n$ consisting of up to $(5/32)n$ 0-bits and up to $(13/32)n$ 1-bits. An initial bit string contains at least $(3/32)n$ 1-bits in the first $(8/32)n$ bits with probability $1 - e^{-\Omega(n)}$ (Chernoff bounds [23]). To reach the global optimum all 1-bits in the first $(8/32)n$ bits need to be removed. A mutation removing some of these 1-bits can only be accepted if the length of the encoded common subsequence does not decrease. As long as there is at least one 1-bit left the length of the total common subsequence is bounded above by $i + (13/32)n$ where i is the number remaining 1-bits in the first $(8/32)n$ bits.

We observe that there needs to be a mutation that removes $\Omega(n)$ 1-bits in a single step. The probability to do that with standard bit mutations is $e^{-\Omega(n)}$. Hypermutations can only do that if all the 1-bits are in a single contiguous region.

That this is the case initially has probability $e^{-\Omega(n)}$. Note that the positions of the 1-bits among the first $(8/32)n$ bits have no influence on the function value: All bit strings with $i + j$ 1-bits, among these i in the first $(8/32)n$ bits, have equal function value. For symmetry reasons this implies that the probability to have $i = \Omega(n)$ 1-bits (with $i \le (5/32)n$) in $(8/32)n$ bits in a single contiguous region remains $e^{-\Omega(n)}$. This implies the result for E_{MAX}.

The proof of E_{LCS} works along the same lines. The longest common subsequence is $1^{(16/40)n}$ encoded by $0^{(24/40)n}1^{(16/40)n}$. Consider a bit string with i 1-bits among the first $(24/40)n$ bits and j 1-bits among the last $(16/40)n$ bits where $i > 0$ and $j > 0$. It encodes a sequence 0^i1^j. Note that this is not a common subsequence. The function value is $\max\{i - j, j - i\}$ under f_{LCS}. If the bit string consider was generated uniformly at random among all bit strings of length n we have $i - j = \Theta(n)$ with probability $1 - e^{-\Omega(n)}$. In order to find the longest common subsequence one needs to get in a situation with $j > i$. As long as $i > j$ holds reducing i in a mutation is only accepted if it leads to a situation where the number of 1-bits in the first part is smaller than the number of 1-bits in the second part and the number of 1-bits in the second part is at least i. Thus, such a mutation needs to change $\Omega(n)$ bits. As above the probability that appropriate bits are in a contiguous region is $e^{-\Omega(n)}$. Thus, the probability for such a mutation by means of hypermutation as well as by means of standard bit mutation is $e^{-\Omega(n)}$ and the claim on the success probability follows. □

Heuristic algorithms are not expected to solve every instance to optimality. Therefore, it makes sense to investigate if they are able to efficiently find approximate solutions. For evolutionary algorithms it is again known that they can fail to do so even for simple problem instances. We cite the following result (Theorem 6 in [18]).

Theorem 3. *For any constant $\varepsilon > 0$, the probabilities that an evolutionary algorithm as defined in Definition 2 using random initialisation finds an $(2 - \varepsilon)$-approximation for the instance A_{MAX} with f_{HJ} or f_{MAX} or an $(2 - \varepsilon)$-approximation for the instance A_{LCS} with f_{LCS} within t function evaluations is bounded above by $t \cdot e^{-\Omega(n)}$ for all settings of p_c, $\mu = n^{O(1)}$ and $\lambda = n^{O(1)}$.* □

Also here the problem-specific algorithm locates an optimal solution in time $\Theta(n^2)$. Again, the B-cell algorithm also fails at finding good approximations.

Theorem 4. *For any constant $\varepsilon > 0$, the probabilities that the B-cell algorithm (Definition 1) using random initialisation finds an $(2 - \varepsilon)$-approximation for the instance A_{MAX} with f_{HJ} or f_{MAX} or an $(2 - \varepsilon)$-approximation for the instance A_{LCS} with f_{LCS} within t function evaluations is bounded above by $t \cdot e^{-\Omega(n)}$ for all settings of $\mu = n^{O(1)}$ and $\lambda = n^{O(1)}$.*

Proof. The proof for A_{MAX} and A_{LCS} follows the same ideas as the proof of Theorem 2. The main observation is that the problem instances share exactly the same structure: The instances E_{MAX} and A_{MAX} are both of the form $X_1 = 0^{a_1}1^{b_1}$, $X_2 = 1^{a_2}0^{b_2}1^{c_2}$, only the concrete lengths of the parts differ. The instances

E_{LCS} and A_{LCS} are both of the form $X_1 = 0^{a_1}1^{b_1}$, $X_2 = 1^{a_2}0^{b_2}$, only the concrete lengths of the parts differ. Therefore, the line of reasoning carries over when one takes care of changing the lengths as appropriate. The second change is a proof that all second best solutions are worse than $(2 - \varepsilon)$-approximations. This is done in the proof of Theorem 3 in [18]. □

4 Performance with Trivial Empty Initialisation

Julstrom and Hinkemeyer [20] demonstrate empirically that evolutionary algorithms benefit if they are started with initial candidate solutions that are not random but the trivial feasible solutions, the empty sequence. In our encoding these are encoded by the all zero bit string. We use this idea here and analyse the performance of evolutionary algorithms as well as the performance of the B-cell algorithm using is deterministic kind of initialisation. We consider exactly the same problem instances as in Section 3. It turns out to be the case that evolutionary algorithms are not able to profit from this change in initialisation in a significant way. The B-cell algorithm, on the other hand, shows drastically improved performance. We prove this rigorously in the following for all four problem instances.

Theorem 5. *The probabilities that an evolutionary algorithm as defined in Definition 2 using initialisation with only trivial empty candidate solutions finds an optimal solution for the instance E_{MAX} with f_{HJ} or f_{MAX} or an optimal solution for the instance E_{LCS} with f_{LCS} within t function evaluations are $t \cdot e^{-\Omega(n)}$ for all settings of p_c, $\mu = n^{O(1)}$ and $\lambda = n^{O(1)}$.*

Proof. We consider E_{MAX} first. The initial bit strings are all 0^n. We remember from the proof of Theorem 1 that the global optimum is $0^{(8/32)n}1^{(24/32)n}$ and it is problematic to have 1-bits among the first $(8/32)n$ bits. Once a bit string with no 1-bits among the first $(8/32)n$ bits and more than $(13/32)n$ 1-bits in the remaining bits is reached new 1-bits in the first $(8/32)n$ bits can only be introduced if the number of 1-bits in the rest falls below $(13/32)n$. We prove that even this situation is not reached with probability $e^{-\Omega(n)}$.

With probability $1 - e^{-\Omega(n)}$ the number of mutations needed to introduce more than $(13/32)n$ 1-bits is $\Omega(n)$. Note that crossover cannot introduce actually new 1-bits. It can only collect 1-bits that have been created by mutation first. Thus, $\Omega(n)$ variation steps are needed with probability $1 - e^{-\Omega(n)}$. As long as the number of 1-bits in the last $(24/32)n$ bits of the bit string is at most $(13/32)n$ it increases the function value if in addition 1-bits are created in the first $(8/32)n$ bits. Thus, with probability $1 - e^{-\Omega(n)}$ there are $\Omega(n)$ 1-bits among the first $(8/32)n$ bits before the number of 1-bits in the remaining part of the bit string exceeds $(13/32)n$ for the first time. The proof of Theorem 1 relies only on the fact that initially there are $\Omega(n)$ 1-bits among the first $(8/32)n$ bits after random initialisation. We see that with probability $1 - e^{-\Omega(n)}$ the algorithm is in the same situation after $\Omega(n)$ variation steps. Therefore, the rest of the claim follows from Theorem 1.

For E_{LCS} the proof follows the same lines of thought. It is important to note that f_{LCS} allows the introductions of 1-bits in the first $(24/40)n$ bits and the last $(16/40)n$ bits simultaneously. If we have 1-bits in both parts the function value is determined by the difference in the number of 1-bits. For the proof of Theorem 1 the crucial observation is that with probability $e^{-\Omega(n)}$ an initial bit string contains $\Omega(n)$ more 1-bits in the first $(24/40)n$ bits than in the remaining $(16/40)n$ bits. This holds since $(24/40)n - (16/40)n = (8/40)n = \Omega(n)$. As for E_{MAX} new 1-bits can only be introduced by means of mutation. Crossover cannot create a 1-bit at a position where no 1-bit has been created before. When b 1-bits are created in an arbitrary number of mutations we have $\Omega(b)$ more 1-bits among the first $(24/40)n$ bits with probability $e^{-\Omega(b)}$. Since we need to create $\Theta(n)$ 1-bits we see that with probability $1 - e^{-\Omega(n)}$ we get in essentially the same situation as if we had random initialisation. Thus, the rest of the claim follows from Theorem 1. □

We see that changed initialisation does not help evolutionary algorithms for these problem instances. We prove that for the B-cell algorithm things are entirely different.

Theorem 6. *The probabilities that the B-cell algorithm (Definition 1) using initialisation with only trivial empty candidate solutions finds an optimal solution for the instance E_{MAX} with f_{HJ} or f_{MAX} or an optimal solution for the instance E_{LCS} with f_{LCS} within $O(\mu\lambda n^2 \log n)$ function evaluations are $1 - e^{-\Omega(\mu\lambda)}$ for all settings of $\mu = n^{O(1)}$ and $\lambda = n^{O(1)}$. For all settings of $\mu = n^{O(1)}$ and $\lambda = n^{O(1)}$ with $\mu\lambda = \omega(n \log n)$ the expected optimisation time is $O(\mu\lambda n^2 \log n)$.*

Proof. The crucial observation for both instances, E_{MAX} and E_{LCS}, is the following. The initial bit strings are all 0^n. There exist positive constants a, b with $1 > a > b > 0$ such that the following holds. If in the very first mutation within a specific contiguous region of length an at least bn bits are flipped to 1 without changing any of the other $(a - b)n$ bits one is in a situation where reaching the global optimum is no harder than optimising the well-known OneMax function that yields as function value the number of 1-bits in a bit string.

We need a lower bound on the probability to achieve this within a single mutation. The probability that a standard bit mutation does not change anything is $(1-1/n)^n \geq 1/(2e)$. For the hypermutation there are $n \cdot (a - 3b/2)$ possible choices for the position p such that there are at least $n \cdot b/2$ choices for the length l. Thus, the probability for such a mutation is at least $(n/(n+1)) \cdot (a - 3b/2) \cdot b/(4e) \geq \varepsilon$ for some constant $\varepsilon > 0$.

In the first round of the algorithm we perform $\mu\lambda$ mutations. Each of these creates one such favourable bit string with probability at least ε. Thus, the probability that such a candidate solution is created in the first round is bounded below by $1 - (1 - \varepsilon)^{\mu\lambda} = 1 - e^{-\Omega(\mu\lambda)}$. A candidate solution with this property can never be lost since all candidate solutions that do not have this property have smaller function values. For $\mu = \lambda = 1$ the number of steps that are sufficient to reach the global optimum are known to be $O(n^2 \log n)$ for OneMax [19]. With μ candidate solutions each creating λ new candidate solutions in each round of the algorithm we obtain the trivial bound of $O(\mu\lambda n^2 \log n)$ for the expected number of steps until a global optimum is found. This implies the first part of the claim.

For the statement about the expected optimisation time we make the following observation. For any bit string we can reach the global optimum by means of standard bit mutations with probability at least $n^{-n} = e^{-n \ln n}$ and do not destroy this by the subsequent hypermutation with probability at least $1/(n+1)$. This implies an upper bound of $O(ne^{n \log n})$ on the expected optimisation time. We already know that the expected optimisation time is bounded above by $O(\mu\lambda n^2 \log n)$ when in the first round of the algorithm a favourable bit string is created and that this happens with with probability $1 - e^{-\Omega(\mu\lambda)}$. For the total expected optimisation time this implies an upper bound of $\left(1 - e^{-\Omega(\mu\lambda)}\right) \cdot O(\mu\lambda n^2 \log n) + e^{-\Omega(\mu\lambda)} \cdot O(ne^{n \log n}) = O(\mu\lambda n^2 \log n) + e^{O(n \log n) - \Omega(\mu\lambda)}$. With $\mu\lambda = \omega(n \log n)$ this is $O(\mu\lambda n^2 \log n)$.   □

We see that the B-cell algorithm benefits from deterministic initialisation here since the use of somatic contiguous hypermutations allows it to introduce a linear number of 1-bits in a region where they are needed in a single step. It is interesting to note that for that bound that we proved it makes no difference how we set μ and λ as long as $\mu \cdot \lambda$ remains unchanged. In evolutionary algorithms the choice of the population size μ and the offspring population size λ are known to have quite different effects [15,28].

We remark that the upper bound of $O(\mu\lambda n^2 \log n)$ is not tight. On the one hand while there is a unique longest common subsequence for each of the instances this unique longest common subsequence does not have a unique encoding. Having much more than a single global optimum in search space makes the task of optimisation simpler than for OneMax so that there is room for improving the upper bound on these grounds. On the other hand extending the $O(n^2 \log n)$ due to Jansen and Zarges [19] to $O(\mu\lambda n^2 \log n)$ is too pessimistic. Taking into account results on the $(\mu+1)$ EA [28] and the $(1+\lambda)$ EA [15] hints at better upper bounds. We do not make this additional effort since the point that the B-cell algorithm outperforms evolutionary algorithms very clearly has already been established in this simpler way.

Just as in Section 3 we also consider approximation in addition to solving the problem optimally. For evolutionary algorithms, again, the different initialisation does not lead to an improved behaviour.

Theorem 7. *For any constant $\varepsilon > 0$, the probabilities that an evolutionary algorithm as defined in Definition 2 using initialisation with only trivial empty candidate solutions finds an $(2 - \varepsilon)$-approximation for the instance A_{MAX} with f_{HJ} or f_{MAX} or an $(2 - \varepsilon)$-approximation for the instance A_{LCS} with f_{LCS} within t function evaluations is bounded above by $t \cdot e^{-\Omega(n)}$ for all settings of p_c, $\mu = n^{O(1)}$ and $\lambda = n^{O(1)}$.*

Proof. The proof can be carried out in the same way as the proof of Theorem 5. With probability $1 - e^{-\Omega(n)}$ after $\Omega(n)$ variations the algorithm is a situation that has all the properties that are required for the proof of Theorem 1. In that situation the proof follows from the result in [18].   □

For the B-cell algorithm, however, we are again able to prove that using trivial empty candidate solutions implies very good performance.

Theorem 8. *The probabilities that the B-cell algorithm (Definition 1) using initialisation with only trivial empty candidate solutions for the instance A_{MAX} with f_{HJ} or f_{MAX} or an $(2 - \varepsilon)$-approximation for the instance A_{LCS} with f_{LCS} within $O(\mu \lambda n^2 \log n)$ function evaluations are $1 - e^{-\Omega(\mu \lambda)}$ for all settings of $\mu = n^{O(1)}$ and $\lambda = n^{O(1)}$. For all settings of $\mu = n^{O(1)}$ and $\lambda = n^{O(1)}$ with $\mu \lambda = \omega(n \log n)$ the expected optimisation time is $O(\mu \lambda n^2 \log n)$.*

Proof. For the instances A_{MAX} and A_{LCS} we have the same as for E_{MAX} and E_{LCS}. We have a probability $\Omega(1)$ that a mutation of the all zero bit string creates a bit string that is close to the global optimum that the optimisation process will not be distracted into areas of local optima with linear Hamming distance to the global optima. Therefore, following the lines of reasoning from the proof of Theorem 6 we obtain the same result.   □

We point out that for the instances A_{MAX} and A_{LCS} the B-cell algorithm actually finds optimal solution in the time given in Theorem 8, not only approximate solutions.

5   Conclusions

We have reconsidered work on randomised search heuristics applied to the problem of computing longest common subsequences. Hinkemeyer and Julstrom [13] have presented an encoding of the problem that allows to employ randomised search heuristics for its solution and have empirically demonstrated that evolutionary algorithms have good performance. Moreover, Julstrom and Hinkemeyer [20] have empirically demonstrated that the performance of evolutionary algorithms becomes even better when the algorithms are not initialised with random candidate solutions but deterministically with the trivial empty solution instead. Jansen and Weyland [18] picked up on the encoding and proved for a large class of evolutionary algorithms with random initialisation that they perform very badly in the worst case and the average case. This was proved by presenting problem instances that are difficult for random search heuristics since they contain bad local optima that are very far away from global optima in the search space.

We considered the difficult problem instances presented by Jansen and Weyland [18] and analysed the performance of the B-cell algorithm [21] on these instances. With random initialisation we proved lower bounds for the B-cell algorithm that essentially match the known lower bounds for evolutionary algorithms. Picking up the insight due to Julstrom and Hinkemeyer [20] we additionally considered deterministic initialisation with trivial empty solutions. We proved that evolutionary algorithms do not benefit from this change in initialisation in the worst case and the average case by obtaining the same bounds as for the case of random initialisation. For the B-cell algorithm, however, we proved that with this deterministic initialisation it is very efficient. It optimises all the

difficult instances we considered almost surely even with a tiny population, i. e.
with probability $1 - \omega(1)$ with $\mu \cdot \lambda = \omega(1)$. Moreover, with a population of
moderate size its expected optimisation time is polynomial, i. e. $O(\mu\lambda n^2 \log n)$
with $\mu \cdot \lambda = \omega(n \log n)$. This demonstrates that the B-cell algorithm can be a
very efficient alternative to evolutionary algorithms. Since it does not make use
of crossover it is in general easier to analyse contributing to closing the gap
between theory and practice.

It remains an open problem to explain the good performance of evolutionary
algorithms that was observed by Julstrom and Hinkemeyer [13,20]. It would be
worthwhile to determine natural and practically relevant classes of problem instances where evolutionary algorithms provably perform well. For such instances
one would like to again compare the performance of the B-cell algorithm to the
performance of evolutionary algorithms.

Computing longest common subsequences is after vertex cover [16] the second
classical combinatorial optimisation problem where the B-cell algorithm is provably a better choice than evolutionary algorithms. It would interesting to see
how the two nature-inspired approaches compare for more and other problems.
A long-term research goal is to gain a principled understanding for which type of
problems the B-cell algorithm should be preferred over evolutionary algorithms.

Acknowledgments. This material is based in part upon works supported by
the Science Foundation Ireland under Grant No. 07/SK/I1205. Christine Zarges
is supported by a fellowship within the PostDoc-Programme of the German
Academic Exchange Service (DAAD).

References

1. Auger, A., Doerr, B. (eds.): Theory of Randomized Search Heurisitcs. World Scientific (2011)
2. Burnet, F.M.: The Clonal Selection Theory of Acquired Immunity. Cambridge
   University Press (1959)
3. de Castro, L., Timmis, J.: An artificial immune network for multimodal function
   optimization. In: Proc. of the 4th Congress on Evolutionary Computation (CEC
   2002), pp. 699–704. IEEE Press (2002)
4. de Castro, L., Zuben, F.: Learning and optimization using the clonal selection
   principle. IEEE Transactions on Evolutionary Computation 6(3), 239–251 (2002)
5. Clark, E., Hone, A., Timmis, J.: A Markov Chain Model of the B-Cell Algorithm.
   In: Jacob, C., Pilat, M.L., Bentley, P.J., Timmis, J.I. (eds.) ICARIS 2005. LNCS,
   vol. 3627, pp. 318–330. Springer, Heidelberg (2005)
6. Cormen, T.H., Leiserson, C.E., Rivest, R.L., Stein, C.: Introduction to Algorithms.
   MIT Press (2001)
7. Cortés, N.C., Coello Coello, C.A.: Multiobjective Optimization Using Ideas from
   the Clonal Selection Principle. In: Cantú-Paz, E., Foster, J.A., Deb, K., Davis, L.,
   Roy, R., O'Reilly, U.-M., Beyer, H.-G., Kendall, G., Wilson, S.W., Harman, M.,
   Wegener, J., Dasgupta, D., Potter, M.A., Schultz, A., Dowsland, K.A., Jonoska,
   N., Miller, J., Standish, R.K. (eds.) GECCO 2003. LNCS, vol. 2723, pp. 158–170.
   Springer, Heidelberg (2003)

8. Cutello, V., Nicosia, G., Pavone, M.: Exploring the Capability of Immune Algorithms: A Characterization of Hypermutation Operators. In: Nicosia, G., Cutello, V., Bentley, P.J., Timmis, J. (eds.) ICARIS 2004. LNCS, vol. 3239, pp. 263–276. Springer, Heidelberg (2004)
9. Dasgupta, D., Niño, F.: Immunological Computation: Theory and Applications. Auerbach (2008)
10. De Jong, K.A.: Evolutionary Computation. A Unified Approach. MIT Press (2006)
11. Dorigo, M., Stützle, T.: Ant Colony Optimization. MIT Press (2004)
12. Droste, S., Jansen, T., Wegener, I.: On the analysis of the $(1+1)$ evolutionary algorithm. Theoretical Computer Science 276, 51–81 (2002)
13. Hinkemeyer, B., Julstrom, B.A.: A genetic algorithm for the longest common subsequence problem. In: Proc. of the 8th Annual Genetic and Evolutionary Computation Conf. (GECCO 2006), pp. 609–610. ACM Press (2006)
14. Jansen, T.: Simulated annealing. In: Auger, A., Doerr, B. (eds.) Theory of Randomized Search Heuristics, pp. 171–196. World Scientific (2011)
15. Jansen, T., De Jong, K.A., Wegener, I.: On the choice of the offspring population size in evolutionary algorithms. Evolutionary Computation 13(4), 413–440 (2005)
16. Jansen, T., Oliveto, P.S., Zarges, C.: On the Analysis of the Immune-Inspired B-Cell Algorithm for the Vertex Cover Problem. In: Liò, P., Nicosia, G., Stibor, T. (eds.) ICARIS 2011. LNCS, vol. 6825, pp. 117–131. Springer, Heidelberg (2011)
17. Jansen, T., Wegener, I.: On the analysis of evolutionary algorithms — a proof that crossover really can help. Algorithmica 34(1), 47–66 (2002)
18. Jansen, T., Weyland, D.: Analysis of evolutionary algorithms for the longest common subsequence problem. Algorithmica 57, 170–186 (2010)
19. Jansen, T., Zarges, C.: Analyzing different variants of immune inspired somatic contiguous hypermutations. Theoretical Computer Science 412(6), 517–533 (2011)
20. Julstrom, B.A., Hinkemeyer, B.: Starting from Scratch: Growing Longest Common Subsequences with Evolution. In: Runarsson, T.P., Beyer, H.-G., Burke, E.K., Merelo-Guervós, J.J., Whitley, L.D., Yao, X. (eds.) PPSN 2006. LNCS, vol. 4193, pp. 930–938. Springer, Heidelberg (2006)
21. Kelsey, J., Timmis, J.: Immune Inspired Somatic Contiguous Hypermutation for Function Optimisation. In: Cantú-Paz, E., Foster, J.A., Deb, K., Davis, L., Roy, R., O'Reilly, U.-M., Beyer, H.-G., Kendall, G., Wilson, S.W., Harman, M., Wegener, J., Dasgupta, D., Potter, M.A., Schultz, A., Dowsland, K.A., Jonoska, N., Miller, J., Standish, R.K. (eds.) GECCO 2003. LNCS, vol. 2723, pp. 207–218. Springer, Heidelberg (2003)
22. Maier, D.: The complexity of some problems on subsequences and supersequences. Journal of the ACM 25(2), 322–336 (1978)
23. Motwani, R., Raghavan, P.: Randomized Algorithms. Cambridge University Press (1995)
24. Mousavi, S.R., Tabataba, F.: An improved algorithm for the longest common subsequence problem. Computers & Operations Research 39, 512–520 (2012)
25. Murphy, K., Travers, P., Walport, M.: Janeway's Immunobiology, 8th edn., Oxford (2011)
26. Tabataba, F.S., Mousavi, S.R.: A hyper-heuristic for the longest common subsequence problem. Computational Biology and Chemistry 36, 42–54 (2012)
27. Wang, Q., Pan, M., Shang, Y., Korkin, D.: A fast heuristic search algorithm for finding the longest common subsequence of multiple strings. In: Proc. of the Twenty-Fourth AAAI Conf. on Artificial Intelligence, AAAI 2010 (2010)
28. Witt, C.: Runtime analysis of the $(\mu+1)$ EA on simple pseudo-boolean functions. Evolutionary Computation 14(1), 65–86 (2006)

Bait a Trap: Introducing Natural Killer Cells to Artificial Immune System for Spyware Detection

Jun Fu[1], Huan Yang[1], Yiwen Liang[2], and Chengyu Tan[2,*]

[1] The 28th Research Institute of CETC, China
{doctorfj,happyfairy106}@163.com
[2] Computer School, Wuhan University, China
ywliang@whu.edu.cn, nadinetan@163.com

Abstract. Artificial Immune System (AIS) achieved some success in malware detection with its distributed, diverse and adaptive characteristics. However, in recent years, malware is evolving quickly in respect of stealth and complexity. This trend has brought a great challenge for AIS, especially when spyware emerged. To solve this problem, natural killer cells (NKs) which can lure latent viruses to expose themselves are introduced to AIS in this paper. We hope their counterparts can enhance the anti-latent capability of AIS by enticement strategy and collaboration with other AIS algorithms. Preliminary results show that artificial NKs can discover tiny abnormalities caused by novel spyware, and then release proper bait (called induction cytokines) to trigger the spyware's actions which will expose itself to further detection by AIS.

Keywords: Natural Killer Cells, Artificial Immune System, Spyware.

1 Introduction

From tricks to means of cyber crimes, malware is evolving quickly in respect of purpose, stealth and complexity. In recent years, with the extensive use of network services, spyware is becoming a new trend of malware evolution [1].

Unlike viruses and worms, spyware is designed to make money by stealing users' privacy or confidential data, rather than harm the computer systems or self-reproduce in the network [2]. Therefore, it usually works in a stealth manner to survive as long as possible. This makes spyware increases sharply, and has become the main threats for Internet users [1, 3].

Detection techniques are effective means to combat spyware. These solutions continue the idea of malware detection, and employ either signature based or behavior based philosophies [4]. Though signature based systems have the advantage of detecting known spyware with a high degree of accuracy, they are incapable of detecting novel threats [5]. Behavior based approaches, on the other hand, can detect partial new spyware [6–9] with acceptable accuracy [10–13], and acquire some anti-latent abilities [3, 4, 14, 15]. But on the whole, the adaptability of the method needs to be further enhanced.

---

* Corresponding author.

C.A. Coello Coello et al. (Eds.): ICARIS 2012, LNCS 7597, pp. 125–138, 2012.
© Springer-Verlag Berlin Heidelberg 2012

Artificial immune system (AIS) is an emerging interdisciplinary subject which encompasses a spectrum of algorithms. Using the human immune system (HIS) that fight against pathogen as inspiration, AIS is a decentralized, diverse and adaptive system, and gradually becomes a promising approach to malware detection [16]. A popular theory in recent years - danger theory, has made good results in behavior based spyware detection [17–19]. However, when detecting more latent spyware, danger theory methods are prone to be evaded because these spyware may not result in obvious danger signals [18].

There are also hidden invaders in human bodies - latent viruses. They lie dormant within cells and reduce activities to escape from most attacks launched by HIS. But HIS still has other weapons to find traces of latent viruses invasions and induce the viruses to exhibit obvious actions. These weapons are natural killer cells (NKs) in innate immune system [20].

The work discussed here is motivated by the interest in the induction mechanism of NKs. We believe this mechanism that works in nature should work for machines. So we introduce NKs to AIS, hoping that their artifacts can deal with the difficulties in latent spyware detection. These artificial NKs we construct work in population. They can capture subtle traces of unknown spyware, and then adaptively release some bait (called induction cytokines) to trigger its actions. If the spyware is interested in the bait, it will exhibit malicious behaviors which expose itself to further detection.

2   Related Work to Spyware Detection

The success of any spyware is determined by its ability to evade detection. Therefore, spyware often uses the following two ways to hide themselves:

1. **Hiding presence**: spyware can hide its files, registries and process with the help of rootkit, making it looks like the spyware does not exist.
2. **Hiding behavior**: most of spyware behaviors are not destructive or forbidden. Besides, these behaviors are blended in with legitimate behaviors.

The latent characteristics above undoubtedly bring a great challenge to both signature spyware based detection and behavior based spyware detection.

2.1   Signature Based Approach

Signature based method constructs a database of all known spyware, and compares the suspected executable to the database entries. Although this method has the advantage of detecting known spyware with high accuracy, it suffers from not being able to detect unknown spyware and variants of known spyware [5].

2.2   Behavior Based Approach

To address the shortcomings of signature based methods, recent work pays attention to the behavior based approach. Adaptivity, low false positive (FP) rate and anti-latent are the goals of these methods.

Early behavior based methods concerned about only one type of behavior, such as sending the intercepted information to remote locations [6, 7], auto-start without invocation [8] and hiding resources (files, processes, etc.) [9]. Although achieved some success, it is hard for these methods to detect spyware accurately, since legitimate applications also perform the same behavior.

To address this issue, methods correlate between different behaviors [10–13] were proposed. They reduced the FP rate by a comprehensive analysis of multiple kinds of behaviors performed by monitored programs. The analysis techniques they utilized include dynamic analysis [10, 11], rule based approach [12] and statistical method [13].

In addition, induction based approaches [3, 4, 14, 15] were proposed to detect latent spyware. These systems such as Siren [3], SpyCon [4] and HoneyID [14] generated crafted human input to trigger spyware's actions, and were difficult to be escaped by specific spyware. Unfortunately, they can not detect different kinds of spyware, because the means of induction were static and lack of adaptability.

Immune inspired algorithms, especially algorithms in danger theory performed well in spyware detection in recent years because of their adaptivity, low FP rate and quick response [17–19]. Inspired by hotly debated 'danger model' [21], they detected spyware by definition, perception and fusion of danger signals. But, when detecting more latent spyware, they are prone to be evaded because these spyware may not result in obvious danger signals.

Overall, the advantages of adaptivity, low FP rate and anti-latent were achieved in some degrees in existing behavior-based methods. But there are no solutions encompassing all of them. This is what we want to overcome in this paper.

3   Introducing Natural Killer Cells

In human bodies, latent viruses escape from recognition and destruction by reducing their own activities and down regulating MHC-I (molecules reflect the state of the cells) production in infected cells. However, recent studies of NKs have showed that they can distinguish between healthy cells and virally infected cells by using a sophisticated repertoire of cell surface receptors that control their activation and effecter functions [22]. After recognition, infected cells are killed and latent viruses within the cells are reactivated and exposed [23]. This is helpful to HIS to further detect latent viruses.

3.1   NK Receptor Signal Transduction

NK has many surface receptors (NK cell receptors, NKRs) which finely regulate the cell functions by signal transduction. They can be classified into two classes: inhibitory receptors (IRs) and activating receptors (ARs), shown in Fig. 1.

NKs recognize MHC I molecules via IRs that deliver signals (inhibitory signals) that inhibit NK cytotoxicity. Accordingly, cells which have lost or expressed insufficient amounts of MHC I molecules may be killed. This frequently occurs when target cells are infected by certain viruses.

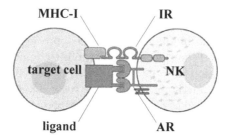

Fig. 1. NK surface receptors and their binding molecules

Viral invasion may change the structures of molecules on cell surface. These changed molecules (called 'ligands') are what the ARs bind. Interaction between ligands and ARs deliver signals (activating signals) that activate NK cytotoxicity.

When inhibitory signals and activating signals are transmitted inside NK by above receptors, the balance between these 'off' and 'on' signals determines the NK cytotoxicity [22]. For healthy cells, NK will not kill them because a lot of inhibitory signals and no activating signals are delivered. But cells infected by viruses will be killed since more activating signals are delivered.

3.2   NK-Mediated Immune Responses

Activated NKs produce proteins, such as perforins, NK cytotoxic factors, to split target cell. This causes the exposure of latent viruses within cells and a certain degree of tissue damage which are beneficial for antigen presenting cells (APCs) to collect danger signals and viral antigen.

Besides, NK interferon (IFN) and tumor necrosis factor (TNF) production are responsible for immunoregulation which include:

- **reactivation of latent virus**: Sometimes, virus latency is caused by the poor condition provided by host cell for virus propagation. The release of IFN and TNF can induce the differentiation of the host cell which provide favorable conditions for virus propagation, and thus reactivate the latent virus to perform obvious malicious activities [23].
- **interaction with dendritic cells**: Many studies have shown that there is a close interaction between NKs and DCs (a kind of professional APC). On one hand, IFN and TNF can promote DC maturation [24, 25]; on the other, cytokines secreted by matured DC can enhance the cytotoxicity of NK [25].

4   Artificial NK Model

The NK model is population based, as in Fig. 2. Every cell in population has the ability to perceive inhibitory signals and activating signals. The concentration of these two signals determines whether the NK can be activated. Once activated,

NK will release induction cytokines (ICs) to lure latent spyware to make additional activities. Meanwhile, stimulation signal is produced by NK population to notify other AIS algorithms (such as DCA) to recognize the activities triggered by ICs to decide the presence of spyware. According to the final decision, other AIS components will feedback the induction effect to help NK population adjust the proportion of various ICs.

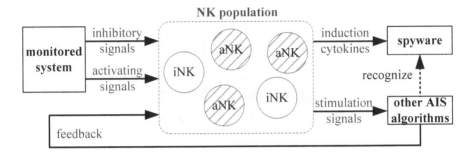

Fig. 2. NK population and the framework of our detection method. aNK stands for active NK and iNK stands for inactive NK.

The detail of every NK's input signals and output cytokines is as follows:

- **Inhibitory signal**: signals that inhibit NK activation. In silico, they are derived from the expression of a program's appearance, such as process, file and registry which are the different sources of inhibitory signals.
- **Activating signal**: signals that promote NK activation. They are derived from the spying behaviors exhibited by a program. Activating signal has multiple sources which reflect different kinds of spying behaviors, such as key logging, information collecting and leaking, etc.
- **Induction cytokine**: cytokines produced by activated NKs. They are implemented by generating bogus user activities in computer systems.

The diverse cells in population recognize different combinations of input signals, and produce different ICs. Under pressure to survive, they will compete with each other, and ultimately promote the evolution of the population.

4.1   Cell Representation

Based on the abstract model of NK behaviors, the artificial NK is represented as follows:

$$NK\ (NKRs,\ Fitness,\ AV,\ Status,\ IC)$$

- **NKRs**: each NK contains N_{NKR} artificial NKRs which are either IR or AR. They together decide whether to activate the NK.

- **Fitness**: inadaptable cell which is measured by fitness will die out in evolution. The higher the value of fitness, the better the adaption.
- **Activating Value (AV)**: cumulative value which increases when activating signals are perceived by ARs, but decreases when inhibitory signals are perceived by IRs.
- **Status**: initial NK is of 'inactive' status in which the cell just perceives signals. When AV exceeds a certain threshold, NK will change status to 'active' and begin to produce ICs.
- **IC**: each NK can produce a specific type of IC. Since the activities tracked by spyware are diverse, NK population maintains the diversity of ICs, and gradually selects an appropriate combination of ICs through evolution.

Artificial NKR is one of the main components of NK. It is used to perceive inhibitory signals or activating signals. NKR is expressed as follows:

NKR (Type, Ligand, Affinity, Weight)

- **Type**: describes whether the NKR is IR or AR.
- **Ligand**: for each type of signal, multiple signals can be defined according to different sources. For example, process, file and registry expressions of a program can be used as different sources for inhibitory signals. Ligand indicates which source does the NKR 'binds'.
- **Affinity**: indicates the degree of the binding between NKR and its corresponding ligand. It determines the value of the signal perceived by NKR.
- **Weight**: the extent of anomaly or normal reflected by signals is different. As a result, the weight of each NKR is not the same. A simple example is that for AR, $Weight > 0$; and for IR, $Weight < 0$.

Each NKR can only perceive signals from one source. Therefore, combination of NKRs is needed to perceive different signals which brings NK not only diversity, but also adaption differences.

4.2   Recognition and Response

To steal valuable data, spyware has to do something which will cause slight changes in monitored system. This information is reflected by signals. The perception of these signals is the beginning of the NK population recognition.

Each cell in NK population has the ability to perceive and accumulate signals. Different combinations of signals determine whether the NK can be activated. The more activating signals the cell experienced, the more likely it will be activated. When many cells are activated in population, it is the sign that the anomaly occurs. The following is the NK population recognition algorithm.

In line 9 of Algorithm 1, the AV is calculated as Equation 1. AV_{before} and AV_{after} are the activating values before and after $mNKRs$ perceive a signal.

$$AV_{after} = AV_{before} + \sum_{mNKRs} Affinity * Weight \qquad (1)$$

Algorithm 1: NK population recognition algorithm

Input: Signals (both inhibitory and activating)
Output: The status of NK (active or inactive)

```
 1 forall the signals do
 2 |   forall the NKs do
 3 |   |   set the affinity of all NKRs to 0;
 4 |   |   get signal s;
 5 |   |   find all NKRs (mNKRs) that match s;
 6 |   |   forall the mNKRs do
 7 |   |   |   mNKR.affinity = s.value;
 8 |   |   end
 9 |   |   calculate the AV of the NK;
10 |   |   if AV ≥ TA (activating threshold) and NK.status == inactive then
11 |   |   |   NK.status = active;
12 |   |   end
13 |   end
14 end
```

Once activated, NK produces ICs to induce spyware which is sensitive to user activities. So, we implement IC by generating bogus user activities. If spyware can not differentiate bogus activities from real ones, they will respond to them and the probability of the spyware avoiding detection will decay exponentially in continuous stimulation by bogus activities [3].

A **induction cytokine (IC)** is defined as a sequence of n bogus user activities $IC = \{UA_1, UA_2, \ldots, UA_n\}$, where $\forall 1 \leq i \leq j \leq n, time(UA_i) \leq time(UA_j)$. Logically, IC can be described as follows:

$$IC(K_{UA}, R, C_0, T_I, T_N, f)$$

- K_{UA}: The kind of IC which specifies the type of user activity to be simulated, such as keystroke, file operation, network request and so on.
- R: The effect of IC is cyclical for continuous stimulation. R is the cycle number. Each cycle is divided into induction period and non-induction period. Only in the induction period the bogus events will be generated.
- C_0: the concentration of IC in the beginning of each cycle. C_0 gives the initial frequency of the simulation in each induction period.
- T_I: the time span of each induction period.
- T_N: the time span of each non-induction period. In this paper, we set $T_I = T_N$. The differences between behaviors exhibited by programs in both periods provide the basis to discover spyware.
- f: the function of the concentration of IC and time in induction period.

There are a great number of different ICs produced by all active NKs. In order to improve the overall induction effect, NK population selects a few kinds of ICs according to the number descendingly, and then merges them according to their kinds. After that, the ICs released by NK population is a sequence of IC ($\{IC_1, IC_2, \ldots, IC_n\}$) where the following properties hold true:

- $\forall i, j \in \{1, 2, \ldots, n\}, IC_i.K_{UA} \neq IC_j.K_{UA}(i \neq j)$
- $\forall i \in \{1, 2, \ldots, n-1\}, time(IC_{i+1}) = time(IC_i) + (IC_i.T_I + IC_i.T_N) * IC_i.R$

In the same time of releasing ICs, NK population releases stimulation signals to guide other AIS components working with ICs cooperatively. By comparing the activities conducted by programs in both induction period and non-induction period, other AIS components will discover spyware lurking in the host.

4.3   Population Evolution

In living organisms, NKs are evolving with the evolution of species to defense pandemic virus. Taking this for inspiration, we proposed the evolution process for artificial NK in which its status changes over time (shown in Fig 3).

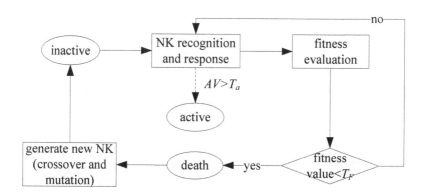

Fig. 3. The lifecycle of NK. Initially, NK is inactive and only perceives signals to accumulate AV. When $AV > T_A$, NK is activated and starts to produce specific IC. After recognizing each signal, the fitness of the cell will be evaluated. When fitness value is less than a certain threshold (T_F), the cell changes the status to death and will be replaced by a new cell which is generated by crossover and mutation processes.

Population Initialization: First of all, all cells in population need to be generated. The initialization process is as follows:

First, the proportions of different IC kinds are set to $p_{K1} = p_{K2} = \ldots = p_{Kn} = 1$. This means that probability of generating each kind of IC is equal according to Equation 2. After initialization, when NK population receives feedback which reflects the effect of the IC it released, the proportion of the kind of that IC will be adjusted accordingly. The bigger the proportion is, the likely the IC of that kind will be generated and arranged to a new NK.

$$prob(Ki) = p_{Ki}/\sum_{j=1}^{n} p_{Kj}, \forall i \qquad (2)$$

Second, all parameters of NK are initialized. Probability-based methods are used in the initialization of NKRs and IC.

Fitness Evaluation: The evaluation process can help NK population to eliminate inappropriate cells. This is done through the calculation of fitness value of NK, as shown in Equation 3. $Fitness_{before}$ and $Fitness_{after}$ are the fitness values before and after $mNKRs$ perceive a signal respectively. C_{decay} is the attenuation coefficient of the fitness value ($0 < C_{decay} < 1$).

$$Fitness_{after} = Fitness_{before} * (1 - C_{decay}) + \sum_{mNKRs} Affinity * |Weight| \quad (3)$$

From Equation 3, it can be seen that if a cell has not perceived any signal for a long time, then its fitness value will decrease continuously. With the death of the cells with low fitness values, NK population will gradually have the ability to adapt to the current environment.

Cell Turnover: After experiencing a few signals, cells in the population will go through a turnover stage following the steps below:

1. Elimination of inappropriate cells: delete cell whose status is death.
2. Generation of new cells by crossover: In this step, parents are selected using Roulette method according to the fitness value of the cell, and single point crossover is performed for their NKR strings. Besides, the IC kind of the offspring is determined by Equation 2, and the fitness value of the offspring is the mean of the parents'. The crossover process will be repeated until the number of cells in population is equal to the original one.
3. Mutation of new cells: In order to enhance the diversity of the cells, new cells generated by crossover need to undergo a mutation process. This involves the substitution of the ligand of each NKR randomly and replacement of another kind of IC according to Equation 2.

5   Experiments

In this section, the induction functionality of artificial NK model will be validated. More specifically, the ability of the IC to lure a spyware to perform obvious behaviors is to be verified. And the ability of the NK population to release different kinds of IC against different spyware is also to be verified.

5.1   Introduction to Spyware Instances

Most spyware are running in the Windows XP environment. Two typical instances of them were selected: *Actual Spy V3.0* and *Spybot V1.2*. Their functions and features are compared in Table 1.

Table 1. Function and feature comparison between *Actual Spy V3.0* and *Spybot V1.2*

Functions/Features	Actual Spy V3.0	Spybot V1.2
Keystroke logging		$\checkmark$
File operation logging	$\checkmark$	
Internet traces logging	$\checkmark$	
Send logging report	$\checkmark$	$\checkmark$
Hiding appearance	$\checkmark$	
Hiding behavior		$\checkmark$

From Table 1, we can see that the user activities that *Actual Spy* and *Spybot* concerned about are different. In addition, their latency is achieved by different ways. *Actual Spy* is able to hide its process, files and registries. And *Spybot* can blend its behaviors in with normal user activities.

5.2   The Prototype Implementation

Data Collection: We collected data from both appearance and behavior of a program according to the functions and features of the spyware instances.

1. **Appearance data**: the information of hidden processes in the host, hidden files and folders in specified directory ($\backslash Windows \backslash System32 \backslash$) and hidden registries (from [8]) which are used by spyware to auto start.
2. **Behavior data**: the Win32 API calls or COM API calls which can be used to collect and leak information (save the data to a file or transmit information to a remote host). These APIs are shown as follows:
   - **Keystroke logging**: *GetKeyboardState, GetAsyncKeyState*
   - **Internet traces logging**: *get_Document, get_LocationURL, get_LocationName*
   - **File access**: *CreateFile, OpenFile, ReadFile, WriteFile*
   - **Network Communication**: *socket, send, recv, sendto, recvfrom*

We adopt a cross-view diff-based approach [9] to obtain appearance data, and implement a hook program to intercept the API calls.

Signals: The inhibitory signal and activating signal in the prototype are defined as follows. Their values are normalized between 0 and 10. Both inhibitory and activating signals have multiple sources (shown in Table 2). They are generated when data from any source satisfy the conditions described below.

- **Inhibitory signal**: derived from the frequency of the hiding appearance behaviors. For normalization, T_{ih} is defined as the maximum frequency that a clear system may have. Thus, if the frequency is higher than T_{ih}, the signal value is 0. Otherwise, the signal value is calculated by applying linear scale.
- **Activating signal**: derived from the frequency of the collecting information behaviors. The collecting behaviors exhibited by spyware are much more than the ones exhibited by normal applications. Therefore, two thresholds

Table 2. Signal sources and corresponding parameters

Signal Sources	Thresholds	NKR weight
inhibitory hidden processes	$T_{ih} = 1$	5
inhibitory hidden files in specified directory	$T_{ih} = 10$	2
inhibitory hidden registries used for auto start	$T_{ih} = 6$	3
activating keystroke logging Win32 API calls	$T_{al} = 100, T_{ah} = 1000$	5
activating Internet traces logging COM API calls	$T_{al} = 3, T_{ah} = 10$	5

are set for the signal normalization. If the frequency is higher than T_{ah}, the signal value is 10. If the frequency is less than T_{al}, the signal value is 0. Otherwise, the signal value is calculated by max-min normalization.

Induction Cytokines: Four types of IC are implemented in the prototype to generate four kinds of user activity that are commonly concerned by spyware:

1. $IC_{Keystroke}$: simulate user keystroke, $IC(Keystroke, 6, 3, 10, 10, f)$.
2. $IC_{FileOper}$: simulate the creation, deletion of files, $IC(FileOperation, 6, 3, 10, 10, f)$.
3. $IC_{WebSurf}$: simulate opening web pages in a browser, $IC(WebSurfing, 6, 2, 10, 10, f)$.
4. $IC_{HTTPReq}$: generate HTTP requests, $IC(HTTPRequest, 6, 2, 10, 10, f)$.

For simplicity, we set $f(t) = C_0 (0 < t < T_I)$ for each IC.

The other parameters in the prototype are: $N_{NK} = 24, T_A = 100, T_F = 200, C_{decay} = 0.15, N_{NKR} = 10$, the mutation probabilities of NKR and IC are $P_{m\_NKR} = 0.25/Fitness$ and $P_{m\_IC} = 0.3/Fitness$.

5.3   Results and Analysis

Two scenarios (S1 and S2) are set for inducing Actual Spy (S1) and Spybot (S2) respectively in the experiment. Each scenario is repeated for five times. The host runs under a Windows XP SP3 OS with a 2.8 Ghz processor and 2G RAM.

As the activities concerned by *Actual Spy* and *Spybot* are different, the IC which can induce them is also different. Theoretically, $IC_{FileOper}$ and $IC_{WebSurf}$ can trigger *Actual Spy* and $IC_{Keystroke}$ can trigger *Spybot*. Figure 4 shows their actual effects on *Actual Spy* and *Spybot*.

Fig 4 shows that *Actual Spy* and *Spybot* behave cyclically under the periodical stimulation by ICs. They are much more active in induction periods (1s-10s, 21s-30s, ...) than in non-induction periods (11s-20s, 31s-40s, ...). This shows that both kinds of ICs indeed trigger the activities of *Actual Spy* and *Spybot*. And the spyware behaviors have a significant difference in induction periods and non-induction periods. In addition, the effect of $IC_{WebSurf}$ is similar to $IC_{FileOper}$ when inducing *Actual Spy*. So it's not depicted in detail.

Fig 5 and Fig 6 show the changes in number of all kinds of ICs during the NK population evolution. The data is derived from one experiment in S1 and S2. Other experiments in S1 and S2 show the same trend in general.

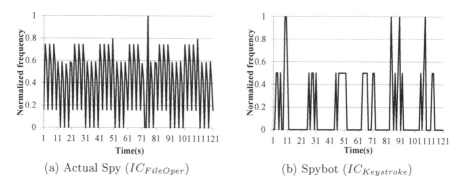

(a) Actual Spy ($IC_{FileOper}$)   (b) Spybot ($IC_{Keystroke}$)

Fig. 4. The information leaking API call frequency of both *Actual Spy* and *Spybot*

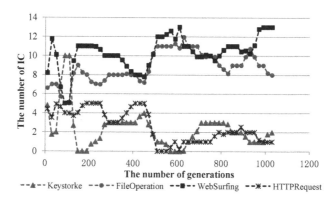

Fig. 5. The changes in number of all kinds of ICs in S1 (Actual Spy)

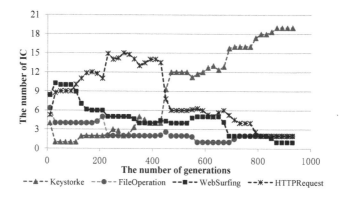

Fig. 6. The changes in number of all kinds of ICs in S2 (Spybot)

Fig 5 depicts that all types of ICs equal in number at the beginning of S1. After 100 generations, $IC_{FileOper}$ and $IC_{WebSurf}$ begin to show their potential among all ICs. 200 generations later, their amounts are always at a higher level than others. In contrast, $IC_{FileOper}$ and $IC_{WebSurf}$ decline in the number over time. It can be seen that the ICs that work on Actual Spy gradually gain superiority during NK population evolution. This advantage makes them a greater probability to be released into the system.

Fig 6 shows the similar trend. Although $IC_{WebSurf}$ and $IC_{HTTPReq}$ reach the largest number one after another before 450 generations, $IC_{Keystroke}$ gains superiority in the following time. This shows that after hundreds of tries and adjustments, the right IC is chosen for Spybot induction.

From the experimental results of the two scenarios, we conclude that NK population can induce different spyware by altering the distribution of all kinds of ICs in the population during evolution.

6   Conclusion

In this paper, we introduce NKs to AIS, hoping that their artifacts can deal with the difficulties in detecting latent spyware. These artificial NKs together form a population which is in constant evolution. They can capture subtle traces of unknown spyware, and then adaptively release some bait (called induction cytokines) to trigger its actions. If the spyware is interested in the bait, it will exhibit malicious behaviors which expose itself to further detection.

Future work will be focused on the immune inspired spyware detection based on the artificial NK model. We will verify the improvement of the detection performance that the artificial NK model brings to AIS through further experiments.In addition, we will give the principles of parameter settings because all parameters used in the experiments in this paper are set by trail and error.

References

1. Gilman, N.: Hacking Goes Pro. Engineering & Technology 4(3), 26–29 (2009)
2. Thompson, R.: Why Spyware Poses Multiple Threats to Security. Communications of the ACM 48(8), 41–43 (2005)
3. Borders, K., Zhao, X., Prakash, A.: Siren: Catching Evasive Malware (Short Paper). In: 2006 IEEE Symposium on Security and Privacy, pp. 78–85. IEEE Computer Society, Los Alamitos (2006)
4. Chandrasekaran, M., Vidyaraman, S., Upadhyaya, S.: SpyCon: Emulating User Activities to Detect Evasive Spyware. In: IEEE Int'l Conference on Performance, Computing, and Communications, pp. 502–509 (2007)
5. Aycock, J.: Spyware and Adware. Springer, New York (2010)
6. Shaw, M., Gribble, S.D.: Reverse Firewalls in Denali. In: 5th Symposium on Operating Systems Design and Implementation. USENIX Association, Berkeley (2002)
7. Borders, K., Prakash, A.: Web Tap: Detecting Covert Web Traffic. In: 11th ACM Conference on Computer and Communications Security, pp. 110–120. ACM Press, New York (2004)

8. Wang, Y., Roussev, R., Verbowski, C., Johnson, A., Wu, M., Huang, Y., Kuo, S.: Gatekeeper: Monitoring Auto-Start Extensibility Points (ASEPs) for Spyware Management. In: LISA: 18th Systems Administration Conference, pp. 33–46 (2004)
9. Wang, Y.M., Beck, D., Vo, B., Roussev, R., Verbowski, C.: Detecting stealth software with Strider GhostBuster. In: International Conference on Dependable Systems and Networks, pp. 368–377. IEEE Press, Los Alamitos (2005)
10. Kirda, E., Kruegel, C., Banks, G., Vigna, G., Kemmerer, R.A.: Behavior-based Spyware Detection. In: 15th USENIX Security Symposium, pp. 273–288. USENIX Association, Berkeley (2006)
11. Egele, M., Kruegel, C., Kirda, E., Yin, H., Song, D.: Dynamic Spyware Analysis. In: 2007 USENIX Annual Technical Conference. USENIX Association, Berkeley (2007)
12. Arastouie, N., Razzazi, M.R.: Hunter: An Anti Spyware for Windows Operating System. In: 3rd International Conference on Information and Communication Technologies: From Theory to Applications, pp. 1–5. IEEE Press, Los Alamitos (2008)
13. Al-Hammadi, Y., Aickelin, U.: Detecting Bots Based on Keylogging Activities. In: 3rd International Conference on Availability, Reliability and Security, pp. 896–902 (2008)
14. Han, J., Kwon, J., Lee, H.: HoneyID: Unveiling Hidden Spywares by Generating Bogus Events. In: SEC 2008. IFIP, vol. 278, pp. 669–673. Springer, Boston (2008)
15. Ortolani, S., Giuffrida, C., Crispo, B.: Bait Your Hook: A Novel Detection Technique for Keyloggers. In: Jha, S., Sommer, R., Kreibich, C. (eds.) RAID 2010. LNCS, vol. 6307, pp. 198–217. Springer, Heidelberg (2010)
16. Kim, J., Bentley, P.J., Aickelin, U., Greensmith, J., Tedesco, G., Twycross, J.: Immune System Approaches to Intrusion Detection - A Review. Natural Computing 6(4), 413–466 (2007)
17. Al-Hammadi, Y., Aickelin, U., Greensmith, J.: DCA for Bot Detection. In: 2008 IEEE Congress on Evolutionary Computation, pp. 1807–1816. IEEE Press (2008)
18. Manzoor, S., Shafiq, M., Tabish, S., Farooq, M.: A Sense of 'Danger' for Windows Processes. In: Andrews, P.S., Timmis, J., Owens, N.D.L., et al. (eds.) ICARIS 2009. LNCS, vol. 5666, pp. 220–233. Springer, Heidelberg (2009)
19. Fu, J., Liang, Y.W., Tan, C.Y., Xiong, X.F.: Detecting Software Keyloggers with Dendritic Cell Algorithm. In: 2010 International Conference on Communications and Mobile Computing, pp. 111–115. IEEE Computer Society, Los Alamitos (2010)
20. Caligiuri, M.A.: Human Natural Killer Cells. Blood 112(3), 461–469 (2008)
21. Matzinger, P.: Tolerance, Danger, and the Extended Family. Annu. Rev. Immunol. 12, 991–1045 (1994)
22. Lanier, L.L.: NK Cell Recognition. Annu. Rev. Immunol. 23, 225–274 (2005)
23. Soderberg-Naucler, C., Fish, K.N., Nelson, J.A.: Reactivation of Latent Human Cytomegalovirus by Allogeneic Stimulation of Blood Cells from Healthy Donors. Cell 91(1), 119–126 (1997)
24. Guan, H., Moretto, M., Bzik, D.J., Gigley, J., Khan, I.A.: NK Cells Enhance Dendritic Cell Response against Parasite Antigens via NKG2D Pathway. The Journal of Immunology 179, 590–596 (2007)
25. Piccioli, D., Sbrana, S., Melandri, E., Valiante, N.M.: Contact-dependent Stimulation and Inhibition of Dendritic Cells by Natural Killer Cells. The Journal of Experimental Medicine 195(3), 335–341 (2002)

AC-CS: An Immune-Inspired Associative Classification Algorithm[*]

Samir A. Mohamed Elsayed[**], Sanguthevar Rajasekaran, and Reda A. Ammar

Computer Science Department, University of Connecticut

Abstract. Data mining is the process of discovering patterns from large data sets. One of the branches of data mining is Associative Classification (AC). AC mining is a promising approach that uses association rules discovery techniques to construct association classifiers. However, traditional AC algorithms typically search for all possible association rules to find a representative subset of those rules. Since the search space of such rules may grow exponentially as the support threshold decreases, the rules discovery process can be computationally expensive. One effective way to tackle this problem is to directly find a set of high-stakes association rules that potentially builds a highly accurate classifier. This paper introduces AC-CS, a novel AC algorithm, inspired by the clonal selection of the immune system. The algorithm proceeds in an evolutionary fashion to populate only rules that are likely to yield good classification accuracy. Empirical results on several real datasets show that the approach generates dramatically less rules than traditional AC algorithms. Hence, the proposed approach is indeed significantly more efficient than traditional AC algorithms while achieving a competitive accuracy.

1 Introduction

The Natural Immune System (NIS) is a distributed, multi-layered, adaptive, dynamic, and life-long learning system. The Artificial Immune System (AIS) is a computational system inspired by the principles and processes of the NIS. The field of AIS has obtained some degree of success as a branch of computational intelligence since it emerged in the 1990s. There have been several successful applications of AIS in computer security, optimization, anomaly detection, and data mining.

Data mining is the process of discovering patterns from large data sets. One of the branches of data mining is Associative Classification (AC). AC algorithms integrate association rules discovery and classification to build a classifier from a training data for predicting the class of unforeseen test data. AC algorithms typically build a classifier by discovering the full set of Class Association Rules (CARs) from the training dataset and then select a subset to form a classifier.

---

[*] This work is partially supported by the following grants: NSF0829916 and NIH-R01-LM010101.

[**] The author is partially supported by Helwan University, Cairo, Egypt.

C.A. Coello Coello et al. (Eds.): ICARIS 2012, LNCS 7597, pp. 139–151, 2012.
© Springer-Verlag Berlin Heidelberg 2012

CARs are association rules of the form $iset \Rightarrow c$, where $iset$ is an item-set and c is a class. Despite achieving high accuracy compared to other classification approaches such as C4.5 [29], the approach suffers from the overhead of exhaustive search through a large pool of candidate rules. Moreover, the rule discovery process in traditional AC algorithms is not well integrated with the classification process.

The main contribution of this paper is AC-CS, a new AC algorithm inspired by the Clonal Selection (CS) mechanism of the NIS. Unlike traditional AC algorithms, the algorithm doesn't search for all association rules and then select a subset of them. Rather, AC-CS directly populates high quality rules through an evolutionary process. This evolutionary process follows the clonal selection process of cloning, mutating, and pruning populations of rules based on both their support and confidence measures. The process is repeated until the generated rules cover all the training data.

The rest of the paper is organized as follows. Section 2 gives a background about the immune system processes and algorithms as well as the associative classification problem. Section 3 describes the proposed algorithm in details. Experimental results are reported in Section 4. Section 5 concludes with some possible future work.

2 Background

In this section, a brief description of the immune system principles and processes, that computer scientists draw inspiration from when designing AIS algorithms, is presented. A brief summary of one of the major AIS algorithms, namely, the clonal selection algorithm, is also presented. In addition, the associative classification approach along with issues of traditional algorithms are discussed.

2.1 The Immune System

The Natural Immune System (NIS) is a complex network of tissues, organs, and chemicals. Its main function is to defend the body against foreign *pathogens* such as bacteria or viruses. NIS recognizes pathogens via a smaller portion on top of them called *antigens*. The main organs of the NIS where the immune cells develop, includes the lymph system, the thymus, and the bone marrow. The immune system protects the body from infection with layered defenses. Physical barriers (e.g., skin) prevent pathogens from entering the body. If a pathogen breaches these barriers, the innate immune system provides an immediate but non-specific response. In many cases, it is able to successfully defend the body. If the innate immune system fails to handle the attack, then the adaptive immune system takes over. The adaptive response is more specific yet slower, resulting in a more effective response. The adaptive immune system can remember past encounters with antigens such that the next time the antigen appears, a more specific and effective response is deployed (the main idea of vaccination).

The main component of the adaptive immune system is lymphocytes which are blood white cells. Lymphocytes consist of two types, namely: *B-cells* and *T-cells*. B-cells get produced and develop in the bone marrow. While the T-cells get produced in the bone marrow and then migrate to the thymus to develop.

There are two main types of B-cells, namely: plasma B-cells and memory B-cells. Plasma B-cells are cells that have been exposed to antigens and produce large amounts of *antibodies* (i.e., Y-shaped receptor molecules bound on the surface of a B-cell with the primary role of recognizing and binding, through a complementary match, with an antigen [8]). While *memory* B-cells created in response to high affinity match with antigens, live for a very long time and provide faster future response. B-cells require co-stimulation from other immune cells (e.g., helper T-cells) in order to activate. B-cells undergo a process called *clonal selection*.

AIS is a relatively young field. The first paper by Farmer et al. [15] in the field was published in 1986. However, it was only in the mid-90's that AIS has become a subject area in its own right. There are several works that form the foundation of AIS. Examples of such works include the work by Forrest et al. [16] in 1994 as well as the work by Bersini [6]. There are five major AIS algorithms that have been popular in the literature, namely: negative selection [16,23], clonal selection [11,9], artificial immune networks [22,30], dendritic cells [18], and danger theory algorithms [27].

2.2   The Clonal Selection (CS)

According to Burnet's 1959 clonal selection theory, activation of lymphocytes occurs on binding with a matching antigen [1]. Once activated, *clones* of the lymphocyte are produced in large numbers with identical receptors of the original lymphocyte that encountered the antigen. Any lymphocytes that bind to self's cells are set to die. During the clonal selection of B-cells, the average antibody affinity increases for the antigen that triggered the process. This phenomenon is called *affinity maturation* and is responsible for the fact that upon a subsequent exposure to the antigen, the immune response is more effective due to the antibodies having a higher affinity for the antigen. Affinity maturation is facilitated by a *somatic hyper mutation* and selection mechanisms that occurs during the clonal expansion of B-cells. Somatic hyper mutation alters the specificity of antibodies by introducing random changes to them.

Researchers have tried to draw some inspiration from the clonal selection process, in particular, the antigen driven affinity maturation process of B-cells along with the hyper mutation mechanism. In [10], the authors highlight two features of affinity maturation in B-cells that can be exploited from a computational point. First, the proliferation of B-cells is proportional to the affinity of the antigen that binds it, the higher the affinity, the more clones are produced. Second, the mutations suffered by B-cells are inversely proportional to the affinity of the antigen it binds. Utilizing these two features, De Castro and Von Zuben [11] developed one of the most popular clonal selection inspired algorithm, CLONALG. There are different variations of clonal selection algorithms in the literature. [9] presents a comparative case study of a handful of such algorithms.

2.3 Associative Classification (AC)

Agrawal, et al. [3] proposed association rules mining for market basket data patterns. Association rules identify correlations among a set of items found in transactions. The input to the association rules mining problem is a set of transactions where each transaction is a set of items. A set of items is also referred to as an *item-set*. A k-item-set is an item-set of size k. There are two measures proposed in [3] that quantify the significance of an association rule, namely, support and confidence ratio. An association rule is an implication $x \Rightarrow y$ where x and y are item-sets in a dataset. The *support* of the rule is the ratio of the number of transactions containing both x and y to the total number of transactions. The *confidence* of the rule is the ratio of the number of transactions that contain y to the number of transactions containing x. The mining of association rules from a set of transactions is the process of identifying all rules having a pre-specified minimum support and confidence. This involves several phases in processing transactions. A k-item-set is said to be *frequent* if the ratio of the number of transactions containing all the items of the k-item-set to the total number of transactions is greater than or equal to the user specified minimum support. Algorithms for finding frequent item-sets typically require multiple passes over the entire dataset.

There are many algorithms for mining association rules in the literature. Apriori [3] is possibly the well-known and most cited algorithm. It uses a breadth-first search strategy and generates candidate item-sets and tests if they are frequent. The key to its success over older algorithms such as AIS [2] and STEM [21] is the fact that it exploits an important property (commonly referred to as Apriori property or downward closure property). This property is the observation that no superset of an infrequent item-set can be frequent. However, generation of candidate item-sets is expensive both in space and time. In addition, support counting involves multiple dataset scans which heavily impact performance. Apriori as well as Apriori-inspired algorithms (e.g., [5]) typically perform well on sparse (i.e., short frequent item-sets) such as the market basket data. However, they perform poorly on dense (i.e., long frequent item-sets) datasets such as census data. This degradation is due to the fact that these algorithms perform as many passes over the database (i.e., high I/O overhead) as the length of the longest frequent pattern [34].

While many algorithms including Apriori use the traditional horizontal data layout, Eclat [35] is probably the first algorithm to introduce a vertical data layout. Eclat is more efficient for long item sets than for short ones. In this algorithm, data is represented as lists of transaction identifiers (one per item). Support counting is performed by simply intersecting these lists. Compared to Apriori and other algorithms, Eclat often performs better on dense rather than sparse datasets. A variation of the algorithm depicted dEclat can be found in [34].

FP-Growth [20] allows frequent item-sets discovery without candidate item-set generation and adopts a divide and conquer strategy. It builds a compact data structure (i.e., FP-Tree) using only two passes over the dataset. The algorithm is more efficient as long as the full tree can fit in memory. However, the tree may need substantial memory in some cases. There are some variations of the algorithm such as H-mine [28].

Liu et al. [25] introduced the Classification Based on Associations (CBAs) algorithm which laid the foundation of the AC approach and other algorithms as well (e.g.,[24],[26]). The basic idea is to mine the full set of association rules from a training dataset into Class Association Rules (CARs) in the form of $iset \Rightarrow c$ where $iset$ is an item-set (i.e, body of the rule) and c is a class (i.e, head of the rule). Rules with high confidence are then selected to form the classifier. During the classification process, all test data that match the rule with the highest confidence are assigned the class of that rule.

AIS data mining applications include classification [36,19,13], clustering [8], and rule induction [4]. Most AISs for classification use an instance-based representation. This includes AIRS [33,32,31] and CLONALG [11,12]. In this representation, the candidate solutions considered by the classification algorithm take the form of a subset of the original data instances, each of them with all its attribute values [17]. Another type of representation is the rule-based one. This representation is used, for instance, in IFRAIS [4]: an AIS for discovering fuzzy classification rules. In this representation, the candidate solutions considered by the algorithm take the form of IF-THEN classification rules, where each rule typically contains a conjunction of a few attribute values [17]. Both representations have pros and cons. In [17], the authors argue that it all depends on the nature of the data being mined, the requirements of the application domain, and how important knowledge comprehensibility is to the user.

In [13] the authors propose an algorithm that employs the clonal selection of the immune system to directly find a subset of rules to form the classifier. Empirical results show that the algorithm is particularly efficient when the support threshold is low. In addition, reported accuracy appears to be competitive with a traditional AC algorithm. The approach in this paper is similar to this work. We reported some preliminary results in [14] and in this paper more results are reported.

3   The AC-CS Algorithm

The AC-CS algorithm is inspired by the clonal selection process, in which rules are populated as if they are B-cells that can be cloned, mutated, and pruned as well. Affinity measurements are determined by the confidence of those rules. The objective is to avoid an exhaustive search for all possible rules in an explosive search space as it is the case in traditional AC algorithms.

Prior to describing the algorithm in details, necessary notations and concepts are defined as follows:

- A *class rule* r can be defined as $iset \Rightarrow c$ where $iset$ is an item-set (i.e, body of the rule) and c is a class (i.e, head of the rule).

- The support of r, $support(r)$, is the ratio of the number of transactions that contain all items in both the head and body of the rule, to the the total number of transaction of the data set. This measure helps remove low-stakes rules.
- The confidence of r, $confidence(r)$, is the ratio of the number of transactions that contain the body item-set to the number of transactions that contain both the body and head item-sets of the rule.
- The coverage of r, $coverage(r)$, is the ratio of the number of transactions that are covered by the generated rules to the total number of transactions. The coverage measure has been previously used in [25] to filter the discovered rules. We use the coverage measure as a termination check to the algorithm. Indeed, if the generated rules managed to cover the whole training data set, then there would be no need to proceed further.
- The clonal rate of r is dictated by the following equation, borrowed from [13]:

$$cloneRate(r) = \frac{n \cdot clonalRate}{\sum_{i=1}^{n} confidence(r_i)} \cdot confidence(r)$$

where n denotes the number of rules at the current generation, and *clonalRate* is a user defined parameter. The clone rate of the rule is proportional to its confidence (i.e., the higher the confidence, the higher the clone rate).

The proposed algorithm AC–CS, depicted in figure 1, accepts a training dataset of transactions and outputs a set of high quality rules that potentially yield a good accuracy classifier. The algorithm starts off by initializing a few data structures namely: the rule populations P, the frequent singleton items I, and finally the memory pool M that contains the high quality rules found throughout the algorithm (line 1). User-defined parameters are initialized at line 2. At lines (3-11), rules with only a single item in the head and have higher support than the given *minSupport* are added to P. In addition, only items that turn out to be frequent are added to the new set of items I. From now on, AC–CS doesn't use the full set of singleton items $\mathcal{I}$. Rather, it uses the refined set I. Note that I is a subset of $\mathcal{I}$.

The algorithm proceeds in generations. In each generation, remaining rules from previous generations are cloned proportional to their confidence (i.e., affinity) which is calculated using the *cloneRate* function above (line 16). For each new cloned rule, the items in the body of the rule are extended (i.e, mutated) by adding one more *new* item (line 19). Only rules with high support are retained (lines 20-21). Next, the remaining rules go through a pruning phase in which redundant rules are removed. For instance, given two rules $r_1 : iset_1 \Rightarrow c$ and $r_2 : iset_2 \Rightarrow c$:

$$iset_2 \subseteq iset_1 \wedge confidence(r_1) > confidence(r_2) \Rightarrow prune(r_2)$$

Upon pruning all the redundant rules, only remaining rules with high confidence are added to the memory pool M (lines 26-30). The process is repeated until either the rules in M cover the entire training dataset or the number of generations exceeds the maximum allowed (line 32).

Note that the whole process is repeated for each class in the dataset. Upon completion, all rules in the memory pool M are sorted in a decreasing order of confidence. Sorted rules are then applied one by one to a test data and the accuracy is reported accordingly.

```
1  P = {}; I = {}; M = {};
2  intialize clonalRate, currentGeneration, maxGenerations;
3  foreach item i ∈ I
4  {
5      set rule r = {i ⇒ c};
6      if(support(r) ≥ minSupport)
7      {
8          set P = P ∪ r;
9          set I = I ∪ i;
10     }
11 }
12 do
13 {
14     foreach rule r ∈ P
15     {
16         repeat cloneRate(r) times
17         {
18             set r̄ = r;
19             set r̄.items = r.items ∪ i where i ∈ I ∧ i ∉ r.items;
20             if(support(r̄) ≥ minSupport)
21                 set P = P ∪ r̄;
22         }
23
24     }
25     prune P
26     foreach rule r ∈ P
27     {
28         if(confidence(r) ≥ minConfidence)
29             M = M ∪ r;
30     }
31     currentGeneration = currentGeneration + 1;
32 }while(coverage(M) < 100% ∧ currentGeneration < maxGenerations)
33 return M;
```

Fig. 1. The AC-CS Algorithm

4   Experimental Results

This section demonstrates the potential of the proposed approach using several benchmarks. The experimental setup is first described followed by a discussion of both the capabilities and limitations of the approach.

4.1   Setup

Experiments were performed on real datasets of different sizes obtained from the UCI Machine Learning Repository[1]. These datasets are shown in table 1 along with their parameters. A few pre-processing steps were performed on the datasets as follows:

- Continuous data were discretized into intervals using the entropy methods with the MLC++ tool[2].
- Any transactions with missing fields were removed. Number of actual instances reflect this fact in table 1.
- Data were converted into a vertical layout for efficient support counting.
- A hash table for item transactions were implemented for easy and efficient access.
- Items in the body of rules were implemented as sets.

The proposed algorithm AC-CS is compared against AC-Apriori, an Apriori based AC algorithm that generates the full set of possible association rules. We use a publicly available implementation of Apriori by Borgelt[3]. This implementation is widely used for academic and commercial purposes.

Execution times are reported in milliseconds, seconds, and minutes as appropriate. They include both the time to extract and apply the generated rules. The minimum support ratios used are 0.5%, 0.75%, 1%, 2%, 5%, 10%. All experiments were performed on a Windows 7 machine with processor speed at 2.80GHz and 3.0GB memory.

Table 1. Datasets & Parameters

Dataset	Instances	Classes	Training	Testing
Adult	45,222	2	30,162	15,060
Iris	150	3	100	50
Letter	20,000	26	13,333	6,667
Nursery	12,960	5	8,640	4,320

---

[1] http://archive.ics.uci.edu/ml/datasets.html
[2] http://www.sgi.com/tech/mlc/
[3] http://www.borgelt.net/apriori.html

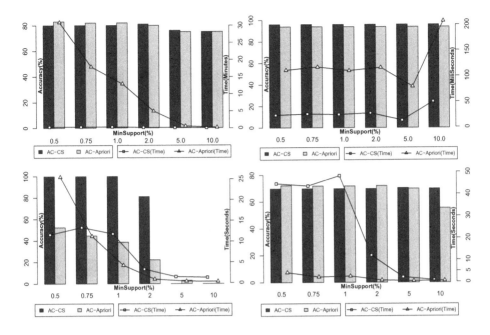

Fig. 2. Accuracy and execution time results for datasets (from top left) Adult, Iris, Letter, and Nursery

4.2 Discussion

In this section, we discuss the performance of the proposed algorithm in terms of accuracy, execution time, and the discovered rules size. We also show how the algorithm compares to one of the traditional AC algorithms.

The bar charts in figure 2 illustrate the accuracy of both the AC-Apriori and AC-CS algorithms on several datasets with different support thresholds. Clearly, on both the Iris and the Nursery datasets, AC-CS has a higher accuracy than that of AC-Apriori in every single case. Meanwhile, for the larger dataset Adult, AC-CS's accuracy is approaching and sometimes rivaling that of AC-Apriori. Similar results were obtained for other values of support.

Similarly, the line charts in figure 2 show the execution times of the two algorithms. For the Adult and Iris datasets, AC-CS has outperformed AC-Apriori in all cases. This is probably due to the significant reduction of rules required as a result of not discovering all possible rules as it is the case with AC-Apriori. Figure 3 shows the dramatic reduction in rules. The reduction is particularly apparent in the case of the Adult dataset. While the rules used by AC-CS grow slowly with lower minSupport, the rules generated by AC-Apriori grow exponentially in some cases. However, when the rules don't differ much like in the case of the dataset *Letter*, the AC-Apriori appears to be faster. It's worth mentioning that the AC-CS algorithm appears to be more efficient than the algorithm proposed in [13] as well.

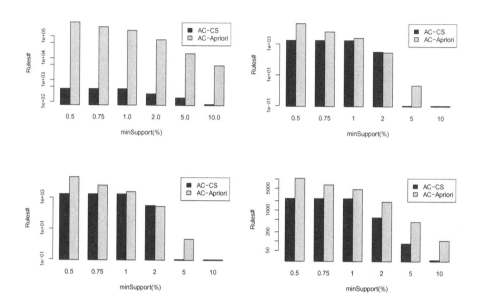

Fig. 3. Rules count, in log-scale, for datasets (from top left) Adult, Iris, Letter, and Nursery.

On an aggregate average over the four datasets, AC-CS has outperformed the AC-Apriori in terms of both time and accuracy. In addition, the AC-CS algorithm is able to integrate the rule discovery along with the rule selection processes, a clear advantage that traditional AC algorithms lack. Moreover, unlike Genetic Algorithms (GA), the employed CS algorithm performs proportionate selection as well as affinity inversely proportional hypermutation with no crossover operation [7]. Moreover, the authors in [11] show that unlike GA, CS algorithm can reach a diverse number of local optimal solutions.

The AC-CS algorithm has two influential parameters, namely, *clonalRate* and *maxGenerations*. The former dictates the rate at which items in rules at a given generation are extended. The later dictates how many generations the revolutionary process may go through. The algorithm ends if the number of generations exceeds this limit or the whole training set has been already covered by the current rules, whichever is sooner. We chose a value of 10 for both the *clonalRate*, and the *maxGenerations* since this was shown to be a reasonable choice in terms of both time and accuracy.

5   Conclusions and Future Work

In this paper, we have introduced AC-CS, a novel AC algorithm inspired by the clonal selection algorithm. The algorithm begins with a small population of frequent single item rules. These rules then go through a process of cloning, mutating, and pruning for several generations. Only high quality rules are added to the memory pool. These rules are applied in turn to classify a testing dataset. Empirical results show that the approach outperforms traditional AC algorithms in running time and quite competitive in accuracy as well. Possible future research directions for this work include:

- Drawing more inspiration from the NIS processes.
- Optimizing the algorithm to improve the running time while keeping the accuracy as high as possible.
- Employing sampling techniques to increase support counting efficiency.
- Conducting more extensive testing with both synthetic & real datasets.
- Comparing the approach against other state-of-the art AC algorithms.

Acknowledgment. The first author is grateful to the the Computer Science Department, Helwan University, Cairo, Egypt for supporting his Ph.D. program at the University of Connecticut.

References

1. http://www.artificial-immune-systems.org
2. Agrawal, R., Imieliński, T., Swami, A.: Mining association rules between sets of items in large databases. In: Proceedings of the 1993 ACM SIGMOD International Conference on Management of Data, SIGMOD 1993, pp. 207–216. ACM, New York (1993)
3. Agrawal, R., Srikant, R., et al.: Fast algorithms for mining association rules. In: Proc. 20th Int. Conf. Very Large Data Bases, VLDB, vol. 1215, pp. 487–499 (1994)
4. Alves, R., Delgado, M., Lopes, H., Freitas, A.: An Artificial Immune System for Fuzzy-Rule Induction in Data Mining. In: Yao, X., Burke, E.K., Lozano, J.A., Smith, J., Merelo-Guervós, J.J., Bullinaria, J.A., Rowe, J.E., Tiňo, P., Kabán, A., Schwefel, H.-P. (eds.) PPSN 2004. LNCS, vol. 3242, pp. 1011–1020. Springer, Heidelberg (2004)
5. Bayardo Jr., R.J.: Efficiently mining long patterns from databases. In: Proceedings of the 1998 ACM SIGMOD International Conference on Management of Data, SIGMOD 1998, pp. 85–93. ACM, New York (1998)
6. Bersini, H., Varela, F.: Hints for adaptive problem solving gleaned from immune networks. In: Parallel Problem Solving from Nature, pp. 343–354 (1991)
7. Castro, L., Timmis, J.: Artificial immune systems as a novel soft computing paradigm. Soft Computing-A Fusion of Foundations, Methodologies and Applications 7(8), 526–544 (2003)
8. Castro, L.N.D., Zuben, F.J.V.: An evolutionary immune network for data clustering. In: Brazilian Symposium on Neural Networks, pp. 84–89 (2000)
9. Cutello, V., Narzisi, G., Nicosia, G., Pavone, M.: Clonal Selection Algorithms: A Comparative Case Study Using Effective Mutation Potentials. In: Jacob, C., Pilat, M.L., Bentley, P.J., Timmis, J.I. (eds.) ICARIS 2005. LNCS, vol. 3627, pp. 13–28. Springer, Heidelberg (2005)
10. De Castro, L., Timmis, J.: Artificial immune systems: a new computational intelligence approach. Springer (2002)

11. De Castro, L., Von Zuben, F.: The clonal selection algorithm with engineering applications. In: Proceedings of GECCO 2000, Workshop on Artificial Immune Systems and Their Applications, vol. 3637 (2000)
12. De Castro, L., Von Zuben, F.: Learning and optimization using the clonal selection principle. IEEE Transactions on Evolutionary Computation 6(3), 239–251 (2002)
13. Do, T.D., Hui, S.C., Fong, A.C.M., Fong, B.: Associative classification with artificial immune system. IEEE Transactions on Evolutionary Computation 13, 217–228 (2009)
14. Elsayed, S.A.M., Rajasekaran, S., Ammar, R.A.: An Artificial Immune System Approach to Associative Classification. In: Murgante, B., Gervasi, O., Misra, S., Nedjah, N., Rocha, A.M.A.C., Taniar, D., Apduhan, B.O. (eds.) ICCSA 2012, Part I. LNCS, vol. 7333, pp. 161–171. Springer, Heidelberg (2012)
15. Farmer, J., Packard, N., Perelson, A.: The immune system, adaptation, and machine learning. Physica D: Nonlinear Phenomena 22(1-3), 187–204 (1986)
16. Forrest, S., Perelson, A., Allen, L., Cherukuri, R.: Self-nonself discrimination in a computer. In: Proceedings of IEEE Computer Society Symposium on Research in Security and Privacy, pp. 202–212. IEEE (1994)
17. Freitas, A.A., Timmis, J.: Revisiting the Foundations of Artificial Immune Systems: A Problem-Oriented Perspective. In: Timmis, J., Bentley, P.J., Hart, E. (eds.) ICARIS 2003. LNCS, vol. 2787, pp. 229–241. Springer, Heidelberg (2003)
18. Greensmith, J., Aickelin, U., Cayzer, S.: Introducing Dendritic Cells as a Novel Immune-Inspired Algorithm for Anomaly Detection. In: Jacob, C., Pilat, M.L., Bentley, P.J., Timmis, J.I. (eds.) ICARIS 2005. LNCS, vol. 3627, pp. 153–167. Springer, Heidelberg (2005)
19. Gu, F., Feyereisl, J., Oates, R., Reps, J., Greensmith, J., Aickelin, U.: Quiet in Class: Classification, Noise and the Dendritic Cell Algorithm. In: Liò, P., Nicosia, G., Stibor, T. (eds.) ICARIS 2011. LNCS, vol. 6825, pp. 173–186. Springer, Heidelberg (2011)
20. Han, J., Pei, J., Yin, Y.: Mining frequent patterns without candidate generation. In: Proceedings of the 2000 ACM SIGMOD International Conference on Management of Data, SIGMOD 2000, pp. 1–12. ACM, New York (2000)
21. Houtsma, M., Swami, A.: Set-oriented mining of association rules. In: International Conference on Data Engineering (1993)
22. Ishida, Y.: Fully distributed diagnosis by pdp learning algorithm: towards immune network pdp model. In: 1990 IJCNN International Joint Conference on Neural Networks, pp. 777–782. IEEE (1990)
23. Ji, Z., Dasgupta, D.: Revisiting negative selection algorithms. Evolutionary Computation 15(2), 223–251 (2007)
24. Li, W., Han, J., Pei, J.: Cmar: Accurate and efficient classification based on multiple class-association rules. In: IEEE International Conference on Data Mining, pp. 369–376 (2001)
25. Liu, B., Hsu, W., Ma, Y.: Integrating classification and association rule mining. In: Knowledge Discovery and Data Mining, pp. 80–86 (1998)
26. Liu, B., Ma, Y., Wong, C.: Classification using association rules: weaknesses and enhancements. In: Data Mining for Scientific Applications, pp. 1–11 (2001)
27. Matzinger, P.: The danger model: a renewed sense of self. Science 296(5566), 301–305 (2002)
28. Pei, J., Han, J., Lu, H., Nishio, S., Tang, S., Yang, D.: H-mine: hyper-structure mining of frequent patterns in large databases. In: Proceedings IEEE International Conference on Data Mining, ICDM 2001, pp. 441–448 (2001)

29. Quinlan, J.: C4. 5: programs for machine learning. Morgan Kaufmann (1993)
30. Timmis, J., Neal, M., Hunt, J.: An artificial immune system for data analysis. Biosystems 55(1-3), 143–150 (2000)
31. Watkins, A.: Exploiting immunological metaphors in the development of serial, parallel and distributed learning algorithms. PhD thesis, University of Kent, Computing Laboratory (2005)
32. Watkins, A., Timmis, J.: Exploiting Parallelism Inherent in AIRS, an Artificial Immune Classifier. In: Nicosia, G., Cutello, V., Bentley, P.J., Timmis, J. (eds.) ICARIS 2004. LNCS, vol. 3239, pp. 427–438. Springer, Heidelberg (2004)
33. Watkins, A., Timmis, J., Boggess, L.: Artificial immune recognition system (airs): An immune-inspired supervised learning algorithm. Genetic Programming and Evolvable Machines 5(3), 291–317 (2004)
34. Zaki, M.J., Gouda, K.: Fast vertical mining using diffsets. In: Proceedings of the Ninth ACM SIGKDD International Conference on Knowledge Discovery and Data Mining, KDD 2003, pp. 326–335. ACM, New York (2003)
35. Zaki, M.J., Parthasarathy, S., Ogihara, M., Li, W.: New algorithms for fast discovery of association rules. In: Knowledge Discovery and Data Mining, pp. 283–286 (1997)
36. Zheng, H., Du Jiaying, Z., Wang, Y.: Research on vehicle image classifier based on concentration regulating of immune clonal selection. In: Fourth International Conference on Natural Computation, pp. 671–675. IEEE (2008)

RC-DCA: A New Feature Selection and Signal Categorization Technique for the Dendritic Cell Algorithm Based on Rough Set Theory

Zeineb Chelly and Zied Elouedi

LARODEC, Université de Tunis, Institut Supérieur de Gestion de Tunis,
41 Avenue de la liberté, cité Bouchoucha, 2000 Le Bardo,Tunisia
zeinebchelly@yahoo.fr, zied.elouedi@gmx.fr

Abstract. The Dendritic Cell Algorithm (DCA) is an immune inspired algorithm based on the behavior of dendritic cells. The performance of DCA depends on the selected features and their categorization to their specific signal types, during pre-processing. For feature selection, DCA applies the Principal Component Analysis (PCA). Nevertheless, PCA does not guarantee that the selected first principal components will be the most adequate for classification. Furthermore, the DCA categorization process is based on the PCA attributes' ranking in terms on variability. However, this categorization process could not be considered as a coherent assignment procedure. Thus, the aim of this paper is to develop a new DCA feature selection and categorization method based on Rough Set Theory (RST). In this model, the selection and the categorization processes are based on the RST CORE and REDUCT concepts. Results show that applying RST, instead of PCA, to DCA is more convenient for data pre-processing yielding much better performance in terms of accuracy.

Keywords: Dendritic Cells, Principal Component Analysis, Rough Set Theory, Core, Reduct.

1 Introduction

The Dendritic Cell Algorithm (DCA) is an immune inspired algorithm developed in [1] as a part of an interdisciplinary research project between computer scientists and immunologists. DCA is derived from behavioral models of natural dendritic cells (DCs). The DCA has the ability to combine a series of informative signals with a sequence of repeating abstract identifiers termed "antigens" to perform anomaly detection. To achieve this and through the pre-processing phase, the DCA selects a subset of features and assigns each one of them to its specific signal type. Each selected feature can be categorized either as Danger Signal (DS), Safe Signal (SS) or as Pathogen-Associated Molecular Pattern (PAMP). DCA combines these signals internally to produce a set of output signals in combination with location markers in the form of antigen to process his

C.A. Coello Coello et al. (Eds.): ICARIS 2012, LNCS 7597, pp. 152–165, 2012.

classification task. According to this procedure, it is clearly noticed that the DCA classification task - the determination of the antigen context - is very dependent on its pre-processing phase which is based on signal selection and signal categorization. More precisely, the selected subset of features and their categorization to definite signal types can influence the DCA classification results.

As the DCA data pre-processing phase would better be automatic to avoid the influence of any external information given by users or experts, in [2], the Principal Component Analysis (PCA) statistical method [3] was introduced in the DCA data pre-processing phase. The use of PCA aims to automatically select the features to retain for the DCA and to perform their categorization to their specific signal types. More precisely and for signal selection, PCA transforms a finite number of possibly correlated vectors into a smaller number of uncorrelated vectors, termed "principal components" which reveals the internal structure of the given data with the focus on data variance [2]. Nevertheless, using PCA as a dimensionality reduction technique presents some shortcomings as it is not necessarily true that the first selected principal components that capture most of the variance are the adequate features to retain [4]. Consequently, choosing these components for the DCA may influence its classification phase by producing unreliable results. Other dimensionality reduction techniques were defined in [5] including correlation coefficient and information gain.

As for feature categorization, DCA uses the PCA ranking of attributes which is based on variability and maps this obtained order to the ranking of the signal categories of the DCA which is in the order Safe, PAMP and Danger implying the significance of each signal category to the signal transformation of the DCA [2]. However, this categorization reasoning which is based on attributes' ranking and where the variability of attributes is equivalent to importance could not be considered as a coherent and consistent categorization procedure. In [5], the signal categorization step is based on the use of the Mean Squared Error (MSE) [6] which is the negative of the expected value of one specific utility function known the quadratic utility function. However, the quadratic utility function may not be the appropriate function to use under a given set of circumstances. Moreover, MSE has the disadvantage of heavily weighting outliers [7]. This is a result of the squaring of each term, which effectively weights large errors more heavily than small ones. Therefore and by applying these methods, the signal categorization step presents a shortcoming that can influence negatively the DCA functioning. Therefore, in this paper, we propose to develop a novel bio-inspired model of the DCA based on a new signal selection and categorization technique. Our new model is derived from the behavioral models of natural dendritic cells and grounded on the framework of Rough Set Theory (RST) for signal selection and signal categorization.

Rough Set Theory (RST) [8] has been employed with much success in different fields as a dimensionality reduction technique [9][10]. It has also been applied to improve the performance and the classification effectiveness of several algorithms [11]. To select features, RST removes the unnecessary attributes while keeping only the most informative ones - a subset termed REDUCT - that preserve nearly the classification power of the original database. Moreover, the assignment of each selected feature to its right signal type (DS, SS and PAMP) is based on the rough set theory main concepts; the REDUCT and the CORE. Our new hybrid computational biological model, named "RC-DCA", is based on the REDUCT and CORE RST fundamental concepts.

The main contributions of this paper are to introduce the concept of rough set theory in the DCA data pre-processing phase and to show how RST can be applied to search for the right and convenient features to retain. In addition, we aim to show how the application of RST can be appropriate for the categorization of each selected feature to its right type of signal. We also present results showing that using RST is well suited to the DCA for the signal selection problem and for the signal type assignment. Applying the RST instead of PCA improves the validity and cogency of the DCA classification results.

The rest of the paper is organized as follows: In Section 2 we describe the dendritic cell algorithm formally, while in Section 3 we describe the basic concepts of rough set theory. Section 4 presents our proposed method based on RST for signal selection and signal categorization. Experiments demonstrating the use of the RST for DCA are outlined in Section 5 and the final Section includes the discussion of the obtained results.

2 The Dendritic Cell Algorithm

Before explaining the functioning of the DCA, we introduce in brief its biological principles used for its classification task.

2.1 Introducing Dendritic Cells

Dendritic cells are potent antigen presenting cells that possess the ability to capture and process antigens and activate specific T cells [12]. DCs differentiate into three main states upon the receipt of signals - PAMPs, danger, safe - from their neighborhood. The first DC maturation state is the immature state (iDCs). The differentiation of iDCs depends on the combination of the various signals received leading either to a full maturation state or to a partial maturation state. Under the reception of safe signals, iDCs migrate to the semi-mature state (smDCs) causing antigens tolerance. iDCs migrate to the mature state (mDCs) if they are more exposed to danger signals and PAMPs than safe signals. mDCs present the collected antigens in a dangerous context.

2.2 Abstract View of the Dendritic Cell Algorithm

DCA was first introduced in [1] and has been subject to several modifications so far [13][14][15][16][17]. The initial step of the DCA is the automatic data pre-processing phase where feature selection and signal categorization are achieved. More precisely, DCA selects the most important features, from the initial input database, and assigns each selected attribute its specific signal category (SS, DS or PAMP). To do so, the DCA applies the principal component analysis (PCA) [3]. For signal selection, DCA applies the PCA that selects the first "principal components" which reveal the internal structure of the given data with the focus on data variance. PCA reduces data dimension, by accumulating the vectors that can be linearly represented by each other [2]. Once features are selected, PCA is applied to assign each attribute to its specific signal type. In fact, PCA performs a ranking procedure by using a sum of the absolute values of the weights used for signal transformation by the DCA. Once ranking is performed, the attributes are mapped into the DCA input signal categories, by correlating the PCA ranking with the ranking of signal categories - which implies the significance of each signal type to the signal transformation of the DCA - which is in the order Safe, PAMP, and Danger [2]. The DCA adheres these signals and antigen to fix the context of each object (DC) which is the step of Signal Processing. The algorithm processes its input signals in order to get three output signals: costimulation signal (Csm), semi-mature signal ($Semi$) and mature signal (Mat). A migration threshold is incorporated into the DCA in order to determine the lifespan of a DC. As soon as the Csm exceeds the migration threshold; the DC ceases to sample signals and antigens. The migration state of a DC to the semi-mature state or to the mature state is determined by the comparison between cumulative $Semi$ and cumulative Mat. If the cumulative $Semi$ is greater than the cumulative Mat, then the DC goes to the semi-mature context, which implies that the antigen data was collected under normal conditions. Otherwise, the DC goes to the mature context, signifying a potentially anomalous data item. This step is known to be the Context Assessment phase.

The nature of the response is determined by measuring the number of DCs that are fully mature and is represented by the Mature Context Antigen Value (MCAV). $MCAV$ is applied in the DCA final step which is the Classification procedure and used to assess the degree of anomaly of a given antigen. The closer the $MCAV$ is to 1, the greater the probability that the antigen is anomalous. By applying thresholds at various levels, analysis can be performed to assess the anomaly detection capabilities of the algorithm. Those antigens whose $MCAV$ are greater than the anomalous threshold are classified as anomalous while the others are classified as normal.

3 Rough Set Theory

Rough Set Theory (RST) [8] has been successfully applied to feature selection problems as it is a robust method for pattern dimensionality reduction. In this Section, we briefly discuss its main concepts.

3.1 Preliminaries of Rough Set Theory

This Section recalls some essential definitions from RST that are used for feature selection. In rough set theory, an *information table* is defined as a tuple $T = (U, A)$ where U and A are two finite, non-empty sets, U the *universe* of primitive objects and A the set of attributes. Each attribute or feature $a \in A$ is associated with a set V_a of its value, called the *domain* of a. We may partition the attribute set A into two subsets C and D, called *condition* and *decision* attributes, respectively [18]. Let $P \subset A$ be a subset of attributes. The indiscernibility relation, denoted by $IND(P)$, is an equivalence relation defined as: $IND(P) = \{(x, y) \in U \times U : \forall a \in P, a(x) = a(y)\}$, where $a(x)$ denotes the value of feature a of object x. If $(x, y) \in IND(P)$, x and y are said to be *indiscernible* with respect to P. The family of all equivalence classes of $IND(P)$ (Partition of U determined by P) is denoted by $U/IND(P)$. Each element in $U/IND(P)$ is a set of indiscernible objects with respect to P. Equivalence classes $U/IND(C)$ and $U/IND(D)$ are called *condition* and *decision* classes. For any concept $X \subseteq U$ and attribute subset $R \subseteq A$, X could be approximated by the R-*lower* approximation and R-*upper* approximation using the knowledge of R. The lower approximation of X is the set of objects of U that are surely in X, defined as: $\underline{R}(X) = \bigcup \{E \in U/IND(R) : E \subseteq X\}$. The upper approximation of X is the set of objects of U that are possibly in X, defined as: $\overline{R}(X) = \bigcup \{E \in U/IND(R) : E \cap X \neq \emptyset\}$ The boundary region is defined as:

$$BND_R(X) = \overline{R}(X) - \underline{R}(X)$$

If the boundary region is empty, that is, $\overline{R}(X) = \underline{R}(X)$, concept X is said to be R-*definable*. Otherwise X is a rough set with respect to R.

The positive region of decision classes $U/IND(D)$ with respect to condition attributes C is denoted by $POS_c(D)$ where:

$$POS_c(D) = \bigcup \overline{R}(X)$$

The positive region $POS_c(D)$ is a set of objects of U that can be classified with certainty to classes $U/IND(D)$ employing attributes of C. In other words, the positive region $POS_c(D)$ indicates the union of all the equivalence classes defined by $IND(P)$ that each for sure can induce the decision class D [19].

Rough set theory defines two important concepts that can be used for feature selection and data reduction which are the CORE and the REDUCT [19].

3.2   Reduct and Core for Feature Selection

The aim of feature selection is to remove unnecessary features to the target concept. It is the process of finding a smaller set of attributes, than the original one, with the same or close classificatory power as the original set. Unnecessary features, in an information table, can be classified into irrelevant features that do not affect the target concept in any way and redundant (superfluous) features that do not add anything new to the target concept.

A simple heuristic is to define a measure that evaluates the necessity of a feature. However, it is difficult to define a heuristic function on these qualitative descriptions of irrelevance and redundance. John et al. [20] defined strong relevance and weak relevance of a feature in terms of the probability of the occurrence of the target concept given this feature. Strong relevant features are *indispensable* in the sense that it cannot be removed without loss of prediction accuracy. Weak relevant features can sometimes contribute to prediction accuracy.

Strong and weak relevance provide a good foundation upon which we can define our basics for defining the importance of each attribute. The set of strong relevant features is equivalent to relative CORE in the RST. The relative REDUCT is a combination of all strong relevant features and some weak relevant features.

In RST, a subset $R \subseteq C$ is said to be a D-*reduct* of C if $POS_R(D) = POS_C(D)$ and there is no $R' \subset R$ such that $POS_{R'}(D) = POS_C(D)$. In other words, the REDUCT is the minimal set of attributes preserving the positive region. There may exist many reducts (a family of reducts) in a information table which can be denoted by $RED_D^F(C)$. The CORE is the set of attributes that are contained by all reducts, defined as:

$$CORE_D(C) = \bigcap RED_D(C)$$

where $RED_D(C)$ is the D-reduct of C. In other words, the CORE is the set of attributes that cannot be removed without changing the positive region meaning that these attributes cannot be removed from the information system without causing collapse of the equivalence-class structure. This means that all attributes present in the CORE are indispensable.

4   RC-DCA: The New DCA Solution Approach

In this Section, we present our RC-DCA model based on RST for the automatic DCA data pre-processing phase including feature selection and signal categorization. Our new proposed approach functions under four levels of abstraction as shown in Fig.1. We will mainly focus on the pre-processing phase which is based on the use of RST.

4.1   The RC-DCA Signal Selection Process

For antigen classification, our learning problem has to select high discriminating features from the original input database which corresponds to the antigen information data set. We may formalize this problem as an information table, where universe $U = \{x_1, x_2, \ldots, x_N\}$ is a set of antigen identifiers, the conditional attribute set $C = \{c_1, c_2, \ldots, c_N\}$ contains each feature of the information table to select and the decision attribute D of our learning problem corresponds to the class label of each sample. As DCA is applied to binary classification problems, the input database has a single binary decision attribute. Hence, the decision attribute D, which corresponds to the class label, has binary values d: either the antigen is collected under safe circumstances reflecting a normal behavior (classified as normal) or the antigen is collected under dangerous circumstances reflecting an anomalous behavior (classified as anomalous). The condition attribute feature D is defined as follows:

$$D = \{normal, anomalous\},$$

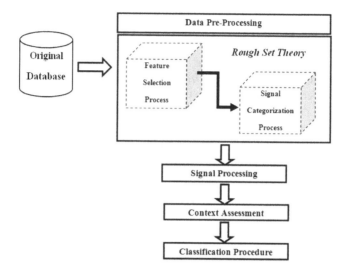

Fig. 1. The RC-DCA Proposed Model

For that, RC-DCA computes, first of all, the positive region for the whole at-tribute set C for both label classes of D: $POS_C(\{d\})$. Based on the RST compu-tations (seen previously in Section 3), RC-DCA computes the positive region of each feature c and the positive region of all the composed features $C - \{c\}$ (when discarding each time one feature c from C) defined respectively as $POS_c(\{d\})$ and $POS_{C-\{c\}}(\{d\})$, until finding the minimal subset of attributes R from C that preserves the positive region as the whole attribute set C does. In fact, RC-DCA removes in each computation level the unnecessary features that may affect negatively the accuracy of the RC-DCA. The result of these computations is either one reduct $R = RED_D(C)$ or a family of reducts $RED_D^F(C)$. Any reduct of $RED_D^F(C)$ can be used to replace the original antigen information table. Con-sequently, if the RC-DCA generates only one reduct $R = RED_D(C)$ then for the feature selection process, RC-DCA chooses this specific R which represents the most informative features that preserve nearly the same classification power of the original data set. If the RC-DCA generates a family of reducts $RED_D^F(C)$ then RC-DCA chooses randomly one reduct R among $RED_D^F(C)$ to represent the original input antigen information table. This random choice is argued by the same priority of all the reducts in $RED_D^F(C)$. In other words, any reduct R of the reducts $RED_D^F(C)$ can be used to replace the original information table.

These attributes which constitute the reduct will describe all concepts in the original training data set. Using the REDUCT concept, our method can guarantee that attributes of extracted feature patterns will be the most relevant for its classification task. An illustrative example related to the REDUCT and the CORE generation can be found in [19]. Once the reduct is generated, our proposed solution moves to its second step which is signal categorization.

4.2   The RC-DCA Signal Categorization Process

The second step of our RC-DCA model data pre-processing phase is feature categorization. More precisely, our method has to assign for each selected attribute, produced by the previous step and which is included in the generated REDUCT, its definite and specific signal category. The general guidelines for signal assignment are presented in the list below [1]:

- **Safe signals :** Their presence certainly indicates that no anomalies are present.
- **PAMPs :** The presence of PAMPs usually means that there is an anomalous situation.
- **Danger signals :** Their presence may or may not show an anomalous situation, however the probability of an anomaly is higher than under normal circumstances.

From the previous definitions, both the PAMP and safe signal are positive indicators of an anomalous and normal signal while the DS is measuring situations where the risk of anomalousness is high, but there is no signature of a specific cause. In other words, PAMP and SS have a certain final context (either an anomalous or a normal behavior) while the DS cannot specify exactly the final context to assign to the collected antigen. This is because the information returned by the DS is not certain as the collected antigen may or may not indicate an anomalous situation. This problem can be formulated as follows:

Both PAMP and SS are more informative than DS which means that both of these signals can be seen as indispensable attributes. To represent this level of importance, our method uses the CORE RST concept. On the other hand, DS is less informative than PAMP and SS. Therefore, our method applies the rest of the REDUCT attributes, discarding the attributes of the CORE chosen to represent the SS and the PAMP signals, to represent the DS.

As stated in the previous step, our method may either produce only one reduct R or a family of reducts $RED_D^F(C)$. The process of signal categorization for both cases are described in what follow.

The Process of One REDUCT. In the case where our model generates only one reduct; it means that $CORE_D(C) = RED_D(C)$. In other words, all the features that represent the produced reduct R are indispensable. For signal categorization and with respect to the ranking of signal categories that implies the significance of each signal category to the signal transformation of the DCA which is in the order Safe, PAMP, and Danger, our method processes as follows:

First of all, RC-DCA calculates the positive region $POS_C(\{d\})$ of the whole core $CORE_D(C)$. Then, our method calculates the positive regions $POS_{C-\{c\}}(\{d\})$ that correspond to the positive regions of the core when removing each time one attribute c from it. Our method calculates the difference values between $POS_C(\{d\})$ and each $POS_{C-\{c\}}(\{d\})$ already calculated. The removed attribute c causing the highest difference value $POS_C(\{d\}) - POS_{C-\{c\}}(\{d\})$

is considered as the most important attribute in the CORE. In other words, when removing that attribute c from the CORE then the effectiveness and the reliability of the core will be strongly affected. Therefore, our method selects that attribute c to form the Safe signal. The second attribute c having the next highest difference value $POS_C(\{d\}) - POS_{C-\{c\}}(\{d\})$ is used to form the PAMP signal. And finally, the rest of the CORE attributes are combined and affected to represent the DS as it is less than certain to be anomalous.

The Process of a Family of REDUCTs. In case where our model produces more than one reduct R, a family of reducts $RED_D^F(C)$, our method uses both concepts: the core $CORE_D(C)$ and the reducts $RED_D^F(C)$. Let us remind that $CORE_D(C) = \bigcap RED_D(C)$; which means that on one hand we have the minimal set of attributes preserving the positive region (reducts) and on the other hand we have the set of attributes that are contained in all reducts (CORE) which cannot be removed without changing the positive region. This means that all the attributes present in the CORE are indispensable.

For signal assignment and based on the positive regions calculation, our method assigns the convenient attributes from the CORE to determine the SS and PAMP following the same reasoning as our method produces only one reduct. As for the DS signal type categorization, our solution chooses first of all, randomly, a reduct $RED_D(C)$ among $RED_D^F(C)$. Then, our method combines all the $RED_D(C)$ features except the c attributes already chosen for the SS and PAMP and assigns the resulting value to the DS.

Once the selected features are assigned to their suitable signal types, our method calculates the values of each signal category using the same process as the standard DCA [1]. The output is thus a new information table which reflects the signal database. In fact, the universe U of the induced signal data set is $U = \{x_1', x_2', \ldots, x_N'\}$ a set of antigen identifiers and the conditional attribute set $C = \{SS, PAMP, DS\}$ contains the three signal types: the safe signal, the pathogen-associated molecular patterns and the danger signal type. The induced signal database which is the input data for the next proposed model steps contains the values of each signal type for each antigen identifier.

Once data pre-processing is achieved, our solution approach processes its next steps which are the Signal Processing, the Context Assessment and the Classification Procedure as the standard DCA does and as described in Section 2.

5   Experimental Setup

To test the validity of our RC-DCA hybrid model, our experiments are performed on two-class databases from [21] described in Table 1.

For data pre-processing, the standard DCA uses PCA to automatically select and categorize signals. As for our method, it uses RST as explained in Section 4. For both DCA and our method, each data item is mapped as an antigen, with the value of the antigen equal to the data ID of the item. In all experiments and for both DCA and RC-DCA, a population of 100 cells is used and 10 DCs

Table 1. Description of Databases

Database	Ref	♯ Instances	♯ Attributes
Spambase	SP	4601	58
SPECTF Heart	SPECTF	267	45
Cylinder Bands	CylB	540	40
Chess	Ch	3196	37
Ionosphere	IONO	351	35
Mushroom	Mash	8124	23
Horse Colic	HC	368	23
Hepatitis	HE	155	20
Congressional Voting Records	CVT	435	17
Labor Relations	LR	57	17
Statlog (Heart)	STAT	270	14
Tic-Tac-Toe Endgame	TicTac	958	10

sample the antigen vector each cycle. The migration threshold of an individual DC is set to 10 to ensure this DC to survive over multiple iterations. To perform anomaly detection, a threshold which is automatically generated from the data is applied to the MCAVs. The MCAV threshold is derived from the proportion of anomalous data instances of the whole data set. Items below the threshold are classified as class one and above as class two. The resulting classified antigens are compared to the labels given in the original data sets. For each experiment, the results presented are based on mean MCAV values generated across 10 runs. Weightings used in all experiments are derived from empirical immunological data. We evaluate the performance of our RC-DCA method in terms of number of extracted features, sensitivity, specificity and accuracy which are defined as: $Sensitivity = TP/(TP + FN); Specificity = TN/(TN + FP); Accuracy = (TP + TN)/(TP + TN + FN + FP)$; where TP, FP, TN, and FN refer respectively to: true positive, false positive, true negative and false negative. We will also compare the classification performance of our RC-DCA method to well known classifiers which are the Support Vector Machine (SVM), Artificial Neural Network (ANN) and the Decision Tree (DT).

6   Results and Analysis

Let us remind that the first step of the DCA classification algorithm is data pre-processing which is based on the use of the PCA. PCA selects automatically the attributes from the original database based on the first principal components that capture most of the variance. Nevertheless, it is not necessarily true that these selected first principal components are neither useful for the DCA classification task nor reflecting the right attributes to retain. Therefore, the choice of the first principal components may generate unreliable and indecisive classification results. Moreover, the DCA uses the PCA attributes' ranking which is based on variability to assign for each selected attribute its specific signal category. Nevertheless, this categorization process could not be considered as a coherent and consistent assignment procedure. In this Section, we show that applying RST to DCA is more convenient than PCA for the feature selection and signal categorization processes. Applying rough set theory for the DCA data pre-processing phase shows that our model, RC-DCA, outperforms the DCA in terms of accuracy. This is confirmed by the results presented in Table 2.

Table 2. DCA and RC-DCA Comparison Results

Database	Sensitivity (%) DCA		Specificity (%) DCA		Accuracy (%) DCA		♯ Attributes DCA	
	PCA	RST	PCA	RST	PCA	RST	PCA	RST
SP	94.15	98.4	94.58	98.49	94.41	98.45	14	8
SPECTF	79.24	88.67	80	87.27	79.4	88.38	11	4
CylB	95.5	97	96.47	97.75	96.09	97.46	16	7
Ch	94.36	98.8	94.3	98.88	94.33	98.84	14	11
IONO	94.44	96.82	96.44	97.33	95.72	97.15	24	19
Mash	99.41	99.55	99.38	99.76	99.4	99.64	7	6
HC	87.5	93.05	90.13	94.73	88.58	93.75	19	14
HE	93.75	96.87	94.3	97.56	94.19	97.41	10	4
CVT	97.02	98.21	95.5	99.25	96.09	98.85	14	8
LR	85	90	89.18	91.89	87.71	91.22	10	5
STAT	81.66	93.33	96.66	98	90	95.92	10	4
TicTac	91.05	95.04	93.67	95.78	91.96	95.3	7	6

From Table 2, we can notice that our RC-DCA model selects fewer features than the DCA when applying PCA (PCA-DCA). This can be explained by the appropriate use of rough set theory for data dimensionality reduction. More precisely, by using the RST REDUCT concept, RC-DCA keeps only the most informative features that should be retained for the algorithm classification task. For example, by applying our RC-DCA method to the CylB data set, the number of selected features becomes only 7 attributes. However, when applying the DCA with PCA to the same database (CylB), the number of the retained features will be 16. From this example and from Table 2, we can notice that PCA preserves more features than RST. These additional features are the result of the PCA overestimation of the number of factors to retain which may affect the DCA classification task by producing unreliable results. On the other hand, RC-DCA based on the REDUCT concept, selects the minimal set of features from the original database and can guarantee that the reduct attributes will be the most relevant for its classification task. In fact, by reducing more the number of features while preserving nearly the same classification power of the original data set, our RC-DCA has the advantages to decrease the cost of acquiring data and to make the classification model easier to understand unlike when applying the PCA with more features.

As for the classification accuracy, from Table 2, we can easily remark that the RC-DCA accuracy is notably better than the one given by the PCA-DCA. For example, when applying the RC-DCA to the Ch database, the RC-DCA accuracy is set to 98.84%. Nevertheless, when applying the PCA-DCA to the same database, the accuracy is 94.33%. Same remark is noticed for both the sensitivity and the specificity criteria where our RC-DCA model is capable of producing relatively higher true positive rates (sensitivity) and higher true negative rates (specificity) than the sensitivity and specificity values of the DCA when using the PCA.

These encouraging RC-DCA results are explained by the appropriate use of RST with DCA for feature selection and their categorization to their precise signal types. As stated previously, the classification results of the DCA depends on its data pre-processing primary step including signal selection and signal categorization. This step is crucial to obtain reliable results. RC-DCA uses the REDUCT RST fundamental concept to select only the essential part of the original input database which can discern all objects discernible by the original information system (the antigen information database). This pertinent set of minimal features (reduct) is the base of RC-DCA feature selection phase and can guarantee a solid base for the signal categorization step. The RC-DCA good classification results are also explained by the appropriate categorization of each selected signal to its right signal type. Using both the REDUCT and the CORE concepts, RC-DCA assigns to each attribute constituting the REDUCT its convenient signal; either the danger signal, the safe signal or the PAMP signal type. Based on these indispensable and most informative features for signal categorization, RC-DCA can produce a coherent signal database for its next classification steps. Rough set theory basic concepts allow the RC-DCA to generate relevant and satisfactory classification results; as it is presented in Table 2.

As for the DCA, by applying the PCA statistical technique, it produces less accuracy in comparison to our RC-DCA method. The fact of selecting the first principal components that capture most of the variance is not necessary the best way to obtain the right set of features to keep for the DCA algorithm. More precisely, the PCA selected attributes are not necessarily the right features to retain since this set may still contain extra features. These extra features may not add anything new to the target concept while increasing the cost of acquiring data. The set may also contain noisy and misleading features which have a negative effect on classification accuracy when they are kept in the model. Furthermore, the DCA categorization step can not reflect a coherent and consistent assignment procedure. These clarifications explain the reasons of the PCA-DCA less classification results in comparison to our RC-DCA model.

We have also compared the performance of our RC-DCA to other classifiers including SVM, ANN and DT. The comparison made is in terms of the average of accuracies on the 12 databases. The parameters of SVM, ANN and DT are set to the most adequate parameters to these algorithms using the Weka software. Figure 2 shows that PCA-DCA has nearly the same classification performance as SVM and ANN and slightly better than DT. It also shows that our RC-DCA outperforms all the mentioned classifiers including the PCA-DCA in terms of overall accuracy. These promising RC-DCA results are explained by the appropriate application of rough set theory to the DCA data pre-processing phase. This makes the DCA a better classifier by generating more reliable and more pertinent results.

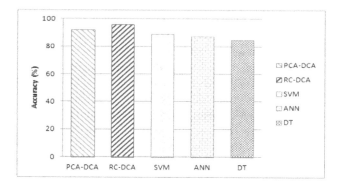

Fig. 2. Comparison of Classifiers' Average Accuracies on the 12 Binary Data sets

To summarize, applying the rough set theory, instead of the principal component analysis statistical method, as a new feature selection technique and for signal categorization is well suited and more appropriate to the standard DCA as it improves its efficiency of classification. RC-DCA selects the minimal and the most informative set of features and assigns to each selected attribute its right signal type. This is based on the REDUCT and the CORE fundamental rough set theory concepts. RC-DCA by applying RST performs much better than the dendritic cell algorithm in terms of classification accuracy. However, it needs more time to process than DCA when using the PCA. It is, also, important to mention that the complexity of our newly-proposed RC-DCA method is more important than the complexity of the standard DCA and despite of this, our hybrid system produces more accurate results than the DCA.

7   Conclusion and Further Works

In this paper, we have introduced a new hybrid DCA bio-inspired model based on RST. Our model aims to select the convenient set of features from the initial database and to perform their signal categorization using the REDUCT and the CORE RST concepts. The experimentation results show that our RC-DCA is capable of performing better its classification task than DCA and other classifiers. As future work we aim to verify further the validity of our method obtained results using more challenging databases and more statistical measures for comparison. We also aim to apply the fuzzy rough set theory for the DCA data pre-processing phase and to compare the results with our solution approach.

References

1. Greensmith, J., Aickelin, U., Cayzer, S.: Introducing Dendritic Cells as a Novel Immune-Inspired Algorithm for Anomaly Detection. In: Jacob, C., Pilat, M.L., Bentley, P.J., Timmis, J.I. (eds.) ICARIS 2005. LNCS, vol. 3627, pp. 153–167. Springer, Heidelberg (2005)

2. Gu, F., Greensmith, J., Oates, R., Aickelin, U.: Pca 4 dca: The application of principal component analysis to the dendritic cell algorithm. In: Proceedings of the 9th Annual Workshop on Computational Intelligence (2009)
3. Jolliffe, I.T.: Principal component analysis. Springer, New York (2002)
4. Cantú-Paz, E.: Feature Subset Selection, Class Separability, and Genetic Algorithms. In: Deb, K., Tari, Z. (eds.) GECCO 2004. LNCS, vol. 3102, pp. 959–970. Springer, Heidelberg (2004)
5. Gu, F.: Theoretical and Empirical Extensions of the Dendritic Cell Algorithm. PhD thesis, University of Nottingham (2011)
6. Garthwaite, P., Jolliffe, I., Jones, B.: Statistical Inference (Hardcover). Oxford University Press (2003)
7. Bermejo, S., Cabestany, J.: Oriented principal component analysis for large margin classifiers. Neural Netw. 14, 1447–1461 (2001)
8. Pawlak, Z.: Rough sets. International Journal of Computer and Information Science 11, 341–356 (1982)
9. Swiniarski, R.W., Skowron, A.: Rough set methods in feature selection and recognition. Pattern Recognition Letters 24(6), 833–849 (2003)
10. Han, J., Hu, X., Lin, T.Y.: Feature Subset Selection Based on Relative Dependency between Attributes. In: Tsumoto, S., Słowiński, R., Komorowski, J., Grzymała-Busse, J.W. (eds.) RSCTC 2004. LNCS (LNAI), vol. 3066, pp. 176–185. Springer, Heidelberg (2004)
11. Zhong, N., Dong, J., Ohsuga, S.: Using rough sets with heuristics for feature selection. J. Intell. Inf. Syst. 16(3), 199–214 (2001)
12. Lotze, M.T., Thomson, A.W.: Dendritic Cells: Biology and Clinical Applications, 2nd edn., no. 794 (2001)
13. Greensmith, J., Aickelin, U.: The Deterministic Dendritic Cell Algorithm. In: Bentley, P.J., Lee, D., Jung, S. (eds.) ICARIS 2008. LNCS, vol. 5132, pp. 291–302. Springer, Heidelberg (2008)
14. Gu, F., Greensmith, J., Aickelin, U.: Integrating real-time analysis with the dendritic cell algorithm through segmentation. In: GECCO, pp. 1203–1210 (2009)
15. Chelly, Z., Elouedi, Z.: FDCM: A Fuzzy Dendritic Cell Method. In: Hart, E., McEwan, C., Timmis, J., Hone, A. (eds.) ICARIS 2010. LNCS, vol. 6209, pp. 102–115. Springer, Heidelberg (2010)
16. Chelly, Z., Elouedi, Z.: Further Exploration of the Fuzzy Dendritic Cell Method. In: Liò, P., Nicosia, G., Stibor, T. (eds.) ICARIS 2011. LNCS, vol. 6825, pp. 419–432. Springer, Heidelberg (2011)
17. Chelly, Z., Smiti, A., Elouedi, Z.: COID-FDCM: The Fuzzy Maintained Dendritic Cell Classification Method. In: Rutkowski, L., Korytkowski, M., Scherer, R., Tadeusiewicz, R., Zadeh, L.A., Zurada, J.M. (eds.) ICAISC 2012, Part II. LNCS, vol. 7268, pp. 233–241. Springer, Heidelberg (2012)
18. Pawlak, Z., Grzymala-Busse, J., Slowinski, R., Ziarko, W.: Rough sets. Commun. ACM 38, 88–95 (1995)
19. Massart, D.L., Walczak, B.: Rough sets theory. Chemometrics and Intelligent Laboratory Systems 47, 1–16 (1999)
20. John, G., Kohavi, R., Pfleger, K.: Irrelevant features and the subset selection problem. In: ICML, pp. 121–129 (1994)
21. Asuncion, A., Newman, D.J.: UCI machine learning repository (2007), http://mlearn.ics.uci.edu/mlrepository.html

Artificial Immune Network Approach
with Beta Differential Operator Applied
to Optimization of Heat Exchangers

Viviana Cocco Mariani[1,2], Leandro dos Santos Coelho[2,3], Anderson Duck[1],
Fabio Alessandro Guerra[4] , and Ravipudi Venkata Rao[5]

[1] PPGEM, Pontifical Catholic University of Parana (PUCPR)
Imaculada Conceição, 1155, Zip code 80215-901, Curitiba, PR, Brazil
viviana.mariani@pucpr.br, andersonduck@gmail.com
[2] Department of Electrical Engineering, Federal University of Parana (UFPR)
Zip code 81531-980, Curitiba, PR, Brazil
[3] PPGEPS, Pontifical Catholic University of Parana (PUCPR)
Imaculada Conceição, 1155, Zip code 80215-901, Curitiba, PR, Brazil
leandro.coelho@pucpr.br
[4] Electricity Department, DPEL/DVSE/LACTEC - Institute of Technology for Development,
Zip code 81531-980, Curitiba, PR, Brazil
guerra@lactec.org.br
[5] Sardar Vallabhbhai National Institute of Technology, Surat-395 007, Gujarat, India
ravipudirao@gmail.com

Abstract. The artificial immune systems combine these strengths have been
gaining significant attention due to its powerful adaptive learning and memory
capabilities. A meta-heuristic approach called opt-aiNET (artificial immune network for optimization) algorithm, a well-known immune inspired algorithm for
function optimization, is adopted in this paper. The opt-aiNET algorithm evolves
a population, which consists of a network of antibodies (considered as candidate
solutions to the function being optimized). These undergo a process of evaluation against the objective function, clonal expansion, mutation, selection and
interaction between themselves. In this paper, a proposed modified opt-aiNET
approach using based on mutation operator inspired in differential evolution and
beta probability distribution (opt-BDaiNET) is described and validated to three
benchmark functions and to shell and tube heat exchanger optimization based on
the minimization from economic view point. Simulations are conducted to verify
the efficiency of proposed opt-BDaiNET algorithm and the results obtained for
two case studies are compared with those obtained by using genetic algorithm
and particle swarm optimization. In this application domain, the opt-aiNET and
opt-BDaiNET were found to outperform the previously best-known solutions
available in the recent literature.

Keywords: artificial immune system, optimization, opt-aiNET, differential
evolution, beta probability distribution, heat exchangers design.

C.A. Coello Coello et al. (Eds.): ICARIS 2012, LNCS 7597, pp. 166–177, 2012.
© Springer-Verlag Berlin Heidelberg 2012

1   Introduction

Natural immune systems are sophisticated and complex defense and maintenance systems. The features of the natural immune systems such as learning, memory, and adaptation are currently being used in the development of artificial immune systems (AIS). AIS are adaptive systems, inspired by theoretical immunology and observed immune functions, principles and models, which are applied to problem solving [1]. During the last decades, novel approaches of AIS have been employed for developing interesting algorithms for optimization applications [2],[3].

The artificial immune network (aiNet) algorithm is a discrete immune network algorithm that was developed for data compression and clustering [4]. Based on clonal selection and affinity maturation, De Castro and Timmis developed the opt-aiNet (artificial immune network for optimization) algorithm [5] which is suitable for function optimization problems. It depicts the interaction of network cells as competition, that is, cells with lower fitness and similar to those with higher fitness are deleted with network suppression. By removing similar network cells, the opt-aiNet prevents cells clustering on a single peak so as to improve diversity of network cells. Furthermore, the opt-aiNet presents a number of interesting features, such as dynamic variation of the population size, local and global search, and the ability to maintain any number of optima. These are highly desirable characteristics, but they are obtained at the cost of a very large number of objective function evaluations.

The opt-aiNet has received a great deal of attentions in the AIS literature and has subsequently been assessed and modified (see examples in [6]-[8]). In this paper, we present a modified and efficient version of opt-aiNET based on mutation operator inspired on differential evolution [9] and beta probability distribution [10] (opt-BDaiNET). It can achieve an improved trade-off between the exploration and exploitation in the solution space.

To illustrate the power of the proposed opt-BDaiNET, three benchmark functions and two case studies of the shell and tube heat exchanger optimization [11] have been considered. Heat exchangers are devices used to transfer heat between two or more fluids that are at different temperatures and which in most of the cases they are separated by a solid wall. Simulation results of the opt-aiNET and the proposed opt-BDaiNET approach are compared with other optimization techniques presented in literature related to the heat exchangers design.

The remainder of this paper is organized as follows. Sections 2 and 3 describe the classical opt-aiNET and a proposed opt-BDaiNET, respectively. The problem formulation for heat exchanger optimization and its assumptions are given in Section 4. Moreover, Section 5 presents the simulation results for two case studies. Finally, the conclusions are drawn and future studies are discussed in Section 6.

2   Fundamentals of the Opt-aiNET

The field of AIS derives inspiration from processes and mechanisms apparent in the biological immune system. Opt-aiNET is an artificial immune system capable of performing local and global search, as well as to adjust dynamically the size of population [12]. Opt-aiNET creates a memory set of antibodies (points in the search space) that represent (over time) the best candidate solutions to the objective function. Opt-aiNET is capable of either unimodal or multimodal optimization and can be characterized by five main features: (i) the population size is dynamically adjustable, (ii) it demonstrates exploitation and exploration of the search space, (iii) it determines the locations of multiple optima, (iv) it has the capability of maintaining many optima solutions, and (v) it has defined stopping criteria [13]. The steps of the opt-aiNET are summarized as follows:

Initialization of the parameter setup

The user must choose the key parameters that control the opt-aiNET, i.e., population size (M), suppression threshold (σ_s), number of clones generated for each cell (N_c), percentage of random new cells each iteration (d), scale of affinity proportion selection (β), and maximum number of iterations allowed (stopping criterion), t_{max}.

Initialization of cell population

Set iteration $t=0$. Initialize a population of $i=1,..,M$ cells (real-valued n-dimensional solution vectors) with random values generated according to a uniform probability distribution in the n dimensional problem space. Initialize the entire solution vector population in the given upper and lower limits of the search space.

Evaluation of each network cell

Evaluate the fitness value of each cell (in this work, the objective of the fitness function is to maximize the cost function).

Generation of clones

Generate a number N_c of clones for each network cell. The clones are offspring cells that are identical copies of their parent cell.

Mutation operation

Mutation is an operation that changes each clone proportionally to the fitness of the parent cells, but keeps the parent cell. Clones of each cell are mutated according to the affinity (Euclidean distance between two cells) of the parent cell. The affinity proportional mutation is performed according to equations (1) and (2), given by:

$$c' = c + \alpha \cdot N(0,1) \tag{1}$$

$$\alpha = \rho^{-1} e^{-f^*} \tag{2}$$

where c' is a mutated cell c, $N(0,1)$ is a Gaussian random variable of zero mean and unitary variance, ρ is a parameter that controls the decay of the inverse exponential function, and f^* is the objective function of an individual normalized in the interval [0,1].

Evaluation the fitness of all network cells

Evaluate the fitness value of all network cells of the population including new clones and mutated clones.

Selection of fittest clones

For each clone select the most fit and remove the others.

Determination of affinity of all network cells

Determine the affinity network cells and perform network suppression.

Generate randomly 'd' network cells

Introduce a percentage d of randomly generated cells. Set the generation number for t = t + 1. Proceed to step of *Evaluation of each network cell* until a stopping criterion is met, usually a maximum number of iterations, t_{max}. The stopping criterion depends on the type of problem.

3   The Proposed Opt-BDaiNET Approach

In the proposed opt-BDaiNET approach, we choose mutation operator based on differential evolution (DE) [9] because DE is an extremely efficient optimization algorithm.

The fundamental idea behind DE is a scheme whereby it generates the trial parameter vectors. In each step, the DE mutates vectors by adding weighted, random vector differentials to them. If the cost of the trial vector is better than that of the target, the target vector is replaced by the trial vector in next generation. It uses a rather greedy and less stochastic approach to problem solving compared to other evolutionary algorithms and is therefore aggressive (at a slightly increased cost of remaining trapped in local minima, which however is not a problem in this context since the search area is a local one and the procedure is repeated from several starting points).

The parameter MF in DE controls the amplification of the differential variation. The parameter MF controls the increase of difference between two individuals in the search space. The difference between two randomly chosen vectors defines the magnitude and direction of mutation. The beta distribution is a good candidate [10] to improve the opt-BDaiNET design can be useful in avoiding entrapment in local optima. A beta probability distribution approach is employed to tune the mutation rate of DE's mutation operator. Beta distribution belongs to continuous probability distributions and it is defined on the interval [0, 1].

In opt-BDaiNET, the stochastic properties of DE's mutation combined with beta probability distribution are used to spread the cells in search spaces as much as possible using information of other cells in the population and the Gaussian distribution is employed to speed up the local exploiting. In terms of implementation, instead of the classical opt-aiNET related to equations (1) and (2), the mutation operator of opt-BDaiNET uses the following procedure to minimization problem:

If F_i < median (F) then
Use the equations (1) and (2) of classical opt-aiNET (*local search*)
Else
Use the differential mutation (*global search using knowledge in population*)

$$c_i' = c_1 + MF \cdot (c_2 - c_3) \tag{3}$$

End If

where F_i is the objective function value of i-th cell c_i, MF is the mutation rate generated with beta probability distribution in range [0,1], c' is a mutated cell, c_1, c_2 and c_3 are three cells ($c_1 \neq c_2 \neq c_3$) choice with uniform distribution of the cell population for each dimension.

4   Heat Exchanger Design

In present study, logarithmic mean temperature difference (LMTD) method is used to specify the characteristic dimensions of shell-and-tube heat exchanger (STHE). The LMTD can be readily computed by knowledge of the hot and cold fluid inlet and outlet temperatures. Problems for which these temperatures are known may be classified as heat exchanger design problems [14].

The design problem is then one of the selecting an appropriate heat exchanger type and determining the size, that is the heat transfer surface area, A, exchanger length, L, and total costs, C_{tot}, including initial costs and operating and maintenance costs. The equations presented in this section are given for I and U type shell and tube heat exchangers.

The total cost C_{tot} is taken as the objective function, which includes capital investment, C_i, energy cost, C_e, annual operating cost, C_o, and total discounted operating cost, C_{od}, like in [15],

$$C_{tot} = C_i + C_{od} . \tag{4}$$

Adopting Hall's correlation given by [16] the capital investment C_i is computed as a function of the heat exchanger surface area

$$C_i = a_1 + a_2 A^{a_3} \tag{5}$$

where $a_1 = 8{,}000$, $a_2 = 259.2$, and $a_3 = 0.91$ for exchangers made with stainless steel for both shell-and-tubes [16]. The total discounted operating cost related to pumping power to overcome friction losses is computed from the following equations,

$$C_{od} = \sum_{j=1}^{ny} \frac{C_o}{(1+i)^j} , \tag{6}$$

$$C_o = P_1 C_e H , \tag{7}$$

where $C_e = 0.00012$, $H = 7{,}000$ and $i = 0.1$.

Considering the pumping efficiency, $\eta = 0.8$, the pumping power, P_1, is computed by,

$$P_1 = \frac{1}{\eta} \left(\frac{\dot{m}_t}{\rho_t} \Delta P_t + \frac{\dot{m}_s}{\rho_s} \Delta P_s \right). \tag{8}$$

In all heat exchanger, there is close physical and economical affinity between heat transfer and the pressure drop. The pressure drop allowance in heat exchanger is the static fluid pressure which may be expended to drive the fluid through the exchanger. In all heat exchanger there is close physical and economical affinity between heat transfer and pressure drop. For a constant heat capacity in the heat exchanger that is to be designed, increasing the flow velocity will cause a rise of heat transfer coefficient which results in compact exchanger design and lower investment cost. However increase of flow velocity will cause more pressure drop in heat exchanger which results in additional running cost. For this reason when designing a heat exchanger pressure drop must be considered with heat transfer and best solution for the system must be found.

The tubeside pressure drop is computed as the sum of distributed pressure drop along the tubes length and concentrated pressure losses in elbows and in the inlet and outlet nozzles from Kern [17], evaluated by

$$\Delta P_t = \Delta P_{tube\,length} + \Delta P_{tube\,elbow}, \tag{9}$$

$$\Delta P_t = \frac{\rho_t V_t^2}{2}\left(\frac{L}{d_i}f_t + p\right)n. \tag{10}$$

Different values of constant p are considered by different authors. Kern [17] assumed $p = 4$, the same value used in this study. The shell side pressure drop is evaluated by,

$$\Delta P_s = f_s\left(\frac{\rho_s V_s^2}{2}\right)\left(\frac{L}{B}\right)\left(\frac{D_s}{d_e}\right), \tag{11}$$

where the friction factor, f_s, is obtained by,

$$f_s = 2b_o\,\mathrm{Re}_s^{-0.15} \tag{12}$$

and $b_o = 0.72$ valid for $\mathrm{Re}_s < 40,000$ by Peters and Timmerhaus [18].

Based on all above calculations, total cost is computed from equation (4). The procedure is repeated computing new value of exchanger area, A, exchanger length, L, total cost, C_{tot}, and a corresponding exchanger architecture meeting the specifications. Each time the optimization algorithm changes the values of the design variables d_0 (tubes outside diameter), D_s (shell internal diameter), and B (baffles spacing) in an attempt to minimize the objective function. The search space is given by $0.015 \le d_0 \le 0.051$, $0.1 \le D_s \le 1.5$, and $0.05 \le B \le 0.5$.

For each case studied the original design specifications, shown in Table 1, were supplied as input to the optimization algorithm. In this paper, the following steps for optimal heat exchanger design are adopted:

Step 1. Assuming values of a set of design variables and estimating heat transfer area of the heat exchanger based on the required heat duty and other design specification;

Step 2. Evaluation of the capital investment, operating cost and objective function;

Step 3. Utilization of the optimization algorithm (opt-aiNET or opt-BDaiNET) to select a new set of values for the design variables;

Step 4. Iteration of the previous steps until that a minimum of the objective function be found.

Table 1. The process input and physical properties used as reference for each case in the numerical optimization of the overall system [15]

Parameter	Case #1		Case #2	
	Shell side: Methanol	Tube side: sea water	Shell side: Kerosene	Tube side: crude oil
Mass flow (kg/s)	27.80	68.90	5.52	18.80
T_i (°C)	95.00	25.00	199.00	37.80
T_o (°C)	40.00	40.00	93.30	76.70
ρ (kg/m³)	750.00	995.00	850.00	995.00
C_p (kJ/kgK)	2.84	4.20	2.47	2.05
μ (Pa.s)	0.00034	0.0008	0.0004	0.00358
μ_w (Pa.s)	0.00038	0.00052		
k (W/mK)	0.19	0.59	0.13	0.13
R_f (m²K/W)	0.00033	0.0002	0.00061	0.00061

5   Optimization Results

Beyond the case studies of heat exchanger design, in order to test the performance of the opt-aiNET and the opt-BDaiNET approaches, a suite of well-known three benchmark functions in Table 2 is evaluated too. The benchmark functions (Rosenbrock, Sphere, and Rastrigin) were implemented in $n = 30$ dimensions.

In relation to the evaluated benchmark functions, Rosenbrock's valley is a classic optimization problem, also known as *banana function* or the *second function of De Jong*. It is important mention here that the Rosenbrock function can be treated as a multimodal problem [20]. It has a narrow parabolic-shaped deep valley from the perceived local optima to the global optimum. To find the valley is trivial, but to achieve convergence to the global minimum is a difficult task.

Sphere function (De Jong's function #1) is a simple and strongly convex function. It is continuous and unimodal. Rastrigin's function has many local minima and maxima, making it difficult to find the global optimum. However, the location of the minima are regularly distributed. Furthermore, Rastrigin's function is a fairly difficult problem for optimization algorithms due to the large search space and large number of local minima. Rastrigin has a complexity of $O\{n.\ln(n)\}$, where n is the number of the function parameters [21].

The initial population of optimization approaches was generated from a uniform distribution in the ranges S specified in Table 2.

Table 2. Adopted benchmark functions, where S for the lower and upper bounds of the search space and $f_{minimum}$ is the minimum value of the function

Benchmark functions	Function name	S	$f_{minimum}$
$f_1(x) = \sum_{i=1}^{n/2} \left(100 \cdot \left(x_{2i} - x_{2i-1}^2 \right)^2 + \left(1 - x_{2i} \right)^2 \right)$	Rosenbrock	$(-30, 30)^n$	0
$f_2(x) = \sum_{i=1}^{n} x_i^2$	Sphere	$(-100, 100)^n$	0
$f_3(x) = \sum_{i=1}^{n} \left(x_i^2 - 10\cos(2\pi x_i) + 10 \right)$	Rastrigin	$(-5.12, 5.12)^n$	0

Choosing suitable control parameter values in opt-aiNET approaches is, frequently, a problem-dependent task. Suitable control parameters are different for different function problems. The difficulty in the use of opt-aiNET and evolutionary algorithms in general arises in that the choice of these is mainly based on empirical evidence and practical experience. The setup of opt-aiNET and opt-BDaiNET adopted in this paper is given by: suppression threshold equal to 50, percentage of newcomers d=50%, scale of the affinity proportional selection using a linear reduction of β with initial and final values of 0.1 and 6, respectively, and the number of clones generated for each cell was N_c=10. The population size N was 50 and the stopping criterion, t_{max}, was 1,000 generations for the opt-aiNET algorithm. A total of 50,000 objective function evaluations were made with each optimization approach in each run to the first and second case studies.

Table 3 presents mean and standard deviation for the opt-aiNET and opt-BDaiNET to the benchmark functions. A result with Boldface means the best value found in Table 3. Opt-BDaiNET performs clearly better than the opt-aiNET for the three benchmarks.

Table 3. Results in terms of objective function (30 runs) applied to benchmark functions

Function	opt-aiNET		opt-BDaiNET	
	Mean	Standard deviation	Mean	Standard deviation
f_1	38.1013	31.2387	**35.2864**	28.4064
f_2	$1.2786 \cdot 10^{-3}$	$2.2126 \cdot 10^{-3}$	**$1.5625 \cdot 10^{-14}$**	$7.8908 \cdot 10^{-15}$
f_3	$2.6418 \cdot 10^{-11}$	$2.5217 \cdot 10^{-11}$	**$9.6226 \cdot 10^{-14}$**	$5.2705 \cdot 10^{-13}$

In terms of heat exchanger design, the effectiveness of the present approach using opt-aiNET and opt-BDaiNET is assessed by analyzing two case studies that were analyzed previously by Patel and Rao [11] using particle swarm optimization (PSO) and Caputo et al. [15] using genetic algorithm (GA). The opt-aiNET algorithm was implemented in Matlab© (MathWorks). In this work, 30 independent runs were made for each of the optimization methods involving 30 different initial trial solutions (parameters of heat exchanger) for the opt-aiNET and opt-BDaiNET.

The setup of opt-aiNET and opt-BDaiNET are the same of benchmark functions, except that in these case studies was adopted the population size N=20 and the stopping criterion, t_{max}, was 100 generations. A total of 2,000 objective function evaluations were made with each optimization approach in each run to the first and second case studies.

The resulting optimal exchangers architectures given by the opt-aiNET and opt-BDaiNET approaches were compared with the original design solution given by [11],[15],[19]. Costs of both the original and the GA, PSO, opt-aiNET and opt-BDaiNET solutions were computed in order to allow a consistent comparison. The following two different test cases, representative of a wide range of applications, were investigated:

Case #1: In this case was used 4.34 (MW) duty, methanol – brackish water exchanger. This case study was taken from [19]. The original design assumed an exchanger with two tubeside passages and one shell-side passage (C=0.249 and n_1=2.207).

Case #2: In this case was used 1.44 (MW) duty, kerosene – crude oil exchanger. This case study was taken from Kern [17]. The original design assumed and exchanger with four tubeside passages, with square pitch pattern and one shellside passage (C=0.158 and n_1=2.263).

In this study the same architecture of Kern [17] and Sinnott *et al.* [19] were retained in the opt-aiNET and opt-BDaiNET approaches. All values of discounted operating costs were computed with n_y = 10 yr, annual discount rate i = 10%, energy cost C_e = 0.12 (€/kWh) and an annual amount of work hours H = 7,000 (h/yr). Table 4 presents the simulation results of objective function F of best solution in 30 runs. A result with Boldface means the best value found in Table 4. In other words, the results reported in Table 4 showed that the opt-BDaiNET outperforms the opt-aiNET with statistically significant differences in their performance for the two case studies.

Table 4. Results in terms of the objective function (F) in 30 runs

F (30 runs)	Case study #1		Case study #2	
	opt-aiNET	opt-BDaiNET	opt-aiNET	opt-BDaiNET
Minimum (best)	47429.76	**47429.75**	19700.61	**19700.56**
Mean	47446.57	**47430.02**	19710.34	**19701.05**
Maximum	47551.75	47430.78	19819.47	19705.82
Standard deviation	37.66	0.26	23.60	0.98

Figures 1 and 2 show the best objective function values (mean of 30 runs) in logscale for the opt-aiNET and opt-BDaiNET approaches for the two case studies, respectively. In the Figures 1 and 2 can be observed that the proposed opt-BDaiNET is less susceptible to premature convergence and less likely to be stuck in local optima that the classical opt-aiNET.

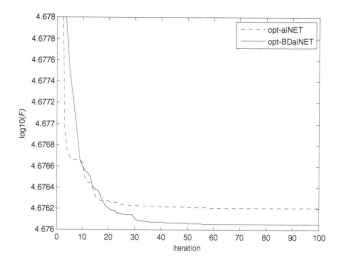

Fig. 1. Convergence of mean of the best F value in logscale for the first case

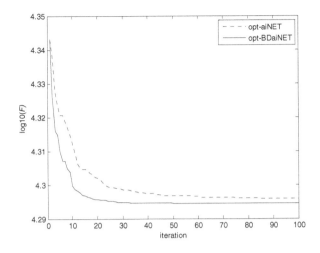

Fig. 2. Convergence of mean of the best F value in logscale for the second case

Table 5 presents the values obtained for the first case study using different optimization approaches. In terms of the cost, the best results were obtained with opt-BDaiNET when comparing with GA from [15] and PSO from [11].

In terms of the second case study, again the opt-BDaiNET presented superior results when compared with GA [15] and PSO [11] approaches in terms of the best solution obtained. An overall cost comparison for the second case study is provided in Table 6.

Table 5. Heat exchanger geometry for case #1 using different optimization methods

Parameter	Ref. [19]	GA [15]	PSO [11]	opt-aiNET	opt-BDaiNET
d_o (m)	0.02	0.016	0.015	0.0150	0.0150
B (m)	0.356	0.5	0.424	0.4436	0.4438
D_s (m)	0.894	0.830	0.810	0.8922	0.8919
C_{tot} (€)	64,480	55,077	53,231.1	47,429.76	**47,429.75**

Table 6. Heat exchanger geometry for case #2 using different optimization methods

Parameter	Ref. [19]	GA [15]	PSO [11]	opt-aiNET	opt-BDaiNET
d_o (m)	0.025	0.02	0.015	0.0150	0.0150
B (m)	0.127	0.12	0.1112	0.1120	0.1117
D_s (m)	0.539	0.63	0.59	0.6489	0.6481
C_{tot} (€)	27,020	20,303	19,922.6	19,700.61	**19,700.56**

6   Conclusion

The classical opt-aiNET and the proposed opt-BDaiNET has been applied to three benchmark functions (Rosenbrock, Sphere, and Rastrigin) and two case studies of shell and tube heat exchanger optimization. In terms of best objective function values, the opt-BDaiNET has a slight advantage in terms of solution quality over the classical opt-aiNET for the two case studies.

Comparing with the results presented in [11],[15],[19] and by classical opt-aiNET, the proposed opt-BDaiNET presented best results in terms of mean objective function value. As future scope of research, one important issue consists of extending the opt-BDaiNET by adapting them to the various classes of problems, such as multi-objective and constrained optimization problems.

References

1. De Castro, L.N., Timmis, J.: Artificial Immune Systems: A New Computational Intelligence Approach. Springer, London (2002)
2. Zheng, J., Chen, Y., Zhang, W.: A Survey of Artificial Immune Applications. Artificial Intelligence Review 34, 19–34 (2010)
3. Campelo, F., Guimarães, F.G., Igarashi, H.: Overview of Artificial Immune Systems for Multi-objective Optimization. In: Obayashi, S., Deb, K., Poloni, C., Hiroyasu, T., Murata, T. (eds.) EMO 2007. LNCS, vol. 4403, pp. 937–951. Springer, Heidelberg (2007)
4. De Castro, L.N., Von Zuben, F.J.: AiNet: An Evolutionary Immune Network for Data Clustering. In: Proceedings of the 6th Brazilian Symposium on Neural Networks, Rio de Janeiro, RJ, Brazil, pp. 231–259 (2000)
5. De Castro, L.N., Timmis, J.: An Artificial Immune Network for Multimodal Function Optimization. In: Proceedings of the Congress on Evolutionary Computation (CEC 2002), Honolulu, HI₃HA, USA, pp. 699–704 (2002)
6. Xu, Q., Wang, L., Si, J.: Predication Based Immune Network for Multimodal Function Optimization. Engineering Applications of Artificial Intelligence 23, 495–504 (2010)
7. Köster, M., Graul, A., Klene, G., Convey, H.: A New Paradigm of Optimisation by Using Artificial Immune Reactions. In: Palade, V., Howlett, R.J., Jain, L. (eds.) KES 2003. LNCS (LNAI), vol. 2773, pp. 287–292. Springer, Heidelberg (2003)
8. Coelho, G.P., Von Zuben, F.J.: omni-aiNet: An Immune-Inspired Approach for Omni Optimization. In: Bersini, H., Carneiro, J. (eds.) ICARIS 2006. LNCS (LNAI), vol. 4163, pp. 294–308. Springer, Heidelberg (2006)
9. Storn, R., Price, K.: Differential Evolution (A Simple and Efficient Heuristic for Global Optimization over Continuous Spaces. Journal of Global Optimization 11, 341–359 (1997)
10. Ali, M.M.: Synthesis of the β-distribution as an Aid to Stochastic Global Optimization. Computational Statistics & Data Analysis 52, 133–149 (2007)
11. Patel, V.K., Rao, R.V.: Design Optimization of Shell-and-Tube Heat Exchanger Using Particle Swarm Optimization Technique. Applied Thermal Engineering 30, 1417–1425 (2010)
12. Campelo, F., Guimarães, F.G., Igarashi, H., Ramírez, J.A., Noguchi, S.: A Modified Immune Network Algorithm for Multimodal Electromagnetic Problems. IEEE Transactions on Magnetics 42, 1111–1114 (2006)
13. Timmis, J., Edmonds, C.: A Comment on Opt-AiNET: An Immune Network Algorithm for Optimisation. In: Deb, K., Tari, Z. (eds.) GECCO 2004. LNCS, vol. 3102, pp. 308–317. Springer, Heidelberg (2004)
14. Selbas, R., Kizilkan, O., Reppich, M.: A New Design Approach for Shell-and-Tube Heat Exchangers Using Genetic Algorithms from Economic Point of View. Chemical Engineering and Processing 45, 268–275 (2006)

15. Caputo, A.C., Pelagagge, P.M., Salini, P.: Heat Exchanger Design Based on Economic Optimization. Applied Thermal Engineering 28, 1151–1159 (2008)
16. Taal, M., Bulatov, I., Klemes, J., Stehlik, P.: Cost Estimation and Energy Price Forecast for Economic Evaluation of Retrofit Projects. Applied Thermal Engineering 23, 1819–1835 (2003)
17. Kern, D.Q.: Process Heat Transfer. McGraw-Hill, New York (1950)
18. Peters, M.S., Timmerhaus, K.D.: Plant Design and Economics for Chemical Engineers. McGraw-Hill Book Company, New York (1991)
19. Sinnott, R.K., Coulson, J.M., Richardson, J.F.: Chemical Engineering Design, vol. 6. Butterworth-Heinemann, Boston (1996)
20. Shang, Y.W., Qiu, Y.H.: A Note on the Extended Rosenbrock Function. Evolutionary Computation 14, 119–126 (2006)
21. Digalakis, J.G., Margaritis, K.G.: An Experimental Study of Benchmarking Functions for Genetic Algorithms. International Journal of Computer Mathematics 79, 403–416 (2002)

A Negative Selection Approach to Intrusion Detection

Patricia Mostardinha, Bruno Filipe Faria,
André Zúquete, and Fernão Vistulo de Abreu

Universidade de Aveiro, Departamento de Física, 3810-193 Aveiro, Portugal
I3N Institute for Nanostructures, Nanomodelling and Nanofabrication
Universidade de Aveiro, Departamento de Electrónica, Telecomunicações e Informática,
3810-193 Aveiro, Portugal
{pmostardinha,brunoffaria,andre.zuquete,fva}@ua.pt

Abstract. An negative selection algorithm is presented for intrusion detection tasks for systems with arbitrary diversity. This algorithm uses two types of agents, detectors and presenters. Presenters present information to detectors; detectors are selected to engage in a maximally frustrated dynamics when presenters present data from a reference state. We show that if presenters present information that has never been available during the selection stage, then presenters engage in a less frustrated dynamics and their abnormal presentation can be detected. The performance of our algorithm is independent of the dimension of the space, i.e., the length of information presented by presenters, and hence does not suffer from the dimensionality curse accompanying current methods.

Keywords: artificial immune systems, self/nonself discrimination, negative selection algorithm.

1 Introduction

Intrusion detection systems (IDS's) have been gaining growing importance in computer security. This is because distinguishing what belongs to a system (self) from what does not (nonself) is a difficult and challenging problem. Two main difficulties exist. First intruders try to mimic self, making evidence scarce. Secondly, IDS's should provide prompt responses, which is difficult to achieve since continuous search for strange or suspicious activities quickly gathers enormous amounts of data.

There are two main approaches of intrusion detection systems in computer security: (i) based on knowledge or (ii) based on the behaviour of the system. In knowledge-based intrusion detection algorithms, the system searches continuously for evidences of attacks based on knowledge accumulated from known attacks [1]. On the other hand, in behaviour-based intrusion or anomaly detection models, intrusions are detected from a deviation of the natural or expected behaviour of the system. The main advantages of the latter models are that 1) they can potentially detect novel attack or penetration attempts (a.k.a., zero-day attacks), 2) they are less dependent on operating systems; 3) they can detect abuse of privilege, and many other types of

C.A. Coello Coello et al. (Eds.): ICARIS 2012, LNCS 7597, pp. 178–190, 2012.

attacks [1]. Several strategies have been explored that led to different behaviour-based models [2, 3]. The artificial immune systems community has been particularly flourishing in this respect[4-11]. Probably the approach providing the best quantitative results so far have been achieved by the negative selection algorithms, first proposed in [3]. These methods have nevertheless limitations. In particular, perfect self/nonself discrimination is not envisageable, at least in principle, for systems displaying arbitrary diversity[12-14].

Here we discuss how perfect self/nonself discrimination can be achieved in a model with arbitrary diversity. Our model uses a different strategy to achieve this goal. Instead of triggering responses when a string belongs to a detector's domain, our model uses a complex system of agents in interaction to generate a dynamics that is perturbed upon the introduction of a foreign string. As we will see, the cellular frustration framework can achieve very specific and prompt reactions. Specificity is guaranteed by a type of generalized kinetic proofreading mechanism embodied in the method[15-17], whereas promptness is guaranteed given that a macroscopic number of agents responds to the foreign string.

This paper is organized as follows. In the next section, we discuss the model and main concepts. In particular, we introduce the principle of maximal frustration and present maximally frustrated systems. Then we discuss a negative selection algorithm that maximally frustrates a systems' dynamics. This algorithm creates a repertoire of detectors that will be used in a monitoring stage. Afterwards, we consider a variety of numerical experiments to illustrate the main mechanisms in operation and the algorithm's performance. This papers ends with a summary of the main results and future perspectives.

2   Conceptual Model

Cellular frustrated systems (CFS) consider a population of agents in interaction. All agents try to establish stable contacts with their preferred agents of the other type. However, stable contacts can only be maintained with one agent at a time. In case of two alternative possible matches, an agent performs a decision, staying in contact with its preferred option. To establish a decision, agents consult a preference (or interaction) list (IList) where all the agents they can interact with are ranked in a decreasing order of preference. Preference lists are an abstract way of encoding the typical affinity strengths between ligands and receptors in cellular interactions. In particular, the many different ways strings can be ranked in ILists could describe different interaction metrics.

The essence of the cellular frustration framework, results from the ability of agents to frustrate each other interactions so that they never reach stable configurations. This can be best understood with a simple example with 2 agent types represented in figure 1. There, presenter agents P_1 and P_2 interact with detectors of type D_1 and D_2. The dynamics of their interaction depends on the strings they present to each other, respectively s_1 and s_2 (presented by presenter agents to detectors) and l_1 and l_2 (presented by detectors to presenters). Strings s_1 and s_2 can be arbitrary and variable from system to system. On the contrary strings l_1 and l_2 are fixed and characterize each detector. Here we assumed that $l_i = i$.

Assume that agent P_1 prefers l_1 to l_2 while agent P_2 does the opposite. Depending on detectors' ILists, agents may never form stable pairs. For instance, if D_1 prefers s_2 to s_1, then P_1 cannot form a stable pair with the detector D_1 because, whenever they meet P_2, P_1D_1 interactions are terminated. On the contrary, if instead detector D_1 prefers s_1 to s_2, stable P_1D_1 pairs could be formed. This example illustrates that selection of detectors ILists can change radically contact lifetimes. The argument applies to more general models. In Figure 1b a more general model is presented. It includes an arbitrary number of agents of each type. It assumes that in principle detectors ILists could be arbitrarily organized, whereas presenters ILists are organized in a cyclic order. I.e., if $L_i = i$ and if $L_i(j)$ denotes the string ranked in the jth position in the IList of presenter agent i, then $L_i(j) = [i+j-1]$, where here $[j]$ denotes j modulus N, N being the total number of agents.

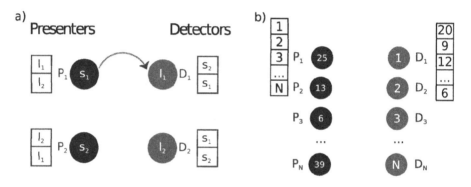

Fig. 1. a) A simple model with two agent types with two subtypes each. On the sides are defined interaction lists, where strings displayed by agents of the other subtype are ranked in decreasing order of preference. b) generalization to include more agents and where presenter agents present an arbitrary set of numbers as strings. ILists for the first presenter and detector agents are also represented.

The Principle of Maximal Frustration[18], establishes that if detectors and presenters are organized in a maximally frustrated set – i.e., a set of agents engaging in a dynamics with minimum lifetimes – then foreign strings introduced in the system will necessarily lead to a less frustrated dynamics involving the cell presenting the new string. As a result, pair lifetimes can signal an intrusion. This mechanism is particularly robust if detectors can organize their ILists according to many different rankings. To understand this it is important to consider the effect of a negative selection process on the selection of detectors ILists. In principle, the organisation of what string is presented by each presenter agent is completely arbitrary. Consequently detectors do not know in which order they should organize their ILists to maximize frustration. In figure 1b we illustrate a generic case. To maximize frustration a negative selection algorithm should eliminate poorly frustrated detectors and replace them by detectors presenting the same string but with random ILists. If negative selection is continuously performed then detectors ILists become ordered in respect to the positions occupied by the ligands detectors interact with. In particular, no detector should have survived that places on the top of its ILists a string presented by a presenter that has higher affinity to that detector. However, and most importantly, strings that were not displayed during the selection process did not shape detectors ILists. Consequently, they will take random positions in detectors ILists. As a result, during the detection phase any foreign string – a string that was not presented during repertoire education - has a 1/N probability of being above the other presented strings. This probability can be small for large systems however other positions below the top one – in fact, a finite fraction of them - can also produce large interaction lifetimes. In any case, this probability is considerably larger than the probability of having an equivalent self-string at the same position. In this work we will show that this mechanism can indeed lead to perfect detections for systems with a reasonable number of presented strings.

3   Computational Algorithm

The algorithm comprises three stages: education, calibration and detection. The algorithm uses a data set characterizing the normal behaviour of a complex system for presentation by presenter agents. At the beginning all detectors *ILists* are generated by a random permutation of all strings presenter agents could display. If the data set has binary strings with N digits, each IList has 2^N strings. Then the frustrated dynamics starts. All agents are given a chance to interact with a randomly selected agent of the opposite type. At this step agents are selected according to a random permutation to avoid giving priority to any of them. If a selected agent was already paired, then it has to evaluate whether the string presented by new agent is placed higher its IList. In that case a similar evaluation has to be done by the new agent. If both benefit from the interaction, a new pair is formed and those agents they were matched with are freed. At this stage, pairing lifetimes are registered. The situation is simpler if any of the agents is not paired. In that case unpaired agents always favour establishing a new pair.

Afterwards, during the education stage any pair that exceeded a *Threshold* lifetime is separated and the detector IList replaced by a new random list. If no pair exceeded the *Threshold* within the last W iterations (typically, W=1000 iterations) then the *Threshold* is updated to the maximum pairing lifetime registered in that period and all detectors ILists registered. The process is repeated until a predefined *Threshold* is reached.

After the education stage, the algorithm runs a calibration stage. Then the frustrated dynamics of the last registered population is analysed to establish the maximum number $n^0(\tau_c)$ of contacts established by *any* presenter that lasted at least τ_c iterations in W iterations (typically, W=5000 iterations). This value is multiplied by a safety factor f (typically 1.05) and establishes a *Detection Threshold* value required to activate the intrusion detection system (IDS) during the detection stage. To measure whether the system discriminates nonself, we compute the ratio that compares the *Detection Threshold* with the number of similar contacts performed by the agent displaying the foreign string :

$$\theta_{NS} = \frac{n_{i=P}^{act}(\tau_c)}{f \, n^0(\tau_c)}$$

We consider that detection can be accomplished if $\theta_{NS} > 1$. This does not imply that a single long contact is required to activate detectors. Rather, it establishes that a rate of long contacts is required to achieve the activation stage. In particular, it establishes that during the W iterations used during the calibration and detection phases the presenter displaying the foreign string established stable contacts more frequently. A similar ratio could be defined involving agents presenting self-strings. Our procedure consists in choosing a sufficiently large safety factor f so that θ is always below 1 for self-agents.

During the last stage, a single string presented by a presenter agent was changed to a string not presented during the education. If more than one string is presented intrusion detection is simpler and consequently these cases will not be analysed here.

4   Numerical Experiments

In this section we analyse numerical experiments that demonstrate that the principle of maximal frustration can indeed constitute a mechanism leading to perfect self/nonself discrimination. First we analyse an artificial system in which ILists are built in order to maximize frustration. This example is interesting because it will allow us to compare the level of discrimination we should expect in an ideal configuration to that of populations in which the repertoire has undergone selection.

4.1   Ideal System

To maximize frustration it should be guaranteed that if a string is ranked on the top of a presenter IList, then the detector displaying that string should have on a bottom position the string displayed by that presenter agent. If detectors ILists are constructed in order to respect this rule, then the dynamics should be extremely frustrated. We considered a system in which presenter agents display as strings the digits of their index: $s_i=i$, and constructed detectors ILists according to the following rule:

$$L_i(j)=[i+j] \qquad i=1,\ldots,100$$

For instance, the first and the last positions in the IList of the first detector would respectively be $L_1(1)=2$ and $L_1(N)=[N+1]=1$. This maximizes frustration relatively to interactions with presenter agent number 1, since that agent has on the top of its IList detector number $L_1(1)=[i+j-1]=1$.

In order to test our numerical experiments in this limiting configuration, we simulated populations with 100 agents of each type, and randomly changed the position of one string on all detectors ILists. In this way we simulated the effect of not having presented that string during a negative selection education process.

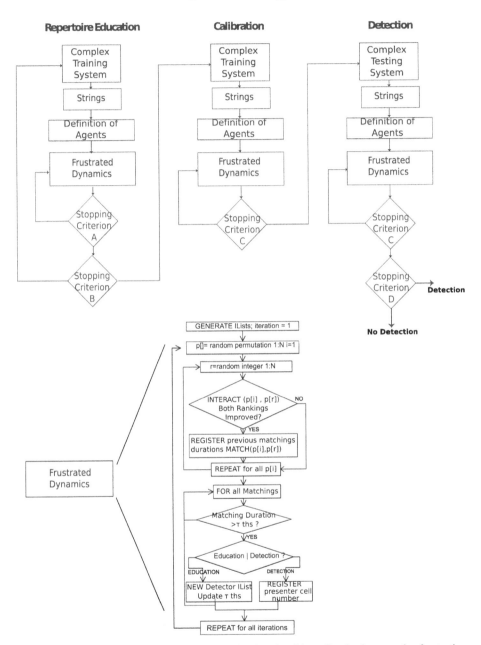

Fig. 2. Flowchart displaying the main steps in the algorithm. On the bottom the frustration dynamics algorithm is presented in detail. During repertoire education, negative selection is applied until a pre-defined *Threshold* (Stopping Criterion A); several repertoires can be educated if necessary (Stopping Criterion B); the calibration and detection stages apply the frustrated dynamics for W iterations (Stopping Criterion C); if a presenter agent exceeds a number given of long contacts consistent with $\theta_{NS} > 1$, detection is signalled for the present repertoire (Stopping Criterion D).

A typical histogram for the frequency of contacts lasting longer that τ iteration steps is shown in Figure 3a. From these results it is possible to verify that foreign string presenters perform considerably longer conjugations and considerably more frequently than self-presenters. Also, it is possible to define an interaction lifetime above which only the invader establishes contacts. This means that in this type of perfectly ordered systems detection could be chirurgical; we could trigger the IDS anytime a contact lasts longer than $\tau=13$ iterations. An alternative approach could be to trigger the IDS following shorter contacts. This may be more convenient for IDS's since these events occur with a higher probability. However, in this case more than a single contact is required to perfectly discriminate between self and nonself. This information is captured by the θ_{NS} ratio. In our analysis we chose τ_C to be equal to two thirds of the maximal conjugation lifetime performed for self-agents (represented by the dash line in Figure 3a). Results would not change qualitatively with a different choice of τ_C, even if the magnitude of θ_{NS} changes. In brief, from the results presented in Figure 3 it is clear that all foreign strings can be detected and in fact these results agree with the results reported for circular frustrated systems in [18]. In the next section, we will discuss how close repertoire education may get to the present ideal results.

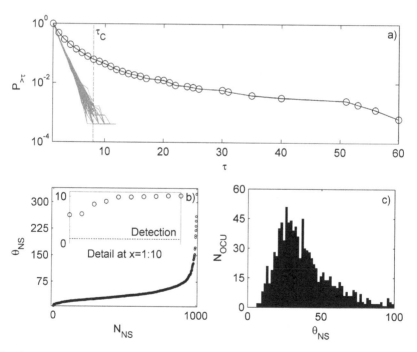

Fig. 3. Numerical results obtained with an ideal system with 100 agents of each type. a) Frequency of contacts lasting longer than τ iterations, for the agent presenting the foreign string (circles) and for the other presenter agents (grey lines), for W=5000 iterations. b) Detection ratio θ_{NS} calculated at $\tau_c = 8$ for all foreign strings and c) respective histogram.

4.2 Educated Systems

To achieve the results obtained in the previous section, it was necessary to order ILists perfectly. There are several reasons why we should not admit that this can be done. The most important concerns the need to compress information. The method we are presenting achieves good results independently of the dimension of the space (i.e., the string length in digital signals). However it requires recording the information contained in ILists which, for the method to work, need to be extremely diverse. To avoid registering the whole information several approximate methods can be used that do not change the results we report here. As we will show in a forthcoming publication, they all assume ILists could be approximated by different random lists. Hence, the problem then concerns that of finding a method to select, among several randomly generated ILists, those that maximally frustrate the agents' dynamics. This requires establishing a selection algorithm which we will discuss here. First we discuss its implementation, the stopping criteria and how ILists evolve. Afterwards, we will present results on intrusion detection experiments. We end by explaining how we can perform perfect self/nonself discrimination.

4.2.1 Repertoire Education

The main goal of the education process is to select a set of detectors that maximize frustration. From the real immune system it is known that lymphocytes that strongly react with self-presenters (APCs) are eliminated and replaced by new incoming cells with random receptors. Within the cellular frustration framework[16, 18], the strength of interactions is measured in terms of their stability. For this reason, the implementation of the negative selection procedure should be changed relatively to traditional approach[3, 5]. Instead of deciding which cell to eliminate based on their position in ILists, negative selection should act on detectors performing a contact longer than a threshold value (see Figure 2, right). This clearly marks a distinctive difference in the two approaches.

In terms of algorithm, every time a detector performs a contact exceeding the threshold value, its IList is reshuffled as if the detector had been replaced by a new detector. This process should end when all detectors perform the shortest contact lifetimes. A dramatic effect on contact lifetimes can indeed be observed in Figure 4 where histograms for all presenters before (a) and after the education process (b) are shown.

Several possible criteria could be defined to stop the education process. Again we used inspiration from immunology where it is known the about 97% of the detectors are deleted[19, 20]. Bearing this value in mind, the education process was applied until contact lifetimes decreased below 75 iterations, which amounted to delete around 90% of the detectors. To perform this relatively small number of replacements the number of iterations required was of the order of 40000 iterations, which represents a fast repertoire education procedure.

To understand how the ordering of ILists is related to an increase in frustration, we analysed the ordering of self-strings in ILists. To this end, we restricted the analysis to the relative position of self-strings in relation to the position they should occupy in the ideal system. We computed:

$$D_j = \frac{1}{N} \sum_{i=1}^{N} [L_i(j) - L_i^{ideal}(j)]$$

where $[j] = j\theta(j) + (j + N)\,\theta(-j)$ represents the deviation from the ideal position. Here $\theta(j)$ is the Heaviside function. For instance, if in the first position of an IList there is a string that should be on the bottom, then this adds a N-1 contribution to the distance. Figure 4c and 4d shows that only a few top positions become ordered and that this ordering is more effective for better educated populations. Furthermore, we should realise that the ordering of ILists is far from perfect, even in top positions. This indeed agrees with the observation of interaction lifetimes histograms(Figure 4a,b): although a remarkable difference in interaction lifetimes has been achieved, the maximum interaction lifetime is considerably larger in educated populations than in the ideal system. The difference is almost of an order of magnitude different.

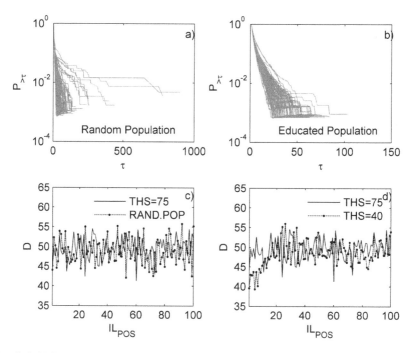

Fig. 4. (a,b) Frequency of pairs lasting longer than τ iteration steps for every self-presenting agents(grey lines) and the average for all agents(black line), for a random and an educated population (THS=75), respectively. (c,d) Average deviation of the value in a given position of the ILists for all detectors in an educated system and a random system, or between two educated systems with different levels of education, respectively.

4.2.2   Intrusion Detection in Educated Systems

Even if considerably lengthier education processes could be applied, results concerning intrusion detection rates would remain qualitatively similar. We tested whether the introduction of 1000 foreign strings could be detected. A disappointing 76% evasion rate was obtained. More lengthy education processes could reduce this number but we verified that it would never reach zero. Typically, no less than 15% non-detection rates should be expected even for the longest education processes.

The problem of achieving perfect self/nonself discrimination has nevertheless a remarkable solution. In the cellular frustration framework the distinctive feature that distinguishes self-strings from foreign strings is that the later can be placed in completely random positions in detectors ILists. One can then question if detection rates could be increased by increasing the number of detector's ILists. One way to achieve this is by educating several detector populations and to use them to sequentially classify a set of strings. The improved detection scheme is shown in Figure 5. The question then becomes that of knowing how much the detection rate can be improved, and how large is the number of repertoire populations of detectors.

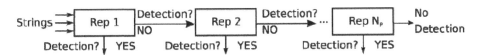

Fig. 5. Detection scheme that uses a sequential application of different detector repertoires during intrusion detection

As in the previous section, we introduced 1000 foreign strings and analysed the dynamics of the system for 5000 iterations. All populations were educated in the same conditions with a threshold of 75, as before. Typical cumulative distributions of interaction lifetimes in one population are presented in 6. In these histograms, the dynamics of the foreign string presenter is marked with circles. Figures 6a and 6b illustrate typical non-detection and detection histograms respectively. Since histograms of self-presenting agents are little disturbed by the presence of the foreign string, when a detection event takes place the histogram line for the foreign-presenting agent is distinctively above all other histogram lines: $\theta_{NS} > 1$. The opposite takes place in case of no detection.

In Figure 6c the number of foreign strings that escaped detection is plotted against the number of consecutive detector populations used. As expected, the number of detectors evading detection decreases exponentially, because these are independent processes. Interestingly, the number of populations required to achieve perfect self/nonself discrimination lies slightly above 30, a reasonable small number. For repertoires with 30 populations, only one foreign string escaped detection. This analysis is compared with the case with non-educated detector populations. Clearly frustration maximization can produce a nontrivial outcome in intrusion detection tasks.

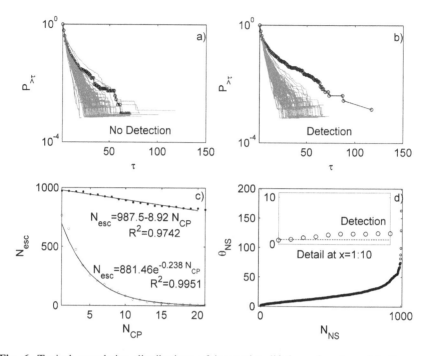

Fig. 6. Typical cumulative distributions of interaction lifetimes for a) no-detection and b) detection cases. Cumulative distribution for conjugation lifetimes are presented in thin grey lines for self-presenters and with circles for the foreign string presenter. c) Number of invaders escaping detection as a function of the number of consecutive detector populations used for educated (circles) or non-educated (dots). d) Maximum detection ratios obtained after the sequence of detections, for each foreign string introduced.

In Figure 6d, all measured detection ratios θ_{NS} are represented in an ordered sequence. The larger θ_{NS} the easier it is to perform prompt detections. In fact, in our analysis we calculated of histograms after 5000 iterations. In practical applications other methods could be more efficient. Intrusion detection strategies could be designed based on the rate of contacts lasting longer than τ_C, triggering the IDS whenever the triggering rate is overcome. In that case, the larger θ_{NS} the prompter responses will be. According to the results displayed in Figure 6d, only 0.5% of the foreign strings have $\theta_{NS} < 2$. This means that 99.5% of foreign strings produce long contacts with at least a frequency twice as higher as self-strings (we chose always τ_C to be equal to 2/3 of the maximal conjugation lifetime performed for self-agents). On the other side, 75% of foreign strings lead to ratios $\theta_{NS} > 10$. This means that for them responses can be prompt and accurate. For instance, if two consecutive contacts are required to trigger the IDS, their probability of occurrence is of the order of $0.05^2 \times 100 = 2.5\%$, which is still a large value. In comparison, the same happen with self-presenting agents with a probability of $0.005^2 \times 100 = 0.025\%$. This clearly shows that the best strategy to trigger an IDS in frustrated systems should be frequency dependent.

5   Conclusions

In a recent work we proposed [18] that a new organisation principle of complex systems – the principle of maximal frustration – could be important to design intrusion detection systems and also to understand the adaptive immune system. Although we demonstrated that certain ideal systems could perform perfect self/nonself discrimination, it had not been shown how, starting from an arbitrary set of data, any foreign string could be detected. Here we showed that models composed by two types of agents, presenters and detectors, can establish a new class of intrusion detection systems. Presenters are agents that present the data to protect, while detectors are agents selected to frustrate maximally the population dynamics. To maximize frustration a new type of negative selection algorithm had to be developed, in which elimination of detectors depended not on the strength of the affinity function, but on the stability of the interactions formed. Our results clearly show that perfect self/nonself discrimination can be achieved when 100 arbitrary strings define the self-set. These results are independent of the length of the strings presented and can also be improved to allow scalability and more efficient computational algorithms (to be presented in another publication).

The present work clearly points to the existence of an alternative approach to perform the self/nonself discrimination task. This should be taken as motivating news: the field of intrusion detection is certainly a very complex one, not only because of the inherent diversity of scenarios but also due to the difficulty in formulating the problem in general terms. Finding methods that give *perfect* solutions in well-defined scenarios will be helpful in the search for a deeper and more general understanding of the intrusion detection problem. In this sense, we believe that, just as the immune system has two main strategies to address the problem – the innate and adaptive immune systems – artificial immune systems may also benefit from several solutions. Only future research can clarify which of them is indeed the most helpful and in which circumstances they can be useful.

Acknowledgments. PM was supported by grant SFRH/BD/37625/2007. The work was supported by Pest-C/CTM/LA0025/2011.

References

1. Hervé Debar, M.D., Wespi, A.: Towards a taxonomy of intrusion-detection systems. Computational Networks (31), 805–822 (1999)
2. Forrest, S., Beauchemin, C.: Computer immunology. Immunological Reviews 216, 176–197 (2007)
3. Forrest, S., et al.: Self-Nonself Discrimination in a Computer. In: Proceedings of IEEE Computer Society Symposium on Research in Security and Privacy, pp. 202–212 (1994)
4. Bereta, M.Ç., Burczynski, T.: Immune K-means and negative selection algorithms for data analysis. Information Sciences 179(10), 1407–1425 (2009)
5. Dasgupta, D., Niño, L.F.: Immunological computation: theory and applications, vol. xviii, p. 277. CRC, Boca Raton (2009)

6. Greensmith, J., Aickelin, U., Tedesco, G.: Information fusion for anomaly detection with the dendritic cell algorithm. Inf. Fusion 11(1), 21–34 (2010)

7. Hone, A., et al.: Theoretical advances in artificial immune systems. Theoretical Computer Science 403(1), 11–32 (2008)

8. Kim, J., et al.: Immune system approaches to intrusion detection – a review. Natural Computing 6(4), 413–466 (2007)

9. Xie, Z.X., et al.: A distributed agent-based approach to intrusion detection using the lightweight PCC anomaly detection classifier. In: Proceedings of IEEE International Conference on Sensor Networks, Ubiquitous, and Trustworthy Computing, vol. 1, pp. 446–453 (2006)

10. Wang, D.W., Xue, Y.B., Dong, Y.F.: Anomaly Detection Using Neighborhood Negative Selection. Intelligent Automation and Soft Computing 17(5), 595–605 (2011)

11. Yang, X., Aldrich, C., Maree, C.: Detecting change in dynamic process systems with immunocomputing. Minerals Engineering 20(2), 103–112 (2007)

12. Ji, Z., Dasgupta, D.: Revisiting negative selection algorithms. Evolutionary Computation 15(2), 223–251 (2007)

13. Stibor, T., Timmis, J.I., Eckert, C.: On the Use of Hyperspheres in Artificial Immune Systems as Antibody Recognition Regions. In: Bersini, H., Carneiro, J. (eds.) ICARIS 2006. LNCS, vol. 4163, pp. 215–228. Springer, Heidelberg (2006)

14. Kim, J., Bentley, P.J.: Negative Selection within an Artificial Immune for Network Intrusion Detection. In: 14th Annual Fall Symposium of the Korean Information Processing Society, Seoul, Korea (2000)

15. Mckeithan, T.W.: Kinetic Proofreading in T-Cell Receptor Signal-Transduction. Proceedings of the National Academy of Sciences of the United States of America 92(11), 5042–5046 (1995)

16. de Abreu, F.V., et al.: Cellular Frustration: A New Conceptual Framework for Understanding Cell-Mediated Immune Responses. In: Bersini, H., Carneiro, J., et al. (eds.) ICARIS 2006. LNCS, vol. 4163, pp. 37–51. Springer, Heidelberg (2006)

17. Lindo, A., Faria, B., de Abreu, F.: Tunable kinetic proofreading in a model with molecular frustration. Theory in Biosciences, 1–8

18. de Abreu, F.V., Mostardinha, P.: Maximal frustration as an immunological principle. Journal of the Royal Society Interface 6(32), 321–334 (2009)

19. Abbas, A.K., Lichtman, A.H.: Basic Immunology: Functions and Disorders of the Immune System. W B SAUNDERS (2010)

20. Janeway, C.: Immunobiology five. Garland Pub. (2001)

Clonal Expansion
without Self-replicating Entities

Danesh Tarapore[1,2], Anders Lyhne Christensen[3],
Pedro U. Lima[1], and Jorge Carneiro[2]

[1] Institute for Systems and Robotics (ISR), Instituto Superior Técnico (IST),
Lisbon, Portugal
[2] Instituto Gulbenkian de Ciência, Oeiras, Portugal
[3] Instituto de Telecomunicacões & Instituto Universitário de Lisboa (ISCTE-IUL),
Lisbon, Portugal

Abstract. The vertebrate immune system is a complex distributed system capable of learning to tolerate the organisms' tissues, to assimilate a diverse commensal microflora, and to mount specific responses to invading pathogens. These intricate functions are performed almost flawlessly by a self-organised collective of cells. The robust mechanisms of distributed control in the immune system could potentially be deployed to design multiagent systems. However, the essence of the immune system is clonal expansion by cell proliferation, which is difficult to envisage in most artificial multiagent systems. In this paper, we investigate under which conditions proliferation can be approximated by recruitment in fixed-sized agent populations. Our study is the first step towards bringing many of the desirable properties of the adaptive immune system to systems made of agents which are incapable of self-replication. We adopt the crossregulation model of the adaptive immune system. We develop ordinary differential equation models of proliferation-based and recruitment-based systems, and we compare the predictions of these analytical models with results obtained by a stochastic simulation. Our results define the operational parameter regime wherein growth by recruitment retains all the properties a cell proliferation model. We conclude that rich immunological behaviour can be fully recapitulated in sufficiently large multiagent systems based on growth by recruitment.

Keywords: Multiagent system, clonal expansion, agent recruitment, crossregulation model.

1 Introduction

The cell collective that constitutes the adaptive immune system has been extremely successful during the course of evolution as evidenced by its presence in all jawed vertebrate species [1]. Central to this success are the T helper cells that orchestrate the system. These cells are capable of dynamically regulating and differentiating themselves into different sub-lineages (e.g., Th1, Th2, Th17, and regulatory T-cells) to initiate appropriate immune responses (e.g., [2–4]).

C.A. Coello Coello et al. (Eds.): ICARIS 2012, LNCS 7597, pp. 191–204, 2012.
© Springer-Verlag Berlin Heidelberg 2012

Importantly, the differentiation and clonal expansion of these cells into different functionally distinct sub-types is decentralised and based solely on the state of the individual cell and local information available to it. Furthermore, cell proliferation and death are fundamental processes underlying clonal expansion, which is the essence of the immune response.

The decentralised and adaptive nature of the immune system, together with the relative simplicity of an individual cell, makes it an appealing model for designers of large scale multiagent systems (MAS). Examples of studies that take inspiration from the immune system include distributed intrusion detection systems [5], fault tolerance systems [6], and behaviour arbitration mechanisms in robotics [7, 8]. In these models, a many-to-one analogy between cells and agents is considered, with the behaviour of the agent dictated by the number and type of cells it possesses. While this approach does facilitate some interesting applications, it requires individual agents to have a high degree of complexity and may consequently not be feasible in certain applications, e.g., involving energy constraints on agents. In this study, we explore an alternative one-to-one mapping between a cell and an agent. An obvious obstacle to this approach is the absence of artificial self-replicating agents to implement clonal expansion by cell proliferation. However, as we demonstrate here, this obstacle can be circumvented by a mechanism of "recruitment" that mimics cell proliferation and cell death within a fixed number of agents.

In our investigation, we use an immune system model of *crossregulation* to compare proliferation and recruitment. The crossregulation model (CRM) [9, 10] postulates a dynamics of interactions between T helper cells, that allows the system to discriminate between antigens based solely on their density and persistence in the environment. The system is able to tolerate body antigens (i.e "self") that are characteristically persistent and abundant, and to mount an immune response to foreign pathogens, that appear as bursts. The model has been used successfully in spam detection (e.g., [11]) and document classification (e.g., [12]) scenarios, making it a good candidate for MAS in other environment classification tasks. In order to determine if and when recruitment can be used to emulate proliferation with reasonably accuracy, we compare two systems: one that relies on proliferation and one that relies on recruitment, respectively. We model both systems analytically and evaluate them in a stochastic simulation environment.

2   The Crossregulation Model

Two principles of multicellular organisation are the foundation of the crossregulation model (CRM). Firstly, the persistence of any cell lineage requires that its cells recurrently interact with other cells in the organism. Cells that fail to interact with other cells eventually die. Secondly, the growth of a cell population involves density-dependent feedback mechanisms controlling individual cell proliferation. These feedback mechanisms involve (i) indirect interactions among cells (such as a competition for limited growth factors), and (ii) direct interactions, such as contact inhibition. Below, we outline the model and highlight its interesting properties that are later replicated with a multiagent system that uses clonal expansion based on recruitment instead of cell proliferation.

The CRM describes the population dynamics of immune cells, based on three mutually interacting cell types: (i) antigen presenting cells (APCs) that display the antigen on their surface; (ii) effector cells T_E that can potentially mount an immune response which, depending on receptor specificity, can be directed against foreign pathogens or self-antigens; and (iii) regulatory cells T_R that suppress the proliferation of T_E cells. Furthermore, individual APCs have a fixed number of binding sites (s) on which T_E and T_R cells can form conjugates.

Dynamics of the T-cell population is regulated by the following density-dependent feedback mechanisms: (i) effector and regulatory cells that are unable to interact with APCs are slowly lost by cell death; (ii) the proliferation of effector and regulatory cells requires conjugation with APCs and direct interactions between T_E and T_R cells co-localised at the APC. The proliferation of the T_E cell population is promoted by the absence of regulatory cells on the APC. In contrast, T_R can only proliferate following co-localisation with effector cells on the same APC. Additionally, T_E and T_R cells interact indirectly by competition for access to conjugation sites on APCs.

2.1 Mathematical Formulation of the CRM

The individual T-cells are in one of the following three states; *free* (i.e., not conjugated with an APC), *conjugated* with an APC, and *activated* (about to proliferate). In our mathematical model, effector cells in the free, conjugated and activated states are denoted by E_f, E_c and E_a, respectively. Similarly, regulatory cells in the free, conjugated and activated states are R_f, R_c and R_a, respectively. Consequently, the total number of T_E cells $E = E_f + E_c + E_a$, and the total number of T_R cells $R = R_f + R_c + R_a$.

T-cell–APC Conjugation: The dynamics of effector and regulatory T-cells conjugated with APCs is described by the following system of equations. For E_c and R_c we have, respectively:

$$\frac{d\,E_c}{d\,t} = \gamma_c A E_f \left(1 - \left(\frac{E_c + R_c}{As}\right)^s\right) - \gamma_d E_c - \delta E_c \tag{1}$$

$$\frac{d\,R_c}{d\,t} = \gamma_c A R_f \left(1 - \left(\frac{E_c + R_c}{As}\right)^s\right) - \gamma_d R_c - \delta R_c \tag{2}$$

where A is the density of APCs, γ_c and γ_d denote the conjugation and dissociation rate constants between APCs and T-cells, respectively, and δ is the death rate of T-cells (parameters in Table 1).

The equations for E_c (eq 1) and R_c (eq 2) have three terms. The first term represents the conjugation of free T-cells with APCs which at least one unoccupied site. The second term accounts for the dissociation of existing conjugates. Finally, the third term represents the process of cell death, assumed to be a simple exponential decay of T-cells.

T-cell Population Dynamics with Cell *Proliferation*: According to the CRM, conjugated effector cells are activated and able to proliferate if and only if there are no regulatory cells conjugated to the same APC. If we let P_E denote the probability that a conjugated effector cell has no neighbouring regulatory cell, the equations describing the dynamics of free E_f and activated E_a effector cells are:

$$\frac{\mathrm{d}\,E_f}{\mathrm{d}\,t} = -\gamma_c A E_f \left(1 - \left(\frac{E_c + R_c}{As}\right)^s\right) + \gamma_d(1 - P_E)E_c + 2\pi_E E_a - \delta E_f \qquad (3)$$

$$\frac{\mathrm{d}\,E_a}{\mathrm{d}\,t} = \gamma_d P_E E_c - \pi_E E_a - \delta E_a \qquad (4)$$

where π_E is the proliferation rate of activated effector cells (parameters in Table 1).

Table 1. Parameters for the CRM

Parameters	Description	Value (a.u.)
A	Density of APCs	–
s	Number of binding sites on an APC	3
E	Total density of effector cells	–
R	Total density of regulatory cells	–
γ_c	Conjugation rate constant of T-cells to APCs	1
γ_d	Dissociation rate constant of T-cells from APCs	10^{-3}
π_E	Proliferation rate of effector cells	10^{-4}
π_R	Proliferation rate of regulatory cells	0.5×10^{-4}
δ	Death rate of effector and regulatory cells	10^{-5}
N	Density of cells, for the recruitment model	30×10^{-3}
γ_r	Recruitment rate constant of cells	10

In the equations for E_f (eq 3) and E_a (eq 4), the conjugated effector cells with no neighbouring regulatory cell on the same APC are selected for activation, and consequently proliferate. By contrast, conjugated effector cells co-localised with one or more neighbouring regulatory cells dissociate without proliferating.

The conjugated regulatory cells can only be activated if at least one effector cell is simultaneously conjugated to the same APC. If we let P_R denote the probability that a conjugated regulatory cell has at least one neighbouring effector cell, the equations describing the dynamics of free R_f and activated R_a regulatory cells are:

$$\frac{\mathrm{d}\,R_f}{\mathrm{d}\,t} = -\gamma_c A R_f \left(1 - \left(\frac{E_c + R_c}{As}\right)^s\right) + \gamma_d(1 - P_R)R_c + 2\pi_R R_a - \delta R_f \qquad (5)$$

$$\frac{\mathrm{d}\,R_a}{\mathrm{d}\,t} = \gamma_d P_R R_c - \pi_R R_a - \delta R_a \qquad (6)$$

where π_R is the proliferation rate of activated regulatory cells (parameters in Table 1).

In the equations for R_f (eq 5) and R_a (eq 6), conjugated regulatory cells with one or more neighbouring effector cells, are selected for activation and consequently proliferate at rate π_R. By contrast, conjugated regulatory cells with no neighbouring effector cell, dissociate without proliferating.

For our system of ODEs, the probability functions P_E and P_R can be expressed with a multinomial approximation [13]. This approximation is reasonable given that the total number of binding sites (summed over all the APCs) is much larger than the number of sites per APC. For three binding sites ($s = 3$) on each APC, we have:

$$P_E = \frac{(R_c - 3A)^2}{9A^2} \quad \text{and} \quad P_R = \frac{(6A - E_c)E_c}{9A^2} \tag{7}$$

Behaviour of Proliferating T-cell Population: The dynamics of the CRM is governed by two key composite parameters representing the effective growth rates of E and R cell populations [9]. These two growth rates are directly proportional to the basic parameters controlling population growth i.e., conjugation and dissociation constants (γ_c and γ_d), proliferation rates of these two types of T-cells (π_E and π_R), and the density of APCs (A). The effective growth rates of the T-cells are also inversely proportional to the death rate (δ) of the corresponding population. The composite E and R growth parameters define four parameter regimes according to the resulting cell population behaviour. Three parameter regimes result in a single stable state that may correspond to either: (i) extinction of all T-cells ($E = 0$, $R = 0$), (ii) immune state ($E > R$), or (iii) tolerant state ($E < R$). The fourth parameter regime corresponds to a bistable system where both immune and tolerant states are stable. A detailed analysis of these parameter regimes is provided in [9].

In the present study, the parameter values have been set so that at low APC densities ($a_E < A < a_R$, Fig. 1a), the system evolves towards a single state composed only of effector cells (immune state). By contrast, at relatively high density of APCs ($A > a_R$, Fig. 1a), the system exhibits bistability and can evolve either into the immune or the tolerant equilibrium state. In the bistable regime, the system develops into the regulatory cell dominated state, provided that the seeding population has sufficient T_R cells (Fig. 1b). By contrast, if T_R cells are initially underrepresented w.r.t. the T_E cells, the latter competitively exclude the former from the system (Fig. 1b).

T-cell Population Dynamics with Cell Recruitment: The T-cell proliferation and death are fundamental processes used by the adaptive immune system to orchestrate an appropriate immune response under varying environmental conditions. Furthermore, these processes are crucial to the density-dependent feedback mechanisms of the CRM. However, in some multiagent systems, new agents cannot be created and existing agents cannot be removed from the system, making it difficult to translate adaptive immune system inspired algorithms

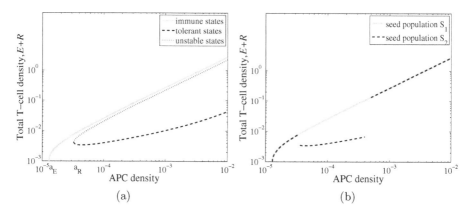

Fig. 1. Equilibrium densities of E and R cell populations as a function of APC densities A with proliferation-dependent growth. (a) Bifurcation diagram of the CRM, representing all possible equilibrium states. The lines indicate the total density of T-cells (sum of the variables, $E + R$) as a function of the APC density (parameter A). (b) Equilibria that are actually reached by solving the system with a fixed seed T-cell population (S_1: $E = 3/4 \times 10^{-3}, R = 1/4 \times 10^{-3}$; and S_2: $E = 10^{-3}, R = 10^{-3}$). Remaining parameter values as in Table 1.

to these scenarios. In this section, we address this problem and describe a model of crossregulation in populations with a fixed number of cells that use *recruitment* instead of proliferation. We also characterise the properties of this modified CRM, and highlight the conditions under which it behaves similar to a proliferation model.

In our recruitment model, the activated T-cells can not "proliferate" without the presence of an idle cell for recruitment. Consequently, in addition to T-cells in free, conjugated, and activated states, we define an intermediate state of T-cells (E_i and R_i, for T_E and T_R, respectively), that are scouting for idle cells. The total number of T_E cells $E = E_f + E_c + E_a + E_i$, and the total number of T_R cells $R = R_f + R_c + R_a + R_i$.

We further define a prefixed total density of cells N. Cells that are neither effectors nor regulator are considered as idle I. The density of idle cells I is defined by the conservation equation, $I = N - E - R$.

The dynamics of the interactions between effector and regulator T-cells with APCs is unchanged when recruitment is used instead of proliferation (eqs 1 and eqs 2 for E_c and R_c, respectively). However, the actual process of cell proliferation is now replaced by the recruitment of an idle cell into the proliferating cells' type (effector or regulator), at recruitment rate constant γ_r. In addition, the process of cell death is simulated by the transition of the effector or regulator T-cell into an idle state. Consequently, the equations of the dynamics of T_E cells are now:

$$\frac{\mathrm{d}\,E_f}{\mathrm{d}\,t} = -\gamma_c A E_f \left(1 - \left(\frac{E_c + R_c}{As}\right)^s\right) + \gamma_d (1 - P_E) E_c + 2\gamma_r E_i I - \delta E_f \qquad (8)$$

$$\frac{\mathrm{d}\,E_a}{\mathrm{d}\,t} = \gamma_d P_E E_c - \pi_E E_a - \delta E_a \qquad (9)$$

$$\frac{\mathrm{d}\,E_i}{\mathrm{d}\,t} = \pi_E E_a - \gamma_r E_i I - \delta E_i \qquad (10)$$

In the equations for recruited E_f (eq 8) and E_a (eq 9), the conjugated effector cells with no neighbouring regulatory cell on the same APC are selected for activation. However, the actual growth of these cells is dependent not only on π_E as with the proliferation model but also the recruitment rate constant γ_r applied to E_i (eq 10), and the density of idle cells I.

Similarly, the equations describing the dynamics of T_R cells are:

$$\frac{\mathrm{d}\,R_f}{\mathrm{d}\,t} = -\gamma_c A R_f \left(1 - \left(\frac{E_c + R_c}{As}\right)^s\right) + \gamma_d (1 - P_R) R_c + 2\gamma_r R_i I - \delta R_f \qquad (11)$$

$$\frac{\mathrm{d}\,R_a}{\mathrm{d}\,t} = \gamma_d P_R R_c - \pi_R R_a - \delta R_a \qquad (12)$$

$$\frac{\mathrm{d}\,R_i}{\mathrm{d}\,t} = \pi_R R_a - \gamma_r R_i I - \delta R_i \qquad (13)$$

where the conjugated regulatory cells with one or more neighbouring effector cells are selected for activation and the growth of these cells is dependent on π_R and γ_r, applied to R_i and I.

Behaviour of *Recruiting* T-cell Population: In the CRM with recruitment, as with proliferation, the effective growth rates of E and R cell populations is directly proportional to: (i) conjugation and dissociation constants (γ_c and γ_d), (ii) "proliferation" rates of the two types of T-cells (π_E and π_R), and (iii) the density of APCs (A). The effective growth rates of the recruited T-cells are also inversely proportional to the "death" rate (δ). For comparison, these parameters are set to the same values as in the proliferation model (Table 1). In addition, with cell recruitment, the effective growth rates of the T-cells is also directly proportional to the recruitment rate constant (γ_r), and the total density of cells (N).

In the CRM, the dynamics of the T-cell population is governed by interactions between T_E, T_R cells and APCs. The consequent density dependent feedback mechanisms involved would not operate if the T-cell population can grow no more, i.e. all the T-cells have been recruited. The maximum density of recruited T-cells is investigated by solving the steady state density of recruited effector cells (E) with no inhibitory regulatory cells ($R_f = 0, R_c = 0, R_a = 0, R_i = 0$), for different A and N (Fig. 2). In order to operate under conditions wherein density of recruited cells is not saturated, we select parameter value $N = 30 \times 10^{-3}$, $\gamma_r = 10$, and A below 10^{-4} (Fig. 2).

In the chosen parameter regime, at low APC densities ($a_E < A < a_R$, Fig. 3a) the stable node composed only of effector cells (immune state) is globally stable,

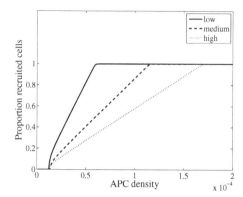

Fig. 2. Equilibrium proportion of recruited effector cells (E/N) as a function of APC densities A for low ($N = 15 \times 10^{-3}$), medium ($N = 30 \times 10^{-3}$) and high ($N = 45 \times 10^{-3}$) total density of T-cells, and recruitment rate $\gamma_r = 10$. Remaining parameter values as in Table 1.

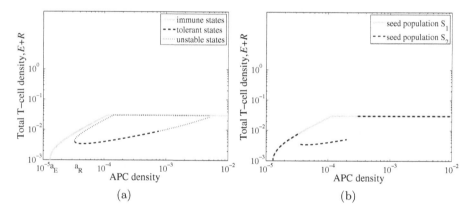

(a)   (b)

Fig. 3. Equilibrium densities of E and R cell populations as a function of APC densities A, with cell *recruitment*. (a) Bifurcation diagram of the CRM, representing all possible equilibrium states. The lines indicate the total density of recruited T-cells (sum of the variables, $E + R$) as a function of the APC density (parameter A). (b) The lines indicate the equilibria that are actually reached by solving the system with a fixed seed T-cell population (S_1: $E = 3/4 \times 10^{-3}, R = 1/4 \times 10^{-3}, N = 30 \times 10^{-3}$; and S_2: $E = 10^{-3}, R = 10^{-3}, N = 30 \times 10^{-3}$). Remaining parameter values as in Table 1.

as was the cases with CRM with proliferation. At relatively high densities of APCs ($a_R < A < 7.5 \times 10^{-4}$, Fig. 3a), the system displays bistability and can evolve into either the immune or the tolerant equilibria, consequent to the proportion of effector and regulatory cells in the seeding population (Fig. 3b).

A Jacobian analysis at the biologically relevant equilibrium points (T-cells densities real and positive and $E + R \leq N$) revealed real and negative eigenvalues for the immune state (stable node). By contrast, at the tolerant state eigenvalues were complex with negative real components, indicating dampened oscillation in the population dynamics. Furthermore, at the unstable equilibrium a mixture of positive and negative eigenvalues were present.

At APC densities above our operational parameter regime ($A > 10^{-4}$), the immune state continues to be stable, with the unstable state and the tolerant state approaching it. At very high APC densities ($A > 7.5 \times 10^{-4}$) the complex eigenvalues of the tolerant state have a mixture of positive and negative real components (Fig. 3a). At these APC densities, the immune state becomes globally stable again.

3   Stochastic Simulation of the Model

A stochastic, spatial, discrete-time simulation is used to compare the CRM using proliferation and recruitment, for different number of APCs. The simulated environment is toroidal and has a size of $S = 1000 \times 1000$ units. The MAS is composed of point-sized entities (APCs) and agents (T-cells). Each APC and T-cell moves at a speed of $v = 0.5$ units/time-step, and has probability 0.01 of changing to a new random direction each simulation step. T-cells can perceive APCs up to a range $w_c = 1$ unit, while they can perceive other T-cells up to a range $w_r = 10$ units.

In our experiments, each T-cell agent can be an effector (T_E), a regulator (T_R) or idle. Furthermore, effector and regulator agents transition between a *free* mode, *attached* mode and an *activated* mode as follows: (i) At the start of the experiment, the agent is free and explores the environment. When an agents detects an APC with a free binding site, it attaches itself to the APC; (ii) Upon detachment from the APC (probability γ_d at each step), effector agents with no regulator agents on the same APC are activated. Similarly, regulator agents with at least one neighbouring effector agent are also activated. The rest of the agents return to the free mode and resume random movement; (iii) Activated agents undergo proliferation with probability π_E and π_R, for effectors and regulators, respectively. In proliferation experiments, the parent and daughter agents return to the free mode. By contrast, in recruitment experiments, the effector or regulator agent, scouts for an idle agent, and upon successful recruitment, the recruiter and recruitee agents return to the free mode; and (iv) The effectors and regulators in all modes are subject to death (probability δ).

The process of proliferation is simulated, either by the introduction of a new agent at the proliferating agent's position (proliferation model), or by the recruitment of an idle agent within range (recruitment model). In both cases, the daughter agent adopts the type of the proliferating/recruiting agent, that is, the daughter immediately transitions either to the effector type or to the regulator type depending on its parent's type. In addition, death is simulated by the removal of the agent (proliferation model), or by switching the agent to the idle state (recruitment model).

3.1 Calculating Agent Parameters

In our stochastic simulations, we set the parameters to connect our experiment results to the ODE model. The simulation probabilities of dissociation, proliferation, and death in each iteration step (τ) are set from the corresponding rates of the ODE model (Table 1) as $\gamma_d\tau$, $\pi_E\tau$, $\pi_R\tau$, and $\delta\tau$, respectively. Furthermore, the T-cell agent's speed (v) and its detection range for APCs (w_c) and other T-cell agents (w_r), and the environment size S, are set as follows. Let us consider the rates μ_c and μ_r, at which an agent encounters an APC and another agent, respectively. These reaction rates can be computed from the corresponding reaction rate constants γ_c and γ_r of the ODE model [14], as $\mu_c = \gamma_c/S$ and $\mu_r = \gamma_r/S$.

As an agent moves through the arena, it sweeps out an area during time interval τ, and will detect an APC or another agent that fall in that area. The detection area can be expressed as is $2w_c v\tau$, for APCs and $2w_r v\tau$ for other agents. Considering that the APCs and agents are uniformly distributed in the arena, the detection rates $\mu_c = 2w_c v\tau/S$ and $\mu_r = 2w_r v\tau/S$.

3.2 Experiments

In experiments with proliferation, the MAS consisted of 1000 T_E agents and 1000 T_R agents. In separate experiments, the number of APCs was set at 20, 40, 60, 80 and 100. The MAS was simulated for 10^7 time-steps (with a constant iteration step $\tau = 1$) at which point the number of effectors and regulators had converged in all experiment conditions. In the case of the recruitment model, an identical set of experiments was conducted, with the total number of agents fixed at 30000 ($I = 28000$).

For both proliferation and recruitment models, since the population dynamics appeared similar at high densities of APCs, cell population dynamics has been shown for the extreme cases of 20 and 100 APCs. In these conditions, we compare the density of T_E (E) and T_R (R) cells from the numerical solution of the model, with the mean density of effector and regulator agents across 40 independent replicates.

The results of the stochastic simulation indicate the population of agents reaches one of two stable states depending on the density of APCs (Fig. 4): (i) an immune state, characterised by the presence of only effectors, and (ii) a tolerant state, consisting of a dominant population of regulators and few effectors. In both proliferation and recruitment growth simulations, the system converged to the immune state in the presence of few APCs (20 in Fig. 4a and b). An increase in the number of APCs in the environment (100 cells in Fig. 4c and d) resulted in convergence to the tolerant state. In addition, the numerical solution of our ODE system appears qualitatively similar to the results from the stochastic simulations, for both proliferation and recruitment models. The quantitative discrepancy between the results of numerical solution of the ODEs and of the simulations (Fig. 4a), reflects: (i) recurrent local interactions between APCs and newly proliferated T-cells; and (ii) sparse and non-uniform distribution of APCs in the simulated environment.

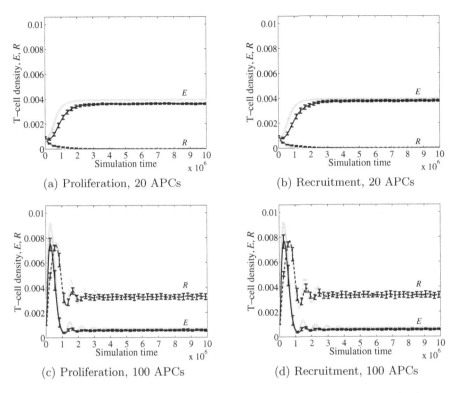

(a) Proliferation, 20 APCs

(b) Recruitment, 20 APCs

(c) Proliferation, 100 APCs

(d) Recruitment, 100 APCs

Fig. 4. Density of effector (E) and regulator (R) T-cells from the numerical solutions (light lines) of the ODE system, and the mean ($\pm$SD) density of effector and regulator agents across 40 stochastic simulation replicates (dark lines)

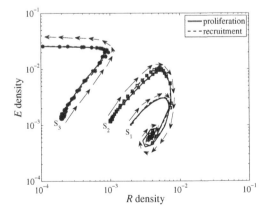

Fig. 5. Trajectory of T-cell population with $A = 10^{-4}$ using proliferation (solid line) and recruitment (dashed line), upon perturbation of tolerant equilibrium state by 50% (seed populations S_1, cross marker), 75% (seed populations S_2, square marker) and 95% (seed populations S_3, star marker)

In stochastic simulations operating in the bistable parameter regime ($A > a_R$), the system developed into the tolerant state (e.g., $A = 10^{-4}$, Fig. 4c and d). In order to evaluate the stability of this tolerant state, we restarted the proliferation and recruitment growth simulations for the extreme case of (100 APCs) and at time-step 10^7, with a perturbed density of effector and regulator agents. The new seed populations were computed by incrementing effectors, and decrementing regulators by 50%, 75% and 95%. The perturbed populations were simulated for 4×10^6 time-steps at which point the number of agents had converged in all six (3 perturbed seed populations each for proliferation and recruitment) experiment conditions. In Fig. 5, we have plotted the density of effector and regulator agents of a single replicate, for 4×10^6 simulation steps, and with population perturbations at 50%, 75% and 95%. For seed populations perturbed up to 75%,the system returned to the tolerant state, irrespective of the mechanism of population growth (proliferation and recruitment) (Fig. 5). At relatively high perturbations (e.g., 95%), the system transitioned to an immune state, with the population dominated by effectors, with no regulator agents present (Fig. 5).

4   Discussion and Conclusions

In this study, we highlighted some of the challenges in deploying immune system inspired algorithms for MAS. We proposed an alternative to the mechanism of clonal expansion, namely recruitment, that may be used in fixed-sized agent populations. We identified and characterised an operational parameter regime, wherein recruitment can be used while retaining the properties of the model. In this operational regime, the analytical models and stochastic simulations of growth by recruitment were shown to recapitulate the same properties of CRM, where growth is dependent on cell division.

In the natural immune system, the total number of T-cells is maintained fairly constant in healthy individuals by homeostatic mechanisms [15], irrespective of the T-cell specificity or differentiation class (e.g. Th1, Th2, and so on). Antigendriven clonal expansion of a subpopulation implies erosion of other subpopulations. The net result of clonal expansion in the presence of strong homeostasis is akin to the recruiment-based growth dynamics we proposed here.

An important issue to note when utilising the recruitment model is the large number of agents needed. In our simulations, 30000 agents had to be present in the population. Additionally, an increase in APCs would demand an even higher number of agents. Another potential approach wherein the total number of required agents may be reduced, would be the recruitment of other cell types, besides idle cells, e.g., in the CRM, an activated regulator cell may be able to recruit an effector cell. However, the outcome of this scenario needs to be explored further, particularly in stochastic simulations with fewer agents, where the discrepancies with the mean field model predictions can be not only quantitative (as in the case of the parameter regime studied here) but even qualitative [16]. Also worth exploration is the impact of random perturbations to the number of agents representing the T-cells or the entities representing APCs, as stochastic perturbations could drive anomalous behaviours akin to relapsing autoimmunity [17].

The CRM, for which our recruitment mechanism has been assessed, describes a dynamics of interactions between T-cells of the immune system, that allows the system to discriminate between "self" and "nonself" antigens based solely on their density and persistence in the environment, and largely independent of their intrinsic characteristics. This property of the model opens up very interesting applications involving decentralised feature classification, wherein our recruitment model may be utilised, circumventing the need for self-replicating units.

In summary, we have shown that our approach to applying immune system inspired algorithms for MAS is promising, particularly for applications involving severe constraints on agents or agents that cannot self-replicate, such as speckled computing or collective robotic systems.

Acknowledgment. This study was supported by the FCT grant PTDC/EEACRO/104658/2008.

References

1. Janeway, C., Travers, P., Walport, M., Shlomchik, M.: Immunobiology: The Immune System in Health and Disease. Garland Science, New York (1997)
2. Park, H., Li, Z., Yang, X., Chang, S., Nurieva, R., Wang, Y., Wang, Y., Hood, L., Zhu, Y., Tian, Q., Dong, C.: A distinct lineage of CD4 T cells regulates tissue inflammation by producing interleukin 17. Nature Immunology 6, 1133–1141 (2005)
3. Mosmann, T., Coffman, R.: Th1 and Th2 cells: different patterns of lymphokine secretion lead to different functional properties. Annual Review of Immunology 7, 145–173 (1989)
4. Sakaguchi, S.: Naturally arising CD4$^+$ regulatory T cells for immunologic self-tolerance and negative control of immune responses. Annual Review of Immunology 22, 531–562 (2004)
5. Nino, F., Beltran, O.: A change detection software agent based on immune mixed selection. In: Proceedings of the 2002 Congress on Evolutionary Computation (CEC), pp. 693–698. IEEE Computer Society, Washington, DC (2002)
6. Bradley, D.W., Tyrrell, A.M.: Immunotronics: Hardware Fault Tolerance Inspired by the Immune System. In: Miller, J.F., Thompson, A., Thompson, P., Fogarty, T.C. (eds.) ICES 2000. LNCS, vol. 1801, pp. 11–20. Springer, Heidelberg (2000)
7. Watanabe, Y., Ishiguro, A., Shirai, Y., Uchikawa, Y.: Emergent construction of behavior arbitration mechanism based on the immune system. In: Proceedings of the IEEE World Congress on Computational Intelligence, pp. 481–486. IEEE Computer Society, Washington, DC (1998)
8. Singh, S., Thayer, S.: Kilorobot search and rescue using an immunologically inspired approach. In: Proceedings of the 6th International Symposium on Distributed Autonomous Robotic Systems, pp. 300–305. Springer, Berlin (2002)
9. Leon, K., Perez, P., Lage, A., Farob, J., Carneiro, J.: Modelling t-cell-mediated suppression dependent on interactions in multicellular conjugates. Journal of Theoretical Biology 207(2), 231–254 (2000)
10. Carneiro, J., Leon, K., Caramalho, I., Van Den Dool, C., Gardner, R., Oliveira, V., Bergman, M., Sepúlveda, N., Paixão, T., Faro, J., Demengeot, J.: When three is not a crowd: a crossregulation model of the dynamics and repertoire selection of regulatory CD4$^+$ T cells. Immunological Reviews 216(1), 48–68 (2007)

11. Abi-Haidar, A., Rocha, L.: Adaptive spam detection inspired by the immune system. In: Proceedings of the 11th International Conference on the Simulation and Synthesis of Living Systems, Artificial Life XI, pp. 1–8. MIT Press, Cambridge (2008)
12. Abi-Haidar, A., Rocha, L.: Collective classification of textual documents by guided self-organization in T-cell cross-regulation dynamics. Evolutionary Intelligence 4(2), 69–80 (2011)
13. Evans, M., Hastings, N., Peacock, B.: 27. In: Statistical Distributions, 3rd edn., pp. 134–136. John Wiley & Sons (2000)
14. Gillespie, D.: A general method for numerically simulating the stochastic time evolution of coupled chemical reactions. Journal of Computational Physics 22, 403–434 (1976)
15. Sprent, J., Surh, C.: Normal T cell homeostasis: the conversion of naive cells into memory-phenotype cells. Nature Immunology 12(6), 478–484 (2011)
16. Figueroa-Morales, N., Leon, K., Mulet, R.: Stochastic approximation to the t cell mediated specific response of the immune system. Behavioral Ecology and Sociobiology 21(295), 37–46 (2012)
17. Velez de Mendizabal, N., Carneiro, J., Sole, R., Goni, J., Bragard, J., Martinez-Forero, I., Martinez-Pasamar, S., Sepulcre, J., Torrealdea, J., Bagnato, F., Garcia-Ojalvo, J., Villoslada, P.: Modeling the effector - regulatory T cell cross-regulation reveals the intrinsic character of relapses in multiple sclerosis. BMC Systems Biology 5(1), 114 (2011)

A Real Time Anomaly Detection System Based on Probabilistic Artificial Immune Based Algorithm

Mehdi Mohammadi[1], Ahmad Akbari[1], Bijan Raahemi[2], and Babak Nassersharif[3]

[1] Iran University of Science and Technology, Computer Engineering Department,
University Road, Hengam Street, Resalat Square, Tehran, Iran
[2] University of Ottawa, 55 Laurier Ave, E., Ottawa, ON, Canada K1N 6N5
[3] Electrical and Computer Engineering Department, K.N. Toosi University of Technology, Iran

Abstract. Artificial Immune System (AIS)-based evolutionary algorithms combine rules and randomness to solve optimization and classification problems. Due to their capability in identifying self and non self samples, they have also gained attention in intrusion detection systems. In this paper, we propose a real-time AIS-based anomoly detection algorithm for intrusion detection. The most important features of the proposed method are its high detection rate, low false alarm, low computational complexity, and real-time response to the incoming samples. We compare our proposed method with several well-known anomaly detection algorithms on various datasets. We demonstrate that the proposed method performs the best among others in terms of false alarm, detection rate and time response.

1 Introduction

Intrusion detection systems are of two principal types: signature matching (or misuse detection) systems and anomaly detection systems. Signature matching systems look for intrusion signatures, which are characteristic indications of known attacks. Anomaly detection systems look for system/application behavior that is anomalous in the sense that it differs markedly from normal, safe behavior. Signature matching systems tend to issue fewer "false positive" alerts than anomaly detection systems, but the former cannot detect new attacks, while the latter can. Signature matching systems need to have a signature database corresponding to known attacks is specified a priori, but anomaly detection systems only need the information about the normal behavior [1].

Anomaly detection systems model the normal network behavior, which enables them to be extremely effective in finding known and unknown or zero-day attacks. This is the main reason why our work focuses on the development of an anomaly-based IDS. In this paper, we have proposed an anomaly detection method based on the artificial immune system (AIS). It uses some observations that are valid for the computer network connections to overcome with the computational cost of the AIS algorithm. These observations are neglected in many works, which have used machine learning technique for IDS (signature or anomaly-based IDSs), and our algorithm applies them to achieve better performance in comparison with other anomaly-based methods. These observations will be discussed in next section.

C.A. Coello Coello et al. (Eds.): ICARIS 2012, LNCS 7597, pp. 205–217, 2012.

2   Artificial Immune-Based Algorithm for Intrusion Detection Systems

Evolutionary algorithms combine rules and randomness to imitate natural phenomena [2]. One of the members of evolutionary algorithms is artificial immune system (AIS), which imitates the human body's immune system. AIS has two main applications in machine-learning techniques. It can be used as an optimization problem solver and as a classifier[3] [4]. There are many uses for AIS in literatures. In [5] the authors use AIS to propose an artificial immune-based feature transformation to achieve better classification accuracy based on the different type of datasets and classifiers. The AIS-based classifiers can be divided into a few categories. Two of the largest categories are positive selection and negative selection algorithms. These two types of AIS-based algorithms can be used as an anomaly detection classifier.

In the training phase of the positive selection method, each sample is considered as a self detector with a fixed radius. In the test phase, the incoming samples, which are placed in at least one detector area, are considered to be self samples. Otherwise, they are considered as non-self or anomaly samples. In terms of IDS, self samples are considered normal and non-self samples are considered as attacks.

In the training phase of negative selection, some random samples are created, and each random sample is considered as a non-self detector with a fixed radius. If one of the training samples is placed in a non-self detector, the non-self detector will be eliminated. However, if none of the self samples is placed in the non-self detector, the non-self detector will be preserved. Lastly at the end of training phase, there are some non-self detectors that do not cover any self samples, and they will be considered as non-self detectors in the test phase. In the test phase, each of incoming samples that is placed in at least one non-self detector area is considered to be anomaly sample. Otherwise, they are considered as a self sample. There are some different versions of positive and negative selection methods.

Real Value negative selection (RVNS) [6] is one of the most famous of these methods. In this paper, we compare our proposed method with positive selection and RVNS algorithms.

In this paper, we propose a combinational AIS-based classifier where the stages of the proposed algorithm are very similar to positive selection. In the next section, we describe the proposed method in more detail.

3   Probabilistic Artificial Immune Method

In this section, we describe the proposed method in detail, starting with the simplest version of the proposed method, and a new attribute of the final algorithm is proposed during each step.

3.1   Simple Probabilistic Artificial Immune Method

The proposed method uses the probability density function (PDF) as the self detector that is why we called this version the Simple Probabilistic Artificial Immune method (SPAI). Fig. 1 shows the diagram of the algorithm.

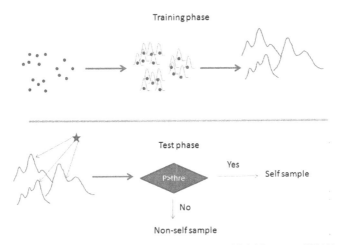

Fig. 1. Block diagram of simple probabilistic artificial immune (SPAI)

As shown in Fig. 4, the SPAI method is a positive selection method, because it considers each sample as a detector. In contrast with the original positive selection method, the SPAI method determines each self sample as a Gaussian probability density with the mean of the self sample and a fixed variance σ. All of the Gaussian densities organize a Gaussian mixture model. In other words, the Gaussian mixture model is a PDF approximation of self samples in the training phase. This process is known as the Parzen window density estimation in much of the literature. Equation (1) shows membership probability for a new incoming sample x.

$$P(x) = \frac{1}{n\sigma^F\sqrt{(2\pi)^{F/2}}} \times \sum_{i=1}^{n} e^{\frac{-(x_i-x)^2}{2\sigma^2}} \tag{1}$$

In this equation, n is number of self samples, F is number of features, x is an incoming new sample, xi is the ith self sample and σ is the variance of each Gaussian distribution.

Using Fig. 1, in the training phase, a PDF is calculated based on all self samples and in the test phase, each new incoming sample is fed into the PDF, and a membership probability is calculated on the whole PDF. Then, in the next step, if the membership probability is higher than a given threshold, it will be considered as a self or normal sample. Otherwise it will be considered to be a non-self sample or an attack.

3.2   Clustering the Self Sample into Some Sub-groups

Using Gaussian mixture-based detectors, the proposed method achieves better detection rates and false alarms in comparison with other AIS anomaly detection methods. However, there is a major drawback for using the SPAI method, namely the computational cost. We incorporate the SPAI method with some machine-learning algorithms based on some characteristics available on the computer network behavior. From now on, in each step, we introduce a new ability that is added to the SPAI method to overcome computational cost without reducing false alarms and detection rates.

In anomaly-based IDS, the definition of normal behavior is always a difficult step. In other words, there is not a plenary profile for normal behavior. Normal behavior can change from time to time, for example, when a new user enters the network or a new application is installed on the network, the network behavior may be changed so any normal activity may generate new normal behavior on the network, and this new network behavior should be added to the existing normal profile. This means that the normal behavior profile contains some sub-profiles for different normal behaviors, and that these sub-normal behaviors can be completely different from each other, because they refer to different kinds of normal behavior of the network. This observation is neglected in many works that have used the machine-learning techniques for IDS (signature or anomaly based IDSs) because there are lots of different kinds of machine-learning applications [7,8], which were trained their classifier based on a normal profile as a normal class, and maybe some different kinds of attack profiles as attack classes, such as DOS, Probe, U2R and R2L. In this paper, we use this fact to improve the performance of the proposed method. Therefore, at first, we cluster the normal profile to some groups that have similar normal behavior. Actually, all clusters represent normal activity, but each cluster represents a different activity in contrast with other normal clusters. Based on the clustering of normal samples, we have proposed the Clustered Probabilistic Artificial Immune (CPAI) algorithm. The diagram of this method is presented in Fig. 2.

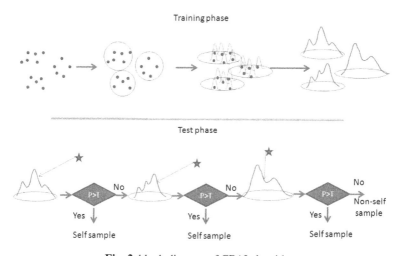

Fig. 2. block diagram of CPAI algorithm

As shown in this figure, the self samples are clustered into some sub-groups, and, for each group, a Parzen window estimation is generated based on the self samples as self detectors, which are the normal detectors of the algorithm. In this stage, each incoming sample is represented in the first detector, and membership probability is calculated. If the probability is greater than a fixed given threshold, the sample will be considered as a self, but if the probability is lower than the threshold, the sample will be introduced into the next detector. If the sample cannot satisfy any of the detectors, it will be considered as a non-self sample. If a normal sample enters the test phase of

CPAI, it will satisfy the threshold of a detector and will exit from rest of the test phase. This produces lower computational cost in comparison with the SPAI method, because the number of normal samples in any kind of network or even network datasets is greater than the number of attack samples. It means that most of the time the new incoming sample represents normal behavior and it will exit in the middle of the detection process.

3.3   Priority Clustered Probabilistic Artificial Immune Method

By using clustering as the pre-process phase of the SPAI, we propose the CPAI method. In CPAI, the new incoming sample is introduced into the first detector but in CPAI there is no mechanism to select the next detector. The next detector is selected randomly or based on the predefined sequence of detectors but in this section we are going to describe an observation that is valid on any typical network connection given and use this observation to propose a new version of our algorithm. In computer network communication, some users start one or more activities in a period of time and then finish one or more of them. It means that the traffic which is generated by the users has identical behavior on a short period of time. In this period of time the samples which are extracted from the network connection are almost identical. Therefore, when these samples enter the CPAI test phase, they are placed in a specific detector because, over a short period of time, they are almost identical and the feature values of these samples may be the same to the other samples which are extracted during this short period of time. The corresponding detector is not changed until the users change some of their activities. Based on this observation, we have proposed another version of our algorithm. We called it Priority Clustered Probabilistic Artificial Immune (PCPAI). Fig. 3 shows the PCPAI diagram.

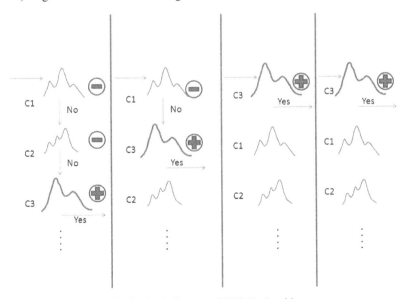

Fig. 3. Block diagram of PCPAI algorithm

As shown in this figure, at first each cluster is given a priority number randomly and these clusters are sorted based their priority values. This means that the highest priority cluster is placed in the first position and so on. When new incoming sample enters the PCPAI test phase, it will be introduced into the highest priority detector (for example C1, based on the Fig. 3) and the membership probability for this detector is calculated. If the membership probability does not pass the threshold, the new sample will be introduced into the next high priority detector (C2). This process continues until the sample is introduced into the next detector (C3). Imagine, in this situation, the membership probability passes the threshold on C3 so the sample is labeled as a self or normal sample, priorities of the previous detectors (C1 and C2) is reduced and priority of the current detector is increased. The current detector moves up to higher priority place. Because of the identical behavior of the network, we hope that the next incoming sample will be very similar to the previous one. In this case, the next sample is introduced into the highest priority detector (C1) and is failed to pass the threshold. At this time, the incoming sample is introduced into the C3 instead of C2, because now this detector has more priority than C2. This means that based on the detection process, the sequence of the cluster will be changed. At this time, the incoming sample is introduced into only C1 and C3, but in previous time the previous sample was introduced into C1, C2 and C3 respectively. So the computational complexity for detecting the new sample is reduced. This process is continued, and C3 detects the second sample too, gaining a greater priority score, and moving up again. The priority of C3 and C1 is changed as shown in the third part of Fig.3 .

Once again, we are hopeful that the next incoming sample is similar to the two previous ones and at this time, C3 has the most priority among the other detectors. So the incoming sample is introduced into the C3, and C3 detects it as a normal sample. From this moment on, the incoming sample only is introduced to the C3 until the behavior of the network changes gradually. It is obvious that the winner detectors are placed on the highest priority rank until the behavior of the network changes seamlessly. These changes can be traced by the PCPAI and detector priorities are changed based on the number of samples they have detected or failed to detect. It can be concluded that the PCPAI can trace the behavior of the network and learn how to adapt with the changes incrementally. As well, the PCPAI can find the suitable detector based on the network behavior.

3.4   Reduced Priority Clustered Probabilistic Artificial Immune Method

By using priority, we have ordered the detector and achieved better performance on PCPAI. There is another major behavior in network connections. In the training phase of the proposed methods (SPAI, CPAI and PCPAI), the normal behavior of the network connection is analyzed, and based on it, the normal signatures are extracted. Within the short period of time the behavior of the network connection is identical so the extracted signatures are almost the same during this period of the time. This means that, in the training phase, there are some repeated samples that describe the same behavior of the network. In other words, not only the repeated sample have a lot of redundant information in training phase, but they also cause the computational complexity of the training phase to increase. We apply a sample reduction method on the training dataset and reduce number of samples in training dataset and incorporated the proposed sample reduction method with PCPAI .We have called this method Reduced Priority Clustered Probabilistic Artificial Immune (RPCPAI).

Let X be the input dataset with N samples, each sample including F features. Sample reduction process can be defined as the function Y=f(X), where Y is the reduced dataset with M samples and F features. Normally M<N, and the ratio of M/N, called reduction ratio, is less than 1.

In [10], we have proposed a new sample reduction method and have applied it to different kinds of intrusion detection datasets. Our experiments have shown that the proposed method has outperformed the other tested methods, which had similar attributes to the proposed method.

In RPCPAI, samples of the self class are divided into some clusters, and then the sample reduction method is applied on the clusters with half of the samples being eliminated from the dataset. The rest of the RPCPAI method is similar to the PCPAI method. This means that this method contains sampling, clustering and priority processes to overcome the computational cost of the SPAI method. In the experimental results section, we evaluate each version of the proposed algorithm separately to show how the RPCPAI is the same as its ancestors (SPAI, CPAI and PCPAI) in terms of detection rate and false alarm and its response time is fastrer than that of the ancestors.

In the next section, we are going to evaluate all versions of the proposed method on various kinds of intrusion detection datasets based on different types of measurements. Lastly, we will compare the proposed method with the other anomaly detection methods on the KddCup99 dataset.

4   Experimental Results

In this section, we evaluate the proposed method using different type of datasets. We use two typical intrusion detection datasets and two new intrusion detection datasets generated in our laboratory. Table (1) shows the details of each dataset.

Table 1. Summary of the Used Datasets

	#features	Self Class	Non-Self Class	#samples Train	#samples test
Darpa98	5	1	2	175359	759334
DataSetMe	10	1	2	8274	9063
IUSTSip	7	1	2	130760	412378
KDD Cup 99	41	1	2 3 4 5	17020	82980

We have introduced two new datasets to our work in our laboratory, and we have named these datasets DataSetMe and IUSTSip. The datasets are designed for anomaly detection purposes. This means that each dataset contains two separate datasets for training and test. The training dataset only includes self samples and the test dataset includes a combination of self and non-self samples. DataSetMe includes a number of different DOS and probes attacks, and IUSTSip contains a number of different attacks on SIP protocol.

For all mentioned datasets in Table (1), the training part contains only self samples and the test part contains a combination of self and non-self samples.

4.1   Evaluation of the Proposed Methods

In this experiment, different versions of the proposed methods are compared in terms of false alarms, detection rates and computational complexity on different datasets. In each sub-section, we have evaluated the methods on a dataset. Each sub-section has a conclusion on the behavior of the method on a specific dataset.

Evaluation of the Proposed Methods on DataSetMe Dataset

In this section, we evaluate our methods on some real datasets, which are captured from the real network and the sequence of the packets are kept in the sequence of the samples. In other words, the close samples in the datasets are calculated from close packets on the real networks. This means that these datasets follow the observations mentioned about typical computer networks, and this means that no one can reorder the sequence of the packets without any logical problems. We will show that, on these kinds of datasets, the proposed method has the best performance based on the different type of measurements. Fig. 4 shows the experimental results on the DataSetMe.

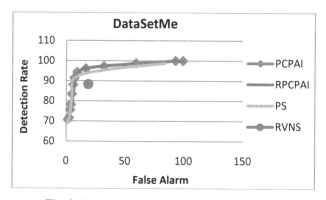

Fig. 4. Experimental results on DataSetMe dataset

There are some important points about this figure. The first one is that, the clustering and priority processes do not reduce the accuracy of the corresponding methods and the results of the first version of the proposed method is similar to the last version of the proposed method (RPCPAI). Another important point is that our final method outperforms the PS and RVNS methods in terms of false alarms and detection rates.

Evaluation of the Proposed Methods on Darpadataset

In this experiment, we evaluate our methods on the Darpa dataset. We look at the first two weeks as the training dataset and the four remaining weeks as the test dataset. In the training dataset, we only used the normal samples for the first two weeks. Similarly to the DataSetMe, the Darpa dataset is calculated on the real network, and the samples of the Darpa follow the real network situation. Fig.5 shows the experimental results of the evaluation.

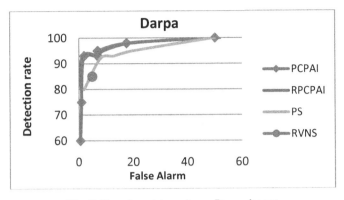

Fig. 5. Experimental results on Darpa dataset

As shown in this Figure , the RPCPAI method is better than the PS and RVNS methods in terms of false alarms and detection rates. It shows that the clustering and priority processes do not reduce the accuracy of the proposed methods and it is better than both PS and RVNS.

Evaluation of the Proposed Methods on the IUSTSip Dataset

In this experiment, we evaluate our proposed methods on another real network dataset, which is captured on SIP protocol in our laboratory. Fig. 6 shows the results of this experiment.

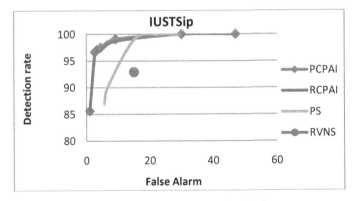

Fig. 6. Experimental results on IUSTSip dataset

Similar to the DataSetMe and Darpa, the results of our proposed methods on this dataset are significant. Our final method, RPCPAI, has low false alarms and high detection rates just like the SPAI method, so it means that clustering, priority and reduction processes do not reduce SPAI accuracy in detecting new incoming attacks. As well, it is better than PS and RVNS.

Lastly, the results of this experiments again prove that our method should work well in real situations and that it does not depend on the type of protocol that transforms the data.

In previous experiments we showed that RCPAI and it ancestors are better than PS and RVNS in term of detection rate and false alarm. In next experiments we will show that not only final proposed method is better that both PS and RVNS but it also better than them based on the response time criteria.

In next figure, we propose the needed time for each algorithm to classify a new incoming sample as normal or as an attack on DataSetMe, Darpa and IUSTSip datasets. We ran the tests on a Pentium IV 2 GHz machine with 1 GB of memory. The tests are written in Matlab in a Windows environment. Fig. 7 compares the needed time for each method on the DataSetMe dataset for processing each sample of the dataset.

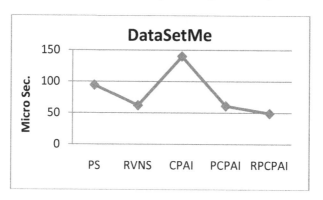

Fig. 7. Response time for different methods based on DataSetMe

As shown in this figure, we compare the PS, RVNS and proposed methods with each other. The value for the SPAI method is about 377 microseconds per sample. This value is significantly greater than the other methods, so we eliminated the SPAI method from the figure. By using the clustering method, we reduced the needed time per sample to 145 microseconds. As well, by applying the priority process, we achieved 70 microseconds per sample. The needed time for the PCPAI method is almost equal to the RVNS method. As we have shown before, the PCPAI method outperforms the RVNS one in terms of false alarms and detection rates. The needed time for the RPCPAI method is about 48 microseconds, with the best results in this figure. This experiment shows that, not only does the RPCPAI method outperform both RVNS and PS in terms of false alarms and detection rates, but also it is better than them regarding computational complexity. Our final method is two times faster than the PS method and 1.3 times faster than RVNS algorithms.

Another important point in this figure is that the dataset samples are calculated based on the two-second analysis of the incoming samples. This means that, for every two seconds, the proposed method needs only 48 microseconds to determine the type of incoming sample, and it can be an acceptable value for detecting an incoming sample. We ran the tests on a Pentium IV 2 GHz computer, which is an ordinary computer that is not very powerful. Fig. 8 represents the results of the experiment on the Darpa dataset.

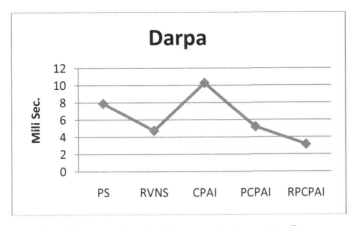

Fig. 8. Response time for different methods based on Darpa

As shown in this figure, we present the time needed per sample for each algorithm on Darpa. We eliminated the SPAI method to make the distinction clearer between other methods. The value of the SPAI method on the Darpa dataset is about 31 milliseconds, and the value is greater than the PS and RVNS algorithms. By using clustering with the CPAI method, we have reduced the needed time to ten milliseconds. This reduction shows the significant effect of using clustering. In the next step, by applying the priority process to our algorithm, we reduce the time to about five milliseconds. It shows that the priority idea works well and has the benefit of reducing the computational cost to half in comparison with the CPAI method. Similar to the previous experiment, the RPCPAI method is the best one among the other methods and could be further proof of the good performance of the proposed method. As it is illustrated in this figure, the RPCPAI method is faster than RVNS and PS algorithms and also outperforms these two algorithms in terms of false alarms and detection rates. The final proposed method is three times faster than PS algorithms and two times faster than RVNS algorithms. Another important thing about the recent experiments is that the performance of the algorithms on these datasets is almost the same, and behavior of the curves on the Fig. 7 and Fig. 8 is almost identical. It can show the independency of the proposed method on the type of protocols, features and other characteristics of the datasets. It proves that the proposed algorithms can be adapted to different environments and computer networks.

Evaluation of the RPCPAI Method in Comparison with the Other Anomaly Detection Methods
In this section, we compare the results of the RPCPAI method with ADWICE, Catsub, FCM, SVM+DGSOT, LIBSVM, and K-Means+ID3[10]. Fig. 9 shows the results of the experiments as an ROC curve as False Alarm and Detection Rate.

As a result of this experiment, we can conclude that the proposed method can compete with other anomaly detection methods and that generally the proposed method is the best approach among these methods. Moreover, the proposed method has acceptable computational complexity and quick response to the changes in network behavior, which some the methods mentioned cannot do. For example, because of the SVM training phase, the SVM-based method cannot be used in real-time applications.

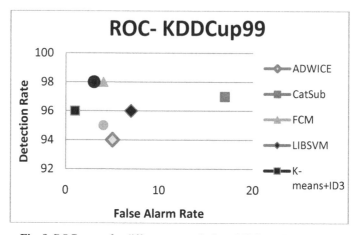

Fig. 9. ROC curve for different anomaly-based IDSs on KDDcup99

5   Conclusion

In this paper, we proposed a real-time artificial immune-based algorithm intrusion detection system. The most important features of the proposed method are its low computational complexity, high detection rate, low false alarm and real-time response to the incoming samples. We demonstrated that our method is designed for real network intrusion detection systems and shows the best performance on the datasets, which are extracted from real network situations. We have measured our proposed method using different measurements on a variety of datasets. Different experimental results show the independency of the proposed method on the type of protocols, features and other characteristics of the datasets. The combinational proposed method has demonstrated good performance in comparison with some of the well-known anomaly detection-based algorithms.

References

[1] Masri, W., Podgurski, A.: Application-based anomaly intrusion detection with dynamic information flow analysis. Computers & Security 27, 176–187 (2008)
[2] Seok Lee, K., Woo, Z.: A new meta-heuristic algorithm for continuous engineering optimization: harmony search theory and practice. Computer Methods in Applied Mechanic and Engineering 194, 3902–3933 (2005)
[3] Zhong, Y., Zhang, L.: An Adaptive Artificial Immune Network for Supervised Classification of Multi-Hyperspectral Remote Sensing Imagery. IEEE transaction on Geoscience and Remote Sensing 50(3), 894–909 (2012)
[4] Delibasis, K.K., Asvestas, P.A., Matsopoulos, G.K., Zoulias, E., Tseleni-Balafouta, S.: Computer-Aided Diagnosis of Thyroid Malignancy Using an Artificial ImmuneSystem Classification Algorithm. IEEE Transactions onInformation Technology in Biomedicine 13(5), 680–686 (2009)

[5] Mohammadi, M., Raahemi, B., Akbari, A., Nassersharif, B., Moeinzadeh, H.: Improving linear discriminant analysis with artificial immune system-based evolutionary algorithms. Information Sciences 189, 219–232 (2012)

[6] Ji, Z., Dasgupta, D.: Real-Valued Negative Selection Algorithm with Variable-Sized Detectors. In: Deb, K., Tari, Z. (eds.) GECCO 2004. LNCS, vol. 3102, pp. 287–298. Springer, Heidelberg (2004)

[7] Bolón-Canedo, V., Sánchez-Maroño, N., Alonso-Betanzos, A.: Feature selection and classification in multiple class datasets: An application to KDDCup 1999 dataset. Systems with Applications 38(5), 5947–5957 (2011)

[8] Tsai, C., Lin, C.: A triangle area based nearest neighbors approach to intrusion detection. Pattern Recognition 43(1), 222–229 (2010)

[9] Gogoi, P., Bhattacharyya, D.: Anomaly Detection Analysis of Intrusion Data using Supervised & Unsupervised Approach. Journal of Convergence Information Technology 5(1) (February 2010)

[10] Mohammadi, M., Raahemi, B., Akbari, A., Nassersharif, B.: Unsupervised Sample Reduction Using Clustering for Intrusion Detection System, Submitted to Security and Communication Network Journal (under review)

CSA/IE: Novel Clonal Selection Algorithm with Information Exchange for High Dimensional Global Optimization Problems

Zixing Cai[1], Xingbao Liu[1], and Xiaoping Ren[2]

[1] School of Information Science and Engineering, Central South University,
Changsha, 410083, P.R. China
zxcai@csu.edu.cn, bxingliu@126.com
[2] National Institute of Metrology, Beijing, 100012, P.R. China
renxp@nim.ac.cn

Abstract. In order to increase the diversity of immune algorithm when solving high dimensional global optimization problems, a novel clonal selection algorithm with information exchange (CSA/IE) is proposed. The main characteristics of CSA/IE are clonal expansion and a novel hypermutation strategy. In addition, a simplex crossover operator is introduced to improve the ability of information exchange. Particularly, a novel performance evaluation criterion is constructed in this paper, by which the performance of different population-based algorithms can be compared easily. The experimental results indicate that CSA/IE outperforms that of the conventional clonal selection algorithms and the three DE variants, in terms of the performance evaluation criterion proposed. Finally, the proposed CSA/IE is generalized to optimize some hyper-high dimensional (such as 100~1000 dimensions) unimodal and multimodal test functions, and the results show that the proposed algorithm performs well in terms of the stability and the solution quality.

Keywords: Artificial immune systems, Clonal selection algorithm, Information exchange, Global optimization problems.

1 Introduction

Nature-inspired computational modals have been utilized to solve the complex scientific and engineering problems. Among them, evolutionary algorithms (EAs), inspired by natural evolution, have attracted more attention. Currently, there are several different types of EAs, including genetic algorithm (GA) [9, 10, 17], differential evolutionary algorithm [22], particle swarm optimization [12,18], ant colony optimization [11], etc. In recent years, a new computational modal, called artificial immune systems inspired by natural immune system, has been paid attention, and some outstanding achievements have been obtained [4]. Moreover, the artificial immune systems have been successfully utilized to many application fields, such as anomaly detection [13], pattern recognition [25], and numerical optimization [6,7,21].

According to Burnet's clonal selection principle [2], the antibodies are stimulated when the antigen, an external entity, trespasses the body barriers. Then antibodies

C.A. Coello Coello et al. (Eds.): ICARIS 2012, LNCS 7597, pp. 218–231, 2012.

match antigens by presenting the receptors to cell surface of antigen. Inspired by the clonal selection principle, De Castro [4] designed a clonal selection algorithm to solve pattern recognition and numerical optimization problems. When CSA is used to solve real-world problems, the process of selection, clone and hypermutation are repeated until some certain terminal criterions are satisfied. The general computational framework of CSA utilized in literature is given as follows [4]:

> *Initialize the population with size NP randomly*
> *Evaluation fitness function for all individuals*
> *While (the termination criterion is not satisfied)*
> > *Select superior individuals from parent population*
> > *Clone the best k individuals according to their fitness values*
> > *Mutate all clones to generate new candidate individuals*
> > *Evaluate all candidate individuals through fitness function*
> > *Select superior individuals*
> > *Update the evolutionary population*
> *End*

Clone and hypermutation operators are the main operators of CSA. These two operators influence significantly on the performance of CSA and, consequently, much research work has been focused on them in recent years [6, 7, 8, 14, 15, 16, 19, 20].

The clones generated through clone operator are the copies of their parents; therefore they need to undergo hypermutation phase in order to become qualified candidate antibodies. Hypermutation mechanism is an interesting and distinguished feature of CSA, and many novel hypermutation operators have been designed, such as distance-based somatic hypermutation [14], adaptive mean hypermutation [16] and fitness-based hypermutation [28]. Compared to other mutation strategies, inversely proportional hypermutation is more interesting [1, 5].

The above work improves the performance and promotes the development of CSA. However information exchange among different antibodies is neglected when designing a novel CSA. To address the aforementioned issues, we propose an efficient algorithm, named CSA with information exchange (CSA/IE), to improve the performance of CSA.

2   Global Optimization Problems

Without loss of generality, the general global optimization problem (GOP) that we are interested in can be formulated as

$$\min_{x \in D} \mathbf{F}(x) = f(x), \quad x = (x_1, x_2, \cdots, x_n) \tag{1}$$

Where x is the decision variable with the domain $D \subset R^n$, R^n denotes the n-dimensional real space, and $F(x) : D \to R$ is a continuous function. The domain D is defined by the lower bound lb_i and upper bound ub_i of each component x_i of x. $x^* \in D$ is called global minimum if and only $\neg \exists x' \in D$ such that $f(x') < f(x^*)$.

3   CSA with Information Exchange

Motivated by the previous observation, we propose a novel CSA/IE, which contains several important novel operators such as a randomized clonal expansion strategy, a somatic hypermutation, and an introduced simplex crossover operator [23].

CSA/IE is divided into the following major process:

(1) Initialize and evaluate antibody population **P**

(2) α-clonal expansion (section 3.1): all antibodies clone themselves according to a random clonal expansion mechanism

(3) Hypermutation (section 3.2): clones undergo a mutation process, and compose a intermediate population **MP.**

(4) Simplex crossover (section 3.3): triple antibody are selected from the intermediate population formed by **P** and **MP,**

The algorithm is run repeatedly until the termination criteria are satisfied. The detailed description of CSA/IE is given in Table 1.

Table 1. The pseudo-code of CSA/IE

Inputs	
	α: the ratio of clonal expansion.
Outputs	
	Gbest: the antibody with best minimum found through the program.
1.	begin
2.	initializing the antibody population **P** randomly;
3.	Evaluating fitness function for all member antibodies in **P**;
4.	while (termination criterion is not satisfied)
5.	**c_P=REC(P**, 0.5); // randomized clonal expansion operator.
6.	**m_P=rand/2Hm(P,c_P)**; // modified somatic hypermutation
7.	Evaluating fitness function for all member antibodies in **m_P**
8.	**inter_PA=[P; m_P]**;
9.	**spx_P=SPX(inter_PA, 2)**
10.	Evaluating fitness function for all member antibodies in **spx_P**
11.	**inter_PB=[inter_PA; spx_P]**;
12.	Sort inter_PB decently based on fitness values.
13.	**P(next)=inter_PB(1:**NP);// select the best NP antibodies to from the next generation.
14.	end_while // end of while loop.
15.	**gbest=P(1,:)**;
16.	end_begin // end of the main program.

3.1   A Novel α-Clonal Expansion Strategy

In CSA/IE, a novel randomized clonal expansion strategy is adopted, where each antibody reproduces clones randomly. The number of clones generated by the parent antibody $\mathbf{x}_i$ is defined as follows:

$$Nc_i = \lceil \alpha \times NP \times \mathbf{Rand}(1) \rceil \qquad (2)$$

where the constant NP is the size of antibody group, **Rand**() is a uniform distribution randomized function, and Rand(1) generates a randomized real number within (0,1]. The control parameter α determines the size of clones reproduced by i^{th} antibody $\mathbf{x}_i$.

From equation (2), the number of clones generated by an antibody is determined by the size of antibody group NP and the control parameter α. Because the parameter NP is a user-defined parameter, therefore the parameter α mainly determines the size of clones.

3.2   Hypermutation Strategy

The hypermutation operator acts on the clones collection **c_P** reproduced by the antibody group, and the number of mutation is fixed to a constant number, which is set to 1 in the paper. Suppose $\mathbf{P}=(\mathbf{x_1},\mathbf{x_2},...,\mathbf{x_n})$, $\mathbf{x}_i=(\mathbf{x}_{i,1},\mathbf{x}_{i,2},...,\mathbf{x}_{i,dim})$, then equation (3) describes the proposed hypermutation operator.

$$\mathbf{new\_x}(j) = \mathbf{x}_{i,j} + w * (\mathbf{x}_{r_1,j} - \mathbf{x}_{r_2,j}) \tag{3}$$

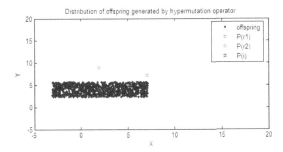

Fig. 1. The figure illustrates the distribution of offspring generated by proposed hypermutation operator

Table 2. Novel Hypermutation Operator

Inputs
P: the evolutionary antibody group;
c_P: the clone group generated through randomized clonal expansion operator.
Output
m_P: the candidate antibody group generated by rand/2 somatic hypermutation operator
1.   **begin**
2.   *count*=**0**; // count the number of clones
3.   **for** *i*=1:*NP*   // *NP* is the size of antibody group
4.   **while (c_P(*i*))>0**// the number of clones generated by i^{th} antibodi is not equal to zero;
5.   U=randperm(*NP*) // select two random antibodies $\vec{\mathbf{x}}_{r_1},\vec{\mathbf{x}}_{r_2}$ from **P**, and $r_j \neq i, j=1,2$
6. $\vec{\mathbf{x}}_{r_1} = \mathbf{P}(\mathbf{u}(1),:); \vec{\mathbf{x}}_{r_2} = \mathbf{P}(\mathbf{u}(2),:);$
7.   w=2*rand(1,dim)-1; // generate a real vector whose members are within [-1,1]
8.   cout=count+1;
9. $\mathbf{m\_x} = \mathbf{x}_i + \mathbf{w} \times (\mathbf{x}_{r_1} - \mathbf{x}_{r_2})$
10.   temp(*count*,:)=**new_x** //save the candidate antibodies
11.   *clone_Ind*= *clone_Ind*-1;
12.   **end**   // the rand/2 somatic hypermutation operator is over for $\overline{\mathbf{X}}_i$
13.   **end**   // the rand/2 somatic hypermutation operator is over for **c_P**
14.   **m_P**=Boundcheck（**temp,lower,upper**）// initialized the variants which is beyond the given domain
15.   return **m_P**;
16.   **END**

where **new_x** is the offspring individual generated by $\mathbf{x}_i$, the antibodies $\mathbf{x}_{r_1}$ and $\mathbf{x}_{r_2}$ are randomly selected antibodies from evolutionary group **P**; the indices r_1 and r_2 are mutually exclusive integers randomly generated within the range[1, *NP*], which are also different from the index i; w is a random real within $[-1,1]$. We describe the modified hypermutation operator with pseudo code in table 2, and figure 1 illustrates the distribution of offspring individuals generated through the proposed hypermutation.

3.3   Simplex Crossover Operator

The simplex crossover generates offspring individuals based on uniform probability distribution and does not need any fitness information of antibodies. In the domain **D**, $n+1$ mutually independent antibodies vector $\mathbf{x}_i$, $i = 1, 2, \cdots, n+1$, form a simplex. The process of generating offspring individuals consists of the following two steps [23]:

(1) Employing a certain ratio to expand the original simplex in each direction ($\mathbf{x}_i$-**O**), where the vector **O** is the center of original simplex. Therefore a new simplex is formed.

(2) Choose one point within the new simplex as an offspring individual.

In order to illustrating the above process, we consider three vector $\mathbf{x}_1$, $\mathbf{x}_2$ and $\mathbf{x}_3$, they form a simplex. When the ratio of expansion is given, the vertexes of new simplex are generated by $\mathbf{y}_i = (1+\lambda)(\mathbf{x}_i - \mathbf{O}), i = 1, 2, 3$. Next, we choose a point $\mathbf{z}$ randomly within the new simplex. i. e. $\mathbf{z} = \sum_{i=1}^{3} k_i \mathbf{y}_i$, where k_1, k_2, and k_3 are randomly selected within [0, 1], and they satisfy $k_1 + k_2 + k_3 = 1$. Figure 2 illustrates the procedure to produce offspring with three-parent SPX in 2-D space.

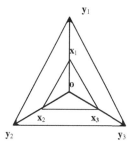
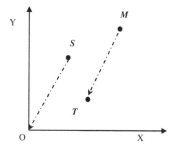

Fig. 2. The convergence of mean vector and standard deviation vector in the process of optimization

Fig. 3. The illustration of simplex crossover operator x1,x2,x3 are parental vectors, their center is the vector o. They expand themselves to the vectors y1,y2,y3, who generate new trial vectors.

The control parameter λ affects the distribution of offspring individuals generated through SPX operator. The parameter is fixed to 3.5 according to reference [23].

4   Performance Evaluation Criterion

Suppose there are k test functions and their best optima are t_1, t_2,..., t_k. so the vector of best optima can be noted as **T**=(t_1, t_2,..., t_k). For a given algorithm, called **A**, employed to optimize the above k test functions, it outputs the best mean vector $\mathbf{M}$ and standard deviation vector $\mathbf{S}$ after a number of independent runs, and $\mathbf{M}=(m_1, m_2,...,m_k)$, $\mathbf{S}=(s_1, s_2,..., s_k)$. Therefore the performance evaluation criterion is given as form (4)

$$\mathbf{PE}v(\mathbf{A}) = 0.5\sqrt{\sum_{i=1}^{k}\frac{(t_i - m_i)^2}{k}} + 0.5\sqrt{\sum_{i}^{k}\frac{s_i^2}{k}} \tag{4}$$

Theorem 1. If an algorithm named $\mathbf{A}$ obtains all best optima when optimizing k test functions, meanwhile, standard deviations obtained by A for all functions are zeros, then PEv($\mathbf{A}$)=0.

Proof. Suppose the vector of best mean obtained by $\mathbf{A}$ for k test functions is $\mathbf{M}=(m_1, m_2,...,m_k)$, and the corresponding vector of standard deviation is $\mathbf{S}=(s_1, s_2,..., s_k)$; The best optima vector for k test functions is $\mathbf{T}=(t_1, t_2,..., t_k)$. Consequently, the value of performance evaluation can be computed through the above form (4). Because $\mathbf{A}$ obtains all best optima in a certain independent runs, therefore $\mathbf{M}=\mathbf{T}$, namely, $m_i=t_i$, $i=1,2,..,k$. Then the item

$$\sqrt{\sum_{i=1}^{k}\frac{(t_i - m_i)^2}{k}} = 0 \tag{5}$$

Meanwhile, the vector of standard deviations obtained by A is a zeros vector, then

$$\sqrt{\sum_{i}^{k}\frac{s_i^2}{k}} = 0 \tag{6}$$

Consequently

$$\mathbf{PE}v(A) = 0.5\sqrt{\sum_{i=1}^{k}\frac{(t_i - m_i)^2}{k}} + 0.5\sqrt{\sum_{i}^{k}\frac{s_i^2}{k}} = 0 \tag{7}$$

Deduction. Suppose two algorithms $\mathbf{A}$ and $\mathbf{B}$ are employed to optimize k test functions. The overall optimization process is independently done for a given times. If $\mathbf{A}$ perform better than $\mathbf{B}$ overall, then $\mathbf{PE}v(\mathbf{A})<\mathbf{PE}v(\mathbf{B})$.

The performance evaluation criterion gives the overall performance in term of solution quality and stability for evaluated algorithm, Figure 3 illustrates the procedure of evaluation.

5   Numerical Experiments and Results

5.1   Experimental Setup

Experimental validation for the proposed CSA/IE is tested on 23 classical benchmarks [27]. Roughly they can be divided into three classes: (1) F_1- F_7 are high dimensional unimodal problems employed to validate the convergence speed of algorithm; and (2) F_8- F_{13} are high dimensional multimodal problems where the number of local optima increases exponentially with the problem dimension, and they are utilized to demonstrate the searching ability of proposed CSA/IE in escaping local optima and tracing the global optima; (3) the rest functions, F_{14}-F_{23}, are lower dimensional multimodal problems with a fewer optima.

5.2 Parameter Tuning

In the experimental studies the parameter α with value 0.0, 0.3, 0.5, 0.7, 0.9, 1.0 and 2.0 are used. In every case, FEs is set to 1E+5. The average results of 10 independent runs are listed in **Table 3**.

Table 3. Experimental results averaged over 10 independent runs. "Best Mean" indicates average of minimum values obtained, and "Std Dev" stands for standard deviation.

Fun	$\alpha=0.0$	$\alpha=0.3$	$\alpha=0.5$	Best Mean Std Dev $\alpha=0.7$	$\alpha=0.9$	$\alpha=1.0$	$\alpha=2.0$
F_1	0.00E+000	0.00E+000	0.00E+000	0.00E+000	.00E+000	0.00E+000	0.00E+000
	0.00E+000	0.00E+000	0.00E+000	0.00E+000	0.00E+000	0.00E+000	0.00E+000
F_2	0.00E+000	0.00E+000	0.00E+000	0.00E+000	0.00E+000	0.00E+000	0.00E+000
	0.00E+000	0.00E+000	0.00E+000	0.00E+000	0.00E+000	0.00E+000	0.00E+000
F_3	0.00E+000	0.00E+000	0.00E+000	0.00E+000	0.00E+000	0.00E+000	0.00E+000
	0.00E+000	0.00E+000	0.00E+000	0.00E+000	0.00E+000	0.00E+000	0.00E+000
F_4	0.00E+000	0.00E+000	0.00E+000	0.00E+000	0.00E+000	0.00E+000	0.00E+000
	0.00E+000	0.00E+000	0.00E+000	0.00E+000	0.00E+000	0.00E+000	0.00E+000
F_5	0.00E+000	0.00E+000	0.00E+000	0.00E+000	0.00E+000	0.00E+000	0.00E+000
	0.00E+000	0.00E+000	0.00E+000	0.00E+000	0.00E+000	0.00E+000	0.00E+000
F_6	0.00E+000	0.00E+000	0.00E+000	0.00E+000	0.00E+000	0.00E+000	0.00E+000
	2.84E-005	3.23E-005	1.95E-005	5.93E-005	5.12E-005	4.50E-005	5.37E-005
F_7	2.89E-005	2.98E-005	9.59E-006	5.33E-005	4.90E-005	1.88E-005	1.99E-005
	-12290.6	-12557.6	-12569.5	-12557.6	-12544.3	-12181.6	-1.17E+004
F_8	3.36E+002	3.75E+001	2.44E-005	3.75E+001	7.45E+001	1.15E+003	1.10E+003
	0.00E+000	0.00E+000	0.00E+000	0.00E+000	0.00E+000	0.00E+000	0.00E+000
F_9	0.00E+000	0.00E+000	0.00E+000	0.00E+000	0.00E+000	0.00E+000	0.00E+000
	8.88E-016	8.88E-016	8.88E-016	8.88E-016	8.88E-016	8.88E-016	8.88E-016
F_{10}	0.00E+000	0.00E+000	0.00E+000	0.00E+000	0.00E+000	0.00E+000	0.00E+000
	0.00E+000	0.00E+000	0.00E+000	0.00E+000	0.00E+000	0.00E+000	0.00E+000
F_{11}	0.00E+000	0.00E+000	0.00E+000	0.00E+000	0.00E+000	0.00E+000	0.00E+000
	4.25E-001	1.81E-014	9.48E-013	4.35E-011	2.68E-010	4.77E-010	1.50E-007
F_{12}	3.23E-001	1.16E-014	1.13E-012	7.96E-011	2.37E-010	2.32E-010	1.66E-007
	2.03E+000	7.32E-013	5.49E-004	4.01E-010	3.61E-009	9.74E-003	2.74E-006
F_{13}	7.72E-001	1.44E-012	2.46E-003	2.31E-010	2.11E-009	3.08E-002	8.50E-007
	1.7619	1.0974	0.9980	0.9980	1.0974	0.9980	1.6856
F_{14}	2.22E+000	3.14E-001	0.00E+000	0.00E+000	3.14E-001	1.05E-016	2.17E+000
	0.0218	0.0044	0.0044	0.0120	0.0044	0.0044	0.0044
F_{15}	1.02E-002	4.03E-011	5.29E-007	2.43E-002	1.51E-007	5.01E-019	9.91E-010
	-1.0316	-1.0316	-1.0316	-1.0316	-1.0316	-1.0316	-1.0316
F_{16}	2.01E-006	0.00E+000	2.28E-016	0.00E+000	0.00E+000	0.00E+000	0.00E+000
	0.4032	0.3979	0.3979	0.3979	0.3979	0.3979	0.3979
F_{17}	4.40E-003	0.00E+000	0.00E+000	0.00E+000	0.00E+000	0.00E+000	0.00E+000
	3.2932	3.0000	3.0000	3.0000	3.0000	3.0000	3.0000
F_{18}	2.49E-001	7.55E-016	2.04E-016	1.26E-015	1.36E-015	9.00E-016	2.48E-014
	-3.7333	-3.8628	-3.8628	-3.8628	-3.8628	-3.8628	-3.8628
F_{19}	4.95E-002	9.36E-016	2.28E-015	9.36E-016	9.36E-016	9.36E-016	9.36E-016
	-3.0054	-3.3268	-3.3268	-3.3268	-3.2899	-3.3268	-3.3268
F_{20}	9.03E-002	0.00E+000	1.37E-015	0.00E+000	5.95E-002	0.00E+000	0.00E+000
	-10.1531	-10.1532	-10.1388	-10.1301	-10.1532	-10.1451	-10.1532
F_{21}	1.91E-004	3.03E-005	6.44E-002	7.29E-002	1.21E-004	2.56E-002	0.00E+000
	-10.4028	-10.4029	-10.4029	-10.4029	-10.4015	-10.1367	-10.2926
F_{22}	1.28E-004	1.87E-015	2.19E-015	1.87E-015	3.01E-003	6.84E-001	3.41E-001
	-10.5362	-10.5365	-10.5364	-10.5365	-10.5338	-10.5187	-10.4664
F_{23}	1.48E-004	1.78E-015	2.91E-004	1.87E-015	6.39E-003	5.61E-002	2.22E-001
PEv	5.82E+001	2.47E+000	**4.48E-003**	2.47E+000	5.25E+000	8.09E+001	1.81E+002

The last row of table 3 lists the performance evaluation value for different ratio of clonal expansion, which shows that significant discrepancy in the value of performance evaluation is observed with the increasing of α. When α is set to 0.0 and 0.3 respectively, the value of PEv are worse than that of α=0.5. The reason behind the observation is that, the diversity of evolutionary population decreases, consequently the ability of escaping local optima becomes weak. Therefore during the following experimental studies, α is set to 0.5.

Table 4. Experimental results averaged over 20 independent runs of CSA/FC, CSA/RC, CSA/SC and proposed CSA/IE. "Best Mean" indicates average of minimum values obtained, and "Std Dev" stands for standard deviation. There are three termination criterions, that are 1E+3, 1E+4 , and 1E+5. Performance evaluation criterion is done for three termination cases.

| | 1E+3 | | | | 1E+4 | | | | 1E+5 | | | |
| | Best Mean Std Dev | | | | Best Mean Std Dev | | | | Best Mean Std Dev | | | |
Funs	CSA/FC	CSA/RC	CSA/SC	CSA/IE	CSA/FC	CSA/RC	CSA/SC	CSA/IE	CSA/FC	CSA/RC	CSA/SC	CSA/IE
F_1	3.17E+003	2.48E+003	3.19E+003	1.15E-018	2.06e-004	8.83E-006	1.48E-004	5.49E-251	5.23E-080	6.25E-090	2.91E-086	0.00
	1.04E+003	5.04E+002	9.17E+002	5.09E-018	3.66e-004	9.58E-006	5.02E-004	0.00	1.50E-079	5.25E-090	9.02E-086	0.00
F_2	1.97E+001	1.15E+001	1.53E+001	1.65E-010	4.75-005	4.49E-006	1.10E-005	4.18E-128	8.51-064	5.36E-069	2.10E-068	0.00
	4.47E+000	3.50E+000	2.94E+000	5.75E-010	6.14-005	2.36E-006	1.05E-005	1.87E-127	1.87-063	1.36E-068	7.80E-068	0.00
F_3	2.64E+4	2.58E+004	2.70E+004	3.27E-016	8.69E+003	4.81E+003	7.50E+003	1.31E-190	1.24E+001	8.55E+000	1.91E+001	0.00
	5.41+3	2.79E+003	6.85E+003	2.13E-016	2.94E+003	1.62E+003	3.15E+003	0.00	2.35E+001	1.80E+000	3.19E+001	0.00
F_4	5.00E+001	4.91E+000	5.14E+001	3.12E-012	2.97E+001	2.72E+001	2.66E+001	3.25E-111	4.34E+000	3.84 E+000	4.93E+000	0.00
	4.38E+000	5.12E+000	4.84E+001	7.32E-012	5.22E+000	3.62E+000	5.63E+000	1.45E-110	3.54 E+000	2.27 E+000	4.58E+000	0.00
F_5	4.40E+4	3.20E+004	4.47E+004	3.23E-024	1.95 E+000	9.12 E+000	1.15E+000	1.24E-258	2.53 E+000	3.19E-002	3.49E-001	0.00
	1.58E+4	2.16E+004	3.24E+004	1.20E-023	1.45 E+000	4.91 E+000	6.33E-001	0.00	3.23 E+000	1.42E-001	3.24E-001	0.00
F_6	2.95E+5	2.19E+003	2.90E+003	0.00	2.53E+001	6.05E+000	2.80E+000	0.00	2.18E+001	2.70E+000	3.75E+000	0.00
	1.01E+3	9.49E+002	8.82E+002	0.00	7.29E+001	8.61E+000	4.42E+000	0.00	8.23E+001	4.43E+000	5.56E+000	0.00
F_7	2.55E+000	1.75E+000	2.10E+000	5.18E-003	1.78E-001	9.52E-002	1.77E-001	4.65E-004	1.50E-002	1.28E-002	1.50E-002	1.95E-005
PEv	9.21E-001	5.43E-001	6.82E-001	1.62E-003	1.02E-001	1.89E-002	8.21E-002	3.42E-004	1.36E-002	6.52E-003	6.76E-003	9.59E-006
	3.29E+004	5.61E+003	8.92E+003	7.09E-004	1.21E+003	6.70E+002	1.11E+003	8.41E-005	1.16E+001	1.57E+000	5.50E+000	3.03E-006
F_8	-4.15E+003	-4.58E+003	-4.21E+003	-5.83E+003	-7.88E+3	-8.73E+003	-8.20E+003	-1.05E+004	-9.05E+003	-9.22E+003	-8.92E+003	-12569.5
	6.73E+003	3.73E+003	6.25E+002	2.14E+003	1.29E+003	1.36E+003	1.48E+003	1.13E+003	1.19E+003	6.45E+002	9.04E+002	2.44E-005
F_9	2.33E+002	2.19E+002	2.31E+002	1.33E+001	9.67E+001	6.12E+001	8.31E+001	0.00	5.37E+001	3.75E+001	5.72E+001	0.00
	2.38E+001	2.42E+001	2.50E+001	1.86E+001	3.72E+001	2.87E+001	3.78E+001	0.00	2.62E+001	9.01E+000	3.43E+001	0.00
F_{10}	1.17E+001	1.03E+001	1.18E+001	1.22E+000	9.77E+001	5.82E+002	6.72E+001	3.68E-010	4.57E-001	1.92E-001	5.77E-001	8.88E-016
	1.28E+000	1.29E+000	1.02E+000	1.19E+000	2.00E+000	3.00E-001	7.19E-001	6.94E-010	7.48E-001	6.01E-001	6.87E-001	0.00
F_{11}	3.42E+000	2.08E+001	3.00E+001	7.34E-001	3.62E-002	3.06E-003	2.91E-002	2.22E-16	9.82E-003	5.94E-003	4.92E-003	0.00
	8.89E+000	9.00E+000	1.11E+001	5.13E-001	6.95E-002	5.60E-003	5.97E-002	9.93E-16	2.35E+001	1.01E-002	8.70E-003	0.00
F_{12}	5.60E+006	3.13E+006	4.00E+006	1.78E+000	6.42E+000	2.68E+000	6.13E+000	3.37E-002	3.18E-001	9.33E-002	6.02E-001	9.47E-013
	5.46E+006	3.71E+006	3.67E+006	8.81E-001	3.55E+000	3.72E+000	4.27E+000	1.09E-002	4.60E-001	1.53E-001	1.79E+000	1.12E-012
F_{13}	1.55E+007	5.94E+006	1.56E+007	3.98E+000	1.46E+001	9.42E+001	5.55E+000	4.10E-001	8.91E-002	5.48E-030	1.77E-001	5.49E-004
PEv	1.36E+003	3.75E+006	1.07E+007	8.43E-001	1.15E+001	1.21E+000	4.84E+000	104E-001	3.56E-001	1.76E-029	7.18E-001	2.46E-003
	3.25+6	1.25E+006	2.85E+006	9.26E+002	6.24E+002	5.42E+002	6.10E+002	3.33E+002	4.91E+002	4.16E+002	1.40E+003	3.14E-004
F_{14}	3.564E+000	2.643 E+000	1.968 E+000	2.345 E+000	1.443 E+000	9.98 E-001	1.54 E+000	1.201 E+000	1.443 E+000	1.340 E+000	1.975 E+000	0.998
	2.77E+000	2.52 E+000	1.29 E+000	1.67 E+000	1.13 E+000	1.25E-016	138 E+000	0.61	1.22 E+000	0.95	3.00 E+000	0.00
F_{15}	0.0103	8.05E-003	1.07E-002	2.77E-002	0.0058	4.36E-003	5.96E-003	4.36E-3	0.0049	5.95E-003	4.36E-003	0.0044
	0.0076	4.69E-003	1.16E-002	1.07E-002	0.0046	6.36E-018	7.17E-003	3.65E-9	0.0024	7.17E-003	1.21E-017	5.29E-007
F_{16}	-1.0316	-1.0316	-1.0316	-1.0327	-1.0316	-1.0316	-1.0316	-1.0316	-1.0316	-1.0316	-1.0316	-1.0316
	0.00	1.19E-011	5.83E-010	1.71E-003	0.00	2.22E-016	2.16E-016	1.97	0.00	2.28E-016	8.94E-016	2.28E-016
F_{17}	0.3987	0.3979	0.3984	0.4286	0.3979	0.3979	0.3979	0.3978	0.3979	0.3979	0.3979	0.3979
	0.0026	3.51E-006	0.0019	0.0528	0.00	0.00	2.67E-015	0.00	0.00	7.94E-016	1.16E-009	0.00
F_{18}	4.35	3.00	4.35	3.04	7.05	4.35	3.00	3.00	3.00	3.00	7.05	3.00
	6.04	1.25E-014	6.04	4.15E-002	9.89	6.04	1.44E-015	9.50E-016	0.00	3.06E-016	9.89	2.03E-016
F_{19}	-3.86	-3.86	-3.82	-3.86	-3.86	-3.86	-3.86	-3.86	-3.86	-3.86	-3.86	-3.86
	0.0026	1.97E-012	0.17	3.43E-003	0.00	2.28E-015	2.28E-015	2.13E-15	0.00	2.28E-015	2.58E-015	2.28E-015
F_{20}	-3.30	-3.31	-3.28	-3.10	-3.28	-3.30	-3.30	-3.33	-3.30	-3.33	-3.30	-3.32
	0.04605	3.81E-002	0.056	0.11	5.97E-002	5.47E-002	5.45E-002	1.99	0.0503	1.37E-015	4.10E-002	1.36E-015
F_{21}	-5.4781	-5.8229	-7.60	-5.3047	-7.47	-8.56	-6.80	-10.1409	-8.6183	-10.1524	-7.9048	-10.1388
	3.5426	3.41	3.30	2.29	3.01	2.88	3.38	2.19E-2	3.0560	3.3638	3.5237	6.44E-002
F_{22}	-6.8379	-7.69	-8.0504	-6.00	-6.737932	-9.58	-8.07	-9.95	-9.2453	-9.6865	-8.3825	-10.4029
	3.5050	3.43	3.0939	2.85	3.323992	2.22	2.97	1.41	2.6761	2.2109	3.0353	2.19E-015
F_{23}	-6.6905	-8.40	-6.4238	-5.13	-7.677755	-10.38	-7.5170	-10.2658	-8.7399	-9.4957	-7.9535	-10.5364
	3.4115	2.47	3.3027	1.83	3.309659	0.46	3.51	1.2105	3.1553	2.5494	3.6243	2.91E-004
PEv	1.73	1.23	1.46	1.36	1.89	0.97	1.14	0.42	0.83	0.50	1.84	0.0083

5.3   Comparison with Conventional CSAs

Three conventional clonal selection algorithms CSA/FC, CSA/RC and CSA/SC are used for comparison with CSA/IE. For the above algorithms, the size of population is 6. In the experimental study, the termination criterion is the maximum function evaluation *FEs*, which is set to 1E+3, 1E+4 and 1E+5. The average results of 20 independent runs are summarized in Tables 4.

The comparison shows that CSA/IE finds the best optima of 18 functions, and performs better than other algorithm. Figure 4 illustrates the convergence characteristic in term of   best fitness value for function $\mathbf{F}_1$, $\mathbf{F}_8$, $\mathbf{F}_{12}$ and $\mathbf{F}_{13}$.

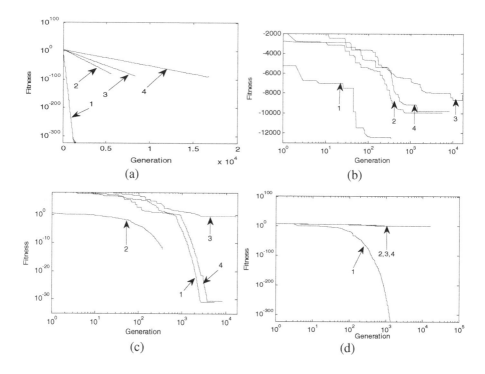

Fig. 4. Average best fitness curves of CSA/FC, CSA/RC, CSA/SC and CSA/IE for selected benchmark functions. (a) Test function F1 . (b) Test function F8 . (c) Test function F12. (d) Test function F13. and the symbols '1', '2','3' and '4' indicate respectively CSA/IE,CSA/FC, CSA/ SC and CSA/RC The above experimental results show that CSA/IE outperforms other three immune algorithms in given FEs. Meanwhile the computational time is important. Figure 5 illustrates the computational time of four algorithms optimizing 23 benchmarks.

5.4   Comparison with Variations of DE

In the experimental study, we compare the proposed algorithm with a self-adaptive differential evolution (SaDE)[3], differential evolution with neighborhood algorithm(NSDE)[26] and a self adaptive differential evolution with neighborhood search(SANSDE)[24]. The size of population for compared algorithms is 100 and that of our proposed CSA/IE is 6 for $\mathbf{F}_1$-$\mathbf{F}_7$ and 30 for $\mathbf{F}_8$-$\mathbf{F}_{23}$, however the FEs is equal each other for certain function. In order to be fair to comparing the different algorithms, the experimental data obtained by SaDE, NSDE and SANSDE is adopted from reference [24]. We also evaluate the performance of four algorithms using the performance evaluation criterion. The average results of 25 independent runs are listed in **Table 5**.

High-dimensional unimodal functions (F_1-F_7). The aim in this case is to get a picture of convergence ratio of the algorithms. As it can be seen, CSA/IE finds all best optima except for function F_7, however SANSDE, SaDE and NSDE do not obtain the best optima for any test functions. Finally, we evaluate the performance of four algorithms by proposed performance evaluation criterion, and the proposed CSA/IE scores 3.61e-06, which is significantly lower than that of SANSDE, SaDE and NSDE, therefore CSA/IE performs better than that of the rest algorithms.

High-dimensional multimodal functions with many local minima (F_8-F_{13}). Function F_8-F_{13} are multimodal functions with many local minima, and the number of local minima increases exponentially as the dimension increases. The aim in this case is to test the ability of algorithms escaping from local optima. According to the performance evaluation criterion SaDE scores 8.34e-09, which means the algorithm performs better than that of others. However, by comparing the results of F_8, F_9, F_{11}, we can see that SANSDE, NSDE and SaDE are unable to approach the best optima, while CSA/IE find the best optima of the above two test functions.

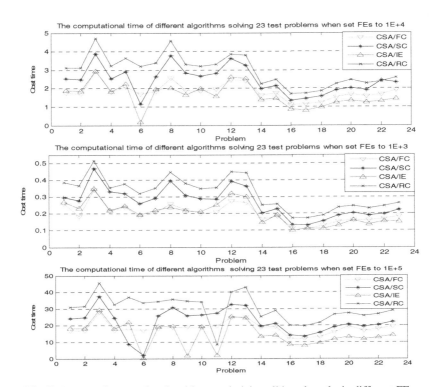

Fig. 5. Average time cost by algorithms optimizing all benchmarks in different FEs

Table 5. Experimental results averaged over 25 independent runs of SANSDE, SaDE NSDE and CSA/IE. "Mean" indicates average of minimum values obtained. Performance evaluation criterion is done for three termination criterions.

Funs	#FEs	SANSDE Mean	SaDE Mean	NSDE Mean	CSA/IE Mean	Best optima
F_1	150 000	3.02E-23	7.49E-20	7.76E-16	**0.00**	0.00
F_2	150 000	4.64E-11	6.22E-11	4.51E-10	**0.00**	0.00
F_3	150 000	6.62E-22	1.12E-18	1.06E-14	**0.00**	0.00
F_4	150 000	1.59E-03	2.96E-02	2.54E-02	**0.00**	0.00
F_5	500 000	4.13E-30	2.10E+01	1.24E+01	**0.00**	0.00
F_6	150 000	0.00	0.00	0.00	**0.00**	0.00
F_7	150 000	7.21E-003	7.58E-03	1.20E-02	**1.73E-05**	0.00
PEv(1-7)	-	**1.54E-003**	**4.38**	**2.59**	3.61E-06	**0.00**
F_8	150 000	-12569.5	-12569.5	-12569.5	**-12569.5**	-12569.5
F_9	150 000	1.84E-05	4.00E-08	7.97E-02	**0.00**	0.00
F_{10}	150 000	2.36E-12	9.06E-11	6.72E-09	**8.88E-16**	0.00
F_{11}	150 000	0.00	8.88E-18	4.68E-15	**0.00**	0.00
F_{12}	150 000	5.94E-23	5.21E-19	5.63E-17	**7.17E-19**	0.00
F_{13}	150 000	3.12E-22	1.75E-19	5.52E-16	**1.50E-16**	0.00
PEv(8-13)	-	**3.84E-06**	**8.34E-09**	**1.66E-02**	1.14E-04	**0.00**
F_{14}	200 00	0.998	0.998	0.998	**0.998**	0.998
F_{15}	150 000	3.07E-04	3.07E-04	3.07E-04	**4.34E-02**	0.0003075
F_{16}	20 000	-1.03	1.03	-1.03	**-1.03**	-1.03
F_{17}	20 000	0.398	0.398	0.398	**0.398**	0.398
F_{18}	20 000	3.00	3.00	3.00	**3.00**	3.00
F_{19}	20 000	-3.39	-3.39	-3.39	**-3.86**	-3.86
F_{20}	20 000	-3.20	-3.20	-3.20	**-3.32**	-3.32
F_{21}	20 000	-10.15	-10.15	-10.15	**-10.15**	-10.15
F_{22}	20 000	-10.40	-10.40	-10.40	**-10.40**	-10.40
F_{23}	20 000	-10.54	-10.54	-10.54	**-10.53**	-10.53
PEv(14-23)	-	**1.01E-01**	**4.42E-01**	**1.01E-01**	9.51E-03	**0.00**
PEv(1-23)	-	**1.01E-01**	**4.40**	**2.59**	9.51E-03	**0.00**

Multimodal functions with only a few local optima (F_{14}-F_{23}): In this case, four algorithms perform well in term of the solution quality; moreover for function F_{14}, F_{16}, F_{17}, F_{18}, and F_{21}-F_{23}, they are all able to obtain the best optima. In addition, the proposed CSA/IE also obtains the best optima for function F_{18} and F_{19}, therefore CSA/IE shows a bit of better performance, and the value of performance evaluation criterion shows the same result.

5.5   Performance for Super-High Dimensional Global Test Functions

In the experimental study, we carry out the CSA/IE when dimension is set to 100, 300, 500, 800 and 1000, the size of population is set to 6 for F_1-F_7 and 30 for F_9-F_{13}.

The function F_8 is not used in the test because its function value increases with the function dimension increases. The average results of 10 independent runs are summarized in **Table 6**. The experimental results show that CSA/IE found the optima of function F_1-F_6, F_9, and F_{11}, in addition, the standard deviation is equal to zero for all cases.

Table 6. Experimental results of high dimensional global test functions averaged over 10 independent runs of CSA/IE. "Mean Best" indicates average of minimum values found, and "std" stands for standard deviation.

funs	100	300	500	800	1000
			Mean best (std)		
F_1	0.00(0.00)	0.00(0.00)	0.00(0.00)	0.00(0.00)	0.00(0.00)
F_2	0.00(0.00)	0.00(0.00)	0.00(0.00)	0.00(0.00)	0.00(0.00)
F_3	0.00(0.00)	0.00(0.00)	0.00(0.00)	0.00(0.00)	0.00(0.00)
F_4	0.00(0.00)	0.00(0.00)	0.00(0.00)	0.00(0.00)	0.00(0.00)
F_5	0.00(0.00)	0.00(0.00)	0.00(0.00)	0.00(0.00)	0.00(0.00)
F_6	0.00(0.00)	0.00(0.00)	0.00(0.00)	0.00(0.00)	0.00(0.00)
F_7	1.97E-005(1.84E-005)	4.25E-005(3.84E-005)	8.33E-006(5.56E-006)	3.67E-005(3.50E-005)	1.54E-005(9.35E-006)
F_9	0.00(0.00)	0.00(0.00)	0.00(0.00)	0.00(0.00)	0.00(0.00)
F_{10}	8.88E-016(0.00)	8.88E-016(0.00)	8.88E-016(0.00)	8.88E-016(0.00)	8.88E-016(0.00)
F_{11}	0.00(0.00)	0.00(0.00)	0.00(0.00)	0.00(0.00)	0.00(0.00)
F_{12}	2.31E-004(2.01E-004)	6.87E-002(9.32E-003)	1.67E-002(3.04E-003)	3.52E-001(2.70E-002)	4.19E-001(5.86E-002)
F_{13}	9.06E+000(2.63E+000)	2.97E+001(5.30E-003)	4.95E+001(6.96E-003)	7.96E+001(8.19E-003)	9.96E+001(5.16E-003)

5.6 Discussions and Analysis

The ratio of clonal expansion α is one of critical factor in the proposed CSA/IE; its value determines the size of intermediate population, which impacts on the number of generation and the diversity of evolutionary population.

It is very clear from **Table 4** that the proposed CSA/IE improved the performance of the conventional clonal selection algorithms significantly for all test functions, especially for high-dimensional unimodal/multimodal functions in 20 independent runs. Under the given FEs, CSA/IE obtained 9 best optima for the cases F_1-F_6, F_8, F_9 and F_{11}, while CSA/RC, CSA/SC and CSA/FC have not found the best optima for the same cases. Even in the cases F_7, F_{10}, F_{12}, and F_{13}, the solution quality of CSA/IE are better than CSA/RC, CSA/SC and CSA/FC. For 10 low-dimensional test function with a few local optima, CSA/IE outperforms than CSA/RC, CSA/SC and CSA/FC in term of best means and standard deviation in 20 independent runs. It is very encouraging that CSA/RC performs better than CSA/FC and CSA/FC for most test functions according to performance evaluation criterion.

The difficulty of obtaining the best optima increases with the dimension increasing for test functions; especially the number of local optima exponentially increases when dimension increase for test cases F_8-F_{13}. However the proposed CSA/IE obtained 6 best optima in unimodal cases and 2 for multimodal functions when the value of dimension increases from 100 to 1000. Therefore, the proposed CSA/IE has the ability to deal with super-high dimensional test functions.

It has been mentioned before, the proposed CSA/IE outperforms than several variations of DE. The result shows that CSA/IE improves the searching ability of CSA significantly, even performs better than the well-known differential evolution.

6   Conclusions and Future Work

In this paper we proposed a novel immune algorithm based on clonal selection principle, called CSA/IE, for global high-dimensional unimodal/multimodal numerical optimization. The main features of CSA/IE are clonal expansion operator, somatic hypermutation operator, and a simplex crossover operator. Finally the simplex crossover operator generates new individuals to increase the information exchange among different antibodies during the evolution search process. We test the proposed CSA/IE on 23 well-known benchmark problems. The experimental studies show that the CSA/IE is suitable for global numerical optimization in term of solution quality and effectiveness. The comparisons with three effective variations of DE have done through our proposed performance evaluation criterion, the results show that the CSA/IE is performs much better than SANSDE, SaDE and NSDE.

As future works, we plan to apply the algorithm in real world problems. Next the proposed performance evaluation criterion is a powerful tool to evaluate performance of algorithms when optimizing benchmarks; therefore we plan to explore its ability.

References

1. Acan, A.: Clonal selection algorithm with operator multiplicity. In: Proceedings of the Congress on Evolutionary Computation, vol. 1- 2, pp. 1909–1915 (2004)
2. Burnet, F.M.: Clonal selection theory of acquired immunity. Vanderbilt Unive. Press (1959)
3. Brest, J., Greiner, S., Bošković, B., Mernik, M., Žumer, V.: Self-adapting control parameters in differential evolution: A comparative study on numerical benchmark problems. IEEE Transactions on Evolutionary Computation 10(6), 646–657 (2006)
4. De Castro, L.N., Von Zuben, F.J.: Learning and optimization using the clonal selection principle. IEEE Transactions on Evolutionary Computation 6(3), 239–251 (2002)
5. Cutello, V., Nicosia, G., Pavone, M.: Exploring the Capability of Immune Algorithms: A Characterization of Hypermutation Operators. In: Nicosia, G., Cutello, V., Bentley, P.J., Timmis, J. (eds.) ICARIS 2004. LNCS, vol. 3239, pp. 263–276. Springer, Heidelberg (2004)
6. Cutello, V., Narzisi, G., Nicosia, G.: An Immunological Algorithm for Global Numerical Optimization. In: Talbi, E.-G., Liardet, P., Collet, P., Lutton, E., Schoenauer, M. (eds.) EA 2005. LNCS, vol. 3871, pp. 284–295. Springer, Heidelberg (2006)
7. Cutello, V., Krasnogor, G., Pavone, M.: Real coded clonal selection algorithm for unconstrained global optimization using a hybrid inversely proportional hypermutation operator. In: ACM Symposium on Applied Computing Dijon, France, pp. 23–27 (2006)
8. Cutello, V., Nicosia, G., Pavone, M.: An immune algorithm for protein structure prediction on lattice models. IEEE Tran.on Evolutionary Computation 11(1), 101–117 (2007)

9. Deb, K.: Multi-Objective Optimization Using Evolutionary Algorithms. Wiley, Chichester (2001)

10. Deb, K., Anand, A., Joshi, D.: A computationally efficient evolutionary algorithm for real-parameter optimization. Evolutionary Computation 10, 371–395 (2002)

11. Dorigo, M.: Optimization, Learning and Natural Algorithms, PhD thesis, Politecnico di Milano, Italie (1992)

12. Eberhart, R., Kennedy, J.: A new optimizer using particle swarm theory. In: Proceedings of 6th International Symposium. Micro Mach Human Science, Nagoya, Japan, pp. 39–43 (1995)

13. Forrest, S., Perelson, A.S., Allen, L., Cherukuri, R.: Self-nonself discrimination in a computer. In: Proc. of IEEE Symposium on Research in Security & Privacy, pp. 202–212. IEEE Press (1994)

14. Gao, S.C., Tang, Z., Dai, H., Zhang, J.: An improved clonal selection algorithm and its application to traveling salesman problems. IEICE Transactions on Fundamentals of Electronics Communications and Computer Sciences E90a 12, 2930–2938 (2007)

15. Gong, M.G., Jiao, L.C., Du, H.F.: Multi-objective immune algorithm with nondominated neighbor-based selection. Evolutionary Computation 16(2), 225–255 (2008)

16. He, H., Qian, F.: Dynamic hypermutation immune algorithms for global optimization. Dynamics of Continuous Discrete and Impulsive Systems-Series B-Applications & Algorithms 14, 113–118 (2007)

17. Herrera, F., Lozano, M., Verdegay, J.L.: Tackling real-coded genetic algorithms: Operators and tools for behavioral analysis. Artificial. Intelligence Review 12(4), 265–319 (1998)

18. Kennedy, J., Eberhart, R.: Particle swarm optimization. In: Proceedings of IEEE International. Conference on Neural Networks, pp. 1942–1948 (1995)

19. Khilwani, N., Prakash, A., Shankar, R., Tiwari, M.K.: Fast clonal algorithm. Engineering Applications of Artificial Intelligence 21(1), 106–128 (2008)

20. Liu, R.C., Jiao, L.C.: Immune Clonal Strategy Based on the Adaptive Mean Mutation. In: Li, K., Fei, M., Irwin, G.W., Ma, S. (eds.) LSMS 2007. LNCS, vol. 4688, pp. 108–116. Springer, Heidelberg (2007)

21. Timmis, J., Edmonds, C.: Assessing the Performance of Two Immune Inspired Algorithms and a Hybrid Genetic Algorithm for Function Optimization. In: Proc. of the Congress on Evolutionary Computation, vol. 1, pp. 1044–1051. IEEE, Potland (2004)

22. Storn, R., Price, K.: Differential evolution-A fast and efficient heuristic for global optimization over continuous spaces. Journal of Global Optimization 11, 341–359 (1997)

23. Wang, Y., Cai, Z.X., Guo, G.Q., Zhou, Y.R.: Multi-objective optimization and hybrid evolutionary algorithm to solve constrained optimization problems. IEEE Transactions on Systems Man and Cybernetics Part B-Cybernetics 37(3), 560–575 (2007)

24. Yang, Z., Tang, K., Yao, X.: Self-adaptive Differential Evolution with Neighborhood Search. IEEE World Congress on Computational Intelligence, 1110–1116 (2008)

25. Yang, X. R., Shen, J. Y., Wang, R.: Artificial immune theory based network intrusion detection system and the algorithms design. In: Proceedings of International Conference on Machine Learning and Cybernetics. Proceedings, vol. 1-4, pp. 73–77 (2002)

26. Yang, Z., He, J., Yao, X.: Making a Difference to Differential Evolution. In: Michalewicz, Z., Siarry, P. (eds.) Advances in Metaheuristics for Hard Optimization, pp. 397–414. Springer (2008)

27. Yao, X., Liu, Y., Lin, G.: Evolutionary programming made faster. IEEE Transactions on Evolutionary Computation 3(2), 82–102 (1999)

28. Zarges, C.: Rigorous Runtime Analysis of Inversely Fitness Proportional Mutation Rates. In: Rudolph, G., Jansen, T., Lucas, S., Poloni, C., Beume, N. (eds.) PPSN 2008. LNCS, vol. 5199, pp. 112–122. Springer, Heidelberg (2008)

An Ecological Approach to Anomaly Detection: The EIA Model

Pedro Pinacho[1], Iván Pau[3], Max Chacón[2], and Sergio Sánchez[3]

[1] Escuela Informätica, Universidad Santo Tomás, Concepción, Chile
ppinacho@ust.cl
[2] Universidad de Santiago, Departamento de Ingeniería Informática, Santiago, Chile
max.chacon@usach.cl
[3] EUIT Telecomunicación, Technical University of Madrid, Spain
{ipau,sergio}@diatel.upm.es

Abstract. The presented work proposes a new approach for anomaly detection. This approach is based on changes in a population of evolving agents under stress. If conditions are appropriate, changes in the population (modeled by the bioindicators) are representative of the alterations to the environment. This approach, based on an ecological view, improves functionally traditional approaches to the detection of anomalies. To verify this assertion, experiments based on Network Intrussion Detection Systems are presented. The results are compared with the behaviour of other bioinspired approaches and machine learning techniques.

1 Introduction

This paper proposes an artificial immune system (AIS) based on a population of evolutionary agents. The model is centered on the effect of environmental changes or perturbations on highly sensitive individuals, employing the concept of bioindicator [15]: that is, the quantification of this effect on the population of individuals in order to detect abnormalities. Because such an environment is the continuous representation of the characteristics of a monitored system, the model must be used for the detection of anomalies in any characterizable system based on a a parameter flow representing its state.

Anomaly detection is a solution to the problem of classification that consists of segregating objects in a set of different classes. In some cases, these classes are predefined and do not change over time. In more complex cases, classes may not be defined a priori, and may change over time. One of the more complex scenarios is Network Intrusion Detection Systems (NIDS). In this realm, the classifying algorithm must deal with at least two fundamental classes: normal traffic and intrusive traffic. These classes are not static, as they change due to the usual variation in the behavior of system users or the presence of a new or unknown attack. Hence, this scenario has been chosen to test the capacities of the classifier proposed in this paper.

The Artificial Indicator Species model (EIA in spanish) proposes an ecological approach, assuming that an agent population that plastically adapts to its

C.A. Coello Coello et al. (Eds.): ICARIS 2012, LNCS 7597, pp. 232–245, 2012.
© Springer-Verlag Berlin Heidelberg 2012

surroundings in order to subsist will develop learning skills, which is its structural modification in this context. This ecological approach is present in Varela's constructivist vision on the Biological Immune System (BIS) [26], which emphasizes self-affirmation and homoestatic potential. This vision is the inspiration for Nanas [20], which implements an adaptive network of terms used for filtering information. Unlike the approach set forth in this paper, it is based on a network and not on a population of agents.

The metaphor of the immune system has been widely used for the detection of intrusions in computer systems because they involve similar targets: the detection and elimination of agents that are not own/harmful/destabilizing. It is precisely this difference of concepts that has given rise to a prolific and diverse set [4] of hybrid techniques collectively called Artificial Immune Systems [10]. All these proposals seek to rescue capacities of identification, threat elimination, failure tolerance and adaptability of Biological Immune Systems through a series of proposals such as Formal Immune Network (FIN) [24], which is based on programmed cell death and cytokine-controlled immunization (messenger proteins), Clonal Selection (CLONALG), which posits a proliferation of detectors capable of detecting antigens and exploring them in order to enhance affinity by means of somatic hypermutation [5], Negative Selection (LISYS) [9] which is based on the maturation of T lymphocytes to produce immunological tolerance [12] and models based on the Jerne immune network [3]. There is evidence that these techniques do not deal with the change of normality in a consistent manner, while they also rely on models that are partial and not fully accepted [28]. Moreover, Bersini also shows that approaches based on the traditional conception of the immune system as a *defensive entity*, which is implicit in the foregoing techniques are incorrect, and it is encountering ever greater opposition among biologists [2]. For Bersini, the real contribution of the BIS model for engineering lies in the concept of endogenous double plasticity [6], which holds that a system adjusts structurally during its functioning in a continuous and plastic manner, integrating new elements and discarding old ones, with the change controlled by its internal dynamic. This is based on simple heuristics such as compensating for weak elements, maintaining diversity and eliminating redundancy, that is, maintaining balances through ecological mechanisms, which is the foundation of the present paper.

The approach in the EIA model possesses substantial operational advantages over the prevailing approach for developing NIDS, which is focused mainly on classifiers which relies on the use of recognized attack signatures or patterns, with the drawbacks of requiring constant updating to be useful, in addition to proving ineffective against unknown attacks [11]. The latter is one of the main points of interest in the development of AIS, which are closer to approaches based on the detection of anomalies. Although they do provide a solution to the problem of novelty attacks, they carry the drawback of being associated to a significant increase in false positives [7].

The structure of the model, its components and the functioning of the prototype elaborated with the multi-agent programming tool Netlogo [23] are presented

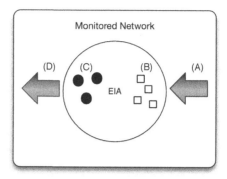

Fig. 1. General System Scheme

in Section II. Section III shows the procedure for transforming agents into bioindicators, and Section IV presents the adaptation of the model to be used as a classifier in the domain of information security. Section V describes the experiments and provides details on the algorithms used for comparison. Section VI gives the results, which were statistically validated with the Wilcoxon sign test [27]. Finally section VII sets forth the main conclusions of the paper.

2   Model

The general model, of which the EIA proposal is an anticipation, envisions the immune system as a symbolic entity that seeks to preserve or find new internal equilibria between chaos transitions generated by perturbations produced by attacks for this study. In this context, system learning is achieved through the progressive adaptation of its agents, which causes a continuous structural modification of the agent population by means of natural selection and the use of a mutation operator. Immunity is understood, in this scheme, as a cognitive system, owing to its recognition, learning and memory abilities [26].

The system model is structurally described in equation 1, where FADS is for *Flow Anomaly Detection System, T*, T is a bidimensional topology inhabited by a set of evolutionary agents, A is the set of agents and X is a set of particles consumed by agents and determined by the medium where the agents are inserted: that is, the system must be monitored.

$$FADS = \langle T, A, X \rangle \tag{1}$$

Figure 1, shows a schematic view of the general operation of the EIA model, which has the following stages:

- *Guest Characteristic Capture (A):* In the first phase, the system hears a continuous characteristics flow which represents the operation of the system under analysis.

- *Model Characteristic Input (B):* Subsequently, the characteristic flow is pre-processed, yielding observable characteristics in the same binary form $\alpha \in X$, which are inputted in topology T of the model.
- *Agent Exposure (C):* Adaptive agents $\beta \in A$ are exposed to elements of X, causing an increase or decrease of their energy, and with this strenghening, their reproduction or death.
- *Population Impact (D):* When observable characteristics (α) impact on agents, they generate effects that can be measured at a population level through two variables of interest: *population size* and *average energy* of the agent population, which are the basis for the developed classifier.

2.1   Artificial Bioindicators

The EIA model has been created with the multiagent programming tool Netlogo. Agents $\beta \in A$ are created, initially, with a random genetic configuration, with the expectation that the fittest will survive and generate decendents. Each agent has a structure $\beta = (\pi, \theta, \lambda)$, where $\pi \subset \Pi$ is the set of rules that determines the conduct of the agent β, θ corresponds to the genetic value of the agent and $\lambda = (\rho, \psi)$ determines the agent's position in the topology T, given by ρ, and the current energy of the same, as given by ψ.

Reproduction of agents is asexual and uses a mutation operator that acts on the vector described in Equation 2, carrying out a permutation between two elements of the vector. The importance of the genetic vector is that it determines the affinity of each agent with the environment. This affinity is constituted by a gene for each particle α of the existing n.

$$\theta = \left\{ (g_0, g_1, \ldots, g_n) \middle| \forall g_k, g_j \left\langle (k \neq j) \Rightarrow (g_k \neq g_j) \right\rangle \right\} \tag{2}$$

When α impacts an agent, it becomes either food or poison, depending on the expression shown in Equation 3, which determines its nutritional value (NV). Where i is the index of gen g_k which represents particle α_k that has impacted the agent, ϕ represents the maximum nutrition that can be provided by a particle α and ϵ is a parameter that determines a linear nutritional loss applied owing to a lack of affinity with particle α.

$$NV = \phi - i\epsilon \tag{3}$$

Agents β are governed by the set of rules (π) described in Table 1, where (1) specifies that agents must achieve a minimum level of energy established by *ReproductionQualityOfLife* (RQL) in order to generate descendants, in (2) it is specified that agents, when losing all their energy due to poisoning – that is, owing to a lack of affinity with particles α in circulation - are eliminated; in (3) agents have a baseline energy consumption determined by the variable *metabolism* and in (4) agents are fed by all the particles impacting on them.

Table 1. EIA World Rules

Agents behavior rules (π)
$(1)\ (agent(\beta) \wedge energyMoreThan(\beta, RQL))$ $\Rightarrow birth(\beta')$.
$(2)\ (agent(\beta) \wedge energyExhausted(\beta)) \Rightarrow kill(\beta)$.
$(3)\ agent(\beta) \Rightarrow energyReduce(\beta, Metabolism)$.
$(4)\ (agent(\beta) \wedge particle(\alpha) \wedge colision(\beta, \alpha)) \Rightarrow eat(\beta, \alpha)$.
World physics rules (ω)
$(i)\ observedParameter(x) \Rightarrow insert(\alpha_x)$
$(ii)\ (particle(\alpha) \wedge outOfRange(\alpha)) \Rightarrow remove(\alpha)$
$(iii)\ (particle(\alpha) \wedge exhausted(\alpha)) \Rightarrow remove(\alpha)$
$(iv)\ particle(\alpha) \Rightarrow LeftMove(\alpha)$

2.2 Topology and Particles

EIA corresponds to a model of artificial life that possesses a set of simple physical rules that regulate the behavior of particles α in the topology T.

The EIA topology $T = \langle E, \Omega \rangle$, is composed of E, to which all the cells in the topology belong, and by the world rules Ω, described in Table 1. The topology of the presented model is linear. Other topologies will be evaluated in future works. As observed in Figure 2, the topology corresponds to a 32x16 bidimensional grid. The rule (i) allows for the input of new particles in the topology when the corresponding characteristic has been observed in the network traffic being monitored; the rule (ii) eliminates a particle of the model when it outputs from the topology; rule (iii) eliminates particles that are exhausted due to the consumption caused by the collision with the agents and rule (iv) is the rule of movement which carries all the particles inserted in a random rightward position in the column (initial position) towards the left. This movement occurs once for each particle α from synchronic iteration of the model

3 Model Sensitization

The structures discussed and the rules on the basis of which they act in EIA constitute a system comprised of an agent population that adapts to the normality of a supervised system. It would be of interest to observe the population reacting in a sensitive and quantifiable manner to disorders caused by abnormalities in the observed system. Hence, the parameters in the model were adjusted and agents were made highly sensitive to these disorders, thus becoming bioindicators.

The flow generation function was used to yield a sequence of variations in the input vectors, thus testing each of the parameters of the model in order to find values that would lend greater sensitivity to the agent population. Tested values

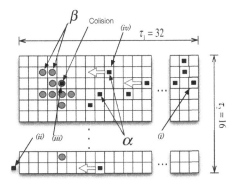

Fig. 2. EIA

in EIA parameters correspond to a variation in values that sensitize agents previously found in an experimental manner. This procedure increased the general sensitivity to flow variations of the EIA model from an average of 35% to 62% in the tests performed.

Figure 3 shows the evolution of the agent population, following the adjustment of these parameters, from their creation to their exposure to an attack. At moment 0, an initial population of 300 agents is created with random genetic vectors. These agents are exposed to habitual network traffic, thus leading to an adjustment consisting of the death of unfit agents and a reduction of the population to fewer than 50 individuals. Subsequently, the most fit agents proliferate and generate descendance by mutation. Until iteration 5570, there is an increase and stabilization of the agent population with an incidence of fractal noise that is intrinsic to ecological systems [19]. In iteration 5570, a probe attack with Satan[1] occurs, causing a significant fall in the size of the population, that is, a quantifiable deviation in one of the model's variables of interest, which is the basis for using the model as a classifier.

4   The Classifier

Once the agent population is sensitized to any perturbations in the environment (achieved through adjustments in model parameters), attention must center on change in the emerging structure established: that is, on the repercussions of environmental changes on the population level. This is achieved by means of monitoring the aforementioned variables of interest.

The variables of interest population size and average population energy exhibit noise in their behavior. Hence, a measurement of their trends for use as discriminators should be considered, and such variables are therefore transformed into classifiers through the incorporation of sliding windows and thresholds with the following parameters:

---

[1] SATAN (Security Administrator Tool for Analyzing Networks).

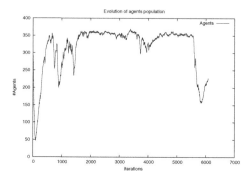

Fig. 3. Evolution of Agents Population

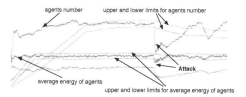

Fig. 4. sliding windows working on Netlogo

Table 2. Detected Characteristics

Detected Characteristics (α)
IP reserved bits, MF, DF, Urg, Ack, Reset, Syn, Fin, Telnet, SSH, FTP, Netbios, rlogin, RPC, NFS, Lockd, NetbiosWinNET, Xwin, DNS, LDAP, SMTP, POP, IMAP, HTTP, SSL, px, Serv, Time, TFTP, NNTP, NTP, lpd, Syslog, SNMP, bgp, Socks

- *Length of sliding windows:* This parameter sets the number of past values used in calculating the current average of the variables of interest. This corresponds to the point of reference used by higher and lower tolerance ranges, which may be observed in Figure 4.
- *Tolerance bandwidths:* Determines the distance of the bands accompanying the variable of interest. If the variable of interest exceeds the upper or lower limit owing to more iterations than those established in the *classifer alarm threshold*, an intrusion alarm is declared.
- *Classifer alarm threshold:* Sets the maximum successive iterations the variables of interest can exceed a tolerance range without triggering an alarm.

These parameters are adjusted in accordance with the domain of computer security, particularly the development of NIDS systems. These systems can be understood as classifiers capable of detecting an attack based on an analysis of network traffic, where this traffic is a continuous flow of data that is captured with sniffing techniques, that is, the capture of all accessible network traffic at the point of connection In this scenario, the flow characterizing the system under study (i.e., the monitored network) is used to feed the agent population in the EIA model package by package, based on information from the transmission and network layers of the TCP/IP stack. This is achieved by transforming through pre-processing forty characteristics of network traffic specified in Table 2, thus allowing the incorporation of their representations in the EIA model by means of particles (α).

The data for running this calibration process were extracted from different sources: samples of normal traffic were obtained from the network of the Department of Information Technology of the University of Santiago de Chile, while the security tools NMAP and Nessus were used to generate hostile traffic. Specifically, these tools generated probe and denial-of-service (DoS) attacks, respectively.

Probe, according to DARPA [18] are related to remote reconnaissance activities carried out by intruders prior to an attack, while DoS attacks consist of any activity aimed at preventing the delivery of a computer service. From this point of view, any attack on the availability of a system falls in this latter category.

Selection of classifier parameters posited a classifer based on the variable of interest agent population size, a second based on the average energy of the population and, finally, a unifying classifier based on the best parameters of the two first classifiers, but recalibrating the alarm threshold. The adjustment was made with the Receiver Operating Characteristic Curves (ROC) technique [8].

To identify the best classifier, a comparison was made of areas under the ROC curves (AUC). These areas have values between 0.5 and 1, where 1 represents a perfect classification and 0.5 signifies complete discriminatory incapacity. Experiments with the results observable in Figure 5, determined that the area under the curve (AUC) of the unified classifer (0,8149) is greater than both that based on population size (0,7860) and that based on average energy (0.7664). Hence, it is selected for the execution of comparative tests based on traffic for a standardized benchmark. The best classifier parameters found may be observed in Table 3. Because the algorithm is non-deterministic, all tests were performed 10 times, with curves generated by means of Bezier approximations.

Table 3. Classifier Parameters

Parameter	Value
Length of sliding window (Agents)	900
Tolerance bandwidth (Agentes)	2
Length of sliding window (Energy)	2800
Tolerance bandwidth (Energy)	0
Joint alarm threshold	200

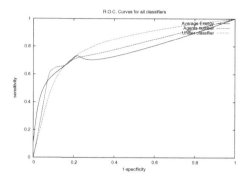

Fig. 5. Receiver Operating Characteristic Curves for all Classifiers

5 Experiments

The experiments specified in this section were posited to verify that a classifier based on notions of ecological systems can attain operational advantages over other automatic learning systems in the classification problem in intrusion detection systems by adaptating to changes in normal conditions and detecting innovative attacks. Comparisons were made with other bio-inspired classification techniques used successfully to develop NIDS, and such techniques were used to verify skill in detecting known and unknown threats.

5.1 Experiment Data

Tests of the EIA model and classifiers in comparison were performed with the widely used DARPA'98 data set. Use was discounted of KDD'99 data, which are considered to be of questionable validity and usefulness [21] , and also poor for the evaluation of anomaly detector systems [25].

5.2 Algorithms Evaluated

The classifier based on the EIA model was subjected to comparative tests to three other classifiers based on biological metaphors as described below:

- *Artificial Neural Network (ANN):* Use of a multilayer perceptron is being considered owing to its good results in the implementation of intrusion detection systems [16]. The network was trained with backpropagation and Levenbeg-Marquard because these reduce the number of false positives [17]. The quantity of neurons in the hidden layer was calculated according to [22] and then adjusted in a calibration process, leading to assignment of 16 neurons in the hidden layer based on an correctness criterion, with the use of 54 input characteristics from the TCP/IP package headings.

– *Formal Immune Network (FIN):* This proposal of immunocomputing (IC), like the neural network, can be considered to fall within the field of computational intelligence. FIN proposes the generation of a Euclidean multidimensional space (FIN space) in which a training process based on application of a discrete tree transform (DTT) [1] and/or a singular value descomposition (SVD) [13] incorporates input data and its initial space, which is optimized to form a set of class representatives for representation called cytokines, following a process of apoptosis and immunization explained in [24]. These cytokines operate according to a proximity principle in the FIN space to determine the class of data reviewed when mapped in the space with the DTT algorithm.
– *Modified Formal Immune Network (FIN+):* The test was conducted against a modified version of FIN (FIN+) developed for this comparation. By incorporating the concept of time and uncertainty, it generates temporary groupings, detecting regions of space with quick growth for classification as attacks, thus improving performance against unknown attacks of the original algorithm.

5.3 Design of Experiments

To evaluate the behavior of classifiers in changing scenarios and in detection of new/unknown attacks. Described algorithms are measured and compared in terms of false positives (FP) or type I errors and correctness determined by Equation 4, where (TP) represents True Positives and (TN) represents True Negatives. The results were statistically validated with the Wilcoxon sign test.

$$Correctness = \frac{(TP + TN)}{n} \qquad (4)$$

The tests were divided into two groups: known attacks and unknown attacks. Tests with known attacks were executed by subjecting the classifiers ANN, FIN and FIN+ to training that includes the attacks to which they will be exposed. Further, the unknown attack group is based on attacks not included in the training sets of classifier algorithms: this distinction does not apply to the EIA-based algorithm because the latter is not trained with attacks, but only exposed to normal traffic of 3000 packets, a time that has been empirically shown to be sufficient for their adaptation or the stabilization of the agent population.

6 Results

Table 4 shows the average FP values and the correctness achieved by the classifier algorithms for tests with known and unknown attacks. It may be observed in the table that for known attacks, EIA (15.56%) yields fewer false positives than other classifiers, with the closest being the modified version of the Tarakanov-Iturbe algorithm (FIN+), with 23.38%, a significant difference ($p \leq 0.05$). For the same type of attacks, EIA achieves better average correctness than the three

Table 4. Main Results

	Known Attacks		Unknown Attacks	
Classifier	FP	Correctness	FP	Correctness
EIA	0.1556	0.7848	0.1556	0.7848
FIN	0.26	0.7017	0.2923	0.6756
FIN+	0.2538	0.6728	0.2762	0.6798
ANN	0.3097	0.6670	0.3477	0.6284

classifiers with which it is compared; but it achieves a significant advantage with ANN and FIN ($p \leq 0.05$), although not with FIN+, of which it does not deliver a significant distance.

In the unknown attacks scenario, EIA (15.56%) yields significantly better results in terms of false positives than the other three classifiers ($p \leq 0.05$)), with the closest being the result of FIN+ (27.62%). The same result repeats in the results of average correctness marks, where EIA attains 78.48% against FIN+ (67.98%), thus attaining a result that is better than the other three by $p \leq 0.05$. The EIA model achieves a specificity of 86%, sensitivity of 95%, and precision of 86%.

6.1   Other Tests of EIA

The EIA classifier was subjected to further tests to check the consistency of the results, as the non-deterministic algorithm means that the results may differ from one experiment to another. Verification was perform by means of tests on characteristic attacks of each of the categories in the DARPA '98 set, which are: DoS, R2L, U2R and Probe. Where R2L (Remote to Local) refers to a category of attacks in which the intruder seeks to gain access to a computer system remotely and U2R (User to Root) refers to an unauthorized attempt to increase privileges.

In Table 5 it may be observed that EIA consistently detects practically all test series in DoS, R2L and probe attacks, whereas it cannot detect U2R attacks as easily, as it successfully did so in only half the experiments. This result is consistent with the general behavior of EIA, where it more easily detected DoS and Probe attacks. This is explained by the fact that variables based on the EIA agent population possess a certain inertia owing to the use of a sliding window and it reacts more readily to more extensive perturbations such as those caused by port scanning or flood attacks in the categories of Probe and DoS, respectively.

In terms of attacks, EIA detected in the first instance 35 of 47 attacks in the DARPA'98 set (74%). Review of undetected attacks revealed that none had sufficient length to activate the classifier because the parameter adjustment based on the ROC curve indicated that the best value of the classifier alarm threshold is 200. Thus, if the attack is not part of a packet trace (with normal background traffic) that is longer than 200, it does not trigger an alarm in the classifier. This

Table 5. Classifier Consistency

Category	Attack	Detections
DoS	Neptune	99/100
R2L	Dict	99/100
U2R	FFB	50/100
Probe	SATAN	100/100

may be related to the fact that the ROC calibration was performed with probe and DoS attacks of a moderate length. In later tests, in which the length of attacks was determined arbitrarily in order to complete at least the 200 packets necessary to sensitize the model, 11 of 12 attacks were detected. It should be noted that non-detection of these attacks in the tests did not significantly affect the comparative results owing to their minor presence in packet terms in the test data set of DARPA' 98.

7 Conclusions

This article provides a report on the proof of concept of a new "Flow Anomaly Detection System" (FADS) in development. The article includes the results of a set of experiments to show the features of the proposal and its applicability.

The analysis of the results verifies that it is feasible the creation of a population of evolutionary agents sensitive to environmental conditions that when subjected to stress can act as a classifier. In this way it is shown that these systems coincide with the biological evidence that the system's sensitivity to environmental changes increases when the genetic diversity of the species (agents) decreases.

When subjected to a complex problem of classification, the model developed has advantages over other bioinspired techniques traditionally used in the problem of intrusion detection network. The most important advantage obtained is the reduction of false positives where the technique of artificial indicator species (EIA) improves the results of three common indicators of both known and unknown attacks. The proposal has also shown competitive in terms of accuracy when attacks are known and even better than the other techniques when the attacks are unknown.

The classifier based on EIA proposes that learning by continuous adaptation has advantages over the machine learning techniques tested (FIN and ANN). Additionally it is shown that can outperform an algorithm with capabilities of online learning such as FIN+.

EIA is the first step in the project of developing a homeostatic control system. The main goal of the homeostatic control system is not to have separate stages of training and production but a unique dynamic and continuing stage to stabilize the host system where it is inserted, facilitating the maintenance of the whole system.

The use of bioindicators respond to partial advance of the system, which tackles the sensing and adjustment of the population of agents. In this context, it is necessary to obtain readings of the population changes, useful model to return to the current inability of the agents car modified their environment. For this reason, the next steps of this project oriented to allow the changes impacting the population of agents into the environment through a continuing dialogue achieved through its structural coupling [14].

References

1. Atreas, N., Karanikas, C., Tarakanov, A.: Signal Processing by an Immune Type Tree Transform. In: Timmis, J., Bentley, P.J., Hart, E. (eds.) ICARIS 2003. LNCS, vol. 2787, pp. 111–119. Springer, Heidelberg (2003)
2. Bersini, H.: Self-assertion versus self-recognition: A tribute to Francisco Varela. In: Timmis, J., Bentley, P.J. (eds.) Proceedings of the 1st International Conference on Artificial Immune Systems (ICARIS), pp. 107–112. University of Kent at Canterbury Printing Unit, University of Kent at Canterbury (2002), http://www.aber.ac.uk/icaris-2002
3. de Castro, L., Von Zuben, F.: ainet an artificial immune network for data analysis. In: Publishing, I.G. (ed.) Data Mining: A Heuristic Approach, pp. 231–259. Idea Group Publishing (2001)
4. Coutinho, A.: A walk with francisco varela from first- to second- generation networks: In search of the structure, dynamics and metadynamics of an organism-centered immune system. Biological Research 36(1), 17–26 (2003)
5. Cutello, V., Narzisi, G., Nicosia, G., Pavone, M.: Clonal Selection Algorithms: A Comparative Case Study Using Effective Mutation Potentials. In: Jacob, C., Pilat, M.L., Bentley, P.J., Timmis, J.I. (eds.) ICARIS 2005. LNCS, vol. 3627, pp. 13–28. Springer, Heidelberg (2005)
6. Dasgupta, D.: Artificial immune systems and their applications. Springer (1998)
7. Estevez-Tapiador, J.M., Garcia-Teodoro, P., Diaz-Verdejo, J.E.: Anomaly detection methods in wired networks: a survey and taxonomy. Computer Communications 27(16), 1569–1584 (2004)
8. Fawcett, T.: An introduction to ROC analysis. Pattern Recognition Letters 27(8), 861–874 (2006), rOC Analysis in Pattern Recognition
9. Forrest, S., Perelson, A., Allen, L., Cherukuri, R.: Self-Nonself Discrimination in a Computer. In: Proceedings of IEEE Computer Society Symposium on Research in Security and Privacy, pp. 202–212 (1994); IEEE, Comp. Soc.; IEEE, Comp. Soc., Tech. Comm. Secur. & Privacy; Int. Assoc. Cryptol. Res. (1994); 1994 IEEE-Computer-Society Symposium on Research in Security and Privacy, Oakland, CA, May 16-18 (1994)
10. Glickman, M., Balthrop, J., Forrest, S.: A machine learning evaluation of an artificial immune system. Evolutionary Computation 13(2), 179–212 (2005)
11. Greitzer, F.L., Moore, A.P., Cappelli, D.M., Andrews, D.H., Carroll, L.A., Hull, T.D.: Combating the insider cyber threat. IEEE Security & Privacy 6(1), 61–64 (2008)
12. Harmer, P., Williams, P., Gunsch, G., Lamont, G.: An artificial immune system architecture for computer security applications. IEEE Transactions on Evolutionary Computation 6(3), 252–280 (2002)
13. Horn, R., Johnson, C.: Matrix Analysis. Cambridge University Press (1986)

14. Humberto Maturana, F.V.: El Arbol del Conocimiento. Editorial Universitaria, Santiago (1976)
15. Jeffrey, D.W., Madden, B.: Bioindicators and environmental management. Academic Press, London (1991)
16. Kukielka, P., Kotulski, Z.: Analysis of Different Architectures of Neural Networks for Application in Intrusion Detection Systems. In: Ganzha, M., Paprzycki, M., PelechPilichowski, T. (eds.) International Multiconference on Computer Science and Information Technology (IMCSIT), Wisla, Poland, October 20-22, vol. 1 and 2, pp. 752–756. IEEE (2008)
17. Linda, O., Vollmer, T., Manic, M.: Neural Network Based Intrusion Detection System for Critical Infrastructures. In: IEEE International Joint Conference on Neural Networks (IJCNN), Int. Neural Network Soc., Atlanta, GA, June 14-19, vol. 1- 6, pp. 102–109 (2009)
18. Lippmann, R., Haines, J.W., Fried, D.J., Korba, J., Das, K.: The 1999 DARPA offline intrusion detection evaluation. Computer Networks-the International Journal of Computer and Telecommunications Networking 34(4), 579–595 (2000)
19. Halley, J.M.: Ecology, evolution and 1f-noise. Trends in Ecology & Evolution 11(1), 33–37 (1996)
20. Nanas, N., de Roeck, A.: Autopoiesis, the immune system, and adaptive information filtering. Natural Computing 8, 387–427 (2009), doi:10.1007/s11047-008-9068-x
21. Olusola, A.A., Oladele, A.S., Abosede, D.O.: Analysis of KDD '99 Intrusion Detection Dataset for Selection of Relevance Features. In: Ao, S.I., Douglas, C., Grundfest, W.S., Burgstone, J. (eds.) World Congress on Engineering and Computer Science, Int. Assoc. Engn., San Francisco, CA, October 20-22. Lecture Notes in Engineering and Computer Science, vol. 1 and 2, pp. 162–168 (2010)
22. Haykin, S.O.: Neural Networks and Learning Machines, 3rd edn., new york edn. Prentice Hall (2009)
23. Sklar, E.: Software review: NetLogo, a multi-agent simulation environment. Artificial Life 13(3), 303–311 (2007)
24. Tarakanov, A.O.: Immunocomputing for intelligent intrusion detection. IEEE Computational Intelligence Magazine 3(2), 22–30 (2008)
25. Tavallaee, M., Bagheri, E., Lu, W., Ghorbani, A.: A detailed analysis of the KDD CUP 99 data set. In: IEEE Symposium on Computational Intelligence for Security and Defense Applications, CISDA 2009, pp. 1–6 (July 2009)
26. Varela, F.: El Fenómeno de la Vida, 2nd edn. OCEANO, Santiago de Chile (2000)
27. Wilcoxon, F.: Indicidual Comparisons by Ranking Methods. Biometrics Bulletin 1(6), 80–83 (1945)
28. Wu, S.X., Banzhaf, W.: The use of computational intelligence in intrusion detection systems: A review. Applied Soft Computing 10(1), 1–35 (2010)

Rethinking Concepts of the Dendritic Cell Algorithm for Multiple Data Stream Analysis

Chris Musselle

Department of Computer Science, University of Bristol, UK

Abstract. This paper begins by stating that the underlying concepts of signals and antigen used by the Dendritic Cell Algorithm are too abstract and arbitrary to be of use in real world applications as they stand. To address this, these concepts are more explicitly defined within a specific application area, namely that of data stream analysis. These new definitions are based around the outputs of the Change Point Detecting Subspace Tracker (CD-ST), a recently developed algorithm for detecting key change points across multiple data streams. Preliminary results demonstrate the utility of this new definition for antigen. The paper concludes by laying the theoretical groundwork for a novel anomaly detection framework for use in data streaming applications. The underlying methodology is to perform anomaly detection via the detection and classification of key change points that occur across the multiple data streams monitored.

1 Introduction

The Dendritic Cell Algorithm (DCA) [10] is an abstraction of the biological function of dendritic cells and can be viewed primarily as a decision making algorithm that uses a set of heterogeneous agents to vote on a binary choice [20], and therefore has applicability to the fields of anomaly detection and classification. The main underlying mechanism is that these virtual agents temporarily correlate multiple real valued time series (termed 'signals'), with a sequence of symbolic events (termed 'antigen') in an attempt to elicit the events that correlate most with a given context, determined by a weighted sum of the signals.

Though the algorithm has been previously applied to many problems [10][19][12][1][17][20], recent analytical and empirical work has cast some serious doubts on the utility of the DCA for real world problem solving.

The work by Stibor *et al.* in [21] presents a mathematical analysis of the DCA's signal processing component, and functionally equates the classification carried out by a single agent to a statically weighted linear classifier. This severely limits the ability of the DCA to discriminate between regions in signal space as the solution must be linearly separable.

Additionally, the work by Gu *et al.* [11] compared the signal processing component of the DCA to machine learning techniques which demonstrated the DCA's inferiority at classification when compared to a linear Support Vector Machine (SVM) whose outputs are filtered with a moving window filter. This

C.A. Coello Coello et al. (Eds.): ICARIS 2012, LNCS 7597, pp. 246–259, 2012.
© Springer-Verlag Berlin Heidelberg 2012

makes it hard to justify using the DCA, which is a fairly complex algorithm with many parameters and interacting components, if superior results can be achieved through the use of simpler traditional machine learning techniques.

The lack of a quantifiable definition for both signals and antigens has also resulted in a variety of subjective user-specified inputs for the DCA in the literature. In addition, further artificial transformations of these inputs (such as the use of antigen multipliers in [12]), or redefinitions of the output metric (such as with the MAC in [1]) have been suggested in an effort to achieve better performance when using this biological analogy. Such subjectivity of the inputs and outputs, coupled with the range of parameters that can also be specified by the user gives the algorithm many degrees of freedom, and increases the likelihood that the DCA is simply being hand-tuned with much trial and error to give the desired results for each application.

The founding argument in this paper is that, as they stand, the concepts of 'signals' and 'antigen' used by the DCA are too abstract and arbitrary to be of any real utility in real world applications, and that for situations where the algorithm has previously been applied, much simpler techniques (such as those used by Gu *et al.* in [11]) are adequate for this purpose.

This paper attempts to extend the underlying ideas of the DCA by explicitly redefining the concepts of 'signals' and 'antigen' for a specific application area, namely that of multiple data stream analysis. Though to do so first requires the introduction of a new algorithm, the Change point Detecting Subspace Tracker (CD-ST), developed to detect significant points of change across multiple co-evolving data streams. These new definitions of 'signals' and 'antigen' are then combined with the capabilities of the CD-ST algorithm in order to lay the theoretical foundations for a novel anomaly detection framework for use in data streaming applications.

The rest of this paper proceeds as follows. Section 2 briefly covers the background of the DCA and the area of multiple data stream analysis. Section 3 covers the methodology of the CD-ST algorithm and the techniques it uses. Section 4 redefines the signal and antigen concepts, and Section 5 covers some preliminary work which gives examples for the new antigen definition. These new definitions are then brought together into a new framework proposed in Section 6. Section 7 presents a summary and the main directions for future work.

2   Background

2.1   The Dendritic Cell Algorithm (DCA)[1]

The function of the DCA is to perform temporal correlation between multiple time series and the symbolic event stream to find out which events are most likely responsible for observed time periods of potentially 'harmful' activity.

---

[1] Here the main features of the DCA are briefly summarised. For a more detailed description of the mechanisms involved, the reader is refereed to [10].

The inputs to the DCA take two possible types; signals or antigens. The signals are a set (two to three) of continuous time series evolving in parallel. The antigens are a stream of symbolic events occurring alongside the time series. The number of events per time step can range from zero upwards, with repeated entries possible both in a single time step and throughout the simulation.

The DCA is viewed as carrying out four interrelated tasks:

1. Classification of time series subsequences into 'safe' and 'harmful' categories. This is achieved by taking a weighted combination of all signals over a subsequence, and thresholding the value at zero.
2. Using a range of subsequence lengths in parallel to conduct classification. The length of the subsequence is determined by comparing a second weighted combination of all signals to a 'migration' threshold, which is varied over a population of virtual dendritic cell agents. Therefore each dendritic cell agent classifies a different length subsequence of signals at a time.
3. Varying the subsequence lengths depending on total signals in a subsequence. As the length of a subsequence depends on the second weighted combination of all signals, this results in longer subsequence lengths when the total signal values are low and shorter subsequence lengths when the total signal values are high. This is the DCAs dynamic filtering property [20].
4. Temporal correlation of subsequences with antigen event stream. The events are ranked according to how frequently they occurred alongside a time series subsequence that was classified as 'harmful' as opposed to 'safe'. The highest ranked are then considered to be anomalous events that are most likely responsible for the 'harmful' time series subsequences.

2.2   Data Stream Analysis

A data stream is an ordered sequence of data instances that typically arrive at a high rate and in high enough volume to prohibit them from all being stored and analysed in main memory. Over the last two decades advancements in information technology have made it possible to generate large amounts of continuous data from a wide range of sources. Examples include transaction logs (credit card, phone), web browsing sessions, computer network traffic, financial data, sensor networks and many others. With such large volumes of data, traditional database management systems are proving insufficient to deal with the continuous queries required in these applications [3].

The following constraints apply when operating on streaming data [8]:

- Limited to one pass through the data at most. Therefore the algorithm must be incremental, that is, capable of utilising and integrating new data points as they arrive.
- Online learning from new data must be possible. This means a way of adapting to new evolving data patterns and of forgetting older data.
- Working with limited computational resources. The computation is often carried out on the sensors themselves, which have much greater limits in their memory and CPU resources.

3   Methods

This section covers all the techniques that are used in redefining the concepts of signals and antigen in Section 4. It begins with an overview of the CD-ST algorithm, then details the components used to synthesis it in Section 3.2 and 3.3. Section 3.4 finishes by covering SAX representation for time series data.

3.1   The Change Point Detecting Subspace Tracker (CD-ST)

The CD-ST algorithm [2, Ch 5-8] was designed to conduct anomaly detection under the constraints of the data streaming scenario, based on the assumption that any anomalies will be associated with a change in the nature of the input data. CD-ST aims to perform a first pass over the data, highlighting key change points for further investigation, whilst using minimal computer resources.

The CD-ST algorithm is build upon a dimensionality reduction technique known as subspace tracking, which is explained in detail in Section 3.2. The CD-ST algorithm can be summarised as performing the following tasks:

1. Compression of the N input data streams into a reduced representation of r hidden variables, where $r \ll N$. This compression occurs along the top r basis vectors of the data space which exhibit the greatest variance.
2. Updating this representation with the arrival of each new data point. The subspace tracking algorithm detailed below makes it possible to incrementally update the top r basis vectors and hidden variables with each new data point. The process is similar to conducting Principal Component Analysis (PCA) [14] in an approximate and iterative fashion. The input history is exponentially discounted which gives the algorithm the ability to forget older inputs and adapt to evolving patterns in the input data.
3. Tracking the squared residual error, SRE, between the original data and the reduced representation. A sliding window of fixed length stores samples of the past SRE values and is updated at each time step.
4. Flagging unexpected change points. A test statistic is derived (Section 3.3) using the sample of SRE and the current SRE. While the SRE contains mostly noise, this test statistic should follow a t-distribution. When this is not the case there is likely to be new unaccounted variance in the current SRE, and so those time steps are flagged as change points.

3.2   Subspace Tracking

The goal of principal subspace tracking is the recursive estimation of the r dominant or leading eigenvalues and the associated eigenvectors of a time-recursively updated covariance matrix [22],

$$\mathbf{\Phi}(t) = \alpha \mathbf{\Phi}(t-1) + \mathbf{z}(t)\mathbf{z}^T(t)$$

where $\mathbf{z}(t)$ is the input data vector of n observations at time t, and α is a positive exponential forgetting factor close to one. We are interested in obtaining estimates for the r dominant eigenvectors in a $n \times r$ matrix V_r which capture the dominant subspace of variance across the data streams, and is related to the $r \times r$ compressed form of the covariance matrix $\Phi_r(t)$ as follows,

$$\Phi_r(t) = \Phi(t)V_r(t)V_r^T(t).$$

These dominant eigenvectors project the original data onto the reduced subspace $\Phi_r(t)$ and thus form a low rank approximation of the original data. More information on subspace tracking can be found in [5] and [7].

The subspace tracking algorithm used by CD-ST and detailed below is the Fast row-Housholder Subspace Tracker (FHST) [22]. A detailed derivation is beyond the scope of this paper, but is available in the original work [22].

The Fast Row-Housholder Subspace Tracker. The majority of subspace trackers are based on the orthogonal iteration principle which is well know [9]. A single orthogonal iteration is applied to the covariance matrix as follows:

$$\mathbf{A}(t) = \mathbf{\Phi}(t)\mathbf{Q}(t-1)$$

$$\mathbf{A}(t) = \mathbf{Q}(t)\mathbf{S}(t): \text{orthonormal factorisation}$$

where $\mathbf{A}(t)$ is an $n \times r$ auxiliary matrix, $\mathbf{Q}(t)$ is the $n \times r$ matrix of the estimated basis for the r dominant eigenvectors, and $\mathbf{S}(t)$ is left as an undetermined $r \times r$ square matrix[2].

Given the dominant basis set $\mathbf{Q}(t)$, the new data vector $\mathbf{z}(t)$ can then be compressed onto a lower dimensional representation as

$$\mathbf{h}(t) = \mathbf{Q}^T(t-1)\mathbf{z}(t).$$

The remainder of the FHST algorithm operates by using row Housholder reflections [4] to update the $\mathbf{Q}$ and $\mathbf{S}$ matrices iteratively, which are then used to calculate the compressed projection or hidden variables $\mathbf{h}(t)$ at each time step. The pseudocode for the FHST algorithm is shown in Algorithm 1

3.3   Change Point Detection in CD-ST

The statistical test requires that the squared reconstruction error, SRE, be calculated at each time step as, $SRE(t) = \|\mathbf{z}(t) - \tilde{\mathbf{z}}(t)\|^2$, where $\tilde{\mathbf{z}}(t)$ is the reconstructed input data based on the reduced representation. A recent sample was then stored in a sliding buffer B for the last w_{ts} time steps as

$$B = [SRE(t - w_{ts}), \ldots, SRE(t)]$$

The entries in B are then differenced so that they have a mean of zero.

$$X(i) = B(i+1) - B(i)$$

---

[2] Note, most subspace trackers use QR-decomposition for this step i.e the S matrix is constrained to be upper triangular. FHST differs here to allow for decreased complexity of the algorithm. Refer to [22] for further details.

Algorithm 1. Fast row-Housholder Subspace Tracker: The algorithm employs Housholder reflections to update the Q and S matrices iteratively [22]

Inputs: $\mathbf{z}(t) \in \Re^N$ # *New data vector*
α # *Decay constant*

Initialise: $\mathbf{Q}(0) = $ random orthonormal matrix
$\mathbf{S}(0) = \sigma\mathbf{I}$ where σ is small and positive
$\mathbf{v}(0) = [0 \dots 0]^T$

for $t = 1, 2, 3 \dots$:
  $\mathbf{h}(t) = \mathbf{Q}^T(t-1)\mathbf{z}(t)$
  $Z(t) = \mathbf{z}^T(t)\mathbf{z}(t) - \mathbf{h}^T(t)\mathbf{h}(t)$
  $\mathbf{u}(t-1) = \mathbf{S}(t-1)\mathbf{v}(t-1)$
  $\mathbf{X}(t) = \alpha\mathbf{S}(t-1) - 2\alpha\mathbf{u}(t-1)\mathbf{v}^T(t-1) + \mathbf{h}(t)\mathbf{h}^T(t)$
  $\mathbf{X}^T(t)\mathbf{b}(t) = Z^{1/2}(t)\mathbf{h}(t) \xrightarrow{solve} \mathbf{b}(t)$ # *LS−solve*
  $\beta(t) = 4(\mathbf{b}^T(t)\mathbf{b}(t) + 1)$
  $\varphi^2(t) = \dfrac{1}{2} + \dfrac{1}{\sqrt{\beta(t)}}$
  $\gamma(t) = \dfrac{1 - 2\varphi^2(t)}{2\varphi(t)}$
  $\delta(t) = \dfrac{\varphi(t)}{Z^{1/2}(t)}$
  $\mathbf{v}(t) = \gamma(t)\mathbf{b}(t)$
  $\mathbf{S}(t) = \mathbf{X}(t) - \dfrac{1}{\delta(t)}\mathbf{v}(t)\mathbf{h}^T(t)$ # *Update S*
  $\mathbf{w}(t) = \delta(t)\mathbf{h}(t) - \mathbf{v}(t)$
  $\mathbf{e}(t) = \delta(t)\mathbf{z}(t) - \mathbf{Q}(t-1)\mathbf{w}(t)$
  $\mathbf{Q}(t) = \mathbf{Q}(t-1) - 2\mathbf{e}(t)\mathbf{v}^T(t)$ # *Update Q*
end

Assuming that under normal conditions the hidden variables capture a large proportion of the input data variance, this then leaves the residual SRE comprising mostly of noisy fluctuations and small amounts of residual variance. Therefore it is assumed that in the absence of an anomaly all the $X(i)$ can be modelled as independent and identically distributed random variables approximated by the normal distribution $N(0, \sigma^2)$. Under this assumption, the sum of k squares of $X(i)$ approximates a chi-squared distribution with k degrees of freedom.

It is known that the ratio

$$T = \frac{Z}{\sqrt{\dfrac{V}{\nu}}}$$

follows the t-distribution, where Z is a random variable from a normal distribution and V is a random variable from a chi-squared distribution with ν degrees of freedom [13]. Therefore the following test statistic TS is derived,

$$TS(t) = \frac{X(t)}{\sqrt{\frac{X(t-L_X)^2+...+X(t-w_{ts}-L_X)^2}{w_{ts}-1}}}$$

where w_{ts} is the length of the buffer and L_X is the lag between the current $X(t)$ and the first $X(i)$ used in the sample[3].

The hypothesis test at each time step is therefore: **H_0** TS continues to follow a t-distribution at time t. Where the significance level of the statistical test is a variable parameter of the algorithm.

A rejection of **H_0** means that TS at that time step is very unlikely to follow a t-distribution given the significance level. Though this implies that the $X(t)$ used to calculate the test statistic is no longer normally distributed, and thus, there is now more than just noise in the most recent residual SRE. The residual now likely contains unaccounted variance present in the input data which the subspace tracker has yet to adapt to. This suggests that there has been a recent change in the variance of the input data, and so any time step that rejects **H_0** is flagged as a change point.

3.4 SAX Representation

The Symbolic Aggregate approXimation technique or SAX [18] was the first symbolic representation for time series data that allows for dimensionality reduction, a lower bounding of the similarity measure, and the ability to operate under the streaming scenario. The technique has been show to be competitive if not superior to other time series representations for many data mining tasks across a wide variety of datasets. An extensive bibliography of over 75 papers that utilise SAX representations is available at [16].

This widely used technique works as follows:

- Two parameters are defined: The word length l which is the number of characters the time series is reduced to; and the alphabet size a which is the number of different symbols used to represent the time series.
- The time series is standardised to zero mean and unit standard deviation.
- The Piecewise Aggregate Approximation (PAA) [15] of the time series is taken, where the time series is divided into l equal subsequences and each approximated with the average value of data points within that subsequence.
- A series of 'breakpoints' $\beta = b_1, \ldots, b_{a-1}$ are then defined which split the area under a Gaussian curve into a equal sizes. Each area is assigned a different symbol from the specified alphabet.
- Each of the l averages is then assigned a symbol based on which area of the Gaussian curve it falls under.
- The result is a SAX word of length l which contains at most a different symbols, as illustrated in Figure 1.

---

[3] Incorporating this small lag helps remove short range dependency between the sampled $X(i)$ and the current $X(t)$. These would be present if the inputs changed as the subspace tracker will take a few time steps to adapt.

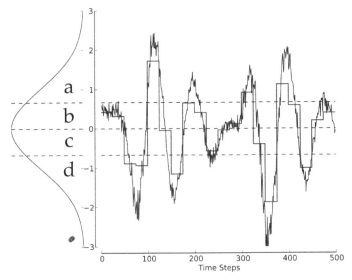

SAX 'word' = b b d d a c d b b c c b a c d a b d b b

Fig. 1. Visualisation of the SAX representation with $a = 4$. A time series is reduced from 500 floating point values to 20 symbolic characters. The stepwise line represents the Piecewise Aggregate Approximation of the time series.

4   Redefining Concepts of the DCA

This section aims to make the signal and antigen concepts of the DCA more useful by reframing them within a specific context, that of data stream analysis using the CD-ST algorithm.

4.1   Redefining the Concept of Antigen

In the DCA the term 'antigen' is used to mean an instance of a symbolic finite set that corresponds to a possible cause of an anomaly in the monitored system. The aim is to find out which of these antigens are genuinely responsible for an anomaly and which are not. This concept overlaps well with the idea behind CD-ST, which is that points of *change* are the likely candidates of anomalous activity in multiple data streams, but that some may also correspond to normal periodic changes in the input data. Further post-processing of these change points could better determine which are genuine anomalies, however to do so requires a method for capturing these change points in adequate detail.

The CD-ST algorithm only outputs the residual error vector for each change point flagged. A better approach would be to take a 'snapshot' of all N data streams consisting of values both before and after the change point. Such a snapshot would be a $N \times w_s$ matrix, where w_s is the snapshot window length, with the time step around $w_s/2$ corresponding to when the change point was first flagged up. One way of doing this is to use the SAX representation described previously to approximate the real values of each snapshot with $N \times l$ symbolic characters from a specified alphabet of size a.

Therefore the term 'antigen' in this scenario can be redefined as a 'SAX snapshot' of all N data streams around change points flagged up by the CD-ST algorithm. Examples of these snapshots are shown in Figure 2.

4.2   Redefining the Concept of Signals

The DCA uses the concept of 'signals' to represent any additional data source that could be monitored over time and used as a heuristic indicator to better characterise the antigen. With 'antigen' redefined as 'SAX snapshots' of the flagged up change points, further information and processing is still also required to better distinguish which correspond to genuine anomalies and which do not. The idea here is to redefine a 'signal' as any feature that can be extracted from the CD-ST algorithm output or SAX snapshots themselves to better aid in characterisation of the change points. These 'signal' features and 'antigen' SAX snapshots can then become inputs to an online machine learning method.

This new definition for 'signals' is still quite broad as many additional possible sources of information could be used (see below), though they are all based on specific statistics or measurable quantities and thus no-longer use arbitrary mappings or rely on expert knowledge of the domain to generate them, unlike with the DCA at current. There will however be a subjective component in the choice of which features to use as the best 'signals' for an anomaly, and this is likely to vary between applications. One solution is to use a training set of data containing the type of anomalies that are of interest, and then analyse the utility of each extractable feature. Possible features include, but are not limited to:

- Absolute time stamp of the SAX snapshot.
- Standard deviation and mean of each data stream.
- Maximum distance between two data streams in a SAX snapshot.
- Number of data streams responsible for the change point.
- Distance between SAX snapshot subsequences from before and after the change point.

Additionally by keeping a record of past SAX snapshot antigen, the following could also be considered as signal features:

- Relative time since last SAX snapshot.
- Distance from most recent SAX snapshot.
- Distance measures from previous SAX snapshots between one of the following: individual streams responsible for change points; SAX subsequences from before and after the change point; or the SAX snapshot as a whole.
- Time steps since a similar SAX representation.
- Frequency of SAX representation in overall and/or recent history.

4.3 Processing the New Antigen and Signals

Assuming that a set of appropriate signal features can be found which are indicative of the genuine anomalies in the application, the final task is to develop a classifier that uses these signal features to better differentiate between normal SAX snapshot antigen and those that are genuinely anomalous. An appropriate classifier for this task is likely to differ depending on the application for the monitored data streams, and so further research on samples of training data would be needed to choose a suitable method for this component of the algorithm.

However a few approaches are considered below, depending on various assumptions about the anomalies. In order of increasing sophistication these are:

1. Using a predefined library of change points that are known to be harmless or 'normal' for the monitored system. Assuming such information is available, simple pattern matching could then be used to filter out these occurrences.
2. Under the assumption that similar, periodically occurring change points are much less likely to be anomalous, a record of recently observed SAX snapshots and the times they occurred could easily be used to construct an online, self-updating version of the filter library suggested in approach 1.
3. Training a linear or non-linear machine learning classifier to take into account a range of the features detailed in Section 4.2.
4. Using online clustering to group the individual SAX snapshots into similar occurrences. This approach would require verification to determine which group corresponds to the genuine anomalies, though this approach would allow for online discovery of new classes or subclasses of change points, beyond simply labelling them as normal or anomalous.
5. Using a combination of some or all of these approaches.

5 Preliminary Results for New 'Antigen' Definition

This section describes the results observed from combining the CD-ST algorithm with 'SAX snapshots' on a real world dataset. Further analysis of the CD-ST algorithm performance can be found in [2, Ch 7&8].

The dataset used consists of internet traffic measurements taken from routers in a data centre and was first introduced in [6]. The dataset contains the number of bits per second averaged at six minute intervals for all gateway links between the main data centre router and the internet. The dataset consists of measurements for 26 links over a total of 897 intervals, which equates to just over three days worth of data. Input values are standardised to zero mean and unit standard deviation so as to compare all data streams on a similar scale.

As shown in Figure 2, the CD-ST algorithm is able to detect multiple types of visually verifiable[4] change points for the dataset. The example SAX snapshots show a single stream peak at $t = 53$, a multi-stream dip at $t = 352$, and a sudden shift in the variance/covariance of all streams at $t = 297$.

---

[4] Quantitative validation was not possible due to the lack of reliable ground truths for the dataset.

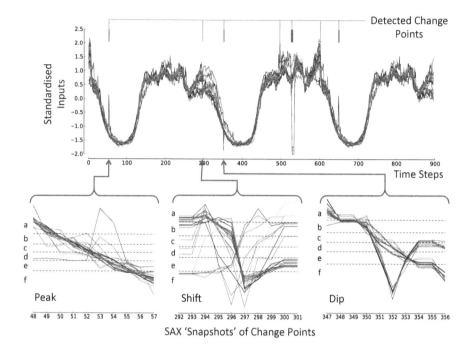

Fig. 2. Change points detected by the CD-ST algorithm on the data centre dataset. The 'SAX snapshot' representation with $\alpha = 6$ and $l = 10$ is also shown for three different change points. Note that the real values for each data stream are plotted here for readability, with the breakpoints β shown as dashed lines. In practice the SAX snapshots would be stored as an array of symbolic values ranging from a-f.

These results are very encouraging, demonstrating CD-STs ability to pickup both subtle (single stream) and glaring (multiple stream) change points, along with the potential for further differentiation of these change points with the addition of SAX snapshot representations.

Though these results give a good example of the utility of the newly proposed definition of 'antigen', further research is needed on an adequately labelled dataset to give specific examples for the new 'signals' definition. However, it is clear from the examples of SAX snapshots in Figure 2 that different types of change points are captured by very different representations. Future work will focus on determining which additional features (Section 4.2) can distinguish between normal or expected change points and those that are genuine anomalies for a given dataset.

6 Overall Framework Foundations

This section discusses the proposed bigger picture of how the change point detection algorithm CD-ST is incorporated with the redefined concepts of antigen as

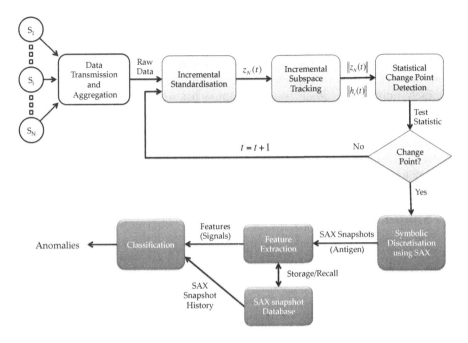

Fig. 3. Overview of larger framework for an online anomaly detection algorithm. The white boxes represent all hardware considerations, the light grey boxes represent the stages carried out by the CD-ST algorithm, and the dark grey boxes represent the proposed future work areas designed to post process the change points in order to pick out the genuine anomalies.

'SAX snapshots' and signals as extracted features, to form a novel online anomaly detection approach. Figure 3 shows an overview of this proposed framework.

The white boxes represent all tasks associated with transmission and aggregation of the raw data from the S_N sources being monitored in the system.

The light grey boxes show the various stages of the CD-ST algorithm itself which include: the incremental standardisation of the raw data; the incremental subspace tracking of the main dimensions of data variance; and the statistical change point detection used to flag up the time step of change.

The dark grey boxes represent all the proposed areas of future research that will carry out further processing of the CD-ST algorithm outputs in order to elicit the genuine anomalies. This area comprises of three steps. The first is capturing symbolic representations of the change points as they occur. This is achieved by the use of SAX snapshot 'antigen' as described in Section 4.1 and demonstrated in Figure 2. These correspond to a symbolic instance that has the potential to be responsible for an anomaly in the monitored system.

The second step is then to extract useful 'signal' features from these SAX snapshots as described in Section 4.2. These correspond to any additional information that can be extracted from the CD-ST algorithm output or SAX snapshots themselves to better aid classification. The number of features can be extended by comparisons to previous SAX snapshots via either a recent record held in memory, or reference to a larger historical database of SAX snapshots.

The last step is to design a machine learning classifier that can utilise both the SAX snapshot antigen and signal features extracted to differentiate between those that are normal or expected in the monitored system, and those that are genuinely anomalous. Some possible approaches are suggested in Section 4.3 though further research would be needed to choose a suitable technique along with the features used to make this decision, as they are likely to be highly dependent on the system being monitored. Reliable training data for an application that monitors multiple data streams would be invaluable in taking this research forward.

7   Summary and Future Work

This paper started with the premiss that the concepts of 'signals' and 'antigen' in the DCA are too abstract and arbitrary for use in real world applications as they stand. These underlying concepts are explicitly redefined for the given context of data stream analysis using the newly introduced CD-ST algorithm. In short, the 'antigen' now correspond to symbolic discritisations of the change points detected by the CD-ST algorithm, and the 'signals' are any additional features that can be extracted from them to aid in their classification. Preliminary work showed the potential utility of the new antigen definition.

By combining these new definitions with proposed extensions to the CD-ST algorithm, this paper has laid the groundwork for a novel approach to anomaly detection in the streaming data scenario through the detection and classification of change points across all monitored data streams.

A promising area for future work will be the implementation of the framework presented on reliable application datasets. The two main unknowns that must be addressed if it is to prove useful are:

1. Identifying which features of the SAX snapshots discriminate between normal change points and genuine anomalies in a real world application.
2. Developing an appropriate classification algorithm to further refine the outputs of the CD-ST algorithm, based on the identified features and the SAX snapshots of change points.

References

1. Al-Hammadi, Y., Aickelin, U., Greensmith, J.: DCA for bot detection. In: 2008 IEEE Congress on Evolutionary Computation (IEEE World Congress on Computational Intelligence), pp. 1807–1816. IEEE (June 2008)
2. Author. Data Fusion Techniques for Temporal Correlation and Anomaly Detection. PhD thesis, Author's Institution (submitted, April 2012)
3. Babcock, B., Babu, S., Datar, M., Motwani, R., Widom, J.: Models and issues in data stream systems. Technical Report 2002-19, Stanford InfoLab (2002)

4. Bojanczyk, A.W., Nagy, J.G., Plemmons, R.J.: Block RLS using row householder reflections. Linear Algebra and its Applications, 188–189, 31–61 (1993)
5. Comon, P., Golub, G.H.: Tracking a few extreme singular values and vectors in signal processing. Proceedings of the IEEE 78(8), 1327–1343 (1990)
6. dos Santos Teixeira, P.P.H., Milidiú, R.L.R.: Data stream anomaly detection through principal subspace tracking. In: Proceedings of the 2010 ACM Symposium on Applied Computing, pp. 1609–1616 (2010)
7. Doukopoulos, X.G., Moustakides, G.V.: Fast and stable subspace tracking. IEEE Transactions on Signal Processing 56(4), 1452–1465 (2008)
8. Gama, J.: Knowledge Discovery from Data Streams, 1st edn. Chapman and Hall/CRC (2010)
9. Golub, G., Van Loan, C.: Matrix Computations, 2nd edn. John Hopkins University Press (1989)
10. Greensmith, J.: The Dendritic Cell Algorithm. Phd thesis, University of Nottingham (2007)
11. Gu, F., Feyereisl, J., Oates, R., Reps, J., Greensmith, J., Aickelin, U.: Quiet in Class: Classification, Noise and the Dendritic Cell Algorithm. In: Liò, P., Nicosia, G., Stibor, T. (eds.) ICARIS 2011. LNCS, vol. 6825, pp. 173–186. Springer, Heidelberg (2011)
12. Gu, F., Greensmith, J., Aickelin, U.: Further Exploration of the Dendritic Cell Algorithm: Antigen Multiplier and Time Windows. In: Bentley, P.J., Lee, D., Jung, S. (eds.) ICARIS 2008. LNCS, vol. 5132, pp. 142–153. Springer, Heidelberg (2008)
13. Johnson, N., Kotz, S., Balakrishnan, N.: Continuous Univariate Distributions, 2nd edn., vol. 2. Wiley-Blackwell (1995)
14. Jolliffe, I.: Principal Component Analysis. Springer Series in Statistics. Springer, New York (2002)
15. Keogh, E., Chakrabarti, K., Pazzani, M., Mehrotra, S.: Dimensionality Reduction for Fast Similarity Search in Large Time Series Databases. Knowledge and Information Systems 3(3), 263–286 (2001)
16. Keogh, E., Lin, J.: SAX Homepage, http://www.cs.ucr.edu/~eamonn/SAX.html
17. Kim, J., Bentley, P., Wallenta, C., Ahmed, M., Hailes, S.: Danger is ubiquitous: Detecting malicious activities in sensor networks using the dendritic cell algorithm. In: Networks, pp. 390–403 (2006)
18. Lin, J., Keogh, E., Lonardi, S., Chiu, B.: A symbolic representation of time series, with implications for streaming algorithms. In: Proceedings of the 8th ACM SIGMOD Workshop on Research issues in Data Mining and Knowledge Discovery - DMKD 2003, p. 2. ACM Press, New York (2003)
19. Manzoor, S., Shafiq, M.Z., Tabish, S.M., Farooq, M.: A Sense of 'Danger' for Windows Processes. In: Andrews, P.S., Timmis, J., Owens, N.D.L., Aickelin, U., Hart, E., Hone, A., Tyrrell, A.M. (eds.) ICARIS 2009. LNCS, vol. 5666, pp. 220–233. Springer, Heidelberg (2009)
20. Oates, R., Kendall, G., Garibaldi, J.: Frequency analysis for dendritic cell population tuning. Evolutionary Intelligence 1(2), 145–157 (2008)
21. Stibor, T., Oates, R., Kendall, G., Garibaldi, J.M.: Geometrical insights into the dendritic cell algorithm. In: Proceedings of the 11th Annual Conference on Genetic and Evolutionary Computation - GECCO 2009, p. 1275. ACM Press, New York (2009)
22. Strobach, P.: The fast recursive row-Householder subspace tracking algorithm. Signal Process. 89(12), 2514–2528 (2009)

Stability-Based Model Selection for High Throughput Genomic Data: An Algorithmic Paradigm[*]

Raffaele Giancarlo[1] and Filippo Utro[2]

[1] Dipartimento di Matematica ed Informatica, University of Palermo,
Via Archirafi 34, 90123 Palermo, Italy
`raffaele@math.unipa.it`
[2] Computational Biology Center, IBM T.J. Watson Research Center,
Yorktown Heights, NY 10598, USA
`futro@us.ibm.com`

Abstract. Clustering is one of the most well known activities in scientific investigation and the object of research in many disciplines, ranging from Statistics to Computer Science. In this beautiful area, one of the most difficult challenges is the *model selection* problem, i.e., the identification of the correct number of clusters in a dataset. In the last decade, a few novel techniques for model selection, representing a sharp departure from previous ones in statistics, have been proposed and gained prominence for microarray data analysis. Among those, the stability-based methods are the most robust and best performing in terms of prediction, but the slowest in terms of time. Unfortunately, this fascinating and classic area of statistics as model selection, with important practical applications, has received very little attention in terms of algorithmic design and engineering. In this paper, in order to partially fill this gap, we highlight: (A) the first general algorithmic paradigm for stability-based methods for model selection; (B) a novel algorithmic paradigm for the class of stability-based methods for cluster validity, i.e., methods assessing how statistically significant is a given clustering solution; (C) a general algorithmic paradigm that describes heuristic and very effective speed-ups known in the Literature for stability-based model selection methods.

1 Introduction

The advent of high throughput technologies, in particular microarrays, for biological research has revived interest in clustering, resulting in a plethora of new clustering algorithms. Indeed, experiments based on them are common practice in biological and medical research to address a wide range of problems, including the classification of tumors [1,2,14,21,32,33,35], where a reliable and precise classification is essential for successful diagnosis and treatment.

---

[*] An extended version of this manuscript appears in [20] and it is presented here as invited contribution to Bio- & Immune- Inspired Algorithms and Models for Multi-Level Complex Systems Workshop within ICARIS 2012.

C.A. Coello Coello et al. (Eds.): ICARIS 2012, LNCS 7597, pp. 260–270, 2012.
© Springer-Verlag Berlin Heidelberg 2012

In the classic statistics and data analysis Literature, there are two essential aspects of clustering: finding a "good" partition of the datasets and estimating the number of clusters, if any, in a dataset. The former problem is usually solved by the use of a clustering algorithm. For recent reviews on clustering algorithms, in particular for biomedical research, the reader is referred to [3,13]. However, the most fundamental issue is the latter problem, referred to as model selection, which is usually solved with the use of internal/relative measures (defined in section 2). The excellent survey by Handl et al. [23] makes the study of those techniques a central part of both research and practice in bioinformatics. It is also worth mentioning that a recent systematic presentation of statistical indices for clustering, with particular attention to microarray data, is given in [18]. Unfortunately, such a beautiful area of statistics has received very little attention both in terms of algorithmic design and engineering. Along with original results, the state of the art regarding those two latter points is described in [19].

The new class of stability-based measures, among others, has gained prominence due to their robustness and predictive power (see [17] and references therein). Although from the theoretic point of view they exhibit shortcomings [4] that seem to be common to other outstanding methods in this area, e.g., the Gap Statistics [38], they work remarkably well in practice. Unfortunately, on benchmark datasets, they also prove to be very slow methods [17], a state that limits their use to datasets with a small aspect ratio, i.e., number of items to classify and number of experimental conditions per item. For one of those stability-based methods, i.e., Consensus Clustering by Monti et al. [31], a speed-up has been proposed [19] that substantially extends the dimensionality spectrum in which that particular method can be used.

The stability-based measures proposed in the Literature have a common root in earlier work by Breckenridge [10] and Breiman [11], which were concerned with cluster validity and classification boosting, respectively, rather than model selection. Common features of those measures have been highlighted by Valentini [40]. In this manuscript, we generalize the techniques due to Breckenridge [10], Breiman [11] and Valentini [40], highlighting a general algorithmic paradigm for stability-based measures able to describe one of the most promising classes of statistical indices known in the Literature.

This paper is organized as follows: section 2 presents a formal statement of the problems we are interested in. For the convenience of the reader, sections 3 and 4 outline essential building blocks of stability-based methods, i.e., data generation procedures and statistical techniques allowing for the establishment of the level of agreement between two clustering solutions. Sections 5-6 and 7 are devoted to the description of the paradigms mentioned earlier. Finally, the last section offers some conclusions.

2   Basic Notions and Definitions

Consider a dataset of n items in a m-dimensional space represented as a data matrix D (of size $n \times m$), in which the rows correspond to the items and the columns to the condition values.

The aim of cluster analysis is to determine a partition of D according to a *similarity/distance* function, with domain D and range $\mathbb{R}_0^+$. There are several ways to formalize such an intuition, depending on the specific objective function one tries to optimize [23]. In what follows, let $P_k = \{p_1, p_2, \ldots, p_k\}$ denote a partition of D obtained via a specific clustering algorithm. Each subset p_i, $1 \le i \le k$, is referred to as a *cluster*, and P_k is referred to as a *clustering solution*.

One of the most fundamental problems in the clustering literature is to assess the "quality" of a clustering solution. It can be expressed in terms of two different methodologies:

(i) *external measure*: they estimate how close the partition of D obtained via a clustering algorithm is to the *reference classification* (or *gold standard solution*). A gold standard solution for a dataset is a partition of the data in a number of classes known a priori. The interested reader is referred to [14,17] for additional details about the notion of gold standard solution.

(ii) *internal measure*: they estimate the quality of a partition according to some suitable criteria using the information contained in D without resorting to external knowledge.

Notice that the two above methodologies try to assess the quality of a clustering solution consisting of k clusters, but they give no indication on what the "correct number" of clusters is. This problem is also referred to as *model selection*. Technically, one is interested in the following:

(iii) *relative measure*: they estimate the relative merits of a set of clustering solutions $P_1, \ldots, P_s$, obtained for instance via the repeated application of a clustering algorithm C. One is interested in identifying the partition that provides the best value for the index. In what follows, let k^* denote the optimal number of clusters according to a given measure.

The interested reader is referred to [25] for a formal definition of the above measures.

2.1 Model Selection with Stability-Based Measures: An Intuitive Description

A "good" clustering algorithm should produce partitions that do not vary much from one sample to another, when data points are repeatedly sampled and clustered. That is, the algorithm must be stable with respect to input randomization. Therefore, the main idea to validate a clustering solution, based on the notion of stability, is to use a measure of the self-consistency of the data, instead of using the classical concepts of isolation and compactness [23,25]. As it will be clear shortly, this framework can be applied to get procedures for (ii) and (iii), since procedures addressing problem (ii) are essential subroutines for those addressing (iii).

In order to obtain a stability-based internal validation method, one needs to specify the following "ingredients":

1. a data generation/pertubation procedure;
2. a similarity measure between partitions;
3. a statistic on cluster stability–it can be used in (ii);
4. rules on how to select the most reliable clustering(s)–it can be used in (iii).

3   Data Generation/Perturbation Techniques

In this section we provide a short description of the most relevant data generation/pertubation methods used in the Literature. The interested reader is referred to [20,39] for an extensive description of each of them. Formally, a data generation/perturbation method can be seen as a procedure, in what follows referred to as DGP, that takes as input a dataset D along with other parameters and returns a new dataset D' of size $n' \times m'$, with $n' \leq n$ and $m' \leq m$.

Subsampling/Bootstrapping is the simplest way to generate a new dataset D' from D, taking random samples from it. Although simple, this approach critically depends on whether the sampling is performed with or without replacement. The former method is referred to as *subsampling* and its aim is to generate a reduced dataset D' that captures the structure (i.e. the right number of clusters) in D. The second method is the well-known *bootstrap* and, although fundamental and of widespread use in statistics [16], it is rarely used in cluster validation as pointed out and discussed in [25,31].

Noise injection is a widely applied perturbation methodology in computer science (see [6,8,27,30,34,41] and reference therein). However, it is not widely applied in clustering. The main idea is to generate D' by adding a random value, i.e., a "perturbation", to each of the elements of D. Perturbations are generated via some random process, i.e., a probability distribution whose parameters can be directly estimated from D.

Randomized dimensionality reduction is an instance of the well known dimensionality reduction class. The technique consists of the use of a family of transformations that try to preserve the distance with an "ε distortion level" between the elements of D. To the best of our knowledge, the Johnson-Lindenstrauss Lemma [26] and *random projections* are the keys to all the randomized dimensionality reduction techniques.

Null models formalize the null hypothesis H_0 "no cluster structure in the data" [24,25]. The most relevant that have been proposed in the clustering Literature [9,22,25,37] are: *unimodality hypothesis, random graph hypothesis, random label hypothesis* and *random position hypothesis*. To the best of our knowledge, only the latter two approaches are suited for microarray data analysis [14,38].

4   Measuring Similarity of Two Partitions

The most used method to assess the similarity of two different partitions of D is via the use of external indices. The interested reader is referred to [12,25] for a detailed description of the use of external indices in cluster analysis.

It is worth pointing out that many stability-based internal validation measures [5,7,10,14] use external indices to establish the similarity between two partitions, one of which is assumed to be the gold standard solution for the dataset, the real one being obviously unknown to the measure. Such a putative gold standard solution is obtained via the use of a classifier/clustering algorithm. The interested reader will find a more detailed discussion about this choice in [14].

5   The Stability Statistic Paradigm

Recall from [25] that a *statistic* is a function of the data capturing useful information about it. In what follows, it is represented by a set S of records. For instance, in its simplest form, a statistic consists of a single real number, while in other cases of interest, it is a one- or two-dimensional array of real numbers.

A statistic assessing cluster stability is, intuitively, a measure of consistency of a clustering solution. The paradigm for the collection of a statistic on cluster stability is best presented as a procedure, reported in Fig. 1. Its input parameters and macro operations are described in abstract form in Figs. 2 and 3, respectively, while its basic steps are described below.

A single iteration of the **while** loop is discussed. The loop is repeated until the condition H is satisfied, i.e., until enough information about the given statistic has been collected. In step 3, a set of perturbed datasets is generated from D_0 by a DGP procedure. In step 4, D_0 and all the datasets generated in the previous step, are split into a learning and training dataset, according to the

---

STABILITY_STATISTIC$(D_0, H, \alpha, \beta, < C_1, C_2, \dots, C_t >, k)$

1   $S_k = \emptyset$;
2   **while** H **do**
3   $\quad$ $< D_1, D_2, \dots, D_l > \leftarrow < \text{DGP}(D_0, \beta), \dots, \text{DGP}(D_0, \beta) >$;
4   $\quad$ $< D_{T,0}, D_{T,1}, \dots, D_{T,l}, D_{L,0}, D_{L,1}, \dots, D_{L,l} > \leftarrow \text{SPLIT}(<$
    $\quad$ $D_0, D_1, \dots, D_l >, \alpha)$;
5   $\quad$ $< G > \leftarrow \text{ASSIGN}(< D_{T,0}, D_{T,1}, \dots, D_{T,l} >, < C_1, C_2, \dots, C_t >)$;
6   $\quad$ $< C_{i_1}, C_{i_2}, \dots, C_{i_q} > \leftarrow \text{TRAIN}(< G >)$;
7   $\quad$ $< \hat{G} > \leftarrow \text{ASSIGN}(< D_{L,0}, D_{L,1}, \dots, D_{L,l} >, < C_1, C_2, \dots, C_t >)$;
8   $\quad$ $< P_1, P_2, \dots, P_z > \leftarrow \text{CLUSTER}(\hat{G}, k)$;
9   $\quad$ $u \leftarrow \text{COLLECT\_STATISTIC}(< P_1, P_2, \dots, P_z >)$;
10 $\quad$ $S_k \leftarrow S_k \bigcup \{u\}$;
11 **return** S_k;

Fig. 1. The STABILITY_STATISTIC procedure

INPUT

- D_0: the input dataset.

- H: a test on the "adequacy" of a statistic S, i.e., it evaluates whether S contains enough information. Note that H could simply be a check as to whether a given number c of iterations has been reached.

- α: a number in the range $[0, 1]$.

- β: a sampling percentage, used by the DGP procedure (described in section 3).

- $< C_1, C_2, \ldots, C_t >$: a set of procedures, each of which is either a classifier or a clustering algorithm.

- k: it is the number of clusters into which a dataset has to be partitioned.

Fig. 2. List of the input parameters used in the STABILITY_STATISTIC procedure

input parameter α. The next two steps train a subset of the classifiers on a subset of the training sets. In step 7, the bipartite graph $\hat{G}$ encodes the association between learning datasets and clustering procedures. In step 8, based on the association encoded by $\hat{G}$, the learning datasets are partitioned. Finally, in step 9, a statistic S_k is computed from those partitions and is given as output.

To the best of our knowledge, there are currently only three incarnations of the stability statistic paradigm: Replicating Analysis due to Breckenridge [10], BagClust1 and BagClust2 due to Dudoit and Fridlyand [15]. In all three cases, the procedures have been proposed to improve a clustering solution for a fixed value of k, rather than to address the model selection problem. The interested reader is referred to [20,39] for a detailed description of each measure and how they can be derived from the STABILITY_STATISTIC procedure.

6   The Stability Measure Paradigm

In this section, the main paradigm of internal stability methods is described. It is best presented as a procedure, reported in Fig. 4. Its macro operations are described in abstract form in Fig. 5, while its basic steps are described below.

For each k in the range $[k_{min}, k_{max}]$ (e.g. $k_{min} = 1$ and $k_{max} = n$), the paradigm collects the statistics S_k computed by the STABILITY_STATISTIC procedure. Then a concise description of S_k, denoted R_k, is computed via the SYNOPSIS procedure. Finally, a prediction of the value of k^* is computed by the SIGNIFICANCE_ANALYSIS procedure and is given as output. There are several incarnations of the stability measure paradigm: Clest [14], Consensus Clustering [31], Levine and Domany [29], Model Explorer [5], MOSRAM [7], Roth et al. [36]. It is worth pointing out that also the Gap Statistics [38], not perceived to be stability-based, is an instance of the stability measure paradigm. The interested reader is referred to [20,39] for a detailed description of each measure and how they can be derived from the STABILITY_MEASURE procedure.

MACRO OPERATIONS

- SPLIT: it takes as input a family of datasets $F_1, F_2, \ldots, F_w$ and a real number $\alpha \in [0, 1]$. The procedure splits each F_i, $1 \leq i \leq w$, into two parts according to α, referred to as *learning* and *training* dataset and denoted with $F_{L,i}$ and $F_{T,i}$, respectively. That is, from each F_i, $\lceil \alpha n_i \rceil$ and $\lfloor (1 - \alpha)n_i \rfloor$ rows are selected in order to obtain the corresponding $F_{T,i}$ and $F_{L,i}$, respectively, where n_i is the number of rows of F_i. Each $F_{T,i}$ and $F_{L,i}$ is given as output.

- ASSIGN: it takes as input a family of datasets and a set of procedures, each of which is either a classifier or a clustering algorithm. It returns a finite set of pairs in which the first element is a dataset and the second one is either a classifier or a clustering algorithm. Such an association is encoded via a bipartite graph G, where the nodes in one partition represent the datasets and the nodes in the other partition the procedures. Notice that the graph is not a matching, i.e., the same dataset can be assigned to different procedures and vice versa.

- TRAIN: it takes as input a set of pairs <dataset, classifier>, encoded as a bipartite graph, analogous to the one just discussed. For each pair, it gives as output the classifier trained with the corresponding dataset. Notice that the number q of trained classifiers returned as output is equal to the number of edges in the input graph.

- CLUSTER: it takes as input a set of pairs <dataset, classifier/clustering algorithm> and a integer $k > 0$. Again, the set is encoded as a bipartite graph. For each pair, it gives as output a partition into k clusters obtained by the classifier/clustering algorithm on the corresponding input dataset. Notice that the number z of partitions returned as output is equal to the number of edges in the input graph.

- COLLECT_STATISTIC: it takes as input a set of partitions. It returns as output the statistic computed on the input set.

Fig. 3. List of the macro operations used in the STABILITY_STATISTIC procedure

7   Approximation Algorithms

The need for very fast algorithms for the computation of stability-based validation measures is evident, as pointed out in [19,28] and well presented in [17,19,39]. To the best of our knowledge, only a speed-up of Consensus Clustering by Giancarlo and Utro [19] is proposed in the Literature.

Here we present the main idea of a general approximation paradigm of the stability-based measures. The idea is to use algorithms that "approximate" the computations involved in the stability-based measures, in the hope that this will grant a speed-up with no substantial loss in predictive accuracy. Intuitively, a large number of clustering solutions, each obtained via a sample of the original dataset, seem to be required in order to identify the correct number of clusters. Indeed, each of the $(k_{max} - k_{min} + 1) \times H$ clustering solutions needed is computed from a *different* sample of the input dataset. However, there is no the-

---

$\text{STABILITY\_MEASURE}(D, H, \alpha, \beta, < C_1, C_2, \ldots, C_t >, k_{min}, k_{max})$

---

1 **for** $k \leftarrow k_{min}$ **to** k_{max} **do**
2     $S_k \leftarrow \text{STABILITY\_STATISTICS}(D, H, \alpha, \beta, < C_1, C_2, \ldots, C_t >, k)$;
3     $R_k \leftarrow \text{SYNOPSIS}(S_k)$;
4 $k^* \leftarrow \text{SIGNIFICANCE\_ANALYSIS}(R_{k_{min}}, \ldots, R_{k_{max}})$;
5 **return** k^*;

Fig. 4. The STABILITY_MEASURE procedure

MACRO OPERATIONS

- SYNOPSIS: it takes as input a statistic and returns as output a concise description of it.

- SIGNIFICANCE_ANALYSIS: it takes as input all the statistics collected, as returned by the SYNOPSIS procedure. It computes the significance level of each statistic. It returns as output, explicitly or implicitly, a prediction about k^*. For instance, an implicit prediction of the value of k^* can be the plot of a histogram or of a curve.

Fig. 5. List of the macro operations used in STABILITY_MEASURE procedure

oretic reason indicating that those clustering solutions must each be generated from distinct samples. It has been also observed that such an approach leads to costly duplications of computations [19], in particular when a measures is used in conjunction with Hierarchical clustering algorithms [25]. Indeed, the ability to quickly compute a clustering solution with k clusters from one with $k + 1$, typical of these agglomerative clustering methods, cannot be used within the measures because, for each k, the dataset changes. The same holds true for divisive methods. Therefore, only H different samples are generated from the input dataset and the $(k_{max} - k_{min} + 1)$ clustering solutions are computed from them using the abilities of the Hierarchical clustering algorithms described above. In this way, the mentioned costly duplications in the computations of an internal stability-based measure are avoided.

8 Conclusion

In conclusion, in this manuscript, we have highlighted:

(A) the first general algorithmic paradigm for stability-based methods for model selection;
(B) a novel algorithmic paradigm for the class of stability-based methods for cluster validity;

(C) the main idea of a general algorithmic paradigm that describes heuristic and very effective speed-ups known in the Literature for stability-based model selection methods.

A detailed description of the results highlighted in this paper is in [20].

References

[1] Alizadeh, A., Eisen, M., Davis, R., Ma, C., Lossos, I., Rosenwald, A., Boldrick, J., Sabet, H., Tran, T., Yu, X., Powell, J., Yang, L., Marti, G., Moore, T., Hudson, J.J., Lu, L., Lewis, D., Tibshirani, R., Sherlock, G., Chan, W., Greiner, T., Weisenburger, D., Armitage, J., Warnke, R., Levy, R., Wilson, W., Grever, M., Byrd, J., Botstein, D., Brown, P., Staudt, L.: Distinct types of diffuse large b-cell lymphoma identified by gene expression profiling. Nature 403, 503–511 (2000)

[2] Alon, U., Barkai, N., Notterman, D., Gish, K., Ybarra, S., Mack, D., Levine, A.: Broad patterns of gene expression revealed by clustering analysis of tumor and normal colon tissues probed by oligonucleotide arrays. Proceedings of the National Academy of Sciences of the United States of America 96, 6745–6750 (1999)

[3] Andreopoulos, B., An, A., Wang, X., Schroeder, M.: A roadmap of clustering algorithms: finding a match for a biomedical application. Briefings in Bioinformatics 10(3), 297–314 (2009)

[4] Ben-David, S., von Luxburg, U., Pál, D.: A Sober Look at Clustering Stability. In: Lugosi, G., Simon, H.U. (eds.) COLT 2006. LNCS (LNAI), vol. 4005, pp. 5–19. Springer, Heidelberg (2006)

[5] Ben-Hur, A., Elisseeff, A., Guyon, I.: A stability based method for discovering structure in clustering data. In: Seventh Pacific Symposium on Biocomputing, ISCB, pp. 6–17 (2002)

[6] Benesty, J., Morgan, D., Sondhi, M.: A better understanding and an improved solution to the problems of stereophonic acoustic echo cancellation. In: ICASSP 1997: Proceedings of the 1997 IEEE International Conference on Acoustics, Speech, and Signal Processing (ICASSP 1997), vol. 1, p. 303. IEEE Computer Society (1997)

[7] Bertoni, A., Valentini, G.: Model order selection for bio-molecular data clustering. BMC Bioinformatics 8 (2007)

[8] Bittner, M., Meltzer, P., Chen, Y., Jiang, Y., Seftor, E., Hendrix, M., Radmacher, M., Simon, R., Yakhini, Z., Ben-Dor, A., Sampas, N., Dougherty, E., Wang, E., Marincola, F., Gooden, C., Lueders, J., Glatfelter, A., Pollock, P., Carpten, J., Gillanders, E., Leja, D., Dietrich, K., Beaudry, C., Berens, M., Alberts, D., Sondak, V.: Molecular classification of cutaneous malignant melanoma by gene expression profiling. Nature 406, 536–540 (2000)

[9] Bock, H.: On some significance tests in cluster analysis. Journal of Classification 2, 77–108 (1985)

[10] Breckenridge, J.: Replicating cluster analysis: Method, consistency, and validity. Multivariate Behavioral Research 24(2), 147–161 (1989)

[11] Breiman, L.: Bagging predictors. Machine Learning 24, 123–140 (1996)

[12] Chen, J., Lonardi, S.: Biological Data Mining. Chapman & Hall (2009)

[13] D'haeseleer, P.: How does gene expression cluster work? Nature Biotechnology 23, 1499–1501 (2006)

[14] Dudoit, S., Fridlyand, J.: A prediction-based resampling method for estimating the number of clusters in a dataset. Genome Biology 3 (2002)

[15] Dudoit, S., Fridlyand, J.: Bagging to improve the accuracy of a clustering procedure. Bioinformatics 19(9), 1090–1099 (2003)

[16] Efron, B., Tibshirani, R.: An Introduction to the Bootstrap. Chapman & Hall, London (1993)

[17] Giancarlo, R., Scaturro, D., Utro, F.: Computational cluster validation for microarray data analysis: experimental assessment of Clest, Consensus Clustering, Figure of Merit, Gap Statistics and Model Explorer. BMC Bioinformatics 9, 462 (2008)

[18] Giancarlo, R., Scaturro, D., Utro, F.: Statistical indices for computational and data driven class discovery in microarray data. In: Chen, J.Y., Lonardi, S. (eds.) Biological Data Mining, pp. 295–335. CRC Press, San Francisco (2009)

[19] Giancarlo, R., Utro, F.: Speeding up the Consensus Clustering methodology for microarray data analysis. Algorithms for Molecular Biology 6, 1 (2011)

[20] Giancarlo, R., Utro, F.: Algorithmic paradigms for stability-based cluster validity and model selection statistical methods, with applications to microarray data analysis. Theoretical Computer Science 428, 58–79 (2012)

[21] Golub, T., Slonim, D., Tamayo, P., Huard, C., Gaasenbeeck, M., Mesirov, J., Coller, H., Loh, M., Downing, J., Caligiuri, M., Bloomfield, C., Lander, E.: Molecular classification of cancer: Class discovery and class prediction by gene expression monitoring. Science 286(5439), 531–537 (1999)

[22] Gordon, A.: Null models in cluster validation. In: From Data to Knowledge: Theoretical and Practical Aspects of Classification, pp. 32–44. Springer (1996)

[23] Handl, J., Knowles, J., Kell, D.: Computational cluster validation in Post-genomic data analysis. Bioinformatics 21(15), 3201–3212 (2005)

[24] Hastie, T., Tibshirani, R., Friedman, J.: The Elements of Statistical Learning. Springer (2003)

[25] Jain, A., Dubes, R.: Algorithms for Clustering Data. Prentice-Hall, Englewood Cliffs (1988)

[26] Johnson, W., Lindenstrauss, J.: Extensions of Lipschitz mappings into a Hilbert space. Contemp. Math. 26, 189–206 (1984)

[27] Kerr, M., Churchill, G.: Bootstrapping cluster analysis: Assessing the reliability of conclusions from microarray experiments. PNAS 98, 8961–8965 (2000)

[28] Kraus, J., Kestler, H.: A highly efficient multi-core algorithm for clustering extremely large datasets. BMC Bioinformatics 11 (2010)

[29] Levine, E., Domany, E.: Resampling method for unsupervised estimation of cluster validity. Neural Computation 13, 2573–2593 (2001)

[30] McShane, L., Radmacher, M., Freidlin, B., Yu, R., Li, M.C., Simon, R.: Methods for assessing reproducibility of clustering patterns observed in analyses of microarray data. Bioinformatics 18, 1462–1469 (2002)

[31] Monti, S., Tamayo, P., Mesirov, J., Golub, T.: Consensus clustering: A resampling-based method for class discovery and visualization of gene expression microarray data. Machine Learning 52, 91–118 (2003)

[32] Perou, C., Jeffrey, S., van de Rijn, M., Rees, C., Eisen, M., Ross, D., Pergamen-schikov, A., Williams, C., Zhu, S., Lee, J., Lashkari, D., Shalon, D., Brown, P., Botstein, D.: Distinctive gene expression patterns in human mammary epithelial cells and breast cancers. Proceedings of the National Academy of Sciences of the United States of America 96, 9212–9217 (1999)

[33] Pollack, J., Perou, C., Alizadeh, A., Eisen, M., Amd, C.F., Williams, A.P., Jeffrey, S., Botstein, D., Brown, P.: Genome-wide analysis of DNA copy-number changes using cDNA microarrays. Nature Genetics 23, 41–46 (1999)

[34] Raviv, Y., Intrator, N.: Bootstrapping with noise: An effective regularization tech-nique. Connection Science 8, 355–372 (1996)

[35] Ross, D., Scherf, U., Eisen, M., Perou, C., Spellman, P., Iyer, V., Jeffrey, S., van de Rijn, M., Walthama, M., Pergamenschikov, A., Lee, J., Lashkari, D., Shalon, D., Myers, T., Weistein, J., Botstein, D., Brown, P.: Systematic variation in gene expression patterns in human cancer cell lines. Nature Genetics 24, 227–235 (2000)

[36] Roth, V., Lange, T., Braun, M., Buhmann, J.: A resampling approach to cluster validation. In: Proceedings 15th Symposium in Computational Statistics, pp. 123–128 (2002)

[37] Sarle, W.: Cubic clustering criterion. Tech. rep., SAS (1983)

[38] Tibshirani, R., Walther, G., Hastie, T.: Estimating the number of clusters in a dataset via the gap statistics. Journal Royal Statistical Society B 2, 411–423 (2001)

[39] Utro, F.: Algorithms for internal validation clustering measures in the Post-genomic era, Doctoral Dissertation, University of Palermo (2011), http://arxiv.org/abs/1102.2915v1

[40] Valentini, G.: Mosclust: a software library for discovering significant structures in bio-molecular data. Bioinformatics 23, 387–389 (2007)

[41] Wolfinger, R., Gibson, G., Wolfinger, E., Bennet, L., Hamadeh, H., Bushel, C., Paules, R.: Assessing gene significance from cDNA microarray expression data via mixed models. Journal of Computational Biology, 625–637 (2001)

Towards an Evolutionary Procedure for Reverse-Engineering Biological Networks

Alberto Castellini, Vincenzo Manca, and Mauro Zucchelli

Verona University, Dept. of Computer Science,
Strada Le Grazie 15, 37134 Verona, Italy
{alberto.castellini,vincenzo.manca}@univr.it,
mauro.zucchelli@studenti.univr.it

Abstract. Metabolic P systems are a modeling framework for metabolic, regulatory and signaling processes. The synthesis of flux regulation functions from time series of substance concentrations is a key task for reverse-engineering biological systems by MP systems. In this paper we present some important improvements to a technique based on genetic algorithms and multiple linear regression for the synthesis of regulation functions. An accurate analysis of generated functions, for the case study of the mitotic oscillator in early amphibian embryos, shows that some knowledge about the regulation mechanisms of biological processes can be inferred from experimental data using this methodology.

1 Introduction

Biochemical systems are characterized by an intrinsic complexity due to interactions among thousands of different molecular species. Unreveling such complex interactions and understanding the internal logic of metabolic, regulatory and signaling processes is very important for dealing with the current challenges of biology and medicine. The current availability of tools for massive data acquisition in molecular and cellular biology enables scientists to tackle this problem by data-centric approaches mainly based on quantitative mathematical modeling [6].

A model is a mathematical tool representing in a formal way some knowledge, usually acquired from sets of quantitative observations, about a specific process. For instance, changes in concentration of substances involved in a metabolic process can be described by a model, as a function of their regulatory interactions. The effectiveness of a model lies in its capability to formalize the knowledge about the biochemical process under investigation, to predict the behavior of the biochemical process in yet untested conditions, and to identify inconsistencies between hypotheses and observations, so as to drive new experiments [2]. Reverse-engineering techniques are used to infer model structure and parameters directly from experimental data.

A variety of mathematical formalisms have been proposed in literature [6,17] (e.g., continuous vs discrete frameworks, static vs dynamical frameworks, deterministic vs stochastic frameworks) and Ordinary Differential Equations (ODEs)

C.A. Coello Coello et al. (Eds.): ICARIS 2012, LNCS 7597, pp. 271–285, 2012.

are one of the most common frameworks for dynamical modeling. An important line of research in systems biology [1,18] aims at defining new classes of discrete models which avoid ODEs limitations.

Metabolic P systems (shortly MP systems) [8,9] are a modeling framework based on P systems [16] and introduced for modeling metabolic processes by means of multiset rewriting grammars. An MP model is mainly composed of a set of *substances* $X = \{x_1, x_2, \ldots, x_n\}$ (e.g., blue circles H, O and $H2O$ in Figure 1), a set of *reactions* $R = \{r_1, r_2, \ldots, r_m\}$ (e.g., grey circles R_1 and R_2 in Figure 1) and a set of chemo-physical *parameters* $V = \{v_1, v_2, \ldots, v_k\}$ (not reported in Figure 1). Reactions act as rewriting rules transforming at each step a certain amount of substances which is tuned by suitable *regulation functions* $\Phi = \{\varphi_1, \ldots, \varphi_m\}$ (e.g., red rectangles F_1 and F_2 in Figure 1). Given an initial state $X[0] \in \mathbb{R}^n$, the *dynamics* of an MP system is computed by the vector recurrent equation *EMA[i]* (*Equational Metabolic Algorithm*):

$$X[i+1] = X[i] + \mathbb{A} \times U[i]. \tag{1}$$

where $\mathbb{A}$ is the *stoichiometric matrix*, $U[i] = (\varphi_1(Z[i]), \ldots, \varphi_m(Z[i]))'$ is the *flux vector*, and $Z[i] = (X[i], V[i]) \in \mathbb{R}^{n+k}$ is the *state* vector of substances and parameters at time i. This equation provides the "next" state of the system (i.e. $X[i+1] \in \mathbb{R}^n$) by adding to the "current" state (i.e., $X[i] \in R^n$) a delta factor $\mathbb{A} \times U[i]$, representing the contribution of each reaction to the variation of each substance.

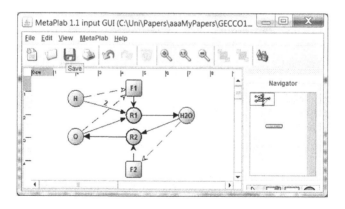

Fig. 1. A graphical representation of a toy MP system having three substances, i.e. H, O and H_2O, two reactions, i.e. R_1 and R_2 and two regulation functions F_1 and F_2.

A key problem in MP modeling concerns with the synthesis of a set of flux regulation functions $\varphi_1, \ldots, \varphi_m$ able to regenerate an observed dynamics $Z^{obs} = (Z^{obs}[i], i = 1, \ldots, t)$ of substances and parameters, where $Z^{obs}[i] = (X^{obs}[i], V^{obs}[i])$ and t is the number of observations [3,11]. Three techniques have been proposed so far to solve this problem. One is based on neural networks [4,3], the second uses *stepwise regression* [11,12,13,14], and the third employs genetic algorithms and multiple linear regression [5].

Here we present some key improvements to the third technique, and we analyze the regulation functions generated for a mitotic oscillator, in order to evaluate the ability of our methodology to infer knowledge from data.

2   Methods

2.1   The Evolutionary Approach

The methodology presented in [5] generates regulation functions in the form of linear combinations of some predefined functions. The set of predefined function is called *dictionary of primitive functions* and each primitive function is also called *regressor*. Genetic algorithms are used as a variable selection technique to identify the best set of primitive functions for each regulation function. Multiple linear regression is employed to compute primitive function coefficients. The main elements of our methodology are listed and briefly explained in the following.

Encoding. In order to describe the subsets of regressors employed by each regulation function we use a vector K, called *chromosome*, such that

$$K = (k_j \in \{0,1\}, j = 1, \ldots, m \cdot d), \tag{2}$$

where d is the number of regressors in the dictionary, $k_j = 0$ if the $(j\%d)$-th regressor is not present in regulation function $\varphi_{(j/m)+1}$ (/ and % are, respectively, the integer division and the rest of the integer division), and $k_j = 1$ if the $(j\%d)$-th regressor is present in $\varphi_{(j/m)+1}$. Figure 2 shows a graphical representation of a chromosome K for an MP system having 7 regulation functions (i.e., $m = 7$) and 6 possible regressors (i.e., $d = 6$).

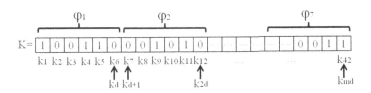

Fig. 2. Chromosome K encoding the subsets of regressors selected in an MP system having 7 regulation functions (i.e., $m = 7$) and 6 possible regressors (i.e., $d = 6$). Function φ_1, for instance, uses the 1st, the 4th and the 5th regressors since $k_1 = k_4 = k_5 = 1$ and $k_2 = k_3 = k_6 = 0$. Function φ_2 uses the 3rd, and the 5th regressors since $k_9 = k_{11} = 1$ and $k_7 = k_8 = k_{10} = k_{12} = 0$ [5].

Fitness Evaluation. Given an MP system M and an observed dynamics $Z^{obs} = (Z^{obs}[i], i = 1, \ldots, t)$, a chromosome K is evaluated by computing:

– the *simulation error* of K, namely, the root mean square error ($RMSE$) between Z^{obs} and Z^{sim} over the first s steps ($s \leq t$) of the dynamics:

$$e_{sim}(K) = \sqrt{\frac{\sum_{j=1}^{n+k} \sum_{i=1}^{s} (Z_j^{obs}[i] - Z_j^{sim}[i])^2}{s \cdot (n+k)}} \quad (3)$$

where $Z_j^{obs}[i]$ ($Z_j^{sim}[i]$) is the state of the j-th element (i.e., a substance or a parameter) at step i of the observed (simulated) dynamics. The simulated dynamics is computed using the regressors selected by chromosome K. Regressor coefficients are estimated by multiple linear regression, employing a *stoichiometric expansion* [11] of the *EMA* equation, which will be described in a future work;

– the *total error* of K, by adding to e_{sim} the weighted contribution of term $e_{\#1}(K) = \sum_{i=1}^{m \cdot d} k_i$, which is the number of 1s in chromosome K (i.e., the number of regressors in the overall model):

$$e_{tot}(K) = e_{sim}(K) + w \cdot e_{\#1}(K) \quad (4)$$

where $w \in \mathbb{R}_0^+$.

Errors $e_{sim}(K)$ and $e_{tot}(K)$ are the fitness functions (to be minimized) used in different stages of our evolutionary process. In fact, we split the evolutionary process in two stages: *(i)* a *start-up* stage, in which only the simulation error is evaluated and the observed dynamics is considered *incrementally* (i.e., $s \leq t$ in Equation (3)); *(ii)* a *main* stage, in which the total error is evaluated and all the t steps of the observed dynamics are always considered (i.e., $s = t$ in Equation (3)). This is because at the beginning of the evolutionary process we have random chromosomes that are unable to reproduce the entire observed dynamics and they accumulate simulation errors which are too large to be dealt with (i.e., infinite or *NaN* values). For this reason, at the beginning of the *start-up* stage we consider only three steps of the observed dynamics (i.e., $s = 3$) and we search chromosomes able to reproduce only these few steps, which is quite a simple task. Subsequently, we increment s, step by step, until all the t steps of the observed dynamics are considered (i.e., $s = t$). This methodology enabled us to generate models providing simulation dynamics very similar to the observed dynamics, as shown in Section 3.

Chromosome Selection. A population of N random chromosomes is generated at the beginning of the evolutionary process (see Figure 3). Afterwards, chromosomes are iteratively selected by *rank selection with elitist replacement* and recombined in order to improve their fitness [15].

Genetic Operators. The chromosome population is evolved by means of two genetic operators (see Figure 3), namely, *crossover* and *mutation*. *Single point crossover* is performed with a probability p_{cross}. The output of this operation is a new couple of chromosomes that are subsequently mutated and inserted in the new population of chromosomes. Mutation is a very important operator in our approach since it makes possible to generate regulation functions incorporating some biological *a-priori* knowledge.

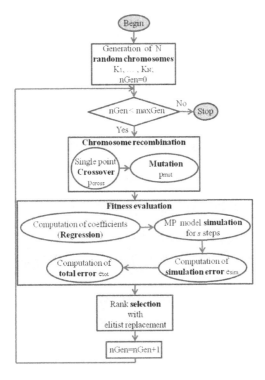

Fig. 3. Overview of the evolutionary process

2.2   An Adaptive Strategy to Minimize the Number of Regressors

The evolutionary strategy described above performs a search in a $(m \cdot d)$-dimensional space in order to find a set of regressors, for each $\varphi_i, i = 1, ..., m$, which minimizes the error e_{tot}. It turns out that parameter w in Equation (4) strongly influences the searching process. In particular, by setting $w = 0$ we achieve only the minimization of the simulation error e_{sim}, while by setting $w > 0$ we obtain the simultaneous minimization of both the simulation error e_{sim} and the number of regressors $e_{\#1}$. The greater the w, the greater the influence of term $e_{\#1}$ in the total error. In our first experiments we noticed that using very large values of w we achieved regulation functions having only few terms (i.e., primitive functions) but the simulated dynamics was quite different from the observed dynamics. On the other hand, using too small values of w we generated regulation functions able to accurately regenerate the observed dynamics but using a very large number of regressors. In order to achieve a good trade-off between simulation error and number of regressors we developed an adaptive strategy, described in the following, for tuning the value of w.

During the entire start-up stage w is set to 0, while during the main stage, the parameter is increased of 0.00001 at each evolutionary step. The increasing continues until the simulation error exceeds the threshold $thr1 = 5e_{sim}^m$, where

e_{sim}^m is the minor simulation error reached until that step. Then, the value of w is kept constant until the simulation error becomes lesser than a second threshold $thr_2 = e_{sim}^m$. When this threshold is reached, the parameter w starts to be increased again and e_{sim}^m is updated.

Using this strategy, at the beginning of the main phase the parameter w usually grows for some evolutionary steps, causing the elimination of some useless regressors from the regulation functions generated in the start-up phase. When the most of the useless regressors have been removed some fundamental regressors are eliminated too, causing the increase of the simulation error. If this increase is "too big" (w.r.t. threshold thr_1), then the growth of w is stopped and the evolutionary process is carried on, in order to bring the simulation error under the threshold thr_2. At that point w starts to be increased again. Results reported in Section 3 were achieved using this strategy.

2.3   Definition of a New Dictionary of Primitive Functions

As explained above, our evolutionary methodology generates regulation functions by putting together, in a linear form, a set of regressors chosen from a "dictionary of primitive functions". The definition of such a dictionary is an important step, since the performance of the generated model, in term of prediction accuracy and capability to formalize biological knowledge, depends on primitive functions.

In [5] we employed a dictionary containing all the monomials with degree -1, 1, 2 and rational monomials of substances in the system. For instance, given a system with substances A and B, the dictionary contained functions A, A^2, $A \cdot B$, $1/A$, A/B, etc. Here, after an analysis of results achieved in [5], we propose to substitute monomials with degree -1 and rational monomials with Hill functions, having the form $\frac{x_i}{\alpha + x_i}$, where x_i is a substance concentration and $\alpha \in \mathbb{R}^+$. These functions have very interesting mathematical properties that make them act as switches. For $x_i = 0$ (i.e., null concentration of substance x_i) their outputs are 0; for $0 < x_i < 100 \cdot \alpha$ their outputs draw a transition from 0 to 1; for $x_i > 100\alpha$ they tend to 1. Moreover, this family of functions has strong biological bases, since it represents one of the simplest and best-known models of enzyme kinetics, i.e., the Michaelis-Menten kinetics. Our experiments show that Hill functions are often selected by the evolutionary procedure and they determine substantial improvements of simulation errors with respect to [5].

3   Experiments and Results

The methodology presented in the last section was first tested on the case study of the *mitotic oscillator in early amphibian embryos* in [5]. Here we report an exhaustive analysis of the regulation functions generated by using *i)* the new adaptive strategy to minimize the number of regressors (see Section 2.2), and *ii)* a dictionary containing Hill functions (see Section 2.3).

3.1 A Brief Introduction to the Mitotic Oscillator

Many cellular changes related to mitosis are triggered by the fluctuations in the activation state of a protein kinase produced by *cdc2* gene in fission yeast and by homologs in other eukaryotes. The simplest form of this mechanism has been observed in early amphibian embryos. In 1991 Goldbeter proposed a minimal model, based on ordinary differential equations (ODE), for the mitotic oscillator [7]. According to this model, the signal protein *cyclin* is produced at a constant rate v_i and controls the activation rate of *cdc2 kinase*, which is considered both in its active (symbol M) and inactive (symbol Mp) form in the model. *Cdc2 kinase* deactivation is performed at a rate V_2 by another kinase which is not considered in the model. The model also represents active (symbol X) and inactive (symbol Xp) forms of *cyclin protease* whose activation is promoted by active *cdc2 kinase*.

In [10] an MP system with an equivalent dynamics to the Goldbeter's model was defined. This model, displayed on top-left of Figure 4, has five substances, namely, C, X, Xp, M and Mp, and seven reactions $R_1, \ldots, R_7$ that determine the stoichiometry of the system. Regulation functions created from differential equations are reported on top-right of Figure 4, and the oscillatory dynamics generated by simulating the MP model for 150,000 steps, with a time interval $\tau = 0.06$ sec, is shown in the bottom of Figure 4. Here our (reverse-engineering) goal is to synthesize, using only a sampled version of the observed dynamics, a set of regulation functions able to regenerate this dynamics. Moreover, we would like the synthesized functions convey some knowledge about the regulation mechanism they govern.

3.2 Tests

We run our evolutionary algorithm 20 times and we analyzed the 10 tests having the smaller simulation errors, corresponding to the set of regulation functions which regenerate the observed dynamics with the best accuracy. Table 1 reports the simulation error of each test, and their mean and standard deviation. Our hypothesis is that, since these functions are able to regenerate the observed dynamics, they should contain in their structure (i.e., function form and coefficients) some knowledge about regulation mechanisms that produced the dynamics.

Simulation accuracy of these tests is very good. Figure 5 shows, for instance, the comparison between the target dynamics (circles) and the dynamics generated by the regulation functions of test 2, which has the smallest simulation error (i.e., 0.0063). This error is much lower than the error achieved in [5] (i.e., 0.0151) due to the new dictionary of primitive functions and the adaptive strategy for tuning parameter w. In both cases the number of used regressors is very small ($e_{\#1} = 20$).

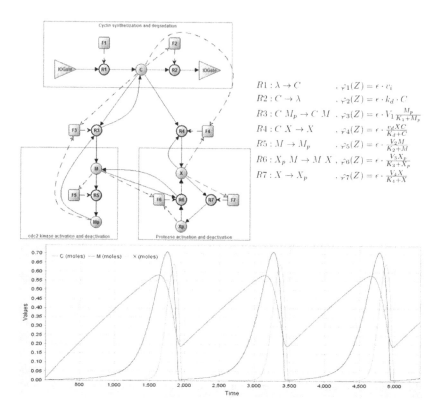

$$R1 : \lambda \to C \qquad \cdot \gamma_1(Z) = \epsilon \cdot v_i$$
$$R2 : C \to \lambda \qquad \cdot \gamma_2(Z) = \epsilon \cdot k_d \cdot C$$
$$R3 : C\,M_p \to C\,M \quad \cdot \gamma_3(Z) = \epsilon \cdot V_1 \frac{M_p}{K_1 + M_p}$$
$$R4 : C\,X \to X \qquad \cdot \gamma_4(Z) = \epsilon \cdot \frac{v_d X C}{K_d + C}$$
$$R5 : M \to M_p \qquad \cdot \gamma_5(Z) = \epsilon \cdot \frac{V_2 M}{K_2 + M}$$
$$R6 : X_p\,M \to M\,X \,, \, \gamma_6(Z) = \epsilon \cdot \frac{V_3 X_p}{K_3 + X_p}$$
$$R7 : X \to X_p \qquad \cdot \gamma_7(Z) = \epsilon \cdot \frac{V_4 X}{K_4 + X}$$

Fig. 4. Target model. An MP system for the mitotic oscillator in early amphibian embryos (on top-left); the related regulation functions (on top-right); the dynamics of the system (in the bottom) achieved from initial conditions $C = 0.01 \mu M$, $M = 0.01$ and $X = 0.01$. Regulation function constants: $\epsilon = 0.001$, $v_i = 0.025 \ \mu M \cdot min^{-1}$, $k_d = 0.01 \ min^{-1}$, $V_1 = \frac{C}{K_c + C} V_{M1}$, $V_2 = 1.5$, $V_3 = M V_{M3}$, $V_4 = 0.5$, $V_{M1} = 3.0$, $V_{M3} = 1$, $K_i = 0.005$, $i = 1, \ldots, 4$, $v_d = 0.25 \ \mu M \cdot min^{-1}$, $K_d = 0.02 \ \mu M$, $K_c = 0.5 \ \mu M$.

Table 1. Simulation errors for 10 tests of our reverse-engineering procedure

Test	e_{sim}
1	0.0141
2	0.0063
3	0.0143
4	0.0114
5	0.0090
6	0.0113
7	0.0115
8	0.0128
9	0.0075
10	0.0140
μ/σ	0.0112/0.0028

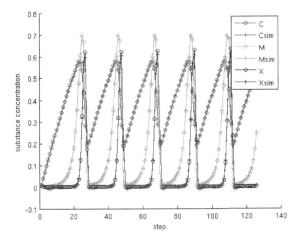

Fig. 5. Comparison between the target dynamics (circles) and the dynamics generated using regulation functions of test 2 (crosses)

3.3   Analysis of Synthesized Regulation Functions

Each test of Table 1 generated a different set of regulation functions $\varphi_1, \ldots, \varphi_7$, since the genetic selection of regressors is stochastic. Here, we analyze these sets of functions in order to understand if they share a common logic and if it is possible to extract some knowledge from this logic. Figure 6 shows heat maps of primitive function coefficients. Each heat map concerns a specific regulation function. Columns represent primitive functions and rows represent single runs (said also tests) of the evolutionary procedure. Notice that the dictionary of primitive functions contains: first order terms (i.e., C, M and X), second order terms (i.e., C^2, M^2, X^2, $C \cdot M$, $C \cdot X$, $M \cdot X$), Hill functions with different transition speed (i.e., $C/(C + 0.5)$, $M/(M + 0.5)$, $X/(X + 0.5)$, $C/(C + 0.05)$, $M/(M+0.05)$, $X/(X+0.05)$, $C/(C+0.005)$, $M/(M+0.005)$, $X/(X+0.005)$) and a constant term (i.e., 1). Substances Mp and Xp, which represent the inactive forms of M and X respectively, were not considered because they are highly correlated with their active forms (i.e., $Mp = 1 - M$, $Xp = 1 - X$), and they would have brought problems of multicollinearity. The generic cell i, j of the heat map contains the coefficient assigned to the j-th primitive function in the i-th test of the evolutionary procedure. From the figure we can see that there exist some regressors which are selected by several tests for a certain regulation function. For instance, regressor M is selected by 5 tests out of 10 in φ_4, and in all the tests the coefficient is negative (black cells). On the other hand, regressor $M/(M + 0.5)$ is selected by 4 tests out of 10 in φ_4, and the coefficient is always positive (white cells). Similar behaviors can be observed in φ_5, where white vertical lines appear for regressors M^2 and X^2, while regressor $C \cdot M$ has always negative coefficients (dark gray line).

From a quantitative analysis of regressor coefficients (see Table 2) we have identified, for each regulation function, the set of regressors that were selected

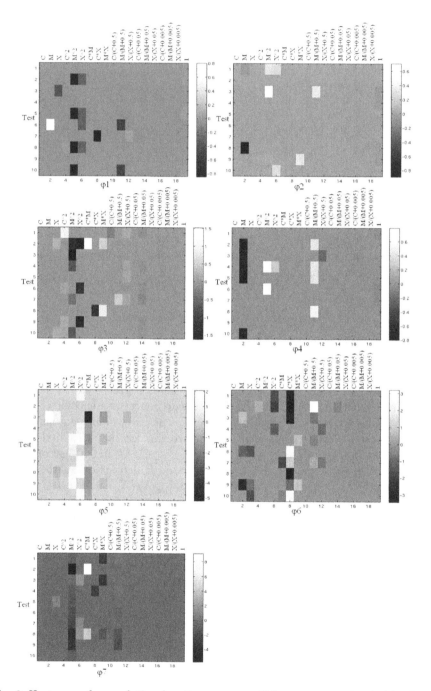

Fig. 6. Heat maps for regulation functions $\varphi_1 - \varphi_7$. Columns represent primitive functions, rows represent single tests of the evolutionary procedure. Cell i, j is colored from white to black according to the coefficient assigned to the j-th primitive function in the i-th test of the evolutionary procedure.

Table 2. Statistical analysis of regressor coefficients. For each regressor (row) and regulation function (column) it is reported the number of tests in which the regressor has been selected for this regulation function (# sel) and the mean and standard deviation of coefficients assigned to that regressor (μ/σ).

Regressor	φ_1		φ_2		φ_3		φ_4		φ_5		φ_6		φ_7	
	# sel	μ/σ	# sel	μ/σ	# sel	μ/σ	# sel	μ/σ	# sel	μ/σ	# sel	μ/σ	# sel	μ/σ
C	0	0/0	0	0/0	0	0/0	0	0/0	1	-0.04/0	1	0.1/0	3	0.01/0.03
M	1	0.8/0	2	-0.5/0.4	2	0.2/0.04	6	-0.6/0.3	1	2/0	3	-1/2	0	0/0
X	1	-0.4/0	0	0/0	4	0.4/0.3	0	0/0	4	-0.03/0.6	3	-1/0.3	1	1/0
C^2	1	0.05/0	1	0.01/0	5	-0.9/0.4	0	0/0	3	-0.2/0.07	1	0.5/0	0	0/0
M^2	4	-0.8/0.02	3	0.4/0.3	3	-1/0.2	2	0.8/3e-16	5	0.9/0.4	0	0/0	9	-2/2
X^2	4	-0.3/0.01	2	0.3/0.0008	1	2/0	1	0.3/0	6	1/0.3	3	-2/0.3	3	2/0.2
$C \cdot M$	0	0/0	0	0/0	2	-1/0	0	0/0	7	-2/1	2	-1/0.7	2	7/2
$C \cdot X$	1	-0.8/0	0	0/0	3	0.7/0.2	0	0/0	0	0/0	8	-0.9/2	1	-3/0
$M \cdot X$	0	0/0	1	0.4/0	3	-0.08/0.1	0	0/0	3	-0.8/0.3	2	0.9/0.03	3	-2/0.8
$C/(C+0.5)$	0	0/0	0	0/0	1	0.5/0	1	0.02/0	0	0/0	0	0/0	1	-0.02/0
$M/(M+0.5)$	2	-0.5/1e-15	1	0.4/0	4	0.1/0.02	4	0.5/0.04	0	0/0	4	0.6/2	5	-0.6/0.7
$X/(X+0.5)$	1	0.06/0	0	0/0	0	0/0	1	-0.2/0	1	-0.6/0	2	-0.8/0.1	0	0/0
$C/(C+0.05)$	1	-0.02/0	0	0/0	6	-0.09/0.04	0	0/0	0	0/0	1	-0.03/0	0	0/0
$M/(M+0.05)$	0	0/0	0	0/0	0	0/0	0	0/0	3	0.05/0.01	1	-0.4/0	0	0/0
$X/(X+0.05)$	1	-0.02/0	0	0/0	0	0/0	0	0/0	0	0/0	0	0/0	0	0/0
$C/(C+0.005)$	0	0/0	0	0/0	0	0/0	0	0/0	0	0/0	0	0/0	0	0/0
$M/(M+0.005)$	0	0/0	0	0/0	0	0/0	0	0/0	0	0/0	2	-0.009/0.02	0	0/0
$X/(X+0.005)$	0	0/0	0	0/0	0	0/0	0	0/0	0	0/0	0	0/0	0	0/0
1	3	0.03/2e-17	4	-0.03/0.002	2	0.02/0.02	3	-0.03/0.005	0	0/0	0	0/0	0	0/0

most frequently (highlighted cells in Table 2), and the mean and standard deviation of their coefficients over the 10 tests (column μ/σ in Table 2). It turns out that some regressors are selected in the majority of the tests, such as, regressor $M/(M + 0.05)$ in φ_3 (6 selections), regressor M in φ_4 (6 selections), regressors X^2 and $C \cdot M$ in φ_5 (6 and 7 selections respectively), regressor $C \cdot X$ in φ_6 (8 selections), and regressor M^2 in φ_7 (9 selections). Many of these regressors have also a good concordance of coefficient values; for instance, regressor M^2 has a negative coefficient in all the 9 tests in which it is selected in φ_7 (see Figure 6 and column μ/σ in Table 2). Other regressors are never selected, such as, $C/(C + 0.005)$ and $X/(X + 0.005)$, or they are selected only a few times. These results show that the proposed methodology is able to discriminate between informative and not-informative primitive functions, and to select highly informative functions.

We notice that the arguments of the regulation functions synthesized from dynamics data seem to agree only partially with the arguments of the original regulation functions reported in Figure 4. This could be due to several reasons, in the following we report a couple of them. First of all, to decrease the number

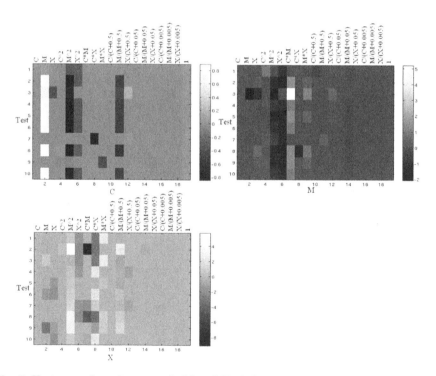

Fig. 7. Heat maps for substances C, M and X. Columns represent primitive functions, rows represent single tests of the evolutionary procedure. Cell i, j is colored from white to black according to the sum of coefficients assigned to the j-th primitive function by all the regulation functions which directly affect the substance, in the i-th test of the evolutionary procedure.

of observations, we sampled the original dynamics with a sampling interval of 1200 points, corresponding to observe the system every 72 sec instead of every 0.06 sec [5], and fluxes are surely influenced by this modification. Second, we observe that in some cases a regressor can be put in more than a single regulation function without affecting the resulting dynamics. Let us explain this concept by a simple example. Substance C is affected by reactions $R1$, $R2$ and $R4$ (see Figure 4), thus the constant term $\epsilon \cdot v_i$ which is added to C at each step by φ_1 in the original set of regulation functions, could be moved to regulation functions φ_2 or φ_4, by changing its sign, without affecting the dynamics of the system.

If we examine functions φ_1, φ_2 and φ_4 in Table 2 we observe that the constant regressor (symbol "1") is selected 3 times in φ_1 with a mean coefficient of 0.03, 4 times in φ_2 with a mean coefficient of -0.03 and 3 times in φ_4 with a mean coefficient of -0.03. We recomputed heat maps and Table 2 using a substance-centric view, that is, given a substance and a regressor we summed together the coefficients of this regressor for every regulation function affecting the substance variation over time. Results are shown in Figure 7 and Table 3 respectively, and show very clearly that the constant regressor (symbol "1") was selected for substance C in 10 tests out of 10, with a mean coefficient of 0.03 and a very small

Table 3. Statistical analysis of regressor coefficients. For each regressor (row) and substance (column) it is reported the number of tests in which the regressor has been selected in a regulation function which directly influences that substance concentration (# sel) and the mean and standard deviation of the sum of coefficients assigned to that regressor in a regulation function which directly influences that substance concentration (μ/σ).

Regressor	C # sel	C μ/σ	M # sel	M μ/σ	X # sel	X μ/σ
C	0	0/0	1	0.037/0	4	0.026/0.070
M	9	0.63/0.32	1	-2.08/0	3	-1.04/1.54
X	1	-0.38/0	6	0.098/0.46	4	-1.24/0.31
C^2	2	0.019/0.034	7	0.31/0.28	1	0.52/0
M^2	9	-0.65/0.26	10	-0.90/0.43	9	2.15/1.62
X^2	7	-0.28/0.008	9	-1.32/0.24	6	-1.59/0.29
$C \cdot M$	0	0/0	8	1.76/1.31	4	-4.00/3.31
$C \cdot X$	1	-0.78/0	1	-1.17/0	9	-0.50/2.60
$M \cdot X$	1	-0.39/0	5	0.75/0.29	5	1.78/0.95
$C/(C+0.5)$	1	-0.02/0	3	-0.084/0.15	1	0.016/0
$M/(M+0.5)$	7	-0.47/0.042	1	0.52/0	9	0.64/1.13
$X/(X+0.5)$	2	0.14/0.08	5	0.24/0.19	2	-0.81/0.10
$C/(C+0.05)$	1	-0.016/0	0	0/0	1	-0.031/0
$M/(M+0.05)$	0	0/0	9	-0.079/0.036	1	-0.37/0
$X/(X+0.05)$	1	-0.018/0	0	0/0	0	0/0
$C/(C+0.005)$	0	0/0	0	0/0	0	0/0
$M/(M+0.005)$	0	0/0	0	0/0	2	-0.0087/0.015
$X/(X+0.005)$	0	0/0	0	0/0	0	0/0
1	10	0.030/0.0029	2	0.022/0.021	0	0/0

standard deviation of 0.0029. This means that our procedure was able to detect a constant contribution of 0.03 in the flux which updates the concentration of C but it could not determine if this contribution came from φ_1, φ_2 or φ_4. Finally, we notice that 0.03 is exactly $\epsilon \cdot v_i \cdot 1200$, thus our procedure automatically inferred the right constant to be used with the sampling interval of 1200 steps. Similar results were achieved also for other regressors. Figure 7 and Table 3 clearly show, for instance, the strong contribution of regressors M, M^2, X^2 and $M/(M + 0.5)$ on the evolution over time of substance C.

4   Conclusions and Future Work

The analysis reported in this paper shows that our methodology has good capabilities to infer some knowledge about regulatory mechanisms of biochemical processes directly from experimental data. However, in specific cases our approach was not able to put flux contributions in the right regulation function because of the lack of appropriate constraints. Work in progress aims at defining such constraints and to implement them within our evolutionary procedure. A second goal of our current work is to validate our methodology by reverse-engineering the network of the yeast Saccharomyces cerevisiae proposed in [2], which is a synthetic network of five genes for in vivo reverse-engineering and modeling assessment. Finally, we are developing a software application which will make available the evolutionary procedure to biologists and modelers by a user-friendly graphical interface.

References

1. Alon, U.: An Introduction to Systems Biology: Design Principles of Biological Circuits, 1st edn. Chapman and Hall/CRC (July 2006)
2. Cantone, I., Marucci, L., Iorio, F., Ricci, M.A., Belcastro, V., Bansal, M., Santini, S., di Bernardo, M., di Bernardo, D., Cosma, M.P.: A yeast synthetic network for in vivo assessment of Reverse-Engineering and modeling approaches. Cell 137(1), 172–181 (2009)
3. Castellini, A., Franco, G., Pagliarini, R.: Data analysis pipeline from laboratory to MP models. Natural Computing 10(1), 55–76 (2011)
4. Castellini, A., Manca, V.: Learning regulation functions of metabolic systems by artificial neural networks. In: Proc. GECCO 2009, pp. 193–200. ACM Publisher, Montreal (2009)
5. Castellini, A., Manca, V., Zucchelli, M., Busato, M.: A genetic approach for synthesizing metabolic models from time series. In: Proceedings of GECCO 2012, Philadelphia, USA (2012)
6. Di Ventura, B., Lemerle, C., Michalodimitrakis, K., Serrano, L.: From in vivo to in silico biology and back. Nature 443(7111), 527–533 (2006)
7. Goldbeter, A.: A minimal cascade model for the mitotic oscillator involving cyclin and cdc2 kinase. PNAS 88(20), 9107–9111 (1991)
8. Manca, V.: The metabolic algorithm: Principles and applications. Theoretical Computer Science 404, 142–157 (2008)

9. Manca, V.: Fundamentals of metabolic P systems. In: Handbook of Membrane Computing, vol. 19, Oxford University Press (2009)
10. Manca, V., Bianco, L.: Biological networks in metabolic P systems. BioSystems 91(3), 489–498 (2008)
11. Manca, V., Marchetti, L.: Log-gain stoichiometric stepwise regression for MP systems. Int. J. Found. Comput. Sci. 22(1), 97–106 (2011)
12. Manca, V., Marchetti, L.: Solving Dynamical Inverse Problems by means of Metabolic P Systems. BioSystems 109, 78–86 (2012)
13. Manca, V., Marchetti, L., Pagliarini, R.: MP modelling of glucose-insulin interactions in the intravenous glucose tolerance test. International Journal of Natural Computing Research 2(3), 13–24 (2011)
14. Marchetti, L., Manca, V.: A Methodology Based on MP Theory for Gene Expression Analysis. In: Gheorghe, M., Păun, G., Rozenberg, G., Salomaa, A., Verlan, S. (eds.) CMC 2011. LNCS, vol. 7184, pp. 300–313. Springer, Heidelberg (2012)
15. Mitchell, M.: An introduction to genetic algorithms. MIT Press (1998)
16. Păun, G.: Membrane Computing. An Introduction. Springer, Berlin (2002)
17. Szallasi, Z., Stelling, J., Periwal, V. (eds.): System Modeling in Cellular Biology: From Concepts to Nuts and Bolts, 1st edn. The MIT Press (April 2006)
18. Voit, E., Neves, A.R., Santos, H.: The intricate side of systems biology. PNAS 103(25), 9452–9457 (2006)

Distributed Computing with Prokaryotic Immune Systems

Niall Murphy[1,2] and Alfonso Rodríguez-Patón[1]

[1] Facultad de Informática, Universidad Politécnica de Madrid, Spain
[2] CEI Campus Moncloa, UCM-UPM, Madrid, Spain

Summary: We propose the *in vivo/vitro* use of prokaryotic adaptive immune systems for distributed learning. In the coming years synthetic biologists will learn to control, program, and modify such systems. We design an enhancement to CRISPR-Cas immune systems and demonstrate the learning potential of the modified system by showing it can approximate solutions to a computationally hard problem. To our knowledge this is the first proposed use of CRISPR-Cas systems for computational purposes.

Biological background: CRISPR-Cas systems are a family of adaptive immune systems found in prokaryotes [1,2]. It allows cells to develop and inherit immunity to viruses and plasmids.

The CRISPR locus is a region of DNA with a "leader" section ($\sim$ 100–500 bp) immediately followed "spacers" ($\sim$ 30–40 bp) interspersed with identical, partly palindromic, repeat sequences. There can be between 20 to 300 spacers in a single CRISPR locus.

The Cas (CRISPR associated) proteins add new spacers just beside the leader sequence. Spacers are typically sections of DNA from viruses and plasmids that have previously infected the cell.

Once the CRISPR locus is transcribed Cas proteins separate the spacers by cutting the mRNA in the middle of the repeat sequences. Each individual spacer is part of a crRNA (CRISPR RNA). If any section of DNA matching a crRNA enters the cell (for example via a virus or plasmid) it is destroyed. However, viruses are constantly evolving in tandem with CRISPR and the mutation of a single base pair may allow a virus to escape destruction.

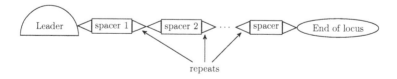

Fig. 1. A schematic of a CRISPR locus showing the location of the leader, spacers and the repeat sequences

C.A. Coello Coello et al. (Eds.): ICARIS 2012, LNCS 7597, pp. 286–288, 2012.
© Springer-Verlag Berlin Heidelberg 2012

Motivation: CRISPR-Cas systems are adaptive and inheritable systems that detect and destroy foreign nucleic acids. They will have important roles and many applications in bio-technology, synthetic biology, and medicine [1]. CRISPR-Cas systems are not yet fully understood but, in the near future, synthetic biologists will be able to modify and control these programmable sets of forbidden DNA sequences. CRISPR loci can also be transmitted from one bacteria to another by conjugation making them a powerful tool to modify the plasmids circulating in a bacterial population.

Synthetic Biology: Currently it is believed that, as a CRISPR locus gets longer, spacers are lost by homologous recombination between the repeat sequences. However, if CRISPR spacers were constantly being removed by some synthetic system (for example, a restriction enzyme and ligase pair that remove the last spacer in the locus) then the CRISPR locus would become a shorter, queue like, DNA memory.

We refer to a CRISPR-Cas system, modified with this engineered method of spacer loss, as a "FORGETR". We assume that the FORGETR uses a CRISPR-Cas system that is not limited to learning proto-spacer regions of viruses [3].

If a bacteria with a FORGETR system is introduced to a population of viruses, we predict that the spacer loss mechanism will put pressure on the bacteria to have the shortest CRISPR locus that still gives full protection against all the viruses in a population. We predict that it would learn the most common or conserved regions of viral DNA.

Bacteria with FORGETR systems have many potential applications such as: a tool to study the mutations and genetic diversity in a wild viral population; to train a CRISPR locus that can be used to harden cells against a wide variety of viruses; and the development of bacteria that remove a particular trait from a bacterial population such as antibiotic resistance.

If we wish to force the CRISPR locus to avoid learning specific sections of virus DNA we could include an engineered plasmid in each bacteria. This plasmid has the unwanted sections of the virus' DNA along with genes for a slow decaying toxin and a fast decaying anti-toxin. If the CRISPR system learns a forbidden section of virus DNA then the plasmid is destroyed. The anti-toxin will no longer be produced and the cell will die. In future, more elegant systems will be possible [4].

Computation: To demonstrate the distributed learning potential of population of bacteria combined with a FORGETR system, we outline how to use it to approximate minimum solutions to HITTINGSET, a classic NP-complete problem [5]. Let (D, P) be an instance of the HITTINGSET problem where $P = (P_1, \ldots, P_m)$ is a collection of subsets of a finite set $D = \{d_1, \ldots, d_n\}$. The minimum hitting set is the smallest set $C \subseteq D$ such that C contains at least one element from each subset in P.

We encode the set D as a set of unique DNA sequences. We encode each subset P_i in the set of subsets P as a virus whose DNA includes a sub-sequence that is the encoding of each $d \in D \cap P_i$.

We consider a well mixed experimental set-up with an infinite supply of each virus in P attacking a population of bacteria with FORGETR. The CRISPR locus, C_b, of each bacteria in the population contains a single potential hitting set solution.

The viruses attack the bacteria. If virus P_i attacks the cell with CRISPR locus C_b and there is an intersection between C_b and P_i then the virus is destroyed and the cell can divide (both children have a copy of the CRISPR locus).

If the CRISPR locus C_b does not have an intersection with P_i then with probability λ it adds an element d in P_i to its CRISPR locus C_b. If this occurs the virus is destroyed and the cell can divide (both cells have a copy of the new improved CRISPR locus).

If C_b has no intersection with P_i and fails to learn an element of P_i then the cell is destroyed and the potential solution C_b lost.

Clearly cells whose CRISPR locus C_b has an intersection with all the viruses of P will survive. To force the system to approximate minimal solutions, we make key use of the forgetting aspect of FORGETR. With a probability ρ the last element of the CRISPR locus is removed.

This setup forces the CRISPR loci to be as short as possible while still retaining as much immunity to the viruses as possible. In simulations we find that the system rapidly reaches the state where the most common sets of spacers in the bacterial population are in fact minimal solutions to the input instance.

We also mention that such a system should be halted before the virus DNA mutates too far from the original instance encoding.

References

1. Horvath, P., Barrangou, R.: CRISPR/Cas, the immune system of bacteria and archaea. Science 327(5962), 167–170 (2010)
2. Terns, M.P., Terns, R.M.: CRISPR-based adaptive immune systems. Current Opinion in Microbiology 14(3), 321–327 (2011)
3. Hale, C., Majumdar, S., Elmore, J., Pfister, N., Compton, M., Olson, S., Resch, A., Glover III, C., Graveley, B., Terns, R., Terns, M.: Essential features and rational design of CRISPR RNAs that function with the Cas RAMP module complex to cleave RNAs. Molecular Cell 45(3), 292–302 (2012)
4. Marraffini, L.A., Sontheimer, E.J.: Self versus non-self discrimination during CRISPR RNA-directed immunity. Nature 463(7280), 568–571 (2010)
5. Garey, M.R., Johnson, D.S.: Computers and Intractability, A Guide to the Theory of NP–Completeness. W. H. Freeman and company, New York (1979)

The Immune System as a Metaphor for Topology Driven Patterns Formation in Complex Systems[*]

Emanuela Merelli[1] and Mario Rasetti[2]

[1] School of Science and Technology, University of Camerino, Italy
[2] ISI Foundation, Torino, Italy

Extended Abstract

Artificial Immune Systems (AIS) [1] include algorithms and systems that use the human immune system as inspiration. The human immune system is a *robust*, decentralised, error tolerant and *adaptive* system. Such properties are highly desirable for the development of novel computer systems, but also - we would like to say - for characterizing complex systems and for contributing to the growth of complexity science.

Complex systems can be defined as systems composed of many non-identical elements, entangled in loops of non-linear interactions. The challenge of the complexity science is understanding the collective emergent properties of these systems, from the knowledge of components to global behaviour. A typical feature of complex systems is in fact emergence of non-trivial superstructures that cannot be reconstructed by applying a reductionist approach. Not only higher emergent features of complex systems arise out of the lower level interactions, but the patterns that they create react back on those lower levels in a possibly infinite feedback-loop. In many of these cases, complex systems possess a characteristic *robustness* with respect to large scale or multi-dimensional perturbations or disruptions, whereby they are endowed with an inherent ability to *adapt* or *persist* in stable forms.

The human system is viewed as the most sophisticated of immune systems in nature. Although its precise function remains undetermined, it is postulated that it has two roles; to protect the body against invading micro-organisms (pathogens), and to regulate bodily functions (homeostasis). Immunologists like to describe the immune system as consisting of two parts, namely the innate immune system and the adaptive immune system. It was originally thought that these were two distinct sub-systems with little crossover, with the *innate system* responding to known threats and the *adaptive immune system* tackling previously un-encountered threats. However, current research suggests that it is the interplay between these two systems that provides the high level of protection required, i.e. the ability to discriminate between self and nonself entities.

In this work we aim to mimic the interplay capabilities of the immune system to identify, classify and learn new patterns, for defining a formal modelling structural patterns allowing us to perform process/data mining in a more efficient way and to extract more easily valuable effectual information.

[*] Thanks to EU for having selected TOPDRIM project.

C.A. Coello Coello et al. (Eds.): ICARIS 2012, LNCS 7597, pp. 289–291, 2012.
© Springer-Verlag Berlin Heidelberg 2012

It is quite natural to see a complex system described as a pair of components $S[B]$, where B represents the behavioural level (or micro level) composed of a large number of autonomous, heterogeneous and discrete entities or agents, continually evolving through non-linear local interactions and S the structural level (or macro level) accounting for the global persistent properties of the system.

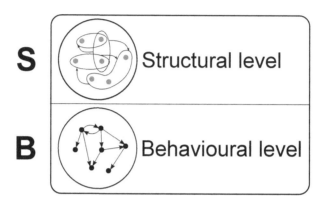

Fig. 1. $S[B]$ system in terms of *topological* (S) and *relational* (B) properties

Starting from our previous works [2,3], the proposed approach will exploit the algebraic topology to derive the structural properties at macro level S from the behavioural micro level B, see Figure 1. The adaptivenees, inspired by the interplay analysis that the immune system naturally performs [1], will be based on a simplified model of immune system represented by a field theory suitable for the analysis of experimental data space, see Figure 2.

Always keeping in mind that:
"... the totality is not, as it were, a mere heap, but the whole is something besides the parts ...", i.e., the whole is greater than the sum of the parts. *[Aristotle, Metaphysics, Book H 1045a 8-10].*
We will discuss the syntax and the semantics of the multi-level system both for proving the correctness of the adaptation and giving rise to a novel class of formal languages suitable to define decision problems in the domains of complexity science [5]. We will give a glance into the new "interactive computation" paradigm proposed by Peter Wegner and we will discuss the features of the "interaction machine", that extends the Turing machine as discussed in [6]. Finally, considerations on "autopoietic machine", proposed by Francisco Varela in [7], as a synthesis of our approach, based on the artificial immune system, will be discussed.

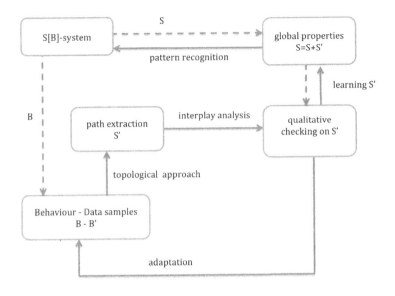

Fig. 2. pattern recognition learning process

References

1. de Castro, L., Timmis, J.: Artificial Immune Systems: A New Computational Approach. Springer, London (2002)
2. Merelli, E., Paoletti, N., Tesei, L.: A multi-level model for self-adaptive systems. In: FOCLASA: 11th International Workshop on Foundations of Coordination Languages and Self Adaptation. A Satellite Workshop of CONCUR 2012, Machester, September 8 (2012)
3. Rasetti, M.: Topology, formal languages and quantum information. Milan Journal of Mathematics (2010)
4. Castiglione, F., Nicosia, G., Motta, S.: Pattern recognition by primary and secondary response of an artificial immune system. Biosciences 120(2), 93–106 (2001)
5. Garrone, S., Marzuoli, A., Rasetti, M.: Spin networks, quantum automata and link invariants. Journal of Physics (2006)
6. Wegner, P., Goldin, D.: Computation Beyond Turing Machines. Communications of the ACM (April 2003)
7. Varela, F., Maturala, H.R.: Mechanism and biological explanation. Philosophy of Science 39(3) (1972)

Author Index